MODERN

BRITISH

POLITICS

By Samuel H. Beer

BRITAIN AGAINST ITSELF

MODERN BRITISH POLITICS

MODERN
BRITISH
POLITICS

PARTIES AND PRESSURE
GROUPS IN THE
COLLECTIVIST AGE

by

SAMUEL H. BEER

W · W · NORTON & COMPANY

New York · London

Copyright © 1982, 1969, 1965 by Samuel H. Beer
All rights reserved.
Published simultaneously in Canada by George J. McLeod Limited, Toronto.
Printed in the United States of America.
First published as a Norton paperback 1982
by arrangement with Alfred A. Knopf, Inc.

Previously published under the title
British Politics in the Collectivist Age

Library of Congress Cataloging in Publication Data

Beer, Samuel Hutchinson, 1911–
Modern British politics.

Rev. ed. of: British politics in the collectivist
age. 1969.
Bibliography: p.
Includes index.
1. Political parties—Great Britain—History.
2. Pressure groups—Great Britain—History.
3. Great Britain—Politics and government. I. Title.
JN1121.B43 1982   324.241   82–6385
AACR2

W. W. Norton & Company Inc. 500 Fifth Avenue, New York, N.Y. 10110
1 2 3 4 5 6 7 8 9 0

ISBN 0-393-00952-1

Preface to the 1982 Edition

This book was originally published under different titles in Britain and the United States. In Britain it was called *Modern British Politics: A Study of Parties and Pressure Groups*. The American title was *British Politics in the Collectivist Age*. I have taken the opportunity of this reprinting to reduce the confusion by combining the titles. Each brought out an important theme of the book.

One theme is the modernization of British politics. When I say "modern" I do not mean simply up-to-date or contemporary in a chronological sense—whatever has come into existence in the past few years. By modernity I mean rather certain values, a distinctive world view, standing in contrast with the traditionalist outlook of the medieval world. Modernization accordingly is the process by which these values have come to be ever more widely shared in Western society in recent centuries and the further complex and often unintended consequences of that growing acceptance. The theoretical underpinnings of this approach to political development were worked out in a course on Western thought and institutions that I taught at Harvard for many years.[1] In the Epilogue to this volume I have made that approach more explicit, suggesting how the five types of political thought and action sketched in Part One characterize the main stages in the modernization of British politics.

The main theme of the book is the development of the most recent of these stages, the collectivist. Most of the book is concerned with tracing the rise of collectivism from the late nineteenth century through the early decades of this century until it

---

[1] This approach and the course are discussed in Melvin Richter (ed.) *Essays in Theory and History: An Approach to the Social Sciences* (Cambridge, Mass.; 1970). See esp. Richter's Introduction and my contribution "Political Science and History."

came to dominate British politics in the postwar years, reaching a certain fulfillment or maturity in the political system that had emerged by the late 1950s and early 1960s.

That political system, however, not only embodied collectivist values; it also engendered pressures, principally "the new group politics," that impelled it toward further development. The Epilogue, written in 1969, identifies some of the resulting tendencies that were undermining the balanced and efficacious system of only a few years before. At that time, it was clear that British politics had entered a period of trouble and transformation, and in the concluding pages of the Epilogue I attempted to suggest some possible futures.

In that attempt I was right to identify a trend toward "a post-collectivist politics." I failed, however, to see how far the change would go. Consequently, when I set out some ten years later to bring the Epilogue up to date, I discovered that that could not be done by adding a mere supplement, but only by writing another book. That new book is being published simultaneously with this reprinting under the title *Britain Against Itself: The Political Contradictions of Collectivism*.

In the original study I laid great stress on the role of ideas in politics—or, to put it more formally, on "political culture as one of the main variables of a political system." [2] Like many political scientists before me, I found that the modernization of British politics had been accompanied by the retention and adaptation of much that was traditionalist. Old values of hierarchy and solidarity had proved to be highly functional to the reassertion of strong government and social responsibility and to the emergence of a system of political parties and pressure groups that sustained the patterns of collectivist policy.

The main fault with the attempt of the Epilogue to discern the shape of things to come is its underestimate of the role that ideas actually played in what took place. I was especially remiss in failing to appreciate the power of the romantic revolt of the 1960s. I did see that challenge,[3] but quite failed to grasp how deeply it was striking at the foundations of the collectivist polity.

[2] p. xii below.
[3] pp. 426-8, pp. 430-1.

I therefore did not appreciate the character and the consequences of the romantic revolt against the massive concentrations of power in the government and politics of the British welfare state and managed economy.

In the new book political culture appears not only as a static condition, but also as a dynamic force. In that analysis the attack upon traditionalist values is the basic change to which the transformation of the British polity in recent years is keyed. This transformation, however, does not mark a departure from modernity. On the contrary, as suggested in the Epilogue to this volume, the romantic values that have shaped the new attitudes spring from the modern spirit and in modern times have repeatedly inspired revolts against authority. Without suggesting any scheme of inevitability, we may, therefore, regard the new post-collectivist phase of British politics as another stage in its modernization. That phase can best be understood if we first look at the collectivist polity of a generation ago that is examined in the following pages.

I am happy again to express my thanks to the sources that helped finance the many visits I made to Britain in the course of working on this book: the Guggenheim Foundation, the Fulbright Scholarships, the Rockefeller Foundation, and the Social Science Research Foundation. Nor shall I neglect to mention my debt to the Rhodes Trust which quite a few years ago made it possible for me to study British history in Britain and for the first time to meet the people who live there.

As for sources of information, I wish to acknowledge my great debt to my British informants. To the established scholars, such as A.H. Birch, David Butler, Bernard Crick, S.E. Finer, the late R.T. McKenzie and Richard Rose, I trust that my frequent footnote references to their published work will also serve to indicate the help I received in conversation. I particularly want to say how much I learned from talking with J.D. Stewart, the author of the first book on British pressure groups. Too numerous to mention, many public figures—meaning by this to include M.P.'s, ministers and ex-ministers, officials of parties, trade unions, trade associations and other organizations—were also generous with their time and comment. There are, however, a few whom I must thank by name, although it would be tedious and sometimes indiscreet to try to say just what I learned from each: David Clarke, the late R.H.S. Crossman, Michael Fraser, the late Richard Fort, Hugh Jenkins, Peter Shore and Eirene White.

On the American side, I must first express my debt to my former teacher, the late W.Y. Elliott. Among others who have shared their insight and criticism, I should like particularly to mention Louis Hartz, Harry Eckstein, George Nadel, Lloyd Rudolph, Melvin Richter, Stanley Rothman, Harvey Glickman, John Saloma III, Harvey Mansfield, Jr., and Michael Walzer. For assistance with specific pieces of research I am indebted to Stephen Elkin, Isabel Robbins, Gad Horowitz, Barbara Haskel and Richard Rothstein. Paul Thomas was a great help when I was working on the 1969 Epilogue.

Cambridge, Mass.
January, 1982   Samuel H. Beer

Contents

Contents

Introduction

Politics is at least a struggle for power. In any political system, people will join together in attempts to win authority or to influence its exercise. The political formations in which they combine vary from age to age and from one system to another. They may be as highly formalized, traditionalist, and enduring as the estates of the realm of a medieval kingdom. They may be as informal and transient as a reformist pressure group of Victorian England. They may be dedicated to violent revolution. Or like the political parties of democratic constitutionalism, they may accept the rules of the game laid down by prevailing conceptions of authority. Describing and classifying these political formations is one of the more interesting tasks that confronts the political scientist. In this book I wish to describe for recent times in Great Britain, and especially for the years since World War II, the principal kinds of political formations and the way they have exercised or influenced authority. My subject, in short, is political parties and interest groups and how they affect public policy.

Because he is himself a contemporary, the student of contemporary politics may fail to notice important features simply because they are common and familiar. Historical comparison can help avert this danger. For that reason, in trying to identify what is distinctive about contemporary formations and their modes of action, I have made comparisons with periods when politics was conducted differently and have prefaced the discussion of contemporary political behavior with a sketch of four different types of politics, corresponding roughly to four different historical periods. To these four I have given the names Old Tory, Old Whig, Liberal, and Radical. The fifth and contemporary type I have called Collectivist. Thus the task of description has also involved an effort of classification.

This classification of various types of political behavior in Britain since the sixteenth century is not by any means intended to be a history of parties and interest groups. It is neither con-

nor comprehensive. It does, I think, characterize the main
in what one may call the modernization of British politics.
rovides, moreover, a typology of political formations that
ı be used in the study of the political development of other
ountries. Its main use in this book, however, is the light it throws
on the study of contemporary affairs. It helps, in the first place,
to bring out the novel features of parties and interest groups in
the period of Collectivist politics. These features, which historical
comparison helps us to identify and which I have characterized
under the headings of Party Government and Functional Representation, entitle and indeed oblige us to classify the politics of
this period as a distinctive type.

In the second place, this historical comparison reveals not only
what is new, but also what is old. It lights up continuities in
British political culture that are fundamental to an understanding
of contemporary British political behavior. I argue, for instance,
that the easy acceptance of group representation in the present
century was facilitated by attitudes favorable to pluralism and
functional representation that had survived from a much earlier
time. Similarly, some of the fundamental traits of British conservatism—traits, incidentally, which radically distinguish it
from what passes for conservatism in the United States—can be
explained only when one sees how Toryism, another survival from
an earlier age, has found and maintained a lodging in the Conservative Party.

In general, as these examples suggest, I lay great stress on
political culture as one of the main variables of a political system
and a major factor in explaining the political behavior of individuals, groups, and parties. Specifically, it is in the political culture
of the time that I have found the most useful clues to the prevailing type (or types) of political behavior. One needs no great
familiarity with the historical evidence to know that in the British
case the types of political formation have changed markedly from
period to period. But it is another task to go on from this impression and develop the characterizations that will accurately
identify each type and sum up its complex of traits.

In each of the five types of political behavior that I discuss,
the characterizing idea is a theory of representation which
was a constituent of the political culture of the time. When I
say "theory" of representation I am thinking of the works of
political philosophers only insofar as these tell us something about

our real object of concern : the images and sentiments that fu.
as operative ideals in a community, or section of a commu
Taken in this sense, each of the five theories of representat
defines a more or less coherent system of roles for political form
tions and their members. My procedure in each section of the
historical discussion is first to set out this theory and then to
examine the corresponding behavior.

Two further points need immediately to be made. I do not
assert, nor have I found, that there is an exact and one-to-one
correspondence between theory and practice. Political culture,
its values, beliefs, and emotional symbols, while a major variable,
is only one of the variables determining behavior. As interesting as
the correspondence of practice with theory are its not infrequent
deviations. There may be irony in these instances, as when the
perfectionism of certain ideals defeats itself by creating institutions that presume for their success a degree of virtue that neither
human nature nor the necessities of a social order will permit.
In any case, structures of political action, like other social structures, often have unanticipated consequences, and the question of
whether these are functional or dysfunctional to the political
system is a matter for inquiry by the political scientist.

Moreover, I do not say that for each period there is only one
type of behavior dictated by a single, reigning theory of representation embraced in a clear, unclouded, and perfectly integrated
political culture. On the contrary, a lack of integration in political
culture may be a main source of conflict in the practical politics
of the day. "A culture," Lionel Trilling has written, ". . . is nothing if not a dialectic." He means this in no technical Hegelian
sense, but simply in the sense that a culture "is not a flow, nor
even a confluence; the form of its existence is struggle or at least
debate."[1] The same is equally true of that aspect of a culture that
we call political. It is often from the "yes and no" (the phrase is
Trilling's) of a country's political culture that major tensions of
its political life derive.

Consider, for instance, the ambiguous meaning of class in
British political culture today. Is class a divisive force in the
community or a unifying one? Is it necessary for social order, or
is it merely an instrument and emblem of privilege? Does it need
only to be rationalized and made functional, or should it be

[1] *The Liberal Imagination* (New York, 1953), p. 20.

ıed? The British political tradition attributes great im-
ınce to these questions. As a body of beliefs widely shared
British society, it confronts Britons generally with such ques-
ɔns and, at the same time, gives support for diametrically opposed
answers. In this way British political culture is today, as it has
been in the past, a source of tension and conflict over fundamental
questions of moral and political philosophy. The difference, for
instance, between what I have called Socialist Democracy and
Tory Democracy is such a conflict over a fundamental question,
and its cultural source is precisely this peculiarly British ambiguity
over the moral and social significance of class. Thus the "dialectic"
within the culture has consequences for behavior.

Politics, as it appears in the following pages, is a struggle for
power, but a struggle that is deeply conditioned by fundamental
moral concerns. The theories of representation with which I shall
deal are constituents of more inclusive conceptions of authority
that lay down how power ought to be distributed in the community and define who may legitimately take part in governing
and how they may do so. These conceptions present quite different answers to a central question of political philosophy : "How
ought we to be governed?" In the periods discussed, the answers
to this question have substantially shaped the way men concerted
and directed their attempts to win and to influence power. The
forms in which they have conducted the struggle for power have
embodied radically different moral perspectives. The question of
legitimate authority has not been simply a subject for talk. Men
have also acted out their answers in the history of parties and
pressure groups.

PART ONE

Five Types of Politics

CHAPTER I

Old Tory and Old Whig Politics

OLD TORY POLITICS

During the debate of the House of Commons on the *Economic Survey for 1947*, Sir John Anderson (later Lord Waverley) attacked the policy of economic equality advocated by the Labour Government, and in warning to his listeners quoted these lines from Shakespeare :

> *Take but degree away, untune that string,*
> *And hark, what discord follows!*

Without saying that Sir John was an Old Tory in the sense in which the word is used here—but without entirely denying it—we may take the passage from which he quoted as a classic expression of the premises and spirit of the Old Tory conception of authority. This conception, which prevailed in the sixteenth and early seventeenth centuries, was part of a larger perspective on social reality and, indeed, the whole cosmos. Ulysses' speech before Agamemnon's tent in *Troilus and Cressida* illuminates the background and its blending of cosmic, social, and political principles. "Degree" and "order" are the central notions with which Old Tory thought was as concerned (we could say obsessed) as later generations were with liberty and self-government.

First, we learn, the cosmos itself is ordered by "degree" :

> *The heavens themselves, the planets, and this centre*
> *Observe degree, priority, and place,*

Insisture, course, proportion, season, form,
Office, and custom, in all line of order;
And therefore is the glorious planet Sol
In noble eminence enthron'd and spher'd
Admidst the other, whose med'cinable eye
Corrects the ill aspects of planets evil
And posts, like the commandment of a king,
Sans check, to good and bad. [I. iii. 85–94]

This same premise explains disorder in the social and political worlds, as in the natural:

O, when degree is shak'd,
Which is the ladder to all high designs,
The enterprise is sick! How could communities,
Degrees in schools and brotherhoods in cities,
Peaceful commerce from dividable shores,
The primogenity and due of birth,
Prerogative of age, crowns, sceptres, laurels,
But by degree, stand in authentic place? [I. iii. 101–8]

Thus, for both the natural and human orders:

Take but degree away, untune that string,
And hark, what discord follows! [I. iii. 109–10]

"Degree" is a distant but powerful ancestor of those attitudes of *noblesse oblige* and deference that still flourish in modern Britain. But we must find strange the premises from which it depended. A "great chain of being"—to use Lovejoy's phrase[1]—stretched from the merest inanimate matter through various planes —vegetable, animal, human, angelic—and finally to God the Perfect Being. From the lower to the higher ranged a hierarchy of value; but also a hierarchy of authority. As Sol, in Ulysses' speech, rules the planets like a king, so man commands all created things "in degree of nature beneath man,"[2] and among men the greater in degree govern the lesser. The "infinite wisdom of God," wrote Raleigh, "which hath distinguished his angels by degrees, which hath given greater and less light and beauty to heavenly bodies, which hath made differences between beasts and birds . . . also

---

[1] Arthur O. Lovejoy, *The Great Chain of Being* (Cambridge, Mass., 1936).
[2] Richard Hooker, *Ecclesiastical Polity* (London, 1907), Vol. I, p. 166.

ordained kings, dukes or leaders of the people, magistrates, and other degrees among men."[3]

The purpose of authority, the function of hierarchy, is to fo the good of the whole: to maintain each subordinate part worki. in harmony with the others. The Old Tory cosmos was organi and hierarchic. So also was the human individual, peculiarly placed as he was at the mid-point in this great chain. And, as in man the head (sometimes it was the heart) ruled the other faculties and corporal members, so in an analogy as old as John of Salisbury, the monarch governed men of lesser degree for the common good.

A Hooker could defend the established order by an argument that permitted men in some far-distant past to choose the form of government they desired, but the sentiments of Old Tory thought were overwhelmingly on the side of personal monarchy. James I was only stating rather pedantically certain common assumptions of the time when he lectured the Parliament of 1609 in these words:

> The state of monarchy is the supremest thing upon earth; for kings are not only God's lieutenants upon earth and sit upon God's throne, but even by God himself, they are called Gods. There be three principal similitudes that illustrate the state of monarchy. . . . In the scriptures kings are called Gods and so their power after a certain relation compared to the divine power. Kings are also compared to fathers of families . . . and lastly, kings are compared to the head of this microcosm of the body of man.[4]

Elizabeth herself had used the head and body analogy to clinch her claim that the monarch has controlling responsibility for the great matters of public policy. At the close of the Parliament of 1566 she warned the House of Commons not to meddle further with the question of the succession and asked rhetorically: "Who is so simple that doubts whether a prince that is head of all the body may not command the feet not to stray when they would slip?"[5]

[3] Sir Walter Raleigh, *History of the World*, as quoted in E. M. W. Tillyard, *The Elizabethan World Picture* (London, 1956), p. 9. On Old Tory cosmology in general, see Theodore Spencer, *Shakespeare and the Nature of Man* (New York, 1942).

[4] Charles H. McIlwain, *The Political Works of James I* (Cambridge, Mass., 1918), p. 307.

[5] J. E. Neale, *Elizabeth I and Her Parliaments 1559–1581* (London, 1952), p. 175.

esentation in Theory and Practice

In any theory of representation, some answer is given to the questions: "How is the community as a whole to be represented?" "Who or what is to represent the common good or public interest, as compared with the more particular interests of the component parts?" In Old Tory thought this right and duty belonged above all to the monarch. This meant that in practice the initiative and decisive influence in the great questions of public policy were the Crown's preserve, entrenched in its prerogative. Starting from Henry VIII's time, it was common for the monarch to have prepared a "government program" for each session of these none-too-frequent Parliaments. And, at least until the end of Elizabeth's reign, the Crown had its way in spite of occasional brushes with the Puritans. The massive Elizabethan economic code, for instance, swept through Parliament with hardly any debate at all. When trouble did occur, it served only to underline the Queen's Old Tory view of her role. As the Lord Keeper warned the Commons at the opening of the Parliament of 1571 : "they should do well to meddle with no matters of state but such as should be proponed unto them and to occupy themselves in other matters concerning the Commonwealth."[6] James I was only repeating this principle when, in 1609, directing his words especially to the lower house, he warned : "that you do not meddle with the main points of government; that is my craft . . . I must not be taught my office."[7]

What were these "matters of state" reserved primarily for the monarch? Elizabeth denied to the Commons the initiative in questions concerning the royal succession; the religious settlement and the church in general; all exchequer matters and the royal administration, including even grants of monopolies by royal patent. Foreign policy and the making of war and peace were, of course, also included. What then were the "other matters" with which Members of Parliament might occupy themselves? In the sixteenth century the older notion that they were delegates or attorneys for their constituencies was still alive.[8] In this view

---

[6] *Ibid.*, p. 189.
[7] McIlwain, *op. cit.*, p. 315.
[8] Neale, *The Elizabethan House of Commons* (New Haven, 1950), p. 158.

their principal function, for which they were given "full
sufficient" power, was to bind their constituencies to make g
the grants of supply to Her Majesty. In return they secured t
redress of grievances. This meant in practice that they were pre
occupied with special and local interests. Neale has put the matter
shortly : if for the Crown Parliament meant subsidies, for the
Commons it meant private bills.[9]

Vast numbers of private bills were promoted, and opposed, on
behalf of boroughs, crafts, companies, and individuals, often in a
context of intensive lobbying. The City of London was particularly well-organized and active as a pressure group and from
the fifteenth century had maintained a handsomely paid agent
to look after its interests in Parliament. Citizens were not to press
any bill without the knowledge and consent of the Lord Mayor
and Aldermen. City companies and crafts with bills to promote
were first to submit them to the Court of Aldermen for consideration and possible amendment. If the bill were approved,
the City's four members of Parliament might be "specially moved"
to further it. Opposition to bills judged injurious to the City's
interests was similarly concerted. Since expenses could be high,
the City provided money for lobbying, briefing, and even feeing
Members of Parliament.[1]

This distinction between the role of monarch and M.P. was
not sharp and mutually exclusive. After all, the monarch did
sometimes seek the advice and often needed the consent of Parliament even in "matters of state." The difference is one of emphasis,
centering on the initiative, but this difference was of the utmost
importance. In the latter part of Elizabeth's reign, the Commons
increasingly took the initiative in matters of state, meddling with
such questions as the religious settlement, foreign affairs, monopolies, and the succession.[2] These first skirmishes foreshadowed
the deep conflicts and changes of the seventeenth century in
which the Old Tory theory of representation was overthrown.

What kind of political groups were legitimized by Old Tory
thought? The ideal of social reality was corporate and hierarchic;

[9] *Ibid.*, p. 383.
[1] *Ibid.*, pp. 384-7.
[2] Wallace Notestein, "The Winning of the Initiative by the House of
Commons," *Proceedings of the British Academy*, Vol. XI (1923-24), pp.
124-76.

.munity of "sundry estates and degrees of men," in Sir Thomas
..t's phrase.[3] Tudor and Stuart social policy, as Tawney has
..1, sought to maintain "an ordered and graded society in which
..ch class performed its allotted function, and was secured such
.1 livelihood, and no more than such a livelihood, as was propor-
tioned to its status."[4] Similarly, the legitimate political formations
were corporate and hierarchic. There were the fixed and corporate
communities of an organic state, whether natural communities like
shires and hundreds or legally created communities like the boroughs and guilds. These might, as we have seen, act through
Parliament. Sometimes several of them might be drawn together
by common interests, as when in 1621 the representatives of the
large towns opposed those of the cattle-raising shires over a bill
to forbid the importation of Irish cattle. But the lines of hierarchy
created other groupings, which might blend with or cut across
these communal ties. Overshadowing all other groups in the political struggles of the time were the factions of the royal court.
There, and in the Council rather than in Parliament, the great
courtiers—a Leicester, an Essex, a Norfolk—found the arena for
their contests. It was an age of dependency; the tie of patron and
client descended from these magnates of the court to followers in
the country, themselves in turn patrons of clients of still lesser
degree. Through this hierarchy the rivalries of the court were
communicated to the country gentry, among whom faction and
feud also had its own independent life.[5]

What were the stakes of these rivalries? Certainly not matters
of public policy or social reform. For themselves the magnates
sought power, prestige, and material advantage—great offices of
state, the grant of manors, even the supreme prize of the Queen's
hand; for their followers, lesser offices and perquisites. In addition
to the hopes of future favor there were ties of personal loyalty and
traditional sentiment. It was a politics not of principle and program, but of honor and interest.

In Parliament there was one major exception. A politics of

[3] "A public weale," wrote Sir Thomas Elyot in 1531, "is a body living,
compact or made of sundry estates and degrees of men, which is disposed
by the order of equity and governed by the rule and moderation of reason."
The boke named The Governor (London, 1907), p. 1.
[4] R. H. Tawney, *Religion and the Rise of Capitalism* (London, 1936),
p. 169.
[5] Neale, *The Elizabethan House of Commons, passim.*

principle on a grand scale was introduced as early as the middle Elizabeth's reign by what Neale calls "the Puritan party."[6] On eve of the Long Parliament, this group, led by Pym, Hampden, and St. John, dominated the House of Commons and, working through the newly created committee system, continually initiated legislation reflecting a Puritan viewpoint.[7] Yet action of this kind lay well outside the bounds of the Old Tory theory of representation. For such transgressions Elizabeth sent members to the Tower. If Charles I could not succeed as well, that was because the country was on the verge of a Civil War which was to bring the era of Old Tory politics to an end.

OLD WHIG POLITICS

If this were a history of British politics, we could not avoid dealing with the new forms of organization and action that were thrown up during the Civil War and Restoration—Britain's great age of revolutionary politics. But these new forms—such as the Presbyterians, Independents and Levellers of the Civil War, or the Whigs and Tories of the Glorious Revolution—did not last, or rapidly changed their character. A stable pattern of thought and behavior only emerges in the eighteenth century. To this politics I have given the name Old Whig.

The Old Whig conception of authority included a theory of representation which, under the growing challenge of Liberal and Radical thought, was given explicit and elaborate form as the orthodox defense of the unreformed House of Commons. Although the men who used it most in the nineteenth century called themselves Tories, this theory was derived from the Whigs of the previous century, among whom the most articulate was Burke.[8] It is fair, therefore, to call it Old Whig in order to suggest its differences from what we have called Old Tory.

The New Justification of Hierarchy

In spite of lip service to Locke, eighteenth-century England was far from being an individualist society and, on the plane of

[6] Neale, *Elizabeth I and Her Parliaments 1584-1601* (London, 1957), p. 221.
[7] Notestein, *op. cit.*
[8] P. A. Gibbons, *Ideas of Political Representation in Parliament 1651-1832* (Oxford, 1914), p. 36.

ative ideals, the image of social reality had a strong corporatist
ge. Again, in Old Whig as in Old Tory thought, the corporatist
as inseparable from the hierarchic ideal. This was pre-eminently
n aristocratic age and the legitimacy of aristocratic rule was
hardly questioned. The equilibrium of the "balanced constitution,"
for instance, was not simply a matter of legal powers. It did not
rest and was not expected to rest, solely on the legal requirement
that, for example, each branch must consent to legislation. It was
also recognized that certain modes of nonlegal influence were
proper and necessary to maintain the balance. In particular, as
Hume observed, the Crown and the peers justifiably influenced
elections to the Commons and its deliberations, since otherwise
the popular house would be too powerful.[9]

The hierarchic ideal suffused Burke's thought even when, in
one of his most liberal moments, he called upon "the people" to
help throw back encroachments of royal power. In a memorable
phrase he says that the House of Commons should be "the express
image of the feelings of the nation."[1] But this is far from an appeal
to the masses—or, as the eighteenth century would say, the "mob."
Nor is it an appeal to the electors as isolated individuals. The force
he wishes to bring into play is "the natural strength of the kingdom : the great peers, the leading landed gentlemen, the opulent
merchants and manufacturers, the substantial yeomanry."[2] It is
through such natural leaders, themselves hierarchically ordered,
that "the people" act. Above all, they act and speak through the
great Whig families, rooted in the country by a "more natural and
fixed influence." The "little platoons," the ancient communities,
the estates, ranks, orders, and interests of realm and empire enter
the political arena through this system of natural hierarchy.

The Old Whig conception of the good society, in short, retained many of the basic features of the Old Tory ideal of the
hierarchic community. Yet the premises on which that ideal depended had shifted radically and in such a way as to permit a far
greater scope for human contrivance and changing circumstances.
The new justification of hierarchy, to put the matter in briefest
form, depended far more on sociology than cosmology. For the
Old Tory, the divine plan of the hierarchic community had indeed

[9] David Hume, "Of the Independency of Parliament," *Philosophical Essays
on Morals, Literature and Politics* (London, 1904) Vol. I, pp. 71–2.
[1] Edmund Burke, "Thoughts on the Cause of the Present Discontents,"
The Writings and Speeches of Edmund Burke (Boston, 1901), Vol. I, p. 492.
[2] *Ibid.*, p. 477.

a sociological sanction in that it was that form of society government which would work best. As Sir Thomas Elyot argu for instance, monarchy would promote order while aristocra and democracy were regimes prone to disorder and tumult. Bu the Old Tory thinker did not trouble himself greatly to seek out in history and illustrate from experience the consequences of various types of regime. His insight into the "similitudes" demonstrated that hierarchy was in itself the right way for men to rule and be ruled.

The eighteenth century had by no means forgotten the language of the older way of reasoning. The phrase "the great chain of being" is taken from Pope's *Essay on Man*, and Burke often seems to embrace an Old Tory cosmology. An instance is that famous passage in which he begins by saying that "society is indeed a contract" and then goes on to describe society (which he takes to be the same as the state) in terms making it the very opposite of a contract : "a partnership of all science; a partnership of all art; a partnership in every virtue, and in all perfection," whose "ends cannot be obtained in many generations." Echoing the imagery of the great chain, he continues :

Each contract of each particular state is but a clause in the great primaeval contract of eternal society, linking the lower with the higher natures, connecting the visible and invisible world, according to a fixed compact sanctioned by the inviolable oath which holds all physical and all moral natures, each in their appointed place. This law is not subject to the will of those, who by an obligation above them, and infinitely superior, are bound to submit their will to that law.[3]

That Burke believed in a Higher Law, sanctioned by our Creator, is not in dispute, although he was less than specific about the content of "that eternal, immutable law, in which will and reason are the same."[4] One can, however, believe in such a Higher Law, to which human law and political institutions must be subject, without accepting the Old Tory and medieval belief in a cosmos of many types of being, each with its *telos*. Scholars disagree violently over the question of whether Burke held to the older teleology.[5] What cannot be doubted, however, is that in

[3] "Reflections on the French Revolution," *Writings and Speeches*, Vol. IV, p. 359.
[4] *Ibid.*, p. 356.
[5] My own reading of Burke supports the interpretation of Paul Sigmund, who writes : "While he believed in fundamental principles of justice, natural law, in the Thomistic sense of a set of teleological goals in man's nature,

e's thought the emphasis had enormously shifted from cosmo-
cal to sociological justification. This is of great interest to the
student of British political culture as one of the many radical
adaptations that the ideal of hierarchy has made during its long
history as an operative ideal.

In his defense of Britain's hereditary monarchy, for instance,
Burke dismisses as foolish, even impious, the notion that monarchy
has "more of a divine sanction than any other mode of justification." Its true defense is pragmatic :

No experience has taught us, that in any other course or method
than that of an *hereditary crown* our liberties can be regularly perpetuated and preserved sacred as our *hereditary right* . . . the un-
disturbed succession of the crown [is] a pledge of the stability and
perpetuity of all the other members of our constitution.[6]

He similarly defends the other "establishments." By means of
the established church, "sublime principles" are "infused into persons of exalted stations" and "a wholesome awe" into "free citizens."[7] Hierarchy likewise has its function : if men are to be incor-
porated into a body politic, there must be differences of rank, a
"habitual social discipline, in which the wiser, the more expert, and
the more opulent conduct, and by conducting enlighten and protect, the weaker, the less knowing, and the less provided with the
goods of fortune."[8] But this aristocracy is not provided by a God-
given body of men with inherent, superior virtue. On the contrary,
it must be formed by favorable circumstances, which Burke sets
forth at great length :

To be bred in a place of estimation to see nothing low and sordid
from one's infancy; . . . to stand upon such elevated ground as to be
enabled to take a large view of the widespread and infinitely diversi-
fied combinations of men and affairs in a large society; to have leisure
to read, to reflect, to converse; . . . to be habituated in the pursuit of
honour and duty; . . . these are the circumstances of men, that form
what I should call a *natural* aristocracy, without which there is no
nation.[9]

does not seem to have been an important concept in Burke's political theory,
except in the early 'Tract on the Popery Laws.'" "Edmund Burke and the
Natural Law," *Natural Law Forum*, Vol. IV, No. 1 (1959), p. 171.

[6] "Reflections," *Writings and Speeches*, Vol. IV, pp. 263–5.

[7] *Ibid.*, pp. 353–4.

[8] "Appeal from the New to the Old Whigs," *Writings and Speeches*,
Vol. IV, p. 174.

[9] *Ibid.*, p. 175.

Thus from environment is that virtue acquired which justifies hierarchy.

There is no one "best model" for all states. In the course of its history, each nation works out the form of government and society appropriate to it. In his arraignment of Warren Hastings and the East India Company, therefore, Burke objected that India should be governed "upon their own principles and not upon ours." At times, "constitutions" need to be restored or even improved. On these occasions a nation should, as Burke advised the French and as they had failed to do, consult its past and build on the old foundations.[1] In this sense, government was an "experimental," not a "theoretical" science. The historical method opened the way for human will to play a large part in the development of states.

The New Distribution of Public Powers

Old Whig differed from Old Tory ideas not only on this high philosophic plane, but also in their allocation of authority. Indeed, although it was advocated by Burke, that great champion of ancient ways, the Old Whig view of the British constitution would have been subversive in the sixteenth century. That aspect in which it contrasts most sharply with the Old Tory view is, of course, the respective roles it gave to monarch and Parliament. The role of representing the community as a whole which, in Old Tory thought, was primarily the monarch's, now was shared by King, Lords, and Commons in what was called the "balanced constitution." While in the sixteenth century the three estates were identified as the Lords spiritual, the Lords temporal, and the Commons, in the eighteenth they were often held to consist of King, Lords, and Commons : the monarch, from being on a plane different from the estates of the realm, had now become one of them. And in this balanced constitution Lords and Commons, as well as the monarch, were charged with deliberating and pronouncing on the public interest and the common good. Although there was a certain recognition of the superior authority of the House of Commons, each branch was considered an independent power, more or less equal.

Our three estates of King, Lords and Commons making up the supreme Legislative power of the nation [wrote one authority in 1716],

[1] Cf. "Reflections," *Writings and Speeches,* Vol. IV, p. 277.

. . . as they are mutual checks and awes on one another so they are to one another mutual lights and assistants. In the equilibrium of this body and the unanimity 'of their deliberations, consists our greatest happiness; while to our further comfort, the nature of their proceedings is such that none of the estates can scarce ever be surprised or seduced into any pernicious measures, but that the other two may seasonably interpose.[2]

But if the King was now, in contrast with Old Tory theory and practice, only one among equals, the period of strong monarchy had left a bequest of the utmost importance to the English polity of later centuries. In Old Tory politics the monarch, assisted by his council, performed the function of what today is called "the Government." He controlled the administration at home, conducted foreign affairs, and monopolized the initiative in financial and other important legislation. In the eighteenth century this function was largely vested in the ministry. Certain members of the Commons and Lords held office and acted both individually and as a body under a prime minister, although hardly yet constituting a modern cabinet. Unlike Old Tory kings and modern cabinets, ministers did not monopolize the initiative in legislation. But in matters of finance they were firmly in control, the famous standing orders of the early part of the century having given them the sole right to initiate proposals for expenditure or taxation. Similarly, in foreign affairs and in the power to make war and peace, their power was decisive.

In this threefold constitution, ministers were in part responsible to the King, who might well have ideas of his own. At the same time it was on the whole recognized that they had to have a majority in Parliament and especially in the House of Commons. That the ministry should have three masters, it may be thought, would be a source of confusion. Indeed it was, particularly under George III. Yet for the theory and practice of British government, it was, and still is, of the utmost importance that there should have survived from the era of strong monarchy this idea of a central initiating, directing, energizing body. Thus was preserved an element around which the vast powers of a modern cabinet could collect. Also there was set before the eyes of the competing factions of Old Whig politics a prize of great value: not merely the individual offices of state, but the comprehensive authority of the

[2] John Toland, author of *The State Anatomy of Great Britain*, as quoted in Betty Kemp, *King and Commons 1660–1832* (London, 1953), p. 83.

"King's Government." To assume that authority, however, m̄
also assuming an obligation—that the King's Government m̄
be carried on. This familiar maxim was at the heart of what Ga⸗
calls the "oligarchic tradition" of politics carried over from th⸗
eighteenth into the nineteenth century.[3] It meant, at the least, that
there were certain needs that must be met, certain tasks to be
performed, whether ministers had or had not so committed themselves by party preference or previous declarations. Something of
the older notions of both the monarch's independent authority and
of his responsibility for the common good shaped the role of
ministry and cabinet.[4]

Parliamentarism and Functional Representation

Whether in making laws or controlling the ministry, the House
of Commons now had the role—consistently denied it by Old
Tory monarchs—of representing the community as a whole as
well as its several parts. Now the members for Bristol, in Burke's
famous words, were not only "members for a rich commercial
city," but also for the "nation which however is itself a part of a
great empire extended by our virtue and fortune to the farthest
limits of the East and of the West." Hence, Parliament was not
"a congress of ambassadors from different and hostile interests,
which interests each must maintain as an agent and advocate against
other agents and advocates." It was rather "a deliberative assembly
of one nation with one interest, that of the whole—where not local
prejudices ought to guide but the general good resulting from the
general reason of the whole."[5]

What we may call the parliamentarism of the Old Whig conception consisted, first, in this notion of the Member of Parliament as
the representative of the whole community as well as of its component interests. He performed this function in Parliament with
his fellows by deliberating on the great questions of state. That is
the second element in Old Whig parliamentarism : deliberation.
It is, so to speak, a "thought" rather than a "will" theory of how
the general good is arrived at. As Burke said to his constituents : "If

[3] Norman Gash, *Politics in the Age of Peel : a Study in the Technique
of Parliamentary Representation* (London 1953), p. xviii.
[4] See Norman Gash, "Peel and the Party System, 1830–50," *Transactions
of the Royal Historical Society,* 5th ser., Vol. I (1951), pp. 47–69.
[5] Election speech of November 3, 1774, *Writings and Speeches,* Vol. II,
pp. 89–98.

rnment were a matter of will upon any side, yours without stion, ought to be superior. But government and legislation are atters of reason and judgment and not of inclination." While a member ought to give "great weight" to the wishes of his constituents, he ought never to sacrifice to them "his unbiased opinion, his mature judgment, his enlightened conscience."[6]

It followed that who was desired as a member was not the typical or the popular man, but rather the man of wisdom and ability. Rotten boroughs and "influence" were defended, therefore, because they could provide seats for those who might not please the ordinary elector but who had high qualities of mind and character. Lord John Russell himself frequently acknowledged the strength of this argument and gave it as his reason for the toleration shown to a number of rotten boroughs by the Act of 1832. For Burke, as Pares says, the House of Commons was "a sanhedrin of skilled legislators" who interpreted "the cries of distress" of the people.[7] They knew (or should know) "the stable and eternal rules of justice and reason," in Burke's phrase. It was their wisdom and experience, not merely their literally representative chearacter, that gave them the right to rule.

Parliamentarism ruled out "authoritative instructions" and "mandates" from the electorate. It also ruled out associations formed outside Parliament for the purpose of determining what Parliament ought to do and for pressing these decisions on it as coming from a higher authority. The Yorkshire Association of 1779–80, which in the minds of some of its supporters would command Parliament as "the principal to the delegate,"[8] was regarded as an "anti-parliament."[9] "The people of England collectively," replied Lord North to the demands of the Association, "could only be heard [through] their representatives in Parliament."[1] For similar reasons, the House of Commons refused even to receive a petition from the Stamp Act Congress in 1766. A major development in the politics of the nineteenth century was the immense growth of such associations, formed for the purpose of putting pressure on Parliament. Through them, public opinion acquired a new and flexible system of channels of political expression.

[6] *Ibid.*
[7] Richard Pares, *King George III and the Politicians* (Oxford, 1953), p. 43.
[8] Herbert Butterfield, *George III, Lord North and The People, 1779–80* (London, 1949), p. 192.
[9] Pares, *op. cit.*, pp. 52–3.
[1] Butterfield, *op. cit.*, p. 341.

But if interests were forbidden the use of this device to obtain a voice in government, that does not mean that the Old Whig theory would exclude them from representation. On the contrary, their representation in Parliament was as legitimate as it had ever been in Tudor or medieval times, and indeed, if we follow Burke, even more necessary. For as he described it, the process of deliberation was not performed in isolation. One of its principal starting points was the array of all the "widespread interests" of nation and empire which in Parliament "must be considered—must be compared—must be reconciled, if possible." Groups interested in influencing legislation were inhibited from forming voluntary associations to put pressure on Parliament and were obliged to proceed through what the Porritts have called "official outlets." This meant that petitions and other expressions of public opinion outside Parliament were normally expected to come from such bodies as the municipal corporations, the universities, deans and chapters of cathedrals, magistrates in petty sessions, and grand juries at quarter sessions and assizes.[2] But so long as interest groups proceeded through such legitimate and restricted channels, they were given a generous role in government. Access to these channels was crucial.

The Old Whig view thus involved a definition not only of the mode of representation, but also of the nature of the interests that were considered legitimate. As compared with Liberal and Radical ideas, it conceived of representation as being not of individuals, but rather of corporate bodies, although not in the strict legal sense of the term. The legitimate interests were not shifting groups of individuals who happened to share similar opinions and wishes, as was the case with the great pressure groups formed as voluntary associations in the nineteenth century. Burke attacked the philosophy of natural rights because, among other things, it proposed "personal representation" and failed to recognize "corporate personality,"[3] and for many years one of the charges against parliamentary reformers was that they championed "individual

[2] Edward and Annie Porritt, *The Unreformed House of Commons: Parliamentary Representation before 1832* (Cambridge, 1903), Vol. I, p. 270. "Cockburn, in describing public opinion in the last twenty years of the eighteenth century, states that it was 'recognized only when expressed through what were acknowledged to be its legitimate organs,' which meant its formal or official outlets."

[3] Speech in the House of Commons on the state of the representation, May 7, 1782, *Writings and Speeches*, Vol. VII, pp. 92–3.

representation" which, in addition to its suggestion of universal suffrage, also implied equal electoral districts in the place of the ancient, unified communities of the old system.

The legitimate interests, in this sense "fixed" and "corporate," were of two broad types, local and functional, although normally in representation one type easily passed over into the other. First there were the local communities, united by ancient ties of interest that M.P.'s might and ought to promote in Parliament. Then there were the broad social groupings not confined to a particular place —the various "estates," "ranks," "orders" and, to use the term most commonly employed, "interests"—of which the nation and empire were composed. Such functional groupings, not individuals, were the basic units of representation along with the local communities. Consequently, virtual representation was possible : the M.P. from Bristol, for example, virtually represented not only that city, but also all other places which did not have actual representation in Parliament, but which, as out-ports and centers of shipping and commerce, had common interests with Bristol.

This notion of functional representation was a principal basis of the defense of the unreformed House of Commons. It was present in Burke's general view of society as well as his idea of representation, and went back to Tudor and medieval times. The existing system brought into Parliament not only the men of wisdom and ability needed for deliberation, but also representatives of all the great functional interests. Variety of franchise was defended against uniformity because it enabled a variety of interests to be represented. Rotten boroughs were justified because they opened a parliamentary career to men of the various professional interests. Along with parliamentarism, the functional representation of interests in the House of Commons was one of the two main poles around which clustered the sentiments and ideas of the Old Whig theory.

While for purposes of exposition Burke's statement of the Old Whig theory has been made central, the leading traits of the theory can be traced through the sixty years of debate over parliamentary reform. They achieve a certain definitive form in the great speech of Sir Robert Harry Inglis in reply to Lord John Russell's motion introducing the first Reform Bill on March 1, 1831. All the essentials are there. Members of Parliament, he said, are not deputies and are not bound by "the cries of a majority of the people" to decide in favor of any change. They represent not a particular place, but the whole empire, and should follow the will of their constituents only if it coincides with their "own deliberate sense of right." At the same time, the House is

the most complete representation of the interests of the people which was ever assembled in any age or country. It is the only constituent body that ever existed, which comprehends within itself, those who can urge the wants and defend the claims of the landed, the commercial, the professional classes of the country; those who are bound to uphold the prerogatives of the Crown, the privileges of the nobility, the interests of the lower classes, . . . the rights of the distant dependencies, of the East Indies, of the West Indies, of the colonies, of the great corporations.

How unnecessary and dangerous to alter a system that provides such wide and balanced representation, which "admits all classes, lets in all interests, and invites all talents"![4]

If at the present moment I had imposed upon me the duty of forming a legislature for any country [the Duke of Wellington had said in eulogy of the unreformed Parliament], and particularly for a country like this, in possession of great property of various descriptions, I do not mean to assert that I could form such a legislature as we possess now, for the nature of man is incapable of reaching such excellence at once, but my great endeavor would be to form some description of legislature which would produce the same results.[5]

The Old Whig theory did not die in 1832. The ideal of parliamentarism was adopted by the Liberals of the nineteenth century; even today it finds advocates, although its practice could hardly be reconciled with the realities of present-day party government. Whatever people may wish or say, in Britain, as on the continent, parliamentarism, as a mode of political action, has been in decline for many years. Functional representation, on the other hand, has had rather greater survival value. The idea was used by both sides in the struggle over parliamentary reform in the 1830's. While virtually all opponents of reform accepted it, even some reformers

[4] *Parl. Deb.*, 3rd ser., Vol. II, 1090ff (1 March 1831). See also for discussion of representation *Parl. Hist.*, Vol. XXI, 686ff (3 June 1780); Vol. XXII, 1416ff (7 May 1782); Vol. XXIII, 826ff (6 May 1783); Vol. XXV, 432ff (18 April 1785); Vol. XXVIII, 452ff (4 March 1790); Vol. XXX, 787ff (2 May 1793); *Parl. Deb.*, new ser., Vol. VII, 51–141 (25 April 1822).
[5] *Parl. Deb.*, 3rd ser., Vol I, 52 (2 November 1830).

found it useful. In their view the Reform Bill, far from being an innovation, simply adapted the existing system to the changed circumstances of the country by giving to the new manufacturing interests, along with the other interests of society, their rightful share in representation. This, for instance, was the line taken by Melbourne and Palmerston in 1831. From the Old Whig theory descended Disraeli's argument for the representation of a "variety of interests" with which he supported his "fancy franchises" proposal in 1859[6] and which was adopted by the "philosophic Liberals," such as Bagehot.[7]

In the Victorian era, however, "class" rather than "interest" came more and more to be the term used to refer to the social units deserving representation and, in the languid contest over the reform of 1867, the Old Whig theory was advocated and attacked as the "balance of classes" argument.[8] This point of view could hardly be stretched to cover the reform of 1885, but we find Randolph Churchill, for instance, resisting majority rule in defense of the representation of a variety of interests and classes.[9] Nor did the arrival of democracy exclude the Old Whig view from public debate over representation. But in the twentieth century a new pluralism, in theory and fact, provided new foundations for functional representation. With these new forces the old attitudes blend, strengthening them and enhancing their legitimacy.[1]

Party in Old Whig Politics

In Parliament, which by the eighteenth century had become the center of political struggle, the leading antagonists were the great aristocratic families with their dependent clients. These "connections" provided the leaders who, in shifting coalitions, fought the parliamentary battles for the power of office and the spoil that went with it. Do we find among these political groups what may be called "party"? A good deal of ink has been spilled over this question, but the answer seems to depend on which of the many definitions of "party" one chooses to follow. If the collective pursuit of office is stressed then the aristocratic connections may be

---

[6] 152 *H.C. Deb.*, 966ff (28 February 1859).
[7] Walter Bagehot, *Essays on Parliamentary Reform* (London, 1883), p. 3.
[8] A. V. Dicey, "The Balance of Classes," *Essays on Reform* (London, 1867).
[9] 285 *H.C. Deb.*, 173–8 (28 February 1884).
[1] See below, pp. 73–9.

called parties.[2] Like the Labour and Conservative parties of today, they sought to win the direct exercise of authority for their leaders. But the differences in structure, purpose, and method are vast. They did not, of course, have "programmes" like those presented to the voters today; nor did they have distinctive social philosophies such as the major British parties have sometimes entertained. Public opinion among the electorate was not, with some exceptions, a force they had to reckon with. Not "organization," but the hierarchic ties of patron and client, landlord and tenant provided the typical channels of electoral influence. Again, looking back to the previous century we see that, unlike the Puritan party of Stuart times, they accepted the reigning conceptions of authority and of the social, economic, and religious order. In method and aim they were anything but revolutionary.

Yet the opportunities of the competitive pursuit of office do not always fully explain their differing stands on public affairs. In particular, between George III and certain of his supporters, on the one hand, and the Rockingham Whigs, on the other, a difference emerges that may be rightly called one of "principle"—a common viewpoint that had some force in holding together the respective sides and in shaping their purposes. George, sharing ideas much like those stated by Bolingbroke in the Patriot King, hated "connection." He wished to break up the system by which the aristocratic leaders formed a government by means of a coalition and, so it seemed to the King, forced him to accept their nominees for the ministry. Thus, in setting up the Chatham administration in 1766, he sought to choose ministers irrespective of their aristocratic alliances and in this sense to establish a non-"party" government.[3]

Like the King, the Rockingham Whigs feared, and thought they saw, an unbalancing of the constitution—but to them the offender was George himself. They were united by their desire to defend the balanced constitution and by their judgment that George was threatening it. This was their justification of a "formed opposition" —of party in Burke's defense—against the King and Court; only by acting in concert, it seemed to them, could they restore the balance of the constitution and maintain the rights of Parliament.

[2] In these aristocratic factions, Namier finds the forerunners of "modern" party. "Monarchy and the Party System," Personalities and Powers (New York, 1955).

[3] I am following Herbert Butterfield, George III and the Historians (London, 1957).

In this Old Whig system, however, we are still far from finding political formations like the Conservatives and Liberals of Victorian times, not to mention the parties of today. In contrast with Old Tory thought and practice, it was legitimate for Members of Parliament, acting in concert, to struggle for office and to initiate legislation or policy proposals on broad matters of national concern. To this extent some progress had been made in legitimizing party in the Victorian and modern meanings of the word. But that such bodies, united on differing principles, should be normal and durable features of political life was in general not accepted and certainly not thought desirable.[4]

THE REPRESENTATION OF INTERESTS

In 1947 the Committee of Privileges of the House of Commons was considering whether it was a breach of privilege for a member and any body of persons outside his constituency to enter into an agreement by which the member should pursue a prescribed line in Parliament in return for a salary. In the course of taking testimony Earl Winterton, then the "Father of the House," observed that the question had never been decided. He went on to remark that, nevertheless, "this situation has existed for a very long time. It must have existed in the eighteenth century when Members' seats were purchased for them?" "That is so, undoubtedly," replied Sir Gilbert Campion, the Clerk of the House.[5]

If we are looking for continuities in the history of the "interested" M.P., one of the most significant aspects of eighteenth-century politics is the relationship between patron and nominee. This relationship provided a principal theme of parliamentary reformers. In presenting the petition of the Society of the Friends of the People in 1793, Lord Grey stressed as his principal objection

---

[4] Although the dominant opinion "condemned party and faction, advocated uniformity of opinion and praised non-partisanship," there were some who regarded party as inevitable or even desirable, as Dr. Caroline Robbins has brought out in her sketch " 'Discordant Parties' : A Study of the Acceptance of Party by Englishmen," *Political Science Quarterly*, Vol. LXXIII, No. 4 (December, 1958), pp. 505–29. See also Peter Campbell, "An Early Defence of Party," *Political Studies*, Vol. III, No. 2 (June, 1955), pp. 166–7 for a favorable view at mid-century.

[5] *Report of the Committee of Privileges, H.C.* 118 (1946–47); minutes of evidence, p. 7.

the "system of private patronage which is so repugnant to spirit of free representation."[6] Historians as well as reformers ha. minutely examined the facts, the most elaborate analysis bein. provided by Namier, who determined that out of 489 English M.P.'s in 1760, 192 had been returned by patrons, along with 32 others returned by Government influence.[7] This relationship normally involved the payment of election expenses by the patron, as well as the exercise of other kinds of influence on behalf of his client, and, on the part of the M.P., a very considerable degree of dependence. "If he does not obey the instructions he receives," said Fox, "he is not to be considered a man of honour and a gentleman."[8] Confirming this, the Porritts say that the code governing the relations of patron and member required the member to resign if he parted company from his patron in his voting in Parliament. No less a man than the younger Pitt, for instance, upon being returned for one of Sir James Lowther's pocket boroughs in 1780, wrote of his relations with his patron that "no kind of condition was mentioned but that if ever our lines of conduct should be opposite, I should give him the opportunity of choosing another member."[9] Even when Pitt was a leading member of the House, he reported to Lowther his refusal of an offer from the King to form a Government and promised to explain further his motives.[1]

The House of Commons seems never to have been without members bearing some such relation to outside persons or bodies. As Gash has shown, aristocratic patronage flourished, although with declining strength, in and beyond the mid-Victorian era.[2] As aristocracy declined, new forms of patronage arose in the latter part of the nineteenth century. The form with which we are best acquainted today is provided by the trade union M.P. who, having secured appointment to the union's panel of candidates and adoption by a constituency party, has his election expenses largely paid by the union and often receives in addition a salary for services in Parliament, where he sits in a "representative capacity"

[6] *Parl. Hist.*, Vol. XXX, 793 (6 May 1793).
[7] L. B. Namier, *The Structure of Politics at the Accession of George III* (London, 1929), Vol. I, p. 182.
[8] Quoted in Porritt, *op. cit.*, Vol. I, p. 311.
[9] R. S. Ferguson, *Cumberland and Westmoreland M.P.s from the Restoration to the Reform Bill of 1867* (London, 1871), pp. 173-4.
[1] *Hist. MMS. Comm.*, 13th Rept., approx. Pt. VII, Lonsdale MSS. (27 February 1783).
[2] Norman Gash, *Politics in the Age of Peel, passim.*

the union.[3] What degree of dependence will in fact be ~~~rated, the House has not made entirely clear. It has refused to ~~~ndemn such arrangements, yet it has said that they must not ~~~nfringe "the complete independence and freedom of action" of Members of Parliament.[4]

What use was made of "sponsored" M.P.'s in Old Whig practice? How far did they act to promote the economic interests of their patrons? From the historians we have learned in abundant detail how they were employed to further their patrons' interests in office, patronage, and emoluments. The basic structure of the aristocratic factions of the time consisted of little clusters of nominees, grouped around their patrons, who formed the complex alliances that provided ministers and their opponents with a considerable part of their followings. Patronage of many varieties was the cement that held patrons in these alliances, and which in turn often provided the patrons themselves with the means of maintaining their influence over elections.

Historians have not yet examined in much detail, however, the role of the sponsored M.P. in relation to the economic interests of his patron. This would especially require detailed inquiry into the processes of private bill legislation, a field that is almost entirely unexplored. But since that inquiry cannot usefully be separated from a broader inquiry into the ways in which interested M.P.'s, whether sponsored or not, sought to represent the great functional interests of the society, it is in this larger context that we shall look at the problem. In general, Old Whig practice fitted closely with the Old Whig theory of representation.

[3] Replying to a Conservative who asked why an M.P. who was an official of the miners' union should not "declare his interest" in pending legislation as would, e.g., a director of a mining company, a Labour member said that the distinction was that the miners' official sat in "a representative capacity." 348 *H.C. Deb.* 1720ff (16 June 1939).

[4] See the debate on the report from the Committee of Privileges mentioned above p. 22, n. 5; 440 *H.C. Deb.* 284–386 (15 July 1947). Mr. R. H. S. Crossman (Lab.) recently wrote : ". . . a considerable number of MPs on both sides of the Commons act as the paid political agents of outside bodies —whether trade unions, churches, business companies or pressure groups— lobbying Ministers on their behalf and sometimes, when they rise to speak, reading aloud almost verbatim, the brief they have received from the body which retains their services." These relations, he continued, only become "unethical if [the M.P.] conceals their existence when he speaks on their behalf. And the only breach of Parliamentary privilege which can occur is if the outside organization brings improper pressure to bear on him, in order to influence his vote." Quoted in Andrew Roth, *The Business Background of Members of Parliament* (London, 1963?), p. xv.

Private Bill Legislation

The eighteenth century, unlike the Victorian era, was not an age of memorable Acts of Parliament. At mid-century, parliamentary activity probably reached its lowest ebb. When one thinks of Government programs even in the quiet times of later generations, it is striking to find that at the opening of Parliament in 1753 the King's Speech, after requesting supply, had nothing further to recommend to the attention of the assembled Houses except the increase in the "horrid Crimes of Robbery and Murder."[5] In the session that followed, some 69 bills were enacted. While 35 were classed as "Private Acts" and 34 as "Publick Acts,"[6] nearly every one would be classed as private by modern standards, and most of them were introduced by unofficial members. This does not mean that they were insignificant. Although few great strides in reform were taken during this century, countless small steps in legislation carried the country a long distance in social and economic development. As Pares has remarked :

most of this legislation was private, local and facultative, setting up local agencies, such as turnpike, paving, enclosure, or improvement commissioners where such things appeared to be desired by the preponderant local interests. . . . Even legislation which was ostensibly national, imposing customs duties or regulating overseas trade, often had local implications and members of parliament handled it as agents of local interests.[7]

A few examples taken from private bill legislation will show Old Whig practice in the concrete and will suggest the general tactics of interest-group politics in the period.

The criterion of the subject-matter of private bills was far from precise in the eighteenth century. In general, they were those bills "affecting the interests of individuals or localities and not of a general public character."[8] Procedure in private bills contrasted sharply with the semijudicial character given it in the nineteenth

---

[5] *Journals of the House of Commons*, Vol. XVI (November 15, 1753).

[6] *Statutes at Large*, Vol. VII (London, 1786).

[7] Pares, *op. cit.*, p. 3.

[8] The words are those of Clifford, who implies that they stated the criterion in the eighteenth century—when also, as he notes, some local bills were included among public bills by being explicitly declared to be public. Frederick Clifford, *A History of Private Bill Legislation* (London, 1885), Vol. I, p. 267. The best eighteenth-century account of procedure, *The Liverpool Tractate*, C. Strateman, ed. (New York, 1937), does not give a

…ury, ample opportunity being given for the intervention of …erested M.P.'s, indeed, as Pares observes, the power of decision …eing largely left to them.[9] In contrast with public bills then and …now, private bills began with a petition from the interested party, alleging a state of affairs which needed legislative remedy and praying that leave be granted to bring in a bill for the purpose. In the normal course, a member from the locality to which the petition related would present it to the House, after which it would be referred to a committee. (A petition for a bill to enclose, however, was not sent to a committee on the petition, but led directly to the introduction of the bill.) While a member could not present a bill for which he himself had petitioned, he could, as we shall see, present a petition and guide the course of a bill which intimately concerned his personal interests.

The committee on the petition was chosen on the following principle : "those best qualified to serve were those who had some personal, local or professional knowledge of the matter, and who represented interests likely to be affected."[1] After the chairman of the committee had reported to the House and it had decided to give leave for the introduction of the bill, members were appointed

---

definition of the scope of private bills. "Broadly speaking the terms *public* and *private* of earlier times correspond to a commonsense division of Acts into those of general and those of local or personal application"; *Acts of Parliament : Some Distinctions in their Nature and Numbering*, H.C. Library, Doc. No. 1 (London, H.M.S.O., 1955), p. 3. Yet, as noted above, judged by the meaning given nowadays to "general" in contrast with "personal" or "local," a very great many Public Acts of the eighteenth century would today be called Private.

[9] This summary of private bill procedure is based principally upon O. Cyprian Williams, *The Historical Development of Private Bill Procedure and Standing Orders in the House of Commons* (London, H.M.S.O., 1948), Vol. I.

[1] Williams, *op. cit.*, p. 30. In a note to the author, Mr. D. McW. Millar, of the clerical staff of the House of Commons, has written : "The principle in the mid-18th century underlying the nomination of local members to committees on private bills was that those best qualified to serve were those who had some personal, local or professional knowledge of the matter, and who represented interests likely to be affected. It was held to be not only a duty, but a right of such members to speak and to vote in committee on matters of which, through local or personal interest, they had special knowledge and decided, if biased, views. . . . In the 18th century, the preamble, or principle, of the Bill was opposed by counsel appearing at the Bar of the House. This afforded an opportunity for discussion of the national, as opposed to the local, interest, so that the committees could devote themselves particularly to the local issues, with the local members present."

to prepare and present the bill, which after a second reading sent to a committee chosen on the same principle of interest representation. Counsel for and against might be heard in committee or in some circumstances, at the bar of the House. Report was made by the chairman (who it appears was normally the member who had introduced the bill) and, after passing through further stages, the bill went to the Lords.

Gradual yet revolutionary in their effect, the enclosure acts are the clearest examples of profound social development brought about by private legislation. From 1719 to 1845 some 4,100 acts were passed, the peak of activity being reached around the turn of the century. Except for a few eccentric poets and divines and an occasional petitioner before the House, opposition was negligible. Of the 5,034 members who sat in the House of Commons from 1734 to 1832, fully three quarters had their principal economic interest in land.[2]

While the passage of the enclosure acts does not provide examples of the conflict of interests in the parliamentary arena, it can be used to illustrate the role of the interested M.P. The painstaking work of W. E. Tate, for instance, "brings out quite clearly," as he says, "the connection which actually existed between the landowning gentry and the Enclosure movement."[3] His elaborate data for Nottinghamshire show that the main burden of preparing, presenting, and reporting the bills fell to the knights of the shire from that county, and their role in reporting implies that they very probably also acted as chairmen of the committees on the bills. For example, Lord Edward Charles Cavendish Bentinck, second son of the second Duke of Portland, a great magnate in the county, presented or reported (or both) some 44 enclosure bills while he was M.P. from Nottinghamshire from 1775 to 1796.

In the light of the reforms of procedure in the nineteenth century, it is worthwhile to try to see just how closely a member might be linked with the interests being favored by the bills he was concerned with. Tate's data permit some inferences as to what was and was not permitted. Personal interest did set some limit on

[2] Gerritt P. Judd IV, *Members of Parliament, 1734-1832* (New Haven, 1955), p. 71.
[3] W. E. Tate, *Parliamentary Land Enclosures in the County of Nottingham during the 18th and 19th centuries* (Nottingham, 1935), Thoroton Society Record Series, Vol. V, p. 137.

part played by the member. An M.P. would not, apparently,
sent or prepare a bill concerning a place of which he was lord
the manor. A son and heir, however, fairly often would prepare
nd present a bill for which his father had petitioned. A nominee
might prepare a bill for which his patron had petitioned. For
example, in 1773 the Rt. Hon. J. Shelley, a boon companion of
the second Duke of Newcastle, helped prepare a bill for which the
Duke had petitioned. Shelley had been returned for Newark in
1768 by the Duke, then the ninth Earl of Lincoln.[4] It also appears
that a member connected with a petitioner by ties of family or
patronage would commonly sit on the committee handling the
relevant bill, although he would rarely be the chairman of the
committee and therefore charged with reporting it to the House.
In all of this, as Tate remarks, the eighteenth century saw nothing
striking, much less scandalous. It was indeed wholly in accord
with the Old Whig theory of interest representation.

The virtual absence of opposition makes the enclosure bills
exceptional. In contrast, Walpole's excise scheme of 1733 was
bitterly and successfully opposed by trading interests in a contest
involving floods of petitions, numerous deputations to Westminster, and an extensive war of pamphlets.[5] Even schemes for
turnpike roads sometimes involved a contest, as, for example, when
towns differed over the proposed route and rival petitions for and
against a pending scheme were received by the House. Proposals
for river navigation improvement, which formed an important part
of private bill legislation from the seventeenth century on, often
met with hostility from land carriers who would be threatened
with competition, from towns that would lose trade, or from local
producers who feared the influx of competing goods. Sometimes
these proposals gave rise to long and fierce parliamentary struggles
carried on by petitions and counterpetitions and by lobbying at
Westminster and in the counties. For twenty-one years at the beginning of the century, for example, opposing interests successfully resisted the enactment of the scheme to improve the River
Weaver.[6]

[4] Tate, op. cit., p. 49; Namier, Structure of Politics, p. 269; and
Debrett's, passim.
[5] E. R. Turner, "The Excise Scheme of 1733," English Historical Review,
Vol. XLII (January, 1927), pp. 34–57. Turner's appendix lists some 700
pamphlets issued during the struggle.
[6] T. S. Willan, River Navigation in England, 1600–1750 (Oxford, 1936),
pp. 34–6.

Canal Politics

For the sake of illustration we may look briefly at the passage of two canal acts in 1762 and 1766, respectively, which set off the canal boom of the late eighteenth century.[7] The first of these, the Longford Bridge scheme, which provided for a canal to cheapen transportation between Manchester and Liverpool, was promoted by the Duke of Bridgewater and executed by James Brindley, the untutored genius of the age of canals. Its passage illustrates how sponsored M.P.'s might be used to promote their patrons' interests and the way in which a private bill might become involved in the general political contests of the time.

The City of Liverpool, being interested in cheaper transportation, naturally sided with the Duke in the parliamentary struggle, lending assistance through petitions and especially through its two members. More important, however, was the support the Duke received from his political connections. Although not taking an active part in politics himself, he was associated through his brother-in-law, the second Earl Gower, with one of the powerful aristocratic factions. This faction, sometimes known as the "Bloomsbury gang," was an alliance of the Duke of Bedford, Lord Gower, and Lord Weymouth and included their nominees, relations, and other followers in the House of Commons. From the mid-forties, it had supported various Whig ministries and shared in high office; by 1761 it formed one of the pillars of the Government of the Duke of Newcastle. Through this alliance the Longford Bridge scheme enjoyed the support not only of the Bedford-Gower group in the House, but also of Newcastle. Opposing the bill were a few groups of traders, certain gentry whose land the canal would pass through or near and, especially, an existing—and lucrative—statutory undertaking, the Mersey and Irewell Navigation Company, which had a monopoly on river transportation between Manchester and Liverpool.

The role of nominees can be briefly sketched. Richard Rigby,

[7] The account of the passage of these two acts is based on the *Journals* of the House of Commons and the House of Lords; Clifford, *op. cit.;* Samuel Smiles, *Lives of the Great Engineers* (London, 1867), Vol. I; J. C. Wedgwood, *Parliamentary History of Staffordshire* (London, 1922), Vol. II, Pt. II; J. Philips, *A General History of Inland Navigation* (London, 1792); and Namier, *Structure of Politics* and *England in the Age of the American Revolution* (London, 1930), which have been particularly useful in identifying nominees and patrons.

.P. for the Duke of Bedford's pocket borough of Tavistock and
manager of the Bedford-Gower group in the Commons, was
chairman of the committee on the petition, reported to the House
for the committee, served on the committee of three to prepare
the bill, and reported for the committee on the bill. Alderman
Marsh Dickinson, who sat for the Duke of Bridgewater's pocket
borough of Brackley, was one of the three members appointed to
prepare the bill and also presented the bill to the House. Among
the tellers on the Duke's side in various divisions, in addition to
Rigby and Dickinson, were Robert Henley-Ongley, M.P. for
Bedford and a nominee of the Duke of Bedford; Lord John
Cavendish and Welbore Ellis, members of the Newcastle group;
and Sir Ellis Cunliffe and Sir William Meredith, M.P.'s for Liverpool.

The passage of the bill took some four months from the presentation of the petition in November, 1761, to the granting of the
Royal Assent in March, 1762, the major struggle taking place not
in committee, but in the House of Commons after the bill was
reported during the last two weeks of February. Numerous petitions for and against were received, counsel were heard at the bar
of the House, and several days were spent in debate marked by
closely contested divisions. On three occasions during this time
the Duke sent out letters—a total of 700—to friends of the measure, explaining it and whipping up support. After a final division
of 133–114, the bill was sent to the Lords where, after report by
the committee on the bill (on which the Duke of Bridgewater and
Lord Gower sat), it was passed without amendment.

A similar pattern of tactics and opposing forces can be traced in
the passage of the Act of 1766, which authorized a canal between
the Trent and the Mersey rivers, linking Hull and Liverpool by
water and passing through the potteries of Staffordshire. Beginning in 1755 interest in the project had been shown by various
parties, among them the City of Liverpool, Lord Gower, who was
a magnate of immense wealth in Staffordshire, Josiah Wedgwood
of the potteries, and other landowners, traders, and manufacturers
of the region. Several meetings in 1765 culminated in a gathering
in Staffordshire at the end of December, over which Lord Gower,
the Lord Lieutenant, presided. Among those present were the
M.P.'s for the county, William Bagot, an independent "Tory"
squire, and George Harry, Lord Grey, a nominee of Lord Gower's
and eldest son of the Earl of Stamford; the M.P.'s for Lichfield,

Hugo Meynell, another Gower nominee, and Thomas Anson, sitting by right of his own family influence and also a close friend of Josiah Wedgwood; the M.P.'s for Gower's pocket borough of Newcastle-under-Lyme, Thomas Gilbert and Sir L. Dundas. Gilbert, a barrister, was land agent for Lord Gower and the manager of his parliamentary interest as well as a promoter of the canal scheme. At this meeting the engineer of the Duke of Bridgewater, James Brindley, who had made the survey for the canal, explained the scheme and it was decided to open a subscription for £101,000 and to apply to Parliament for an act to authorize the canal.

Proceedings in Parliament ran from mid-January to mid-May, 1766, and were accompanied by the usual petitioning for and against, lobbying by parties concerned, argument by opposing counsel, and promotion by members of the House of their own and their patrons' interests. Opposition came mainly from two river navigation commissions, threatened by competition from the proposed line of transportation, and from a number of Cheshire gentry whose lands would be affected by the canal. The principal part in guiding the bill through the House was taken by one of the promoters of the scheme, William Bagot. He also sat on the committee on the petition, helped prepare the bill, presented it to the House, sat on the committee on the bill, and took the bill to the House of Lords. Thomas Gilbert, like Bagot a promoter of the scheme, similarly sat on the committee on the petition and helped prepare the bill, and after serving, probably as chairman, on the committee on the bill, reported it to the House. Robert Wood, a nominee of the Duke of Bridgewater, sat on the committee on the petition and Sir L. Dundas sat on the committees on the petition and on the bill. In the House of Lords, Lord Gower himself reported for the committee on the bill.

These cases serve to illustrate the pattern of interest-group politics in the Old Whig period. More could be said about the activity of commercial centers in promoting or opposing legislation, both private and public, related to their interests. Isaac Gascoyne, M.P. for Liverpool from 1796 to 1831, for example, is said to have promoted some 200 bills at the instigation of his constituents. From the seventeenth century on, merchants, sometimes acting through the great chartered companies, pressed for "legislation to protect their special interests."[8] And legislation was not the only sphere in

[8] Dorothy Marshall, *English People in the 18th Century* (London, 1956), p. 23.

which advantage could be sought. In 1763 the influence of the West Indian sugar planters has been called decisive when, at the Peace of Paris, Canada was retained and the French sugar islands were returned to France.[9] The powers of administrative bodies might also be influenced by individuals or groups.[1] And no general sketch would be complete without mention of the long-continued, influential, and complex political activities of the East India Company. Its power rested less upon its bloc of M.P.'s than upon its immense financial resources; moreover, it not only penetrated Parliament, but was itself penetrated by political factions struggling to control its board of directors.[2]

The politics of the middle decades of the eighteenth century did not consist solely in the struggle of aristocratic connections pursuing power and patronage. At times one can also detect the clash of principle. Moreover, as I have stressed, groups vigorously pursued their economic self-interest in a manner fully legitimized by Old Whig norms. Over a period of time this group politics might produce significant shifts in policy, as in the case of the enclosure acts. Yet on the whole it presupposed a wide consensus within the active political community. Almost without question, the members of that community accepted not only the aristocratic order and the balanced constitution, but also the mercantile system. Indeed, the ideology of mercantilism had as great a hold upon the age as free trade came to have on the nineteenth century. Hence, although the members of the landed interest held the commanding heights of political power, this did not mean that the claims of commerce were neglected. On the contrary, in their minds, as in the minds of the other great interests, commerce was "the dominant factor" in the existence and well-being of Britain.[8] The self-interest of group and faction was conditioned by this wide agreement on the economic and social order. So conditioned it could be freely pursued without danger to that order.

[9] *Ibid.*, p. 17.
[1] See, for instance, what appears to have been the successful lobbying of the Treasury Board by Sir James Lowther, the notorious borough-monger, to have an exception made in his favor regarding the duty on coals. *The Jenkinson Papers 1760–1766*, Ninetta S. Jucker, ed. (London, 1949), pp. 34–6.
[2] See especially Lucy S. Sutherland, *The East India Company in Eighteenth Century Politics* (Oxford, 1952); also C. H. Philips, *The East India Company, 1784–1834* (Manchester, 1940).
[8] Namier, *England in the Age of the American Revolution*, p. 35.

CHAPTER II

Liberal and Radical Politics

The growing demand for popular government in the nineteenth century voiced an individualism that broke sharply with the hierarchic and corporatist ideal. In politics, as in other spheres, these new views enlarged the freedom of the individual, loosening his ties to the established social groupings with their fixed interests, and enhancing his ability to create new associations in pursuit of new demands. On this Liberals and Radicals were at one and must be distinguished from the Old Whigs. The distinction is particularly important for the study of American politics. For in this country the Old Whig, as well as the Collectivist, current of thought has been feeble, while the principal and contending theories of representation derive respectively from Liberal and Radical premises. These can be illustrated from American as well as from British sources.

Like the Old Whigs, the Liberals were committed to parliamentarism. The member of the legislature was not a delegate sent merely to reflect the will of the people; he was a representative charged with deliberation on the common good. On these grounds Lord John Russell, for instance, opposed the Radical demand for shorter parliaments and for pledges by candidates to voters. When presenting his plan for reform in 1831, he declared that

in such an assembly the representatives of the people will consider not with whom they are voting but for what measure they vote. The measures of such an assembly will be deliberately weighed and will be carefully designed to remedy the evils which may have been brought upon the country by bad laws and to rescue it from their operation.[1]

[1] Lord John Russell, *Selected Speeches* (London, 1870), pp. 364–5.

Madison treats representation in the tenth Federalist. It is not device adopted merely because it is impossible to assemble all the people, but a means by which the public views may be refined "by passing them through the medium of a chosen body of citizens, whose wisdom may best discern the true interest of their country." Thus the force of faction and partial interests may be broken and a representation of the national interest achieved.

LIBERAL INDIVIDUALISM

But when we ask *what* was represented, a gulf opens between the Old Whig and Liberal views. For the Liberals gave a new stress in their political thought to the representation of individuals rather than corporate bodies, ranks, orders, or "interests." In their politics, as in their economics, the source of action was (or ought to be) the rational, independent individual. From this individualism there followed in political thought the notion of equal electoral districts, which in Britain was gradually expressed in various schemes for redistribution until finally, in 1885, the ancient communities of shire and borough ceased almost entirely to be the basis of representation. Then, writes Ensor, "the individual for the first time became the unit, and numerical equality ('one vote, one value') the master principle."[2]

This concern with the individual appears in the Liberal arguments in favor of the property qualification for the franchise. Often in these discussions Liberals reasoned from the premise that the main end of government is the preservation of property. Not inconsistent was the view that property shows something about the individual that entitles him to political power : it is, so to speak, the best rough index of his intelligence and good will. In 1859 Bagehot wrote that, in recruiting intelligence for the electorate, the most practical test is property.[3] In the earlier struggles for reform the same point had often been made. Property was "the certificate of probity and good behavior."[4] According to one reformer, since there was no public provision for education "a certain degree of income was the only general and practical cri-

[2] R. C. K. Ensor, *England 1870-1914* (Oxford, 1936), p. 88.
[3] Walter Bagehot, "Parliamentary Reform" (1859), in *Essays on Parliamentary Reform* (London, 1883), p. 42.
[4] Norman Gash, *Politics in the Age of Peel: A Study in the Technique of Parliamentary Representation* (London, 1953), p. 18.

terion of a required degree of intelligence."[5] In 1822 Ru
argued that that change in the state of the people which nec
sitated a change in representation consisted not only in an increa
in wealth, but also in a great improvement in knowledge, whic
he illustrated by noting the vast growth in the numbers of
books and newspapers being sold.[6] Similarly, Macaulay contended,
against the democrats, that it is not by numbers, but by "property
and intelligence" that the country should be ruled.[7]

This attempt to make a certain kind of individual the basis of
representation meant there would be uniformity of franchise
rather than a variety, as under the Old Whig regime. On these
premises, it was logical not only to extend the franchise to the
rational and independent, but also to withdraw it from such poor
and ignorant as had previously enjoyed it on the grounds of
variety. And this was in fact done in the case of those few constituencies where the old franchise had been broader than the new.

But what of the reformers' emphasis upon the "middle class" and
its right to political power? Is this not reasoning in the Old Whig
or Old Tory vein and a severe qualification on Liberal individualism? To be sure, in a country such as Britain where from time
immemorial "degree" has so profoundly colored all social relations,
individualism will always be qualified. From one era to another the
principle will be differently expressed: the various categories of
men will differ in numbers, in function, in relations to one another
—from the "sundry estates and degrees of men" of Old Tory
times to the "ranks, orders and interests" of the eighteenth century; to the "upper, middle and lower classes" of Victorian and
Edwardian days; and indeed to the occupational hierarchy of
modern bureaucratic Britain, where the leading position goes not
to "His Grace" or a "gentleman" but to one of the "Top People."
All in different forms express some deeper and abiding social value
and tendency. Call it hierarchy, or precedence, or even the class
system; we would hardly recognize English society or English
politics without it, although more than one school of reformers
has set up as its enemy.

Among those would-be enemies of hierarchy were the Liberals
of the early nineteenth century. They thought of it in a new and
special way. The term "middle class" was first used only in 1812,

[5] *Ibid.*
[6] *Parl. Deb.*, new ser., Vol VII, 51–141 (25 April 1822).
[7] 2 *H.C. Deb.*, 1190ff (March, 1831).

ı general the terminology of class, especially in its reference ıe upper, middle, and lower classes, became common usage ıy in the nineteenth century.[8] It can therefore be misleading to ıe the term "class" of previous centuries when social categories ıad quite different meanings. Sometimes in the early reform period of the nineteenth century the use of "class" was Old Whig, as when, for instance, Inglis spoke of the many classes and interests of the empire. But in the mouths of the reformers it had another meaning. For one thing, they were less likely to think of society as consisting of as many categories as did the Old Whigs or Old Tories, and spoke rather of only a three-fold division of society.

But what is much more important, they did not, as did the men of the ranks and orders of the eighteenth century, accept their position as only one among several components of a permanently hierarchic order. On the contrary, they felt peculiarly representative of the whole society. Or, as Ruggiero has said, speaking of the Liberal middle class of Europe as a whole, they regarded themselves as "the general class." Suffering from neither the compulsions of poverty nor the temptations of great riches, they were, to quote Brougham, the "genuine depositaries of sober, national, intelligent and honest English feeling."[9] "The middle class," wrote Macaulay, "that brave, honest and stout-hearted class, which is as anxious for the maintenance of order and the security of property, as it is hostile to corruption and oppression."[1] With this vision and with these abilities it is only right that they should have the largest voice in government. And this vision was strongly individualist.

To say that the Liberal reformers were individualists is hardly novel. But their individualism expressed a new view of society as a whole—a point worth stressing because the usual account of this period portrays the reformers as concerned mainly with the welfare of the middle class and with a reordering of the economy and policy that would favor the interests of the owners of industrial and commercial capital.

There is much truth in this interpretation. In the era of Conservative-Liberal rivalry that began in the years after Waterloo,

[8] Asa Briggs, "Middle Class Consciousness in English Politics, 1780–1846," *Past and Present*, Vol. I (1956), pp. 65–74.
[9] *Speeches* (London, 1857), Vol. II, p. 41.
[1] T. B. Macaulay, "Hallam," *Critical, Historical and Miscellaneous Essays and Poems* (Boston, n.d.), Vol. I, p. 386.

party division roughly followed class division. To be sure, c. lines were not sharply drawn. The Conservatives benefited fro a large deferential vote from the middle class and the Liberals drev many leaders from the upper class. Earl Grey's cabinet, which won the great victory for the middle class in 1832, could hardly have been more aristocratic. Still, the usual textbook picture is right : the upper class, consisting of aristocracy and gentry and strongly rooted in the ownership of land, rural and urban, was predominantly Conservative, while the middle class, embracing owners, large and small, of industrial and commercial capital, tended strongly toward the Liberals. Moreover, these rising—indeed, demanding, pushing, pressuring—middle-class types recognized that they formed a separate class in the community which would benefit from the program of the reformers.

Yet their values were not those of narrow class interest. On the contrary, they broadened into a vision of a classless society. For the middle class was the class that would bring all classes, all hierarchy, to an end. It was not asking for hegemony. Rather it sought only to strike down privilege and open the doors to economic, social, and political advancement to all persons. Its members were, as Asa Briggs has said, "middle class Marxists" in the sense that they, like Marxists of a later time, thought of themselves as representing—indeed, embodying the virtues of—the society of the future. Cobden, who was perhaps a little inclined to see what he wanted to see, found in America the image of that self-reliant, acquisitive, atomistic Britain of the future.[2] Accordingly, he not only fought against "monopoly" and the privilege of the warlike aristocracy, he also advised the workingmen of England that not government action, but they "alone individually" could work out their regeneration.[3] From being a social problem in Old Tory thought, the "masterless man" had become the ideal man, rational and independent, joined to others not by traditional status, but by his own free contracts.

In their parliamentarism and individualism, the Liberals of Britain and America were in accord. They were a good deal alike also in their attitudes toward interest groups and parties. Their fear of interests, deriving from their individualism, was in Britain

[2] John Morley, *Life of Cobden* (London, 1881), pp. 39–40.
[3] *Ibid.*, p. 467.

...iceable and in America pronounced. While in Britain hostility the corporatist society of the past did not go to the extremes in thought or action that were reached in France, British Liberals, in contrast with the Old Whigs, were nevertheless cool to the representation of interests.[4] In America, of course, the fear of special interests in politics was given classic expression by Madison. The diversity of the faculties of men as well as the fallibility of their reason set up insuperable barriers to "a uniformity of interests." From this diversity of interests proceeded "faction," whose malign effects, it was hoped, would be offset by the device of representation and the wide extent of the Republic.[5] Madison is often cited as one of the first Americans to observe the role of interest groups in politics. This does not mean that he approved of them or wished to encourage their activity : quite the contrary. His thought on representation is neither that of the Old Whig nor that of the modern pluralist. Individuals, not interest groups or classes, were the basic units of his ideal polity.

What did the Liberals think of party? As represented by Madison, as well as John Adams, George Washington, and the Federalists, their hostility was emphatic : party and faction were interchangeable terms to them, and the bane of free governments. They disliked party in theory, and in practice Hamilton himself had great difficulty in getting the Federalists to organize. The view of the British Liberals, however, was more complex. Both individualism and parliamentarism agreed poorly with the idea of party government, and we do not expect to find advocates of rigid party discipline or great extra-parliamentary organization among Macaulay and his friends. With regard to extra-parliamentary organizations, the Liberal point of view was restrained. Even after mid-century, leading men in the Liberal Party organization denounced the very registration societies that they directed.[6] And it was only Radical initiative that led to the founding of the National Liberal Federation in 1877. In general, the period between the First and Second Reform Acts was "the golden age of the private M.P."[7]

[4] P. A. Gibbons, *Ideas of Political Representation in Parliament 1651–1832* (Oxford, 1914), p. 47.

[5] *The Federalist*, No. 10.

[6] M. I. Ostrogorski, *Democracy and the Organization of Political Parties* (New York, 1902), Vol. I, pp. 156–8.

[7] Richard Pares, *King George III and The Politicians* (Oxford, 1953), p. 192.

The highest respect, as Macaulay correctly states, was reserved f
the independent politician in the sense not of one who was outsic
party, but one who was in party solely because of his conscientious
opinion and perhaps traditional association. . . . All members and all
candidates claimed to be independent in their opinions and votes because it was the contemporary ideal of what a politician should be,
however far removed from reality that ideal was.[8]

The ideal member of Parliament, like the ideal constituent, was
the independent rational man. His "conscientious opinion," however, might lead him to agree and vote with others. So to act in
concert, Lord John Russell observed, was in accord with Burke's
precept and constituted no sacrifice of conscience. Parties so conceived not only did not violate independence, but also positively
enhanced it by attaching individuals to "steady and lasting principles," thus protecting them against the seductions of money and
patronage.[9] And while one of the functions of party was to embody the various opinions of the nation, this did not make of
M.P.'s mere delegates. On the contrary, a great merit of party,
according to Russell, was that it made possible the passage of laws
which had not yet caught popular favor.

In one sense, contemporary ideals marked a further step in filling
out the meaning of party as a legitimate political group. Now
party in the Burkean sense was tolerable, even desirable, although
this meant contention over principle and the continuance of a
"formed opposition." The phrase "His Majesty's Loyal Opposition," first used in 1826 derisively, came to express acceptance of
the party system.[1] Yet to all this the Liberal added an all-important
qualification : the independence of the member must be respected,
a provision that could only work against party unity and party
discipline.

RADICAL DEMOCRACY

In the spring of 1956, Harry Truman, reaching for a cliché,
declared that the task of his party was to take the government out

---

[8] Gash, *op. cit.*, p. 109.
[9] *Essay on the History of the English Government and Constitution*
(London, 1823), Ch. XVII.
[1] Caroline Robbins, " 'Discordant Parties' : A Study of the Acceptance
of Party by Englishmen," *Political Science Quarterly*, Vol. LXXIII, No. 4
(December, 1958), p. 512.

the hands of "the special interests" and return it to "the people." these phrases Truman was using the central symbols of the Radical tradition. In the history of political philosophy the leading exponent of the Radical idea is Rousseau. Yet even in countries such as America and Britain, where Rousseau's direct influence was slight, the tradition has had its strenuous advocates. In that tradition "the People" certainly does not mean, as it did for Burke, the various ranks and orders of men speaking through and acting under their "natural" leaders. Nor does it mean simply a miscellany of individuals, a mere set of rational, independent men. It means rather a body of individuals bound together and guided forward by a unified and authoritative will. In spite of apparent diversity, this unity of will and direction is there, forming the ultimate and only sovereign in the polity—supreme, morally infallible, even sacred. For that reason those corrupting influences that divide the community, creating special and partial goals in conflict with the ultimate unity, are supremely reprehensible. They are the "special interests" (the "sinister interests," in the Benthamite phrase). Toward them the Radical is not, like the Liberal, simply suspicious; he is positively hostile. He would not only not listen to them or consult with them, but would indeed drive them out of political life. For they are not data from which thought proceeds toward the common good, but selfish promptings seeking continually to breach the unified will of the people. "The interests are always awake," said Mr. Gladstone during his last and democratic phase, "while the country often slumbers and sleeps."[2]

These ideas leave little place for parliamentarism. Jefferson, defining a republic, called it "a government by citizens in mass, acting directly and personally according to rules established by the majority," and said that, although this could not be fully achieved beyond narrow limits of space and population, the ideal by which forms of government were to be measured was the degree of "direct action of the citizens."[3] Very different was this view from the Federalist notion of government based on a limited franchise

[2] In 1883, defending the organization of the National Liberal Federation, Joseph Chamberlain said that "private interests are like a disciplined regiment while the public good was defended by an unorganized mob." Quoted in Simon Maccoby, *English Radicalism, 1853–1886* (London, 1938), Vol. II, p. 284.

[3] Quoted in Alfred de Grazia, *Public and Republic : Political Representation in America* (New York, 1951), p. 105.

and refining the public views "by passing them through the m_
dium of a chosen body of citizens."

The contrast of Liberal and Old Whig parliamentarism with
Radical direct democracy is fundamental. For the latter, as directly as possible, the will of the majority should decide major
questions of policy.[4] The aim of democratic theory, wrote Dicey
in 1867, is to make the majority of the nation the arbiter of the
nation's destiny.[5] According to H. H. Fowler, the idea of the proposed reform of 1884 ". . . was that the majority should regulate
the policy of the nation."[6] "At last," commented Joseph Chamberlain a year later, "we have a Government of the people and by the
people."[7]

Did the Radicals believe that the majority has the right to do
whatever it liked? Surely not. The Radicals in America or Britain
were no more crude majoritarians than Jefferson. The majority
should rule, not because it is arbitrarily sovereign but because it,
and it alone, can be trusted to speak with the voice of the whole
people. It is the one will in the community that can be trusted to
speak the general will. The majority, as John Bright said in Britain
and John Taylor of Caroline in America, is the only body which
has no interest opposed to that of the whole. It is therefore
through the will of the majority that the people carry on their war
against the special interests and for the national interest.[8]

How is the Radical attitude likely to affect people's views of
interest groups and parties? Hostility will be sharp to the group
openly asking for some particular benefit for itself. This will be

[4] For a complete survey of the Radical tradition in England one would
need to start with the Levellers of the seventeenth century. See, for instance, the famous passages in the Putney and Whitehall Debates, A. S. P.
Woodhouse, ed., *Puritanism and Liberty* (London, 1936), Pt. I. Representative spokesmen in the nineteenth and twentieth centuries would be the early
John Bright, Joseph Chamberlain, Charles Dilke, and Lloyd George. Yet
there is no doubt that the Radical current is a good deal weaker in Britain
than in the United States. De Grazia, *op. cit.*, who holds that the Radical
view is the "most indigenous to American life and buried most deeply in
the American spirit," has traced its course through the Jacksonian, Populist,
and Progressive periods.

[5] A. V. Dicey, "The Balance of Classes," *Essays on Reform* (London,
1867).

[6] 285 *H.C. Deb.* 167 (28 February 1884).

[7] *Annual Register, 1885*, p. 152.

[8] Against the argument that extension of the franchise to the working
classes would swamp every other class, Roebuck said in the House (March
31, 1859) : "People who use this argument do not make this important

case especially if its members are wealthy, well-educated, or some way outstanding. For the unity of "the People" is not cooperative solidarity, but rather homogeneity, likeness, similarity of condition and wants : [9] they are, in Truman's imagery, "the little people," "the ordinary citizens." Or in rather more elevated imagery, they are men considered simply as "moral persons" and without regard for class or other distinctions.[1] At the same time the Radical ideal, with its appeal to direct democracy, confirms the right of the people to associate in order to press their views on government. There could be no question of such associations being "unconstitutional," as the Old Whigs said of the Yorkshire Association. On the contrary, they will—and indeed on Radical premises they must—claim to be "the voice of the people." This claim is less implausible the wider the organization. And we may note that both in Britain and America, although at different times, it was the Radicals who took the initiative in setting up the vast extra-parliamentary organizations of political parties.

This does not mean that the Radical welcomes a system of parties. Indeed, given his belief in the unity, or at least the potential unity, of the people, rival partisanship can only seem wicked, a conclusion that John Taylor of Caroline did not hesitate to draw when he stated : "Truth is a thing, not of divisibility into conflicting parts, but of unity. Hence, both sides cannot be right."[2] Liberalism is a more likely source of the legitimacy of a system of competing parties. It is readier to admit that diversity is inevitable and opposition useful.

Moreover, Radicalism, while it justifies party organization, at the same time undermines party unity. It serves poorly, there-

---

distinction—the majority of a country can have no interest inimical to the interests of the country. If you give power to a minority, that minority may have interests at variance with the interests of the country; but the majority cannot—if they understand their own interests." 152 *H.C. Deb.*, 3rd ser., 1225.

[9] Jefferson, wrote Herbert Croly, "conceived a democratic society to be composed of a collection of individuals, fundamentally alike in their abilities and deserts." For this reason, continued Croly, Jeffersonian doctrine was hostile to "intellectual and moral independence" and favorable to "intellectual and moral conformity." *The Promise of American Life* (New York, 1909), pp. 44–5.

[1] See Broderick and Dicey in *Essays on Reform*.

[2] *A Definition of Parties* (Philadelphia, 1794), quoted in Benjamin F. Wright, *A Source Book of American Political Theory* (New York, 1929), p. 343.

fore, as a rationalization for party government. The flaw is its individualist bias. Ideally, "the people" act as one; yet they achieve that unity by a series of individual acts of mind. The Radical differs from the Liberal in believing that property is not a necessary qualification for the vote. But the ultimate unit for him also is not class, estate, rank, or interest, but the rational, independent man. Presumably by discussion the ultimate atoms will be led to discover their general will and thus to unity of action.

But what are the restraints on the individual who finds his judgment at variance with that of the organization? The principle of majority rule is such a sanction. Yet one can always question whether the organization's decision truly reflects its majority and, indeed, whether this majority truly represents the majority of that larger and vaguer entity, "the people." A Radical party lacks that further strengthening of solidarity given to a party explicitly based on class and the agencies of a class, such as trade unions. Certainly a robust party discipline cannot be easily founded upon Radical premises. In American history the Radical, although the founder of party, is also its persistent critic. Forever disillusioned with the actual tones in which party speaks, he seeks to eliminate interference by bosses, corruption, and special interests and to tune in the authentic voice of the people by regulating party processes, by setting up a direct primary, by instituting the initiative and referendum. The strength of the Radical ideal in America is one major reason for the weakness of our parties. In Britain, while the Radical ideal has not had so great an influence, it has also been inadequate as a moral foundation for party government. Only in Collectivist thought do we find the necessary sanctions.

POLITICAL ASSOCIATIONS AND PARTY DEVELOPMENT

In nineteenth-century politics the most striking change from the eighteenth century was probably the rise of public opinion.[3] We get rather closer to the facts if we use the plural, "public opinions," for then we are likely to focus attention on the vast proliferation of voluntary associations formed for political purposes. Notable examples can be found in the eighteenth century, for instance, that product of Wilkes' agitation and vehicle of his

[3] See Pares' discussion in relation to the declining role of the monarchy, *op. cit.*, Ch. 6.

ns, the Society for Supporting the Bill of Rights (1769). Other
odies aiming at parliamentary reform were the Yorkshire Association (1779) and the Associated Counties, The Society for Constitutional Information (1780), The London Corresponding Society
(1792), The Society of the Friends of the People (1792).

These eighteenth-century associations, however, were on the
whole failures. The structure of society and the climate of opinion
were against them, and during the wars with revolutionary France
many were brutally suppressed. But in 1807 Wilberforce's Committee for the Abolition of the Slave Trade won a striking success,
and from the 1820's political associations became increasingly a
power—a new kind of power—in British politics. Among them
were the Political Unions of the 1830's, O'Connell's Catholic Association, the London Workingmen's Association and the Chartist
groups, the Anti-Corn Law League (1839), the Short Time Committees for the Ten Hours Bill (1840's), the Liberation Society
(1853), The National Reform League (1865), the National Education League (1869).[4]

Much of the old hierarchic, corporatist discipline remained :
aristocracy, country gentry, the Church, Inns of Court, universities. But alongside it and, so to speak, up through it, the new
structure pushed its way, providing new and flexible channels for
expressing and for forming public views. These new modes of
political action were legitimized by Liberal and Radical values,
especially the latter. Indeed, in the course of the century, one can
discern a certain Radicalization of political organization, culminat-
ing in the creation of the massive extra-parliamentary political
party.

These associations were a distinctive type of political formation.
Our first inclination is perhaps to call them "modern." And surely
in structure, spirit, and method they departed sharply from Old
Whig models. While they might use the town or county meeting, their effort was precisely to create a body that cut across the
aristocratic structure of power. They were not bodies established
by law, ancient custom, or natural hierarchy, but, as certain opponents of the Yorkshire Association had charged, merely "self-
created assemblies."[5] Their members did not gather at one of the

---

[4] For a survey on the Radical side, see Simon Maccoby, *English Radicalism, 1762-1914* (London, 1935-55), 5 vols.

[5] Butterfield, *George III, Lord North and The People 1779-80* (London,
1949), p. 250.

traditional meetings to agree on and forward a petition and then disperse. They remained in contact and pursued their agitation until, so they hoped, their aims had been realized. Very commonly, however, their aims embraced only a single major piece of legislation, and when they had achieved this end the association might well disband.

These bodies were indeed "self-created"; their members thought themselves united by the free acts of individual minds. Hence, each new effort required, so to speak, a new "compact." They were, precisely, associations, not communities. They were united not by tradition, personal loyalty, or ancient communal ties, but by a common opinion individually arrived at. Not unlike the limited liability companies that were springing up at this time, they were limited in purpose, embraced only one segment of the individual's life, and had only a contractual claim upon his energies.[6] In terms of American political experience, they were pressure groups of the type illustrated by the Anti-Saloon League.

But all this does not make them "modern," if by that one means that they resemble the major organized interest groups of British politics today. On the contrary, the Liberal-Radical groups were not based explicitly on a productive function, did not have important nonpolitical functions, and lacked the bureaucratic structure, complex goals, and continuing engagement of the later Collectivist types. Indeed, it would not be a quibble to argue that the present-day organizations have at least as much in common with the Old Whig as with the Liberal-Radical groups.

This contrast is not only a matter of structure, purpose, and social base. There is something about the whole tone and spirit of these Victorian associations that clashes with the atmosphere of group politics in the eighteenth century or today. Perhaps the simplest way to describe it is to call it their moralism, or moralistic reformism. Many of the manufacturers who supported the Anti-Corn Law League, for instance, were sharply aware of the economic benefits promised by repeal. Moreover, the association as a whole, although it did win some genuine working-class support, was predominantly middle class and recognized that it was fighting

---

[6] In his *Parliamentary Parties, 1868–1885* (Unpublished Ph.D. dissertation, 1953; Harvard Archives), Barry McGill notes the parallel between business, religious and political organizations (pp. 2–4) and characterizes the period 1868–1885 as "the era of joint stock politics" in contrast with the previous period of "laissez-faire politics" (pp. 355–6).

r the interests of this class. Yet a certain moral exaggeration, not ɔ say self-righteousness, colored its advocacy. "While they" (i.e., the contributors to the League) "abstained from the claim of being actuated by unmixed benevolence," wrote the historian of the League, who was also a leader of it, "I have seen the tears run down the cheeks of many a manly countenance, when the great employer spoke of the wretched condition of hundreds and thousands who looked to him for employment when none was to be had."[7]

To be sure, it is usual for pressure groups to claim that their goals accord with the national interest and, as we have remarked, this may well have some substance of truth. Yet the extreme moralism of these Victorian pressure groups is worlds apart from the straightforward language of wool-growers or sugar-importers in the eighteenth century or a trade union or trade association today. The source, no doubt, was the Evangelicalism that was as strong an influence in forming their sentiments and rhetoric as Liberal and Radical ideas. What is more, these associations, however limited and specific their goals in any particular instance, were genuinely moved by a vision of a new social order. As one student of the League has said, they saw in the Corn Laws "the symbol of aristocratic misrule" against which they asserted in all sincerity "the nobility and dignity of commerce and industry."[8] Free Trade in their minds would bring prosperity and, still more important, peace to the whole world.

Although the constitutional history of these associations has not been much studied, a few comments about organization and tactics may be risked. One model was provided by the Yorkshire Association, which included three elements : primary assemblies at the base; then committees of correspondence linking the various local units; and at the top an assembly of deputies to speak for the whole. Ford traces the organization of American parties back to the corresponding committees of the days of the Sons of Liberty and the Stamp Act Congress.[9] While the committee of correspondence as a political device was presumably of American origin, it has early parallels in religious organization, such as the Quaker

[7] Archibald Prentice, *History of the Anti-Corn Law League* (London, 1853), Vol. I, pp. 94–5.

[8] Norman McCord, *The Anti-Corn Law League 1838–1846* (London, 1958), p. 23.

[9] Henry Jones Ford, *The Rise and Growth of American Politics* (New York, 1898), pp. 7–8.

Committee of Sufferings.[1] In the face of laws forbidding the fede
ation of political bodies, it was adopted in Britain.[2] It was used nc
only by the Yorkshire Association, but also by the London Corresponding Society and similar bodies during the period of the
French Revolution and by Wilberforce in his agitation against the
slave trade. But correspondence too fell under legal prohibition
and could not be used by the political unions inspired by Attwood's agitation.

The Anti-Corn Law League was an alliance of local associations,
direction being put in the hands of a council composed of the
more substantial contributors and including at least as nominal
members the leaders of the principal local associations.[3] Day-to-
day activity was directed by the executive committee of the
League.[4] The local associations were in great measure independent
of the League's control, although management of financial matters
was centralized in Manchester. In the period, generally, there is a
trend toward greater centralization, as the form of organization
approximates that of the extra-parliamentary political party fathered by the National Liberal Federation in 1877.[5]

The tactics of these associations included mass meetings, petitioning, and intensive lobbying of M.P.'s and ministers. Petitioning,
indeed, grew in quantity, reaching its peak from 1868 to 1872,
after which it fell off, declining to negligible proportions in the
twentieth century. Yet, as compared with that of the eighteenth,
the petitioning of the nineteenth century took on a new character
when it was converted into a means of appealing to public opinion.
In the case of the great mass petitions, such as those of the Chartists
and the Corn Law Repealers, it merged with the new techniques
for appealing to and "educating" an active political public many
times larger than it had been in the eighteenth century.[6]

[1] See Arnold Lloyd, *Quaker Social History 1669–1738* (London, 1950).

[2] Graham Wallas, *The Life of Francis Place 1771–1854*, 3rd. ed. (London,
1919), p. 22.

[3] McCord, *op. cit.*, pp. 53–54 and 177.

[4] Prentice, *op. cit.*, Vol. I, p. 106.

[5] See with regard to the National Reform League of 1865, Maccoby,
English Radicalism 1853–1886, Vol. II, pp. 85–87, 91–92; and with regard
to the National Education League of 1869, *Report of the First General
Meeting of the National Education League* (Birmingham, Eng., 1869).

[6] On petitioning in general see Colin Leys, "Petitioning in the 19th and
20th Centuries," *Political Studies* (February, 1955). Leys shows the immense increase in petitioning from the latter part of the eighteenth century
until debate on petitions threatened to become the sole business of the
House!

'All you want," Cobden told the League in 1842, "is to have the opportunity of disseminating those stores of information which are now lying bound up in Parliamentary returns or the productions of writers on this question; all you want is that this information be disseminated in order to insure the success of the question at the next meeting of Parliament."[7] Inspired by this article of the Liberal and Radical faiths, the League performed prodigies of propaganda, sending paid lecturers on tour throughout the country, distributing millions of tracts, subsidizing the foundation of the *Economist*, and in general making of itself "a peripatetic university." Yet the League was more than a propaganda body. It also came to the point of organizing deliberate intervention in elections to procure the return of free trade candidates.[8] The contrast with the tactics of Wilberforce is interesting; in appealing to "the justice and humanity of the nation," he distributed tracts and sent out lecturers on tour through the provinces. But he opposed the holding of a great public meeting in London, disavowed a "systematic agitation," and did not intrude the slave trade question into parliamentary elections.[9] Francis Place similarly did not resort to electoral intervention in bringing pressure to bear for the repeal of the Combination Acts.[1] In the course of later years, however, there seems to be an increasing tendency for the pressure groups to resort to this tactic.

From Wilberforce's Abolition Societies to the National Education League, the line of development in form of organization and in tactics is from Liberal to Radical models—away from parliamentarism and toward direct democracy. Perhaps the most interesting aspect of this process of "Radicalization" in political methods is its connection with party. Let us look at some of the characteristics of the political party in this period.

Liberalism and Political Parties

The time between the First and Second Reform Acts, as we have noted, has been called the "golden age of the private M.P."

[7] Prentice, *op. cit.*, Vol. I, p. 393.
[8] McCord, *op. cit.*; and Henry D. Jordan, "The Political Methods of the Anti-Corn Law League," *Political Science Quarterly*, Vol. XLII (March, 1927).
[9] Robert I. and Samuel Wilberforce, *The Life of William Wilberforce* (London, 1839), Vol. I, p. 299 and *passim*.
[1] Wallas, *op. cit.*

Breaking free from the heavy hand of Old Whig patronage a. not yet subject to the still heavier hand of modern party discipline the Member of Parliament could, if he chose, plausibly imagine himself falling not far short of the Liberal ideal. Not all chose to think of themselves in this way. Some members were beholden to patrons, others to what they took to be public opinion; and by various means party influenced the votes of many. Yet in general the private member was probably more independent than he had ever been before or was to be thereafter.

The reformed Parliament inherited a rudimentary organization of party from the age of the aristocratic connections. By custom, ministers occupied the front bench to the right of the Speaker, leading members of the opposition the front bench facing them, while supporters ranged themselves behind their respective leaders. The Leader of the Party was not elected, but achieved his position upon being made Prime Minister. To provide for the house of which he was not a member, he might appoint a leader on his own decision; or the choice might be made by a gathering of the great men of the party. In 1830 Lord Althorp had been elected leader of the Commons at a well-attended meeting of M.P.'s, an election, however, that Grey felt it needful to confirm when he became Prime Minister later in the year. Appointed by the Leader, the Whips, who dated from the eighteenth century, had as their main task to keep in touch with back-benchers and muster them for divisions of the House. Leaders sometimes called meetings of M.P.'s in order to explain some plan or policy, or possibly to plead for better attendance at Parliament. Policy and tactics were the prerogative of the great men of the party, but after 1832 their control was shaken by the decline in party unity and the rising independence of members.[2] In 1846 Peel exercised this prerogative in the name of statesmanship, but his party broke under the strain.[3]

Only by doing considerable violence to the facts can we classify the members of the House into two parties. But if, following Lowell, we do so, we find that what he calls party voting, at the start of the period weak enough by present-day British standards,

[2] A. Aspinall, "English Party Organization in the Early 19th Century," *English Historical Review*, Vol. XLI (1926), p. 393.

[3] Norman Gash, "Peel and the Party System, 1830-50," *Transactions of the Royal Historical Society*, 5th ser., Vol. I (1951), pp. 47-69.

ı almost vanished by 1860.[4] Those he classifies as "Liberals" ere more independent than those he calls "Conservatives," but among both, nonparty voting was high. Majorities and minorities were composed of shifting groups, sometimes in bitter conflict. And after the repeal of the Corn Laws in 1846, parties in the House resembled the bloc system of continental parliaments far more than the two-party system that we identify with Britain. From the opening years of the reformed Parliament, Peel, representing the oligarchic tradition of strong and stable government, was deeply disturbed by the absence of reliable majorities. In 1859 Lord Derby, then Prime Minister, declared that while he was not ready to say that parliamentary government itself had come to an end, with regard to a two-party system in which leaders commanded the votes of their followers and exercised a species of parliamentary discipline, "Those days are gone, and are not likely to return."[5]

Looking back with the benefit of hindsight, we can see that party organization among the electorate can, in the right circumstances, greatly enhance the power of party and party leaders in Parliament. But although extra-parliamentary organization spread rapidly after 1832, it was not of the sort to have this effect. It took the form of local registration associations in the constituencies, whose creation was variously instigated—by the candidate, by the parliamentary Whips, by local notables. Membership was small, even in the context of the modest constituencies of the time (half the borough constituencies, for instance, had less than two thousand voters).[6] Their purpose was to get the names of local supporters on the electorial register and to canvass voters at election time. They were therefore instrumental in getting out the vote and in making it a party vote. And in 1841, for the first time, a Government was defeated in a General Election by an organized opposition.

But we are more interested in what the local associations were

---

[4] Lowell defines a party vote as one in which more than nine tenths of the members of a party vote on the same side. He found that the proportion of divisions in 1836 where both parties cast party votes on opposite sides was 22.65%; in 1860, 6.22%. A. L. Lowell, "The Influence of Party upon Legislation in England and America" (Washington, D.C., 1902), pp. 326–7.

[5] 153 *H.C. Deb.* 1269 (4 April 1859).

[6] G. S. R. Kitson Clark, "The Electorate and the Repeal of the Corn Laws," *Transactions of the Royal Historical Society*, 5th ser., Vol. I (1951), pp. 109–26.

not. They were not a means of nominating candidates, who st■
with the acquiescence, or possibly at the request, of local notable
or parliamentary leaders, "offered themselves" to the electorate.
They were not a means of calling members to book for votes in
Parliament or for failure to support the party. They were assur-
edly not bodies for discussing policy and program and for taking
part in party decisions on these matters.

A link between the parliamentary leaders and local notables was
provided by the great political clubs : the Carlton, founded in 1832
by the Tories, and the Reform, founded in 1836 by Whigs and
Radicals. Explicitly political in purpose, they provided a social
center for party members in both houses and influential supporters
in the provinces, as well as a home for party management and
organization. In them the Whips had their offices; from there,
with the aid of their chief party agents, they kept in touch with
constituencies, collecting information, bringing candidates and
constituencies together, maintaining contact with local associations
and local party agents. But it was only in the years after the reform
of 1867 that the local associations took their part in an organization
that was able to contribute to party solidarity in Parliament and
to the forming of party policy.[7]

The tradition that "H. M. Government must be carried on" still
shaped the behavior of leaders such as Wellington and Peel. But
patronage had declined as a means of holding together majorities
and the later foundations of party discipline had not yet been
created. As a result, the political structure gave "too little power
to the executive, too much to the private member; too much to
interest and too little to principle."[8] As we shall see, this gave
opportunities to the interested M.P.[9] It also reduced the barriers in
the way of the reformist political associations. We should not
exaggerate their influence. Even the formidable Anti-Corn Law
League did not play the decisive role in repeal, which was rather
the product of Peel's statesmanship. Yet the League's influence was
substantial in bringing around Lord John Russell and his followers.
And in general, as has been observed, the political associations
rather than parties or Governments were the source of new ideas
in policy.[1]

[7] Gash, *Politics in the Age of Peel*, Ch. 15, "Club Government."
[8] *Ibid.*, pp. xviii–xxi.
[9] *Ibid.*, pp. 61–8 below.
[1] Jordan, *op. cit.*

adicalism and Political Parties

The new organization of parties that grew up after 1867 owed a great deal to the example of the political associations. Yet the process of "Radicalization" of political methods, which in its first phases enhanced the activity of the associations, in the course of time worked to restrict it. For its culmination was the founding in the 1870's of the massive extra-parliamentary party organization constructed to emphasize program and to enforce discipline on M.P.'s. The clear case is what happened to the Liberal Party in this period.

The sustenance offered the followers of the Birmingham Caucus and the National Liberal Federation was the pure milk of Radical democracy. In 1867 the Birmingham association was reorganized on representative lines. Of this new structure Joseph Chamberlain said :

It has become necessary . . . that the people at large should be taken into the counsels of the party, and that they should have a share in its control and management. Hence, the new constitution upon which the Liberal Association of Birmingham is founded, according to which every Liberal in the town is ipso facto a member by virtue of his Liberalism, and without any other qualification. The vote of the poorest member is equal to that of the richest. It is an Association based on universal suffrage.[2]

The summons to the conference of 1877 at which the National Liberal Federation was launched read :

The essential feature of the proposed Federation is the principle which must henceforth govern the action of the Liberals as a political party, namely, the direct participation of all members of the party in the formation and direction of policy and in the selection of those particular measures of reform and of progress to which priority shall be given.[3]

The Radical theory of government by the people—with its strong implication of government by a single party—is particularly clear in the words of William Harris, secretary of the Birmingham association, to the assembled delegates :

Why should they not at once and for all form a federation which, by collecting together the majority of the people in all the great

[2] M. I. Ostrogorski, op. cit., Vol. I, p. 174.
[3] Reproduced in National Liberal Federation Report 1887, p. 30.

centres of political activity, should be able to speak on whatever questions arose with the full authority of the national voice.[4]

Two new functions were to be performed by this representative
organization. First, as we have seen, it was to enable the people to
take part in framing the party program. Second, and hardly less
important for the future, the constituency association would provide, in the words of William Harris, "a more popular body" for
selecting candidates—"a body which should not only be a reflex
of popular opinion, but should be so manifestly a reflex of that
opinion that none could doubt it." The consequence was quite
logical, as Harris added : "Gentlemen aspiring to the honourable
position of representing Birmingham must abide by the vote of
the selecting body and the Liberal electors must do so."[5] Perhaps
this dual requirement may be logical; but it was not realized fully
in practice until well into the next century.

One reason given for the foundation of the N.L.F. was that it
would avoid the waste of having separate reformist organizations
such as an Education League, a Reform Union, or a Liberation
Society by providing one body that could speak on any question
that might arise with "all the authority of the voice of the nation."[6]
Springing from long experience with reformist agitation and
guided by men rooted in this agitation rather than parliamentary
life, the N.L.F. can be regarded as the self-conscious fusion of
separate pressure groups with specific ends into a national party
organization with a broad program.[7] Now, as the founders of the
Federation had urged, the initiative in program and in presenting
the issues to the voters was often exercised by the extra-parliamentary organization. In the passage of the First and Second Reform Acts, for instance, agitation had come very largely from
nonparty associations, such as the political unions of the 1830's and
the National Reform League of the 1860's. In the case of the act of
1884, however, the movement was launched in 1883 by the N.L.F.,
which largely carried out the work of spreading propaganda and
organizing meetings to forward the measure.

Not quite yet, however, can we identify the Federation with the
Liberal Party. In its early years it was controlled by those who on
many points were opposed to the parliamentary leaders of the

[4] A. L. Lowell, *Government of England*, Vol. I (New York, 1926), p. 517.
[5] Ostrogorski, *op. cit.*, Vol. I, pp. 161–2.
[6] *Ibid.*, pp. 175–6.
[7] For this observation I am indebted to Dr. Hugh Berrington.

:ty. In these conflicts of Radical democracy with the parliamentarism of the Whig Liberals, the Federation employed, and often with effect, the new power assumed by its local associations as nominating bodies.[8] After the loss of some of the more conservative elements in the break-up over Home Rule, this tension relaxed. Yet, as we shall see, the forces that spoke through the Federation and in the accents of Radical democracy continued to press upon the traditional autonomy of the parliamentary party.

PARTY PROGRAMS AND GOVERNMENT POLICIES

The Liberal Party that was created after 1867 is a distinctive type of political formation. And in its novel features we may fairly see an expression of the Radical ideal. On a large scale, party supporters were organized throughout the country and brought together in a representative structure, which included a large annual conference, the Liberal Council. Through this structure influence could be exerted on the party program and on Members of Parliament. With its help, leaders, and especially the Leader, made an appeal to an electorate numbered in millions. Thanks in part to its sanctions, party unity in the House of Commons had risen sharply from its low point at mid-century.[9] But old traditions and old structures still flourished, not only within the parliamentary party, but also throughout the political system as a whole. This was, as Feiling has observed, "the last age of aristocracy, but also the one and only age of an ascendant upper-middle class."[1] Quite apart from the remaining limits on the suffrage, and within its enfranchised circles, Britain still had a "governing class." Within the Liberal Party itself, the new representative structure encroached on, without overcoming, the old autonomy of the parliamentary leaders.

May we say that at last the "modern political party" has made its appearance? Not if by that you mean the present-day political party. Twentieth-century Collectivism has brought changes in political attitudes, structures, and methods of action that oblige us to create a new party model. Of this new type, the Labour Party is the leading example. In comparison with it the Liberals, even at

---

[8] Ostrogorski, *op. cit.*, Vol. I, p. 209; Lowell, *op. cit.*, Vol. I, p. 522.
[9] See below Ch. IX, Tab. 9.1.
[1] Keith Feiling, *History of England* (London, 1948), p. 898.

the height of Radical influence, belong to a different order
political formation. The relation between programs adopted
the Liberal Council and policies followed by Liberal leaders an
Governments will bring out this contrast and will illustrate one
aspect of the distribution of power in the Party. We may examine
this relation during the Governments of Gladstone and Rosebery
from 1892 to 1895, and of Campbell-Bannerman after 1905.

The party election program, which states authoritatively what
a Government based on the party will do and which has been
drawn up by some recognized procedure within the party, is not
an old device in British politics. Even in the years following the
Second Reform Act, according to Hanham, "the party election
manifesto was still a personal appeal from the party Leader, not a
statement of future policy prepared and endorsed by the leading
men in the party."[2] During a campaign, declarations by individual
candidates and leading personalities in a party might well disagree,
even contradict one another. One result was that party leaders,
once in office, were left "relatively uncommitted to any particular
scheme of reform."[3]

An aggressive Radical faith inspired many of the founders of
the National Liberal Federation and Lowell could fairly conclude
that some of these expected that "the initiative on all the greater
issues, so far as the Liberal party was concerned, would be largely
transferred from the Treasury Bench to the Federation."[4] The
conference did exercise a varying, and at times substantial, influence on the parliamentary party. Yet neither in theory nor
practice did it ever win the authority which the conference of
the Labour Party has enjoyed. And with regard to claims only,
not even among the Radical militants was there a consistent
assertion of the ultimate sovereignty of the rank and file over the
party.

The call for the meeting at which the Federation was founded
in 1877 declared that its "essential feature" was "the participation
by all members of the party in the formation and direction of its
policy, and in the selection of those particular measures of reform
and progress to which priority shall be given."[5] The rules of the

---

[2] H. J. Hanham, *Elections and Party Management : Politics in the Time
of Disraeli and Gladstone* (London, 1959), p. 200.
[3] *Ibid.*, p. 201.
[4] Lowell, *op. cit.*, Vol. I, p. 518.
[5] See above, p. 52.

...eration themselves made it an object of the organization "to ...mote the adoption of Liberal principles in the government ... the country" and "to ascertain and give expression to the ...pinions of the Liberal party." These generalities left a good deal of leeway for differing views of the role of the Federation. The highpoint of the assertion of the Federation's authority—as well as the highpoint of its actual influence—came in the early 1890's when its Newcastle Programme of 1891 was strongly pressed on the Liberal Government of 1892–95.

At the first meeting of the Federation after the election of 1892, its president, Dr. Robert Spence Watson, took an exalted view of its authority. "The Liberal party," he said, "had fulfilled its part : they had told them [the party leaders] what their wishes were." The Newcastle Programme expressed the "immediate will of the Liberal party." What then was the function of the leaders? "It was theirs to decide how, and how best, and how most speedily the wishes of the Liberal party might be carried into execution." "The Leaders were where they were by the exertion of the Liberal party and they [the party] had every confidence that, given fair play . . . [by the time of the next election] good progress would have been made with every item of the Newcastle Programme."[6]

These are high claims, and they suggest three questions. First, was it generally believed in the party that the Federation alone had sufficient authority to make a program binding on a Liberal Government? The answer to this question is clearly "no." Even in this period of Radical ascendancy, the endorsement of the Leader was felt to be necessary. In 1894 the General Committee, in its address to Gladstone on the occasion of his retirement, said that "the schedule of reforms . . . styled the Newcastle Programme, largely gained its definite character and prompt acceptance by your powerful endorsement of it at one of our greatest meetings."[7] The object of the Federation, Dr. Watson told the Council in 1896, is to ascertain the will of the party and get it carried into law. If this is to be done, however, he observed, the Council's resolutions must be accepted by the leaders of the party.[8]

[6] N.L.F. *Report* 1893, p. 30.
[7] Dr. Robert Spence Watson, *The National Liberal Federation : From Its Commencement to the General Election of 1906* (London, 1907), p. 161.
[8] N.L.F. *Report* 1896, pp. 54, 58.

A second question is whether Gladstone did in fact author the Newcastle Programme as a statement of what a Liberal Go ernment would try to do. Even on this point there is room fo. doubt. In his history of the Federation, Watson wrote that "the appeal to the country had practically been upon the Newcastle Programme of reforms."[9] The Executive Committee of the Federation was more emphatic, declaring that the party had "fought the general election of 1892 on the Newcastle Programme."[1] To that program, said a speaker at the Council in 1893, "the voice of the people had given confirmation as strong as Holy Writ."[2]

On the other hand, Gladstone never explicitly endorsed the Programme by name or reference, nor did he lend his advocacy to every one of the many resolutions and sub-resolutions of which it was composed. At the mass meeting at the close of the conference of 1891, he spoke favorably of most, but not all, its proposals.[3] His election address of the next year, while not going beyond the Newcastle proposals, again did not mention it specifically and included only a selection of items from it.[4] With some reason, therefore, Lord Rosebery, Liberal Leader in the Lords, could warn during the campaign that the Newcastle Programme was still unauthorized.[5]

How did the record of the Liberal Governments compare with the Programme? Not many reforms of consequence were enacted; the Lords stood in the way. But in spite of the ambiguous status of the Programme, the coincidence between its proposals and what the Government attempted is striking. The Executive Committee was not far wrong in saying, after the Conservatives had come back, that the Liberal Governments had "made every endeavor, when they were in power, to redeem the pledges that Programme had contained."[6] Rosebery himself accepted this judgment in large part. His Government fell, he told the Council, because "it determined to fulfill all the pledges that it had given

[9] *The National Liberal Federation*, p. 46.
[1] N.L.F. *Report* 1896, p. 24.
[2] *Ibid.*, p. 46.
[3] When one counts them up, there prove to be twenty-six separate items in the Newcastle Programme. Of these Gladstone referred to only fifteen in his speech. See N.L.F. *Report* 1891.
[4] See *Annual Register, 1892*, pp. 110–111.
[5] *Ibid.*, p. 107.
[6] N.L.F. *Report* 1896, p. 24.

Opposition" and, moreover, "it had, I think, given too many edges—partly owing to you, Dr. Spence Watson."[7] He did not, however, regard the Programme or the resolutions of Council as the sole source of the Government's policies. These, he said, came not only from meetings of the Federation, but also from declarations of leaders and "the inherent necessities of the case."[8] With the view that the Newcastle Programme had been a powerful, if not dominating, influence on the Government's action, Lowell also concurred. Like Rosebery, of course, he thought this a source of weakness because, in his view, it hampered the Government's initiative in policy.[9]

After the fall of Rosebery's government, a reaction set in against policy-making by party conference and programmatic pledges by party leaders. In the campaign of 1895, Rosebery had warned against "a many-headed programme" and later, as we have seen, he attributed the Government's fall in part to its overcommitment to pledges deriving from the party conference. As strenuously as Rosebery, Campbell-Bannerman refused to commit himself to "any fixed programme for action." What a Liberal Government would do, he told the Council in 1899, would depend on circumstances, the feeling of the nation and the size of its majority.[1] In his speech to the mass meeting at the party conference of 1905, he reviewed approvingly a series of reforms, many of which had figured in council resolutions. This was much in the manner of Gladstone in 1891, except that, unlike Gladstone, he took care quite plainly to say : "This is no conclusive list; I am not here to frame or to propound any programme whatever."[2]

During the campaign of 1906 Campbell-Bannerman also kept a free hand. His tactic, at times a little devious, is worth examining. In his election address of January 6, he raised high the banner of Free Trade and, in his broad attack on Conservative policy, by implication committed the Liberals to take action to reduce expenditure and do something with regard to education, licensing, and the rating system. Otherwise he promised only to maintain

[7] *Ibid.*, p. 119.
[8] N.L.F. *Report* 1895, p. 111.
[9] *Op. cit.*, Vol. I, p. 517.
[1] N.L.F. *Report* 1899, pp. 86–7.
[2] N.L.F. *Report* 1905, p. 77.

the "time-honoured principles of Liberalism," remarking t.
Liberal policy was "well-known" and referring electors to h
recent speech at Albert Hall for detail.[3]

In that speech he had indeed stated a Liberal position on a
number of topics : the administration of India, Chinese labor in
South Africa, military expenditures, Ireland, land law and the
rating system, the law of combination, licensing, and especially
Free Trade. At the same time he was very careful to say that this
was not a program, neither a "particular programme of work"
for a session of Parliament; nor indeed "a general programme, a
policy" such as comes at a general election. After such a long
period of Tory rule, he said, "great allowances" must be made
for a Liberal Government.[4]

So far as explicit commitment was concerned, the Government
emerged from the campaign of 1906 with a freer hand than Gladstone had had in 1892 and (to anticipate the later discussion) a far
freer hand than Labour had in 1945. But can we go further and
agree with Lowell's judgment that the Council had been "effectively muzzled"?[5] Was the opinion of the Federation, expressed in
Council resolutions, no longer an accurate guide to Liberal action
in office?

In the decade before 1906 the views of Federation spokesmen
had receded from the peak of self-assertion reached in Dr. Watson's declaration of 1892. They did not entirely deny the Council's
program-making power, yet neither did they unambiguously
assert it. The Council, in its practice, moved away from the
custom of proposing each year a long catalogue of specific proposals—a custom from which the Newcastle Programme had
emerged—and the Omnibus Resolution, which in 1891 had included nine proposed reforms, was dropped in favor of a general
resolution expressing adherence to Liberal principles. Yet it seems
to have been hard to damp the Radical spirit. At its five meetings
from 1901 to 1905, the Council accumulated a set of proposals
that was hardly less voluminous and far-reaching than the Newcastle Programme and which indeed included the main headings
and many of the details of that document. Lowell's judgment

---

[3] *The Liberal Magazine*, February, 1906, pp. 47–50.
[4] Speech given December 21, 1905. Reprinted in Pamphlet 7, Liberal
Publications Dept., 1906.
[5] Lowell, *op. cit.*, Vol. I, p. 547.

:t its resolutions "never again reached anything resembling the
:nge, the well-nigh revolutionary propositions . . . of the New-
:astle Programme" does not square with the facts.[6]

When we compare these resolutions with the record of the
Campbell-Bannerman Government—as in 1892–95 we must include legislation attempted, as well as legislation achieved, since
once again the Lords often stood in the way—we find a substantial coincidence. Self-government for South Africa; reduction
of military estimates in 1906, 1907, and 1908; the Education Bill
of 1906; the Licensing Bill of 1908; the Plural Voting Bill of 1906;
the taxation of land values in the budget of 1909; the repeal or
reduction of certain food taxes; the four land bills of 1907; the
cessation of the recruitment of indentured Chinese labor; the
Trade Disputes Act of 1906—all these had been foreshadowed in
resolutions of the previous five years. All also, it is fair to say,
were in the spirit of Gladstonian and Victorian Radical reform.

The Government's Radical reforms mirrored not unfaithfully
the party opinion that had been previously expressed by the
Federation. But along with these, however, was another body of
measures that embodied a new spirit and turned reform in a new
direction—the direction of social reform. Among them were the
Provision of Meals Act of 1906, the Old Age Pensions Act of
1908, the Coal Mines (8 hours) Act of 1908, the Wages Boards
Act of 1909, the Labour Exchanges Act of 1909, the Act of 1906
greatly extending the coverage of Workmen's Compensation
and, one should certainly add, the introduction of a graduated
income tax by the budget of 1909 that levied super-tax for the
first time. These reforms, which involved Government intervention in the economy to favor the working classes, even to the
point of a redistribution of income, have been called the most
original work of the Government.[7] Yet, with only minor exceptions, they were not anticipated by resolutions of the Federation.

To be sure, as these bills were introduced and passed into law
(the Lords, incidentally, treated social reform more kindly than
they did Radical reform) they were welcomed by the Council.[8]
But it was not the extra-parliamentary Party that took the initia-

---

[6] See *ibid.*, p. 599. Between 1901 and 1905 the number of resolutions passed
is just about the same as the number contained in the Newcastle Programme.

[7] W. Lyon Blease, *A Short History of Liberalism* (London, 1913), pp.
324–30.

[8] See *Reports* of N.L.F. Council for 1907, 1908, and 1909.

tive in suggesting them. The free hand that Campbell-Bannerma had maintained for his Government was used to introduce far-reaching measures that had not been anticipated by the Federation. For that matter, neither had they been anticipated, to any great extent, by the declarations of the leaders of the Party. Certainly that economy and reduction of taxation which party leaders, as well as the Federation, had strenuously preached was incompatible with the increase in expenditure for which social reform was in no small part responsible.

These reforms reflect a growing Collectivism in policy. The political means by which they were pressed on M.P.'s and the Government were similarly new. Often the infant Labour Party was the immediate source of the proposal and sometimes even the bill embodying it. But the Government, with its overwhelming Liberal majority, was not dependent on Labour votes in the House. The Government and Liberal M.P.'s, however, responded to the initiative of the same forces that were bringing forward the Labour Party. In particular, the trade unions were displaying a new effectiveness as pressure groups. The structure of power as well as the pattern of policy was developing along Collectivist lines.

THE INTERESTED M.P. IN THE
LIBERAL–RADICAL PERIOD

Reviewing a book on pressure groups in 1958, a writer in the *Times Literary Supplement* wrote :

The ideal back-bencher would be one who is wholly unfettered by any obligation to particular bodies, and who is sufficiently well off financially not to depend on the patronage of any kind of pressure group.[9]

This ideal flourished in the early Victorian era and suggests what the role of the interested M.P. was at that time. If he was barred from receiving subventions from patron or party, or a salary from the executive, he was obliged—as Macaulay observed —to be well-to-do on his own account. In short, so far as the Liberal ideal of independence was realized, the member would

[9] *Times Literary Supplement* (February 21, 1958), p. 94; review of J. D. Stewart, *British Pressure Groups* (Oxford, 1958).

ery likely have strong outside economic interests of a personal kind. "It is because I have made a fortune and am independent, that I come here to ask for your suffrages to send me to Parliament," said George Hudson, the Railway King, to the voters when he first stood for the House in 1845.[1] As his later actions at Westminster showed, he meant anything but independence of his vast railway interests.

It is tempting to think of the new type of "interested" M.P. as the middle-class businessman. While, as Jennings and Thomas have shown, members with interests in business enterprise did greatly increase in number through the century, land too was a source of wealth that legislation might affect.[2] The type must be rather general : the member who owns property of one sort or another, possibly being a director or shareholder of a joint stock company. Looking back, we may contrast him with the Old Whig client; looking forward, with the member who through office-holding or membership is connected with one of the great producers' organizations of the twentieth-century economy.

To say that there were M.P.'s with personal economic interests which might affect their decisions in Parliament is not to say that Liberal or Radical ideals legitimized such influences. Quite the contrary; in contrast with Old Whig attitudes, the new spirit —with a certain lack of realism—found it hard to find a legitimate role in government for special interests. Certain reforms in legislative procedure illustrate this spirit.

We have seen how tolerantly the Old Whig viewed the use of parliamentary power to favor group and personal economic interests, especially in the field of private bill legislation.[3] Beginning early in the nineteenth century, procedure in this field was gradually reformed, the general direction being toward assimilating it to a quasi-judicial model. The principal reform was the elimination of members with local and personal interests from private bill committees.

Under the system of appointing committees that existed in the early nineteenth century, every opposed private bill became a battlefield for interested parties. Lobbying of M.P.'s was intense and was sometimes conducted by parliamentary agents, already an

[1] Richard S. Lambert, *The Railway King, 1800–1871 : A Study of George Hudson and the Business Morals of His Time* (London, 1938). p. 152.

[2] W. Ivor Jennings, *Parliament* (London, 1939), p. 37

[3] See above Ch. 1, pp. 22–32.

established profession.[4] Deputations headed by their attorneys regularly came to Westminster from the localities concerned. Promoters and opponents distributed statements, visited the homes of members, and otherwise sought to win the support of members and especially of those on the committee on the bill. Costs were high : one witness said that during one session the promoters of the Great Western Railway bill spent £40,000—a not unusual amount, he claimed—and at that the bill failed.[5] There were dark suggestions not merely of lobbying, but of "rather more than that." It was even said that sometimes committee members with land that would be bought up under a proposed scheme threatened to oppose the bill unless they were offered a higher price.[6]

The Select Committee on Private Bill Procedure of 1825 recognized the difficulties that arose from the presence on committees of members whose constituents were locally interested in the results, and of members who had themselves a personal interest in the subject of bills. It was willing to go no further, however, than to reflect that "abstractedly considered, that mode would undoubtedly be most desirable which should assimilate committees, by a limitation of numbers and an exclusion of all bias from interest, to the form and character of juries."[7] Through the next twenty years such a reform was resisted on the grounds—typically Old Whig—that the local knowledge possessed by members was valuable and that it was wrong to abolish their right and duty to represent their constituencies in committee as well as in the House. At last in 1844 the House, impelled by Gladstone, resolved to send all bills for competing railway lines to committees whose members were obliged to sign a declaration of noninterest, both local and personal. In the same year the House forbade members with a direct pecuniary interest from voting in any committee on a private bill. Eleven years later local representation on opposed private bill committees was abolished.[8]

Efforts to eliminate personal interest from procedure in the

---

[4] *Parl. Papers*, Vol. XXIII, *Report from Select Committee on Private Business* (1837–38).

[5] *Ibid.*

[6] *Ibid.*, minutes of evidence, pp. 14–19.

[7] *Parl. Papers*, Reports from Committees, Vol. II, *Report from the Select Committee on the Constitution of Committees on Private Bills* (1825), p. 2.

[8] Cyprian Williams, *The Historical Development of Private Bill Procedure and Standing Orders in the House of Commons* (London, 1948), Vol. I, p. 88.

House itself were more complex and less successful. In 1811 Speaker Abbott said that it was a rule established some two hundred years before, and even then spoken of as an ancient practice, that "a personal interest in a question disqualified a member from voting."[9] In the field of public legislation Speaker Abbott's ruling had so narrow a scope as to be almost meaningless. The interest, according to the Speaker, "must be a direct pecuniary interest, and separately belonging to the persons whose votes were questioned, and not in common with the rest of His Majesty's subjects, or on a matter of state policy." As a result, in the whole history of the House there has been only one case in which votes of members on public business have been disallowed on this ground.[1]

Whatever very ancient practice may have been in the field of private business, it is clear that the rule to which Abbott referred did not prevent members in the eighteenth century from taking an active part in promoting bills in which they were intimately and pecuniarily interested—subscribers to a canal company, for instance, voting in the House on the bill to authorize the company.[2] In the first half of the nineteenth century there was a substantial tightening up of procedure in this respect. Not only, as we have seen, were members with a direct pecuniary interest excluded from private bill committees; their votes on relevant private bills in the House were also subject to disallowance, a step that was frequently taken.[3] Yet it does not seem

[9] *Parl. Deb.*, Vol. XX, 1012 (17 July 1811).

[1] In 1892 the votes of three members, two of them directors and the other a shareholder in the British East Africa Company, were disallowed on a grant of public funds to that company. *Report from the Select Committee on Members of Parliament* (Personal Interest); with proceedings, minutes of evidence and an Appendix; *H.C.* 274 (1896). It is highly unlikely that objection to voting in similar circumstances would be upheld today, since the Speaker would surely rule that such a grant is a matter of public policy. This is the opinion of Sir Edward Fellowes, Clerk of the House. See *Special Report from Select Committee on the House of Commons Disqualification Bill; H.C.* 349 (1956); minutes of evidence, Q. 777.

[2] See above, p. 31. In 1800 Mr. Tierney told the House that he knew that gentlemen frequently sat on committees and voted on canal and turnpike bills in which they were personally interested, "but," he claimed, "this was an exception, not the rule of the House." See Appendix, Report of 1896 (Personal Interest).

[3] Sir Thomas Erskine May, *Parliamentary Practice*, 16th ed. (London, 1957), pp. 440, 442. See also Appendix Report of 1896 (Personal Interest), for examples under the heading "Personal Interest (Private Legislation), objections sustained."

that the rule was strictly applied throughout the century a
directors or shareholders in a joint stock company might guic
through the House a bill concerning their company and vote or
the bill in the House,[4] a fact that was particularly disturbing to
many members on the Liberal side.[5]

Railway Politics

In spite of Liberal and Radical reforms, therefore, ample opportunity was left the "interested" M.P. What use did he make of
this opportunity? Railway politics provide illustrations and at the
same time indicate the interplay between economic interest, on
the one hand, and party and ideological commitment, on the
other.

It was generally recognized that certain members represented
the railways in the House of Commons and, while there were
protests against the parliamentary strength of the companies,
there were, to my knowledge, none against the fact of their being
represented. In addition to shareholders (who Gladstone in 1844
thought constituted a majority of the House) there were many
directors. Of the 815 M.P.'s who sat from 1841–47, some 145
were railway directors;[6] in 1867 the number was 179;[7] in 1886 it
was 90.[8] Considerably smaller than these figures suggest, the hard

[4] See Report of 1896 (Personal Interest), Appendix, Sect. II, under heading "objections not sustained." Cases in which objection was not sustained
in the latter part of the century are discussed in Barry McGill, "Conflict of
Interest : English Experience 1782–1914," *Western Political Quarterly*, Vol.
XII, No. 3 (September, 1959), pp. 808–27.

[5] The division on the disallowance of the votes in 1892 was practically
a party vote : a majority composed mainly of Liberals and Home Rulers
voted against a predominantly Tory opposition. As a result of Liberal
representations, the Select Committee on Personal Interest was appointed.

[6] W. O. Aydelotte, "The House of Commons in the 1840's," *History*, Vol.
XXXIX (October, 1945), pp. 249–62.

[7] Bernard Cracroft, *Essays, political and miscellaneous* (London, 1868),
Vol. I, *The Analysis of the House of Commons, or Indirect Representation
in the year 1867*, p. 95. Incidentally, Cracroft's comment on the role of the
fifty or sixty directors of insurance companies is worth quoting : ". . . when
Mr. Sheridan, the recognized leader of this influential phalanx, rises in his
place to plead for the remission of the Fire Duty, or expound any other
grievances connected with those offices, his statements are listened to, quite
independently of himself, with an attention and a care conceded to one
who speaks not only with knowledge and authority, but with a certain well-
understood if undefined power at his back" (p. 98).

[8] Philip Williams, "Public Opinion and the Railway Rates Question in
1886," *English Historical Review*, Vol. LXVII, No. 262 (January, 1952),
p. 52.

e of railway M.P.'s busied themselves with both private and
~blic legislation. A private bill was needed to authorize a new
~ie and also to make major changes thereafter. As a result, railway bills poured through Parliament, some 4,000 being sanctioned
in the half century after 1830. Sometimes, especially in the early
days, the initial bill involved prolonged and bitter conflict with
existing interests, such as turnpike trusts and canal companies,
and the pattern of politics was essentially that of the struggles
over the canal acts of 1762 and 1766. Such, for instance, was the
case with the struggle over the Liverpool and Manchester Railway
from 1824–26, which involved parliamentary expenses of £80,000,
mostly for "canvassing," i.e., lobbying.[9]

Once the railway age had been launched, however, the principal
contests were between opposing projects in which the growing
amalgamations were often pitted against one another. A classic
example was the bitter parliamentary fight between George Hudson and Edward Denison, also an M.P., over the latter's scheme
for a London-to-York line, which was finally enacted at a cost
to all parties of £523,000 for legal controversy, lobbying, and
wire-pulling.[1]

In the field of public legislation, however, the railway M.P.'s
were likely to act together, as they did, for instance, when resisting
Gladstone's proposals of 1844.[2] These proposals, intended to provide some comprehensive guidance for railway policy that otherwise was left to the countless *ad hoc* decisions of private bill
committees, would have given the state a direct control, including
effective power of revising rates. Although recognizing that the
railways had "perhaps the strongest interest in regard to direct
influence upon the votes" of M.P.'s, Gladstone, then President
of the Board of Trade, took a high line against the companies in
the second reading debate. The usual deputations and lobbying
went on, however, and very probably through Peel[3] the bill was
drastically amended as desired by the companies. The point of
interest is that the strength of the companies proceeded not just
from the brute number of railway M.P.'s in the House, but also

[9] O. Cyprian Williams, *op. cit.*, Vol. I, p. 54. See also George S. Veitch,
The Struggle for the Liverpool and Manchester Railway (Liverpool, 1930).
[1] Lambert, *op. cit.*, p. 185.
[2] This account is based mainly on Edward Cleveland-Stevens, *English
Railways: their Development and their Relation to the State* (London, 1915).
[3] Gustav Cohn, *Englische Eisenbahnpolitik*, 2nd ed. (Leipzig, 1875), Bd. I,
p. 164.

from the fact that members generally, including the Prime Mi=
ister, did not believe in state intervention. For the same reasons
similar efforts to frame and enforce a comprehensive policy in
later years also failed.

By 1888, when the act providing the first effective regulation
of rates was passed,[4] two important and interrelated changes had
taken place. First, there had begun that general shift away from
laissez faire which one may associate with Radical rather than
Liberal influence in policy. This tendency of policy—provision
for free, compulsory education is a leading example—is not
properly called Collectivist. It involved certain exceptional acts
of state intervention to provide a service or to correct some undesirable consequence of the free economy. Unlike later Collectivist policy, it was not an effort to reshape the economic system
as a whole or to alter its foundations. In this view, railways in
particular were regarded as exceptions to the usual rules of orthodox economics; as potential or actual monopolies they might be
regulated by the state. And when the bill was being contested in
the House in 1886, the press as a whole showed little sympathy
with the complaints of the companies.

The second change was the rise of a new kind of pressure
group, which opposed the railways' claims and favored the bill.
Concern over railway monopoly had already been shown in the
early seventies by the trading community, which expressed itself
by means of petitions from various chambers of commerce; and
in the mid-eighties there arose a formidable opposition, based on
organizations of traders, manufacturers, and agriculturists. The
Associated Chambers of Commerce, founded only a few years
before, strongly supported the bill. So also did the Central Chambers of Agriculture, the Association of Municipal Corporations,
and the recently formed Railway and Canal Traders' Association
that brought together some twenty-six trade and manufacturing
associations such as the Mining Association of Great Britain and
the British Iron Trades Association. Like the railways, many of
these bodies had their "interested" M.P.'s, and the committee
consisting of their representatives and formed to coordinate their
parliamentary action included fifteen peers and forty-five members of the House of Commons. In terms of "interested" M.P.'s,
the two sides were about evenly matched, forty-five on the side

[4] Philip Williams, *op. cit.*, gives a brilliant analysis of this episode.

the railway customers and an equal number constituting the ~~rd~~ core of railway members. The opinion of the House, however, was so overwhelmingly against the railways that the latter did not even challenge a division when the bill had its second reading in 1886. While for various extraneous reasons the measure was not enacted until two years later, the contest showed that the railways, once dominant in these matters, now, as Williams concluded, could only win brief victories "in the dark."[5]

The bill was not an item of party policy. Governments, whether Liberal or Conservative, exerted little influence on the outcome; their effort was to find a position midway between the traders and the railways. If in this sense the struggle was mainly one of pressure politics, it was pressure politics waged with very different weapons from those used by the railways in the 1840's or by the reform associations of the previous generation. The rise of nation-wide associations of manufacturers and traders was introducing a new element into the politics of the country. The essence of this change was the formation of bodies based on a productive function and their affiliation as national organizations, the principal examples being trade unions and trade associations. The latter were growing up in the last quarter of the century, in reaction partly to the growth of trade unions and partly to the price-fall that began in the mid-seventies.[6] Behind both developments lay large changes in the British economy at home and in its relations to the international economy. By the nineties British managers had made their first large-scale experiments with industrial combination. On the plane of economic development, the way was being prepared for the rise of Collectivism.

[5] *Ibid.*, p. 73.
[6] Sir John Clapham, *An Economic History of Modern Britain* (London, 1932), Vol. II, p. 155.

CHAPTER III

Collectivist Politics:
Socialist and Tory Democracy

We expect a political party to take a distinctive approach to public policy. It is likely also to have its own view of how political power should be organized and exerted. In this century, the Labour Party introduced the question of Socialism into British politics. It has also been the principal means by which a new theory of representation has been propagated. It introduced into the political culture of Britain not only a new concept of public policy—Socialism—but also a new view of political organization which we may designate as "Socialist Democracy." This includes a distinctive view of party, interest groups, and indeed of the British constitution and the meaning of democracy.

But in Britain the old—and not least, the very old—often blends with the new. The Toryism of the Conservative Party is a case in point. This pre-capitalist, pre-individualist, pre-liberal creed ought surely to have died out in the nineteenth century. Yet not only has it survived into the era of the Welfare State and the Managed Economy, it can also claim credit for having helped create them. British Tories are in some degree Collectivists, not only in certain aims of policy, but also in certain methods of political action. In both respects, they often have more in common with Socialists than with their contemporaries in the Liberal Party. Old traditions of strong government, paternalism, and the organic society have made easier the massive reassertion of state power that has taken place in recent decades, often under Conservative auspices. Old ideals of authority have been adapted to the conditions of mass suffrage in a theory of representation which we may call "Tory Democracy."

ocialist Democracy and Tory Democracy have a great deal common. Both of course accept the basic legal structures of modern British government—universal suffrage, periodic elections, freedoms of speech and press, an elected legislature, a career civil service. Both accept the basic conventions of Cabinet Government, although there are aspects of these conventions that are interpreted differently. But what is most interesting is the extent to which they agree on how political power is to be organized within this legal and constitutional framework. This agreement sets both Tory and Socialist Democracy apart from nineteenth-century political individualism and constitutes a common theory of politics in the Collectivist era. This theory is not confined to the closets of political philosophers, but pervades the political culture of twentieth-century Britain and functions powerfully as an operative ideal in daily political life.

The major theme of this Collectivist theory of representation is party government; its minor theme, functional representation. In this Collectivist guise, democratic thought legitimizes a far greater role for group and party than did Liberal and Radical thought. To put the matter negatively : both Tory and Socialist Democracy reject parliamentarism. Both reject the notion that Members of Parliament should freely follow their own judgment when deciding how to vote and that the House of Commons is, or should be, in Bagehot's phrase, in "a state of perpetual choice." On the contrary, both demand that the M.P. should be not a "representative" but a "delegate" (although, to be sure, a party delegate, not a local delegate), and that the Government's majority should stand stoutly with it, as should the Opposition's minority.[1] Both accept the great organized producer groups of a modern industrial society and attribute to them an important role in government and administration. Both, in short, depart in major respects from the political individualism of the nineteenth century.

---

[1] Sometimes the Burkean ideal of the "representative" pops up in the most implausible contexts. In 1948, for instance, the National Executive of the Labour Party warned candidates not to pledge themselves to particular measures outside the field of declared Government policy or of the party manifesto. "Otherwise," concluded the warning, "Members of Parliament are liable to find themselves in the position of instructed delegates rather than representatives who have a duty to give their vote in Parliament after they have heard the pros and cons of debate." *Annual Report of the Labour Party for 1949*, p. 5. (Cited hereafter as *LPCR*.)

But the political culture of a country is rarely monolithic. .
modern Britain Liberal and Radical currents of opinion still ru.
strongly. Even more important, however, is the dialectic between
Tory and Socialist Democracy within the consensus of Collectivist
politics. Conflict exists between Tory and Socialist views over
the function of party and the meaning of democracy—and it is
tempting to call this conflict fundamental.

FUNCTIONAL REPRESENTATION

The notion of functional representation I take in a broad sense,
applying it not only to Old Tory and Old Whig, but also to
modern Collectivist views. A few words to define it and distinguish
it from other theories may be helpful.

In this book the term refers to any theory that finds the community divided into various strata, regards each of these strata
as having a certain corporate unity, and holds that they ought
to be represented in government. From one historical period to
another, such groupings have been differently named—estates,
ranks and orders, interests, classes and vocations—and have differed
greatly in their internal structure, relations with the community,
and mode of representation. The similarity lies first in the fact
that they are regarded as performing an important function in
the community as a whole (as the order of knights in medieval
society performed the function of defense, or as the workers in
some industry carry on an activity necessary to the economy
of modern Britain). Moreover, the unity of such a stratum is not
that of mere voluntary association which stresses common ideas
and moral judgments. On the contrary, its integration is seen
as arising especially from objective conditions that give its members a function and are the ground for deeply rooted, continuing
—even "fixed"—interests. Recognizing this function and these
common interests, the members act as a unit and find in the group
a sphere of moral fulfillment and an instrument of political action.
This anti-individualist bias is common both to older corporatist
attitudes and to modern pluralism.

It is conventional and correct to distinguish functional from
territorial representation, although the two notions are not necessarily incompatible. A theory of territorial representation may,
for instance, conceive of the constituency represented as itself a

ialler community within the larger, having a coherent set of interests or purposes that its representative can advocate. So the ancient communities of shire and borough were conceived in the eighteenth century and before. Such a view of territorial representation permits functional representation—as in the case of an eighteenth-century port that was at once a community and a section of the great "commercial interest" of the Empire. The incompatibility of territorial and functional representation arises, however, as territorial representation is viewed from individualist perspectives. The concern with functional status or membership in established communities gives way to the individualist emphasis on the identity and equality of all rational men, and arithmetical equality among election districts becomes an overriding criterion.

Should one also distinguish functional from interest representation? The two notions can be separated analytically, but historically they almost always go together. Interest representation rests on the belief that certain social elements ought to be represented simply because they have a mode of existence that is part of the legitimate social order quite apart from any functions they may or may not perform for the community. The design of the good society legitimizes their needs; hence, their wishes, reflecting the needs of this mode of life, ought to have a voice in government. Such a view is reflected, for instance, in Hugh Cecil's interpretation of medieval representation, which he finds to have been based on the "principle" that "no tax should be imposed except by the consent of the class of taxpayers who paid it." "This consent," he claimed, "was the safeguard against oppression. Individuals might be coerced, but not classes."[2] In general the "balance of classes" or "balance of interests" argument reveals an attitude of this sort. The basic contention is not so much that each element performs a function which makes its representation necessary for the good governance of the whole, as that it deserves a share of power to protect and promote its just needs.

Such attitudes, however, usually also have overtones of functionalism. The needs of the class or interest in question should be considered not simply because they are legitimized by the design of the good society, but also because this element (whether stratum or lesser community) carries out a function important to the social whole. This justifies giving it power to protect itself. But

[2] *Conservatism* (London, 1912), p. 155.

what is especially relevant in modern society, it also means that the knowledge of those performing this function may well be necessary for the good governing of the wider community. They have special skills, experience, *expertise* which government must have at hand if it is to understand and control the complex and interdependent social whole. Even the mighty sovereign of Tudor times felt some need for the advice of representatives of his subjects. But a special emphasis is given this need by the conditions of government in modern industrial society. As control extends into the complex and technical affairs of the economy, government must win the cooperation of crucial sectors and show sensitivity to their values and purposes. Not least, it must elicit their expert advice. These sectors are the seat of technical, professional, and scientific knowledge indispensable to effective policy making. In various periods of history the contribution of representatives has been thought of sometimes as primarily "reason," at other times as "will." For the proponents of functional representation in modern times, this contribution is especially "knowledge."

The New Pluralism

From the functionalist perspective, the unit of representation is generally a social stratum having a certain corporate unity and performing an important function. These give it the ability to be represented as well as the persisting interests and special knowledge that deserve to be represented. It is tricky to generalize, of course. For one thing, a theory of functional representation is usually involved with some larger view of the nature of the social reality that is represented, a view that may derive from a comprehensive cosmology, sociology, or philosophy of history. This was true not only of the older, pre-liberal pluralisms, in terms of which functional representation was justified, but also of the "new pluralism" that emerged in European thought in the present century. On the Continent divergencies within this current of thought were pronounced and fundamental. United in its opposition to individualism and its advocacy of functionalism, the new pluralism there was inspired by social philosophies as radically opposed in basic premises as those of revolutionary syndicalism and fascist corporatism. Continental thought had no small influence on British pluralism. But as is usually the case when the weapons of ideological war are shipped across the Channel, the edge of their fierce polemic was blunted. Still, one can detect differences between a functionalism of the Left and of the Right, and these differences suggest opposing social philosophies. The principal difference is in the Left's advocacy of representation of only workers (enlarged in some contexts to include workers "by brain" as well as "by hand") and the Right's familiar plea that "all classes, all interests" be given a share of power.

In Britain at the turn of the century, there were signs of a general shift in the climate of opinion toward legitimizing functional groups, in particular the new organized producer groups of the modern industrial economy. The causes of this change were economic as well as ideological. Certainly the movement away from the individualist and polycentric economy of the earlier nineteenth century played a part. By the seventies and eighties the joint stock company with limited liability was beginning to supersede the old common law partnership as the dominant form of business organization, and in the nineties British managers used the new corporate forms to make their first large-scale experiments with industrial combinations. If the rise of the large business corporation was the central thread in economic development, the rise of trade unions, trade associations, and indeed of cooperatives was part of the same general tendency away from individualism and toward collectivism. In this emerging society, as W. H. B. Court writes, while direct personal relations between "master and servant" were by no means extinguished, "over a large part of the field they were beginning to be replaced by corporate and associate life in many forms, not only among the business men, but also among the industrial workers as trade unions grew." Parallel to these changes in economic and social forms were intellectual developments. "The significance of the rise of corporateness," Court continues, "was recognized as early as 1900 by a deep legal thinker who was also sensitive to the atmosphere of his time, F. W. Maitland."[3] From these years onward, an interest in group life became an important concern of academic and scholarly thought.

The main thrust behind the new pluralism, however, came not from pure scholars, but from men deeply engaged in political action as Socialists. "The attack on 'arithmetical democracy' and

[3] *A Concise Economic History of Britain from 1750 to the Present Time* (London, 1954), p. 216.

in favor of 'communal representation,' which had been a conservtive cry in the 1830's," writes Professor W. J. M. MacKenzie "began to be an advanced cry in the 1890's."[4] In the course of succeeding decades, proponents of some such revision of British parliamentary democracy included the outstanding intellectuals of the Labour Party : Cole, Tawney, Russell, Brailsford, Laski, even the Webbs. Guild Socialism was, of course, the sharpest statement of this current of thought. In their proposals, the Guildsmen made a frontal attack on British representative institutions. For a House of Commons based on territorial representation, they would—as proposed by Cole—substitute a series of guilds, each based on a branch of industry and possessing a council through which the "workers by hand and brain" in that industry would govern themselves. On the national plane, a "Commune" would coordinate the activities of the guilds, but without powers of coercion.[5] These syndicalist proposals were resisted by leading Fabians. But even the Webbs were strongly influenced. For while they rejected the vocational parliament of the Guildsmen, their proposed constitution for a Socialist Britain provided for a large measure of industrial self-government. Their Social Parliament, for instance, would supervise the economy by means of standing committees, each concerned with a main sector of the economy and operating through boards, one of which would carry out tasks of supervision and management and would include representatives selected by the Parliament from nominations put forward by the workers, administrators, and consumers.[6] Guild Socialism reached the height of its influence during the life of the National Guilds League (1915–25), but the idea of workers' control, which they had done much to foster, deeply influenced the trade unions and was not finally put to rest until Labour took office in 1945. By that time other channels of power—we shall examine them in Chapters VII and XII—had been firmly established for trade unions and other producer groups.

While the main thrust came from the Left, the Right also produced its advocates of pluralism and functional representation.

---

[4] "Representation in Plural Societies," *Political Studies*, Vol. II, No. 1 (February, 1954), p. 59.

[5] G. D. H. Cole, *Guild Socialism, A Plan for Economic Democracy* (New York, 1920), pp. 109–10.

[6] *A Constitution for the Socialist Commonwealth of Great Britain* (London, 1920).

the nineteenth century, some writers cultivated a nostalgia for the *noblesse oblige* of feudalism. In 1877 Ruskin founded his "Saint George's Guild," an organization for workingmen designed to develop agriculture and industry cooperatively. In a letter to workmen he promised them ". . . no liberty . . . but instant obedience to known law and appointed persons . . . no equality . . . but the recognition of every betterness and the reprobation of every worseness. . . ."[7] A follower of Ruskin, Arthur J. Penty, proposed in his *Restoration of the Guild System*, published in 1906, a system of producers guilds, whose political organs would consist of a Lower House elected by the people "in their private capacity" and an Upper House, nominated by the guilds, thereby securing both the "leadership of the best and wisest" and "a balance of power between the various interests of the State."[8] Nor is it unfair to include among the conservative currents of functionalism the proposals of the Whitley Committee in 1917 that joint industrial councils including both employers and workmen be established to review and improve industrial relations.[9]

A strong flavor of functionalism clings to the proposal made by Winston Churchill in his Romanes lecture of 1930 that there be established a "non-political" "sub-Parliament" for economic affairs, which would include, along with certain M.P.'s, other persons "possessing special qualifications in economic matters." L. S. Amery's ideas were more radical; in a debate on the suffrage in 1931, for instance, he granted that British democracy in the nineteenth century had the fault of not representing the working classes. In rectifying this wrong, he continued, they should not, however, destroy the representation of "all interests, all classes."

Manual labour, important as it is, is after all only one element, one function in the life of the nation, and it would be entirely contrary to any true interpretation of democracy if that one element should by its numerical majority occupy a preponderating place in the House of Commons.[1]

Amery again picked up this theme when in 1947 he called for "a new and far-reaching Reform Act which will recognize

[7] Fors Clavigera," *The Works of John Ruskin*, E. T. Cook and A. Wedderburn, eds. (London, 1903–12), Vol. I, p. 96.
[8] Pp. 70–1.
[9] See J. B. Seymour, *The Whitley Councils Scheme* (London, 1932).
[1] 249 *H.C. Deb.* 668 (5 March 1931).

the growing economic organization of the national life as a necessary basis of representation." "This conception of functional representation," he continued, "has . . . its own independent history in this country," going back to the medieval House of Commons when the knights of the shire represented agriculture and the burgesses a variety of localized industrial and commercial interests.[2] To Amery's proposal Harold Macmillan, in a speech of March 5th, 1949, lent his support. Or to take the thoughts of a "new Conservative," we may consider a speech of David Eccles of January, 1948, in which he set forth his conception of a "balanced society with a purpose . . . in which the greatest number and variety of legitimate interests are all welcome and all have an assured place" and urged that Conservatives "deliberately encourage such groups and associations and make maximum use of them to carry out government policy."[3]

We may doubt whether a parliament of industry will ever be set up in Britain. Its advocacy, however, illustrates a general shift in the climate of opinion toward legitimizing the representation of groups—and more particularly the representation of the new organized producer groups of the modern economy. In their relation to practice, two other lines of thought have been more important. One of these, again descending from a distant past, is the continuing recognition of the legitimate role in Parliament of the "interested" M.P. There have, of course, been great changes in the character of the interests represented and the methods by which they gain a voice in Parliament since Old Whig and Victorian days. Along with M.P.'s who have interests arising from directorships, investments, and the like, the House includes, as Churchill has said, "those people who come to represent particular bodies, particular groups of a non-political character." "We are not supposed to be an assembly of gentlemen who have no interests of any kind and no associations of any kind," he continued. "That is ridiculous. That might happen in Heaven, but not, happily, here."[4]

Even more important, as we shall see, has been the growing

---

[2] *Thoughts on the Constitution* (London, 1947), pp. 63–5.
[3] *Conservatism: 1945–1950* (London, 1950), pp. 87–9. See also the proposals for an industrial parliament in Christopher Hollis, *Can Parliament Survive?* (London, 1949), Chs. 8 and 9.
[4] *Report*, Committee of Privileges, *H.C.* No. 118 (1946–47), minutes of evidence, p. 8. See also above pp. 22–4.

recognition of the need to associate representatives of interest groups with government administration. In many instances this has taken statutory form, as when, for instance, members of the relevant professions, trade unions, or branches of business have been appointed to committees charged with administrative duties; and an elaborate system of committees advisory to ministers has been developed in recent decades. The Education Act of 1921 required every local education authority to have an education committee that included persons experienced in education and persons acquainted with the needs of various kinds of schools, these persons to be nominated by outside bodies. The National Health Insurance Act of 1924 provided for the functional representation of specific interests, such as the medical profession and the suppliers of drugs, medicines, and appliances, on the various committees charged with administering the system of social insurance. There were analogous provisions in the minimum wage legislation enacted in the Trade Boards Acts of 1909 and 1918. Beyond these formal provisions, however, there has been legitimized a system of continuous, informal contact between departments of state and trade unions, trade associations, and similar vocational bodies. The long struggle by trade unions for such "recognition" by government—long after they had won recognition by employers—illustrates the development. But other groups, such as the teachers, have also helped change attitudes and have benefited by that change. So far has the climate of opinion come to accept these practices, that today it is a rare and serious charge that a Government has made policy without consulting with the organized interests involved. In the Second Reading debate on the National Health Service Bill in 1946, the Conservative Opposition hinged its attack on the failure of the Government to "negotiate" with the doctors. Also, at the time of the Anglo-Japanese trade agreement of 1954, the Labour Opposition pressed as a serious charge the fact that the Government had made policy without first consulting the special interests concerned, in particular the representatives of the Lancashire cotton industry.[5]

The most important of these relationships have been those between the government on the one hand and the organized producers groups representing capital and labor on the other. We

[5] See Harry Eckstein, *Pressure Group Politics: The Case of the British Medical Association* (London, 1960), p. 24; and *Manchester Guardian*, February 11, 1954; and *Economist*, February 13, 1954.

shall have occasion to examine these relationships in some detail. We may note here that they involved representation on high-level committees such as the Economic Planning Board and the National Production Advisory Council on Industry, the most ambitious effort being the National Economic Development Council set up in 1962. With representatives of the Government, the management of private and public industry, and the Trades Union Congress as well as independent experts, the Council, it was hoped, would not only point the way toward more rapid economic growth, but also be a means for securing cooperation for this end among the bodies represented on it.

PARTY GOVERNMENT : SOCIALIST VERSION

Functional representation has been broadly accepted in Britain by both Conservatives and Labourites. But the major theme of the Collectivist attitude toward representation has been party government. We shall look first at the Socialist and then at the Tory version.

Like the Radical, the Socialist rejects the parliamentarism of the Liberal and the Old Whig. The House of Commons is there to ventilate grievances and, especially by means of an organized Opposition, to provide responsible criticism of the Government. But its function is not to deliberate and decide on major questions of policy or—except in the rarest circumstances—the fate of Governments. For that would be usurping the role of the electorate, which by giving a majority to a party has endowed it with authority to govern. "The Government's majority exists to support the Government," writes Jennings in words that are not only descriptive, but also normative; "through the party system, it is the Government that controls the House of Commons."[6]

So far the logic, though rather more stringent, is in accord with Radical premises. But if we look further, we see that Socialist thought profoundly alters and strengthens the foundations of party government, making of party a political formation quite different from that conceived by Radicals. It leads to this conclusion, first, by way of its view of policy and, second, by way of its view of the social bases of party.

[6] *Cabinet Government*, 3rd ed. (Cambridge, Eng., 1958), pp. 472-3.

The Socialist approach to policy diverges not only from laissez faire, but also from the piecemeal intervention of Radical reform. The Radical policy of free public education and of "Three Acres and a Cow," for instance, would indeed mean that the wealth of some would be used for the benefit of others. Some writers have taken such redistribution to be the mark of Collectivism in policy. I have not followed this usage, but have taken Collectivism to characterize government intervention with the economic and social system *as a whole*.

The contrast between the Socialist and the Radical approach to policy is pronounced in this respect. To be sure, the Radical approach to particular measures did, broadly speaking, reflect certain distinctive values, certain attitudes toward society as a whole. In particular it was guided by the desire to eliminate unfair advantage. "Nearly all the questions submitted to the conference," said John Morley to the National Liberal Federation in 1891, "turned upon the principle of privilege."[7] But even though the Radical sought so to reform the system as to reduce privilege and promote equality, the system he supported would still be an individualist system, the struggle an individual struggle. "Our ideal," said Joseph Chamberlain in 1885 at the height of his Radicalism, "should be that an honest, a decent and an industrious man should be able to earn a livelihood for himself and his family, should have access to some means of self-improvement and enjoyment and should be able to lay aside something for sickness and old age."[8] Twenty years later Campbell-Bannerman spoke in the same vein, when he told the N.L.F. that the Liberal purpose was to end every privilege and every monopoly injurious to the interests of all and to give every man the chance to develop in his own way his faculties and opportunities.[9]

The government intervention advocated by the Socialist is inspired by very different values and beliefs. Not only is there a different conception of the conditions of liberty and a greater stress on equality; it is especially the Socialist's commitment to "fellowship" that fundamentally distinguishes his approach from that of the Radical.[1] For private ownership he would substitute public ownership; for production for profit, production for use; for competition, cooperation. A cultural and ethical revolution

[7] *Annual Register, 1891* (London, 1892), p. 181.
[8] *Annual Register, 1885* (London, 1896), p. 140.
[9] N.L.F. *Report* 1905, p. 85.
[1] Discussed in more detail below, Ch. V, pp. 126–32.

would also take place, and motives that had aimed at individual benefit would now aim at common benefits. Industry, which had been governed by individual decisions within the competitive system, would be subject to collective and democratic control. The upshot is that government intervention would consist in comprehensive and continuous planning and administration. These were not the views only of early ideologues or Left Wing extremists. Writing in 1937, Clement Attlee, Leader of the Party and already a moderate, declared that "economic liberty" cannot be achieved "by the extension of private property," but only by "collective control." "The issue before the country is Socialism versus Capitalism—and Socialism is not a matter of degree."[2]

Such "system-thinking" is a good deal less common in the Labour Party of recent years. Yet the Welfare State and the Managed Economy of these days involve government intervention that is profoundly different in kind from even the most ambitious thoughts of Radicals. Such commitments mean not simply that ministers must be protected against an undisciplined House "carrying some provision of a bill which might in appearance be trifling, but would destroy its coherence."[3] In these words Bryce himself, although indeed fearful of the growing power of party discipline, admitted the necessity for such discipline. The scope and depth of economic policy today require far more. For if the economy is to be managed successfully, the main decisions of economic policy must be coherent, harmonizing with one another and joined together over time by a comprehensive view of means and ends. Moreover, if Governments are to carry out such policy, the need for "mechanical majorities"[4] is heightened not only in economic matters; they must also be protected against defeat in other fields, if they are to have the time to mature their schemes.

Like a Radical Government, a Socialist Government will need such control over its majority as will enable it to prevent amendments that muddle the purpose of a bill. It will also wish to see its

[2] *The Labour Party in Perspective* (London, 1949), pp. 34, 91, and 102. (First published in 1937.)

[3] James Bryce, *Modern Democracies*, new edn. (London, 1921), Vol. I, p. 120. On the incoherence in a bill arising from the fact that two different majorities have voted two different clauses, resulting in a "medley of motives," see Walter Bagehot, *The English Constitution*, new edn. (London, 1872), p. 107.

[4] The phrase comes from Disraeli, who complained of Gladstone's "mechanical majority" used in passing the bill for the disestablishment of the Irish Church in 1869.

distinctive social values expressed in all branches of policy. But Socialist policy imposes still further demands for coherence. These flow especially from its approach to economic affairs. Economic planning—or to use the milder term, economic management—deals with variables that are highly interdependent. In the same degree, programs dealing with these aspects of the economy must be fitted coherently to one another. From this necessity follows a new and compelling sanction for party unity and party discipline.

The "casual majorities" constituted *ad hoc* from both parties which we see in the American Congress will not do. Party government means government by a cohesive majority of one party. Opening the party conference of 1937, Clement Attlee said :

A Socialist Government coming in will come in with a definite objective and that objective is the Socialist Commonwealth. A Socialist Commonwealth cannot be attained by one or two legislative measures. It means that the Government must inform its entire administration with the Socialist ideal : that every Minister in his office must be working to a common end by a common plan. Therefore, we must have a coherent Government. A Labour Government coming in will proceed to plan this country . . . the essential planning that a Labour Government must do is this : It must take this country as an economic whole. It must consider the relationship of all the workers of the country to each other, and it must try and get the greatest amount of well-being for all and see that there is a fair distribution.[5]

Herbert Morrison hammered home the same point to delegates at the Labour conference on the eve of the 1945 election : "Only by a Labour majority—a coherent Labour Majority—can our programme be put through. I make no promise about what will happen to that programme if we do not get a clear and coherent and united majority. . . ."[6] "The British people," he wrote in a more scholarly mood a few years later, "rightly attach importance to a party being sufficiently coherent and united to give the country a Government not only of sound policy but of adequate strength and unity of purpose."[7]

Class Representation and Party Unity

How does Socialist thought reconcile this demand for strict party unity with its emphatic belief in democracy and popular

[5] 1937 *LPCR*, p. 182.
[6] 1945 *LPCR*, p. 92.
[7] *Government and Parliament : A Survey from Inside* (London, 1954), p. 162.

participation? The argument rests on the Socialist's view of the social reality that is represented in the political system. For him the basic units of representation are not so much individuals, as social groups : not merely the many sub-groups that underlie the great vocational associations of the modern economy, but primarily the two major classes of industrial society.

When the National Liberal Foundation was founded, its purpose was to enhance the representation of "the people." When the Labour Representation Committee was set up, its task was to ensure that "working class opinion" was represented in Parliament. In 1918 the new constitution of the Labour Party cited "the workers by hand and brain" as the more particular beneficiaries of the efforts of the party and, at the same time, by its provisions for individual membership opened the way for middle class Socialists to join and take an active part. But in imagery, both popular and sophisticated, Labour remained the party of "the workers." For the Webbs in 1920 the rationale of its organization was "a recognition of the solidarity of interest . . . among the great mass of wage-earning folk," along with some blackcoated workers, and the conviction that "the aspirations and desires of the wage-earners and the salariat can be formulated in a programme for legislation and public administration that will command their general assent."[8] In the thirties Laski wrote that "the essential direction of the party . . . is in the hands of the working-class with a small admixture of 'intellectuals' and minor business men," and that the program of the Labour Party, like that of any other party, is implied by the economic interests of its supporters.[9] About the same time Clement Attlee declared that although there are not two sharply contrasted classes—since, e.g., some workers own some property—yet there is "a vital conflict in the community between the classes that live by mere ownership and those that live by labour." For both Attlee and Laski the dominant issue confronting the voters was "Socialism versus Capitalism" and it was "the workers" who through the Labour Party sought to resolve the issue in favor of Socialism.[1]

An instance from the postwar period will suggest how this rhetoric is put to work by a skillful party manager. At the conference of 1947 Herbert Morrison was making a plea for higher production, directing his words especially to the trade unions. At

[8] A Constitution for Socialist Britain (London, 1920), p. 84.
[9] Parliamentary Government in England (New York, 1938), p. 63.
[1] Attlee, op. cit., pp. 91–3 and passim.

the same time he could not forget that the party drew marginal, but critical, support from the middle class. He reminded delegates that he had devoted the greater part of his life to the Labour and Socialist cause and "with no greater wish than to further the permanent well-being of the working class in which I was born and to which I am proud to belong." What then is the role of the middle class? "If they stand the strain," he said, "with no undue grousing but with patience and understanding, then they are our partners in the great social enterprise on which we have embarked."[2] The imagery is clear : to be a "partner" is not the same as being one of the "we" who are doing this work.

One must not oversimplify. The mixture of traditions means that spokesmen of the Labour Party can without insincerity sometimes make an appeal to "the people" that is typically Radical in its rhetoric. Moreover, as party leaders interested in getting votes wherever they can be found, they will wish to avoid offense to voters of any class. Few, if any of them, failed to deplore the class-war overtones of Aneurin Bevan's famous "vermin" speech.[3] Nor is this merely a consequence of electoral opportunism. When Herbert Morrison said, on the occasion just referred to, that "ours is not a sectional policy; it represents the long term interests of all the constructive elements in the community . . . every worker by hand or brain . . . every useful member of every so-called class . . . ," this is quite compatible with a class theory of party. Here Morrison is thinking of the working class in much the way nineteenth-century champions of the middle class thought of themselves : as the "representative" class, the class that would lead the way for all.

What is the bearing of the class theory of representation on party unity and party discipline? When he was a young miner in a South Wales colliery, writes Aneurin Bevan, he was concerned with one practical question : "Where does power lie in this particular state of Great Britain and how can it be attained by the workers?" This question, he says, did not shape itself in some such fashion as "How can I get on?"

---

[2] 1947 *LPCR*, p. 136.

[3] "No amount of cajolery, no amount of ethical or social seduction can eradicate from my heart a deep burning hatred for the Tory Party. . . . They are lower than vermin." Speech at Manchester, 1948, as quoted in Mark M. Krug, *Aneurin Bevan : Cautious Rebel* (New York, 1961), pp. 91–2.

The texture of our lives shaped the question into a class and not into an individual form. . . . For us power meant the use of collective action designed to transform society and so lift all of us together. . . . We were the products of an industrial civilization and our psychology corresponded to that fact. Individual initiative was overlaid by the social imperative. The streams of individual initiative therefore flowed along collective channels already formed for us by our environment. Society presented itself to us as an area of conflicting social forces and not as a plexus of individual striving.[4]

It has often been remarked that the severe discipline that the Labour Party sought to impose on its M.P.'s was derived from the tradition of "solidarity" of the trade unions from which the party sprang.[5] One may follow Bevan in believing that this psychology was determined by the environment of an industrial civilization. If so, party discipline, one might say, springs ultimately from factory discipline.

In any case, to base party explicitly upon class and vocation is very different from basing it upon that natural consensus of individual minds which the Radical conceived to be the foundation of his political organizations. Once you accept the class image, for instance, you face no problem of looking about for other like-minded individuals : your political associates are unmistakably defined as all those who share your class status. And as it becomes easy to identify your party, so also it becomes correspondingly hard to break with it. For this presents itself not as the simple task of disassociating yourself from certain other free individuals who, in your opinion, have mistaken the common good. It is rather to break with your class, an objective social fact. Moreover, the class upon which the party is based, although solidary, is not undifferentiated (as are "the people") but consists of sub-groups organized as trade unions or cooperatives. Again party authority is strengthened, for it is doubly difficult for the workingman to deny that his union's party represents his interest when he sees the union doing precisely that in its daily relations with employers. The basis of his party allegiance is not so much that he *agrees* as that he *belongs*.

By such attitudes that stringent demand which Labour makes

[4] *In Place of Fear* (New York, 1952) pp. 1, 2.
[5] James MacColl, M.P., "Public Attitudes to Politics," *Political Quarterly,* Vol. XXX, No. 1 (January/March, 1959), p. 16. And see Ramsay Muir, *How Britain is Governed* (London, 1932), p. 125.

of its members for unity in both the parliamentary party and the extra-parliamentary organization is legitimized. We must have a sense of these attitudes, of these images rooted in the emotion and thought of members and adherents, if we are to understand such phenomena as the behavior of the party in 1931.[6] For the remarkable thing about that behavior was not so much that the Big Three in the party's leadership—MacDonald, Snowden, and Thomas—tried to lead it into coalition; nor that in the ensuing election they swung some two million votes away from Labour. The striking thing was that the party itself did not split. On the contrary, MacDonald carried over only a handful of M.P.'s, who with him were expelled from the party. And not a single constituency organization or prominent trade union leader followed the "National Labour" line. Such solidarity in the face of a major defection among leaders would have been inconceivable in a party inspired by Liberal or Radical ideals. The individualism of their approach to politics has continually undermined the efforts of the Liberal Party to maintain its unity against the splintering that has been chronic in its history in the nineteenth and twentieth centuries. Labour's class image of politics, as well as its Collectivist view of policy, made it a distinctive type of political formation.

DEMOCRACY BY PARTY GOVERNMENT

The class theory supplies an indispensable element to the Socialist model of democracy by party government. It enables one to accept the functional need for strict party discipline imposed by Collectivist policy and yet maintain that government is still fully democratic. We need to dwell on this point because in a community with millions of voters it is not easy to reconcile democratic premises with a party system dominated by two tightly united parties. It seems highly implausible that there are only two sides to any question, or only two major groupings of interests and ideals. If the actual diversity of the community is to be reflected in politics, the two-party system, it would seem, must at least be loose and fluid and permit frequent cross-voting in the legislature. Otherwise there will surely be grave distortion of the popular will. Potential majorities will be frustrated simply because they cut across party lines. Or perhaps the two great party

[6] Discussed below, Ch. VI, pp. 159–61.

machines will become engines for grinding out conformity, manu-facturing that two-sided opinion which they claim merely to rep-resent.[7]

Objections such as these are averted by the Socialist theory that there are only two major classes. The working class has a system of interests and aspirations that are reflected in the party's social philosophy and articulated, as the times require, in its pro-gram. Democracy is interpreted to mean, primarily, periodic con-tests between two such programmatic parties. Deriving from such a comprehensive social philosophy, program makes an emphatic claim to coherence. The voter cannot find himself liking parts of each party's program. His preference for one party's policy in one field will be linked with his prefence for that party's policies in other fields. Hence, the choice presented to him is meaningful in two senses. The voter has a choice between two coherent and distinctive programs. Moreover, he knows that the victorious party will surely be able to carry out the program to which it is pledged. Democracy itself—government by the people—as well as the need for strong and stable government, legitimizes the strictest party unity. "Representative government," to quote Herman Finer, "is Party Government."[8]

In this view of democratic politics, the M.P. is no longer a rep-resentative in the Old Whig or Liberal sense. He is a party man, indeed a party delegate. If he belongs to the majority party, his task is to carry out the party program, for it is through program that the voters have given party a mandate to govern. Lord Attlee has written :

The candidate of one of the major Parties stands for a connected policy and for a certain body of men who, if a majority can be ob-tained, will form a Government. This is well understood by the electors. If the Member fails to support the Government or fails to act with the Opposition in their efforts to turn the Government out, he is acting contrary to the expectation of those who have put their trust in him.[9]

This mandate, however, is not a local mandate. Party has dis-tilled the interests and aspirations of a class into a comprehensive

[7] See below, Ch. XII, pp. 346-9.
[8] *The Theory and Practice of Modern Government*, rev. edn. (New York, 1949), p. 237.
[9] "Party Discipline Is Paramount," *National and English Review*, Vol. CXLVIII, No. 887 (January, 1957), p. 15.

social philosophy. The program deriving from this philosophy, while favoring one class over another, is conceived to be in the long-run interests of the whole nation. It makes sure that the voter—in Rousseau's phrase—asks himself "the right question," ruling out merely local representation and giving the voter only a choice between two national viewpoints. Thus, the old problem of whether the M.P. should represent his constituency or the nation is given a new solution. The function of representing the national interest, once attributed to the Sovereign and later to Parliament, is now performed by party. Party—to echo Herman Finer's phrase — is indeed "king."[1]

Intraparty Democracy and Party Unity

Party solidarity outside Parliament and within it is further legitimized by the Socialist conception of how the party comes to decisions. The party's social philosophy must be articulated as the times require in the party program. The only possible agency that could properly be charged with this task is the mass membership of the party through which the working class—along with others expressing its "opinion"—finds its authentic voice. Discretion as to details, timing, and so forth, must, no doubt, be left to the organs charged with leadership. But the decisive will and the main thrust of ideas must come from the rank and file.

Such has been the official theory of the Labour Party : in the plain words of the party constitution, in what speakers at conference say about its powers, in the public utterances of party leaders. Indeed, one might logically infer from the party constitution not only that conference controls program, but also that the National Executive has the right to instruct the parliamentary party. According to the constitution, the party program is framed by conference, which "shall decide from time to time what specific proposals of legislative, financial or administrative reform" shall be included. Every member of the party must "accept and conform" to the program and it is the duty of the National Executive to "enforce the Constitution . . . by way of disaffiliation of an organization or expulsion of an individual or otherwise."[2] From these premises it would seem clearly to follow that if a Labour M.P. fails to "accept and conform" to the party program, he may,

---

[1] Finer, *op. cit.*, p. 274.
[2] Party Constitution, Clause V (1); Clause VIII (2) b.

and indeed should, be expelled from the party by the Executive, subject to this action being overruled by Conference. The plain words of the law make no exception for M.P.'s, Ministers, parliamentary leaders, or indeed a Prime Minister.

The Executive has not exercised such powers over the parliamentary party—and party leaders have denied that it has them —although, to be sure, in 1931 the Executive did expel from the party a man who was then Prime Minister. The issue came up sharply in the famous exchange of letters between Churchill and Attlee in 1945. Churchill suggested that a Labour Government "would be subject to the directions" of the Executive and that the Executive had "a right . . . to express opinions which are binding on Ministers . . . or on the Cabinet itself."[3] This Attlee acidly denied, asserting that while the Parliamentary Labour Party had frequent consultations with the Executive, it was not answerable to it or under its direction.[4] His denial is entirely consistent with the Socialist theory of democracy, which entitles one to argue that M.P.'s elected on the basis of a certain program are the proper body to interpret what it means and how it should be carried out.

According to party theory, however, the power to make program still rests with the extra-parliamentary party, as Attlee consistently maintained. While asserting in his exchange with Churchill that the parliamentary party "has complete discretion in its conduct of Parliamentary business and in the attitude it should adopt to legislation tabled by other parties," he limited this discretion by the qualifying phrase : "within the programme adopted by the annual party conference."[5] Again in 1954, when conference took up the question of German rearmament, Attlee conceded it the same power. Attacking an amendment that would commit the party to oppose German rearmament, he declared that if it were passed, it would send any future Labour Secretary of State for Foreign Affairs into negotiations with the Russians

---

[3] Morrison, *op. cit.*, p. 142.

[4] *Ibid.*

[5] *Ibid.*, pp. 142-3. By 1961, however, Attlee had shifted his emphasis. He said : "In the Labour Party the Annual Conference passes resolutions which are party policies . . . But as far as work in the House goes, they must always be interpreted and dealt with in the light of circumstance by the Parliamentary Party. They are a guidance to the Parliamentary Party, not an absolute mandate." Francis Williams, *A Prime Minister Remembers : the Memoirs of The Rt. Hon. Earl Attlee* (London, 1961), p. 91.

"already tied and bound."[6] The same point was made by Herbert Morrison when he pleaded with delegates not to put a Labour Government in a position "in which we are tied and fettered."[7]

The ideal of intraparty democracy may seem unfeasible and to some even foolish. Yet one must note that it is not the product of some casual or accidental development in the history of the Labour Party or of political thought, but derives logically from a deep strain of democratic theory. It is a basic principle of Socialist —as of Radical—democracy that, in one way or another, the voters may and should tell those who have authority, or who aspire to have it, what they want done—and these in turn are obliged to try to do what they have been told. How is this to be accomplished? Conceivably, the initiative can be taken by voters individually. Or groups may get together in a constituency in order to exact pledges from candidates. Or they may organize an association that uses its combined electoral power to sway ministers, M.P.'s, and candidates. But Socialist thought, even more strongly than Radical, makes party the main device by which voters take the initiative. According to this theory of democracy, voters organize or join a political party and by means of its conference agree on a program; they then nominate candidates who advocate this program before the electorate at large. Candidates elected on this program must stand by it. This is precisely how they fulfill their responsibility to the electorate. In short, if British democracy is "government by the people," then program-making by a party conference is a perfectly reasonable device for putting into effect this basic principle. The internal structure of the party depends upon the function that party is expected to perform in the system as a whole.

In actual practice, leaders may at times—and perhaps even most of the time—have exercised far greater power over program-making than this theory would allow. It cannot be seriously denied, however, that the pervasive belief of the party has been that ultimate control over program belongs to the members acting through the democratic structures of the party constitution. Because it has been so derived—or has been thought to be so derived —party program acquires a moral claim to the conformity of the Labour M.P. and indeed the ordinary party member. He may, of course, disagree with how his leaders interpret the program and

[6] 1954 *LPCR*, p. 94.
[7] *Ibid.*, p. 109.

what they do to realize it. But the program itself, issuing from conference, has a high claim to the solidary support of all.

Two-party competition, tight cohesion among partisans in the legislature, executive, and country, a program deriving from a comprehensive social philosophy, party allegiance founded primarily upon economic class and giving the party a mass membership, a party structure providing for intraparty democracy, especially in the framing of program : such are the main ingredients that are condensed and so, of course, often blurred and distorted in the Socialist image of democracy by party government. By this means, a massive concentration of political power is legitimized.

TORY DEMOCRACY

The phrase "Tory Democracy," coined by Randolph Churchill, has usually been employed to refer to the concern that Conservatives have sometimes shown for "the condition of the people" and their readiness to accept and even to initiate social reform. But Tory Democrats before as well as after Randolph Churchill have also had distinctive ideas about political organization. In particular, they have adapted older Tory ideas of authority to the conditions of mass suffrage. In these pages, Tory Democracy refers not to their attitude toward policy, but to their views on the organization of power and especially their views on the political party.

Like Socialist Democracy, Tory Democracy legitimizes a massive concentration of political power. It too provides a theory of party government, rationalizing tight party cohesion and stiff party discipline. It arrives at these conclusions by a very different —and less familiar—sequence of ideas. But in one respect it shares an important premise with Socialists. Like them, modern Conservatives—and especially those who pride themselves on the title of Tory—accept a broad and continuous, indeed a Collectivist, intervention by government in society and especially in economic affairs.

This is not just a development of post-World War II days. The state-controlled capitalism developed by Conservative Governments during the interwar years involved large interventions in the economy.[8] The Conservative shift to protection, for in-

---

[8] Discussed in detail in Ch. X below.

stance, was not merely a matter of giving up free trade and raising tariffs. It included a whole system of economic guidance that linked foreign, imperial, and domestic policies. State power was reasserted throughout the economy and tied in with the action of cartels and trade associations in the name of "industrial rationalization." Since World War II, Conservative policy has taken a different turn, but it is still committed to wide and systematic intervention. Like Labour, the Conservatives are committed not only to the Welfare State, but also to a Managed Economy. Although with differing emphasis, a Conservative Government also would be concerned in recent years with the inflationary or deflationary climate of the economy as a whole, with the balance of payments and its relations to the domestic economy, with increased productivity and economic growth. Such tasks of economic management require strong and stable government.

But we must recognize that a moral foundation facilitating the acceptance of these new necessities is provided by certain values and beliefs of Tory thought stretching back to Tudor times—and indeed to an even more ancient past. The essential proposition is that fundamental of Old Toryism : Order requires Hierarchy. "In any group of men pursuing a common purpose," David Clarke wrote in a Conservative Party pamphlet, "whether it be a nation or a family, a factory or a farm, there must be those who exercise authority and those who obey."[9]

The Socialist theory of representation, as we have seen, is a theory of class. So also is the Tory theory of representation, although for Toryism, ancient or modern, class has a different meaning and function. Both the Tory and the Socialist conceive of society as divided into different strata and each recognizes that social stratification has an impact on and importance for politics. But while, for the Socialist, social stratification is a force dividing society and separating parties, for the Tory it is a force uniting one level of society with others and the leadership of a party with its followers. One sees, and approves, horizontal division. The other sees, and approves, vertical integration.

Authoritative leadership is a permanent social necessity for the Tory; no social order, no body of men, large or small, can function effectively without such leadership. Whatever the social order of the nation may be and however it may develop, a governing class is necessary. This is as true in the age of democracy, mass

[9] *The Conservative Faith in a Modern Age* (London, 1947), p. 14.

parties, and free institutions as it was in the age of monarchy and aristocracy. Tory Democracy is the adaptation of this basic insight to the conditions of the new age.

In the Tory view, to maintain and to develop (or at any rate to adjust) a social order is a task requiring high and exceptional talents in the governor. To govern, as a publication of the Conservative Political Centre has put it, is a "specialized vocation" requiring a "habit of mind" which can be acquired only by "specialized preparatory training" in home and school.[1] This art of governing, to be sure, does not consist merely in expertness or technical skill, but rather in an ability to handle men and affairs that depends more on character than on knowledge. Still, like any other specialized vocation, it can be practiced successfully only if its practitioners are given a large discretion. The nature of the task itself inexorably implies inequality in power. Qualified as it may be according to time and conditions, the essential point remains : some must decide and command, others must accept and obey.

In one sense, Toryism, as compared with Radicalism or Socialism, plays down the importance of politics. In its view, men have higher and more promising tasks than governing one another. If politics is conceived as an instrument of change, then those who resist change may well depreciate politics. But in its stress on the pervasive need for hierarchic authority, Toryism is strongly political. "Inequality of natural ability," writes David Clarke, "necessarily results in class. Some men will always rise superior to others." And—this is the heart of the matter—"Indissolubly linked with class is the exercise of authority."[2]

We misunderstand Toryism if we neglect this stress on the political and the primacy it gives to governing. The principal defining characteristic of the governing class is precisely that it has the talent to govern. Toryism is not a theory of oligarchy—a theory that the rich should rule because they are rich—although, no doubt, this is a corruption to which it is susceptible and an interpretation that its opponents are prone to put on it. The Tory argues that property should be adapted to the needs of the state, not vice versa. He does not argue, as Liberals sometimes did, that the protection of private property is the main end of the state and that, therefore, the well-to-do ought to rule. He does indeed

[1] Sir Geoffrey Butler, *The Tory Tradition* (London, 1957), p. 68.
[2] *Op. cit.*, p. 14.

say that the governing class ought to have wealth and social status. But these are not the justifications of its power. On the contrary, they are conditions auxiliary to its social function; they are "privileges" necessary to enable it to rule effectively and well. "Responsible government demands certain privileges in the way of leisure and culture," writes A. K. White. "Only those who are economically secure can acquire the culture which . . . enables [them] to rule responsibly."[3] The governing class is not primarily an owning class or a class of elegance and culture. It is rather a class that governs—in business, education, and political party; in church, army, and state. From this superiority its title to other superiorities is derived. If we may think of the class theory of the Socialists as essentially a theory of "economic" class, we may contrast the Tory view as a theory of "political" class.

That social order requires hierarchy, that the art of governing can and will be acquired only by a few, that good government calls for a governing class trained—perhaps even bred—for the task : these are ancient tenets of Toryism. Other schools of political thought have looked with more optimism to other sources of social order. Economic Liberals, for instance, with their faith in the automatic mechanisms of the market, found that order in economic life required only a slight and occasional exercise of hierarchy. On a deeper level, the moral philosophy of Liberalism held that a large part of the citizenry were capable of understanding and respecting the foundations of the social order. Such mutual acceptance of common purpose and interest, according to their way of thinking, opened the way to popular government and dispensed with the need for paternalistic guidance. Radicals developed still further the possibilities of free and rational discussion in a democratic community as the source of direction in the state. All these currents of thought have influenced modern Conservatism. But it still retains a strong emphasis on the old belief that without "degree" there can be no "order." "Untune that string, and hark what discord follows."

The British Constitution : Tory View

The Tory approach leads to a distinctive view of the British constitution, of the meaning of democracy, and of the role and structure of the political party. L. S. Amery has developed this view of the constitution. In the Tory tradition (which Amery

[3] *The Character of British Democracy* (London, 1945), pp. 17 and 20.

regards as "the British political tradition") "all the emphasis," he says, "lies on the strength and stability of government."[4] In harmony with this emphasis, the British Constitution from medieval times has developed around two basic elements. On the one hand is the Crown, the central governing, directing, and initiating element; on the other hand is the nation in its various "estates," classes, and communities. At one time the Monarch performed the function of initiation and direction. Nowadays it is the Government, while the House of Commons, and especially the Opposition, perform the function of checking, criticizing, and ventilating grievances.

Parliamentary government and the mass suffrage have been grafted onto and adapted to the ancient bipolar structure of authority. But the democracy it permits is Tory Democracy. Amery sharply distinguishes his conception of democracy from that view which derives from the French Revolution and which gives the initiative to the people and makes political power wholly a delegation from the voter to the legislature and the executive (the view, in short, that I have called Radical Democracy and from which Socialist Democracy has arisen). In contrast, according to Amery, the British system "has never been one in which the active and originating element has been the voter, selecting a delegate to express his views in Parliament as well as, on his behalf, to select an administration conforming to those views."[5] The function of the voter in this system is "essentially passive." He chooses between the two alternatives presented to him by the leaders of the Government and the Opposition: alternative records, alternative promises, and especially alternative teams of leaders. British democracy therefore is "democracy by consent and not by delegation." It is a system of "government of the people, for the people, with, but not by, the people."[6]

This is surely a fair rendering of what democracy means to the Tory. On crucial questions this conception of the constitution and of democracy differs from Radical thought and certainly from the Socialist adaptation of Radical thought. For both the Radical and for the Socialist, democracy is "government by the people." And this means that the initiative in government belongs to and comes from the people and that the authority of government is based on delegation from them. The voters do not merely present griev-

[4] *Thoughts on the Constitution*, 2nd ed. (London, 1953), pp. 4 and 10.
[5] *Ibid.*, p. 15.
[6] *Ibid.*, p. 21.

ances which their governors then remedy with appropriate policies. They do not merely choose between alternative policies that
are presented to them by alternative leaders of Parliament. They
also originate policies as well as decide between them. To be sure,
the voters need not decide questions of detail or of parliamentary
timing—although the extreme versions of Radicalism that supported the referendum and other devices of direct government
have that implication. Presumably, there is also a place in the
making of policy for technical expertise. Still, in an important
and fundamental sense, the directing force in policy-making is
public opinion. Exercising a reasonable, but limited, power of
discretion, the task of Parliament and Government is to carry
out its mandate.

Tory Democracy gives the voters power. But it is the power
of control, not initiation, exercised under government by consent,
not by delegation. With its acceptance of mass suffrage, Tory
Democracy blends the "oligarchic tradition" and the old conception of bipolar authority. Leaders take heed of the public's grievances. Like Disraeli, they are concerned with "the condition of
the people." They take into account the voice of public opinion,
but without necessarily being guided by it. For it is their task to
initiate and determine policy in the light of what they think necessary and desirable. In turn the voters are expected to recognize
that what has been done is for the best and therefore to renew
their trust. "A British government," wrote Amery, ". . . is an independent body which on taking office assumes the responsibility
of leading and directing Parliament and the nation in accordance
with its own judgement and convictions."[7]

The British Constitution embraces democracy. But which kind
of democracy : Socialist or Tory? The authorities are divided.
If Amery declares for the old theory of bipolar authority and the
essential passivity of the voter, Herman Finer takes the other side,
sharply criticizing Amery for overstressing the initiating powers
of the Cabinet and of parliamentary leaders and for undervaluing
the role of party in making general policy.[8]

Sir Ivor Jennings, perhaps the leading authority on the constitution, has entertained views that could hardly be reconciled with
Tory Democracy. "The electorate," he wrote, "is the basis of all
governmental power. . . . The Government exists only because

[7] *Ibid.*, p. 31.
[8] Finer, *op. cit.*, p. 396n.

the majority of the voters have approved a certain broad policy."[9] "Democracy as we understand it," he says, "means that the people choose the rulers and the rulers govern according to the wishes of the people." British parties are not mere electioneering organizations, but are "truly based on competing political principles." "In preferring one party to another, therefore, the electorate not only prefers one Government to another but prefers one line of policy to another." Because of the party system, "public opinion can operate" and there is "close relation between the policies followed by Government and the general ideas of the majority of the electorate." "We have government by the people," he writes, "not merely because the people exercise a choice freely and secretly at short intervals, but also because it follows from the fact that the whole machinery of government—the House of Lords in part excepted—is keyed to public opinion."[1]

For the Tory Democrat, on the other hand, the voters choose a Government, a team of leaders, rather than "a certain broad policy." This Government, while no doubt it considers the wishes, and certainly the feelings and grievances of the people, makes policy primarily in the light of what it thinks best and necessary. To be sure, the Conservative Party is not a mere electioneering organization; but its "principles"—to which Tory Democracy is central—mean that it is much less inclined than the Radical or Socialist Party to offer a program spelling out the policies it will adopt if given power. Public opinion does indeed "operate" when the voters approve the policies of a Conservative Government and renew the grant of power to it. But this judgment is rendered after the event—after decisions have been taken by Government and worked out over a period of time. This means that public opinion is strongly influenced and shaped by the initiative taken by Government, as voters are informed and educated by the policies that have originated at the top. In no small degree the volitions of the "will of the people" are called into life by Tory leadership.

Contrasting the attitudes of the Conservatives and of Labour, McCallum and Readman wrote of the general election of 1945 :

They [the Conservatives] tended to place more confidence in a leader who could be relied on to take appropriate action as occasion should arise, rather than in a thorough-going plan developed in ad-

[9] *Cabinet Government*, pp. 455 and 486.
[1] *The British Constitution* (New York, 1941), pp. 209, 212, 229.

vance. Moreover, they considered futile any attempt by the electorate to direct or restrict the leaders by a specific mandate for any particular legislative measure.[2]

PARTY AND GOVERNING CLASS

These two conflicting conceptions of the British constitution have consequences for the Conservative and Labour views of party—its function in the political system and its internal structure. Amery, elaborating this point, finds the basis of the British two-party system not in the division of society into two economic classes, each giving rise to a party; rather he starts from the bipolar conception of authority that gives "all the emphasis" to strong and stable government. The two-party system, he continues, is "the natural concomitant of a political tradition in which government, as such, is the first consideration and in which the views and preferences of voters or of members of Parliament are continuously limited to the simple alternative of voting 'for' or 'against.' "[3] Party unity, then, is as important in Tory as in Socialist thought, but for different reasons : not because a body of voters have mandated their M.P.'s to support a program; not because a class with unified interests and aspirations has sent delegates to the legislature; but because strong and stable government is a necessity of social existence. The new functions of government in recent times only make this necessity more urgent.

It follows also that if the initiative in making and proposing policies rests with parliamentary leaders, then the extra-parliamentary party will be essentially an electioneering body, although it may also be given the opportunity to offer advice to leaders. So indeed runs the Conservative Party's official theory of its function and structure. The extra-parliamentary party does not originate and decide what policies the party will advocate in Parliament or before the electorate. Overriding authority in this sphere is vested in the Leader—the leader of the parliamentary party. As the Committee on Party Organization reported in 1949, "endorsements and pronouncements on Party policy are the prerogative and responsibility of the Leader."[4] Resolutions on policy may be passed by the representative assemblies of the

[2] *The British General Election of 1945* (London, 1947), pp. 60-1.
[3] *Op. cit.*, p. 17.
[4] Interim and Final Reports of the Committee on Party Organization, National Union of Conservative and Unionist Associations (London, 1949), p. 36.

party and detailed programs may be adopted by them, but these are advisory only.

Indeed, program as a statement for future policy will tend to be given a definitely secondary role in the party's relations with the electorate. The Tory conception of the wide and independent authority of Government and parliamentary leaders implies that they will have a very free hand to do what they think best. As Churchill told the annual conference in 1949, even while accepting the elaborate program it had just approved :

All I will promise to the British electorate in your name, and the only pledge that I will give on behalf of the Conservative party is that if the government of Britain is entrusted to us at this crisis in her fate, we will do our best for all, without fear of favor, without class or party bias, without rancor or spite, but with the clear and faithful simplicity that we showed in the days of Dunkirk.[5]

Moreover, the Tory theory of the constitution and of the role of party is inseparable from its conception of the governing class. Mass parties are unavoidable in a time of universal suffrage. But in the Tory view, party should be built around the relation of governing and governed—an ancient relationship in which class distinctions do not divide, but rather integrate and unify. According to Tory sociology, this distinction is inevitable in any functioning society. But there is need also for the Tory tradition to guide and shape it. Both leaders and followers need to be instructed in their roles. As essential as the tradition of *noblesse oblige* and public service among the governing is the tradition of deference among the governed.

The "good society" in the Tory view is characterized by the "proffer and acceptance of reciprocal advantage," according to G. M. Young, writing in a party publication. "Whatever natural superiority a man may enjoy, he is expected to put at the service of society." But the duties are reciprocal. "Because, if it is the duty of the learned to instruct the ignorant, it is no less the duty of the ignorant to allow themselves to be instructed, of the clumsy to be guided."[6] "Indissolubly linked with class must be the exercise of authority," writes David Clarke, "and authority implies duty both by those who exercise it and those who respect and submit to it."[7]

[5] *Report 70th Annual Conference*, National Union of Conservative and Unionist Associations (London, 1949), p. 119. Cited hereafter as *CPCR*.
[6] G. M. Young *et al.*, *The Good Society* (London, 1953), pp. 10 and 12.
[7] *Op. cit.*, p. 14.

As anyone who has ever known England can report, these sentiments are shared by many of the governed as well as by the governing. In the masses of Victorian England, as the *Times* remarked, Disraeli found the Tory workingman "as the sculptor perceives the angel prisoned in the block of marble." Today, the deferential voter among the British working class remains indispensable to a party that gets half its electoral support from that stratum of the population. Summarizing a study of working-class opinion, R. T. McKenzie reported that many voters, who by any objective criterion must be called working class, perceive the Labour Party "as being less competent than the Conservatives and 'less fit to rule.' " "This," he continues, "is partly because a considerable section of the British electorate positively prefers to be ruled by its social superiors, who have presumably either inherited their competence or at least demonstrated it by achieving high social status."[8]

The Socialist theory that class divides the two parties can be traced widely among the British electorate, especially those who support Labour. For them the Labour Party "stands for" the working class, while the Conservatives stand for only the interests of the middle and upper classes. But the sentiments of Tory Democracy are also strong among the working class. These people vote Conservative, but they see power in the party as belonging to a governing class to which they are ready to defer.

The Conservative Party is the gentlemen's Party. They're the people who have got the money. I always vote for them. I'm only a working man and they're my guv'nors.

The Conservatives have got more idea of what they're doing than the people who come up from the working class—the mines and such like. Working-class people are not the sort to run the country, because I don't think they understand it really. I'm sure I wouldn't if I got up there.

The Conservatives have had more experience over the centuries. It's in the blood for them, running the country. There's more family background in the Conservatives, more of the aristocratic families, more heritage.[9]

Such evidence could be multiplied indefinitely. It only fills out what any traveler's everyday conversations confirm.

[8] *The Observer* (July 19, 1959).
[9] Ralph Samuels, "The Deference Voter," *New Left Review*, No. 1 (January/February, 1960), pp. 9–13.

Tory Democracy accepts class rule—this derives from its essential and ancient Toryism : "hierarchy is the order of nature," as a Conservative writer put it recently.[1] But Tory Democracy is also democratic in its own way. Although it is not, in Amery's words, government by the people, it is nevertheless government with the people. It provides a role for the people, specifically for the working class. What is this role?

Within the formal structure of the state (though not in other spheres of the social system), the people as electors choose their rulers. Essentially, when all goes well on both sides according to Tory theory, this is an act of renewed confidence in the governing class. Tradition has established certain external signs—accent and mode of speech, education at the great public schools and at Oxford or Cambridge, famous family names, the possession of wealth—as means by which the governed may identify those whom they may wisely choose for office. These are not the only bases on which the Tory voter will judge. Tory thought has so far adjusted to Radical democracy as to concede that the voter can in some degree assess the results of the rule of the governing class. "Those who exercise authority," Clarke can write, "will be respected if they show themselves fit to exercise it."[2] But this judgment of fitness is rendered after the event. It is a judgment on what has been done in the past rather than a projection of what is willed for the future—in short, an act of control, not initiation. Moreover, because of the two-party system, this act of control can at most only shift power from one team of leaders to another. At the time of an election, according to Amery, the voter's "function is the limited and essentially passive one of accepting one of the two alternatives put before him."[3] Perhaps one should also add that in most cases the voter properly makes an independent judgment only with regard to matters that touch him closely and which therefore he can intelligently assess. "I win their confidence," a Tory M.P. once said of his supporters, "because of their experience with the things they know about. They know, for instance, that I'll get them an extra shilling on their pensions—not as fast as they'd like, but ultimately. Therefore, they trust me in other matters."

Indeed, the art of governing itself includes the capacity to inspire trust and win deference. It is the ability not only to deal with

---

[1] R. W. White, *The Conservative Tradition* (London, :957), p. 18.
[2] *Op. cit.*, p. 14.
[3] *Op. cit.*, p. 16.

great matters of state, but also to "handle men." The Tory governor faces two ways: toward the problems of government and toward the forces of public opinion. As a party leader bent on winning the support of these forces, he cannot rely simply on the external signs that mark him as a member of the governing class. In this respect he is in a more trying position than his predecessor in the ages of aristocracy. For he must pay attention to public opinion, interpreting to voters the manner in which he has discharged his trust and winning a renewal of their confidence.

Such subtle and complex qualities of leadership also belong to his "specialized vocation." "Many men can rule in a way," writes A. K. White, "but few rule with that effortless grace which inspires loyalty without loss of self-respect in those who are ruled."[4] It is such "effortless grace" in leadership that the great public schools seek, above all, to impart to their pupils.

Of Conservatism, Hearnshaw wrote:

its very genius affirms on the one hand, the solidarity of the nation and the unity of all classes in the whole; on the other hand, the propriety of leaving predominant political control in the possession of those who are by descent, by character, by education, and by experience, best fitted to exercise it.[5]

On the one side, leadership; on the other side, deference. These pre-eminently political qualities mark out the line between classes. But in the view of Tory Democracy, it is a line that integrates their action for the common good by means of the Conservative Party.

The Labour Party, Harold Macmillan has said, is "a class party. . . . They build on division. We are a national party. We build on unity."[6] One might criticize these statements for exaggeration or a certain obliviousness to fact. For the Labour Party too is a national party, according to its own conceptions. And if there is anything in the preceding exposition, the Conservative Party can also be called a class party. Yet the beam in Mr. Macmillan's eye is part of an elaborate and impressive intellectual construction, the theory of Tory Democracy. Millions of Britons of all classes do accept the class system as an integrating force in country and in party. They accept these ideas and their political behavior cannot be understood unless one recognizes that fact.

[4] *Op. cit.*, p. 20.
[5] *Conservatism in England* (London, 1933), pp. 293-4.
[6] *Conservatism, 1945-50*, p. 102.

PART TWO

The Labour Party

CHAPTER IV

A Coalition
of Pressure Groups

What I have called the model of Socialist Democracy has provided the Labour Party with a picture of itself for much of its lifetime. To the outside observer this self-portrait must be tinged with implausibility. One need not be a Tory to doubt that the ideal of intraparty democracy can be realized in a modern mass party and to wonder how much real influence the rank and file can exert in comparison with their national chiefs. Nor is it easy to believe that the many members of such a party—even if we think only of the activists—can be united on a significant ideology or social philosophy. Such a political formation, it would seem, would have to be a coalition, embracing many interests and points of view. One must also be skeptical of the possibility of programmatic party government with its formula of party program : electoral mandate : government by mandated program. Surely this formula is far too mechanical to be fitted to the changing, complex, and unpredictable actualities of governing.

PLURALISM, ELITISM, IRRATIONALISM

These common-sense doubts are reinforced and developed by three broad currents of political thought : pluralist theory, elitist theory, and irrationalist theory.

Pluralism in the guise of group theory raises doubts about the Socialist conception of the party's purpose. That conception is that the party members are, by and large, united in their acceptance of an ideology—a distinctive party view of the common good for society—and that in consequence some actions of the party can be understood only in terms of this unifying common purpose. Pluralism implies no fixed view of what the purpose and structure of a political party, or of the Labour Party, must be. It strongly suggests, however, that we consider favorably the hypothesis that the party is essentially a coalition of groups, each with its distinctive aim or goal and that in consequence any action of the party as a whole can be understood by analyzing it into the action of these component groups. The party as a whole, for instance, supports a common program. But according to the pluralist hypothesis, this program is a composite, deriving from the goals of the various member groups. Leaders of the party function as brokers, mediating between groups in the party and, of course, trying also to attract other groups into it, or to its support. Thus, in the composition of the party program, they combine the demands of groups belonging to, or to be attracted to the coalition with such compromise, ambiguity, and gloss of principle as they find necessary and effective.

The critical and most suggestive assertions in this hypothesis are that the component groups have different goals and the equally important denial that all groups share the same goal. The coalition purpose is formed basically by "logrolling," each group supporting the achievement of the goals of the others only because of their help in achieving its own goals. While the resulting program is a composite formed by addition, when goals are similar to one another, their statement can be generalized. For instance, several trade unions, each of which seeks better legal protection for its rights of organization, may state their objectives in the form of a general demand for such legislation applying to all trade unions. Such generalizing of goals, however, only masks the essential instrumentalism of the bonds holding together the coalition.

This illustration may suggest that the goals of the members of a coalition are self-interested and no doubt the logic of building and maintaining coalitions is most readily illustrated when their members aim at benefits to themselves. But group theory is not necessarily wedded to utilitarianism. The goal of a group may be sternly other-oriented, encompassing benefits for persons in no way connected with the group, and yet retain the essential trait of being separate and distinct from the goals of other groups in the coalition. Thus educational or penal reformers might join a political party like Labour and support its program, but solely in order to enhance the chances of their particular reforms.

If one follows this pluralist line of thought, one will think of the Labour Party as a coalition that includes various groups, such as trade unions and reformers with special concerns, each component group aiming at its particular goal. In this coalition, the "socialists" are nothing more than one member.[1] Their goal, to be sure, is very broad, a state of affairs described as the "Socialist Commonwealth." This means that there is some overlapping of goals, the miners, for instance, wanting the benefits that come to miners in a Socialist society, although perhaps less urgently thàn more immediate improvements in their conditions of life and work. Except for this overlapping, each group has different goals and it is still denied that the party entertains a distinctive common purpose.

While pluralist doubts attack the communitarian assertions of the Socialist view of the party, elitist theory contradicts its claims to democracy. The central proposition of elitism is that in such a massive political formation as Labour, the initiative and certainly the decisive power must be exercised by leadership. This general notion can be developed in various ways. Attention may be directed toward the role of a single leader, or of a unified leadership group, or of competing elites. The structure of leadership might be sharply bipolar, a single body of national leaders confronting the rest of the party as followers. It is possible and more likely, however, that instead of a single elite, or leadership group, we should find various circles or echelons of influential persons as we move from the literal rank and file—the mass of dues-paying members— through the activists of local parties and trade unions and delegates to the annual conference, on up to parliamentary and national trade union circles to the top political and industrial chiefs. In particular, elitist theory poses this question : What has been the role of the party conference in party decisions, especially those relating to program and policy, and what influence has conference exerted as compared with that of the parliamentary and trade union chiefs?

[1] "The Labour Party," Bernard Crick has written, ". . . is a coalition of diverse class, union, regional, ideological and even ethnic interests. . . . And socialism itself, except in a very broad sense, is only one element in this coalition . . . certainly subsidiary, in both electoral and historical terms to the Labour Party as the representative of the interests of organized labour." "Britain's 'Democratic Party,' " *The Nation*, Vol. CXCI, No. 20 (December 10, 1960), p. 453.

The techniques by which influence is exerted can be of various kinds, the rationalist-irrationalist distinction providing one broad criterion. Conceivably an elite might win and exercise influence by purely rational persuasion, monopolizing the power of decision simply because again and again it wins over its followers in free and sober debate. This ingredient may be larger in leader-follower relations than political theorists usually allow. Commonly, however, exponents of elitist theory find that the influence of leaders is founded upon a capacity to induce what Graham Wallas called "subconscious, non-rational inference."[2] Whether by reliance upon traditional deference, demagogic manipulation of sentiments, charismatic appeal, or other "psycho-technic means," and whether unified or in competition with one another, they "manufacture"— the word is Schumpeter's[3]—the opinion of the group and impose it upon their followers.

This is not to say, however, that the penetrating but rather amorphous insights of irrationalism are inevitably tied to elite theory. Powerful sentiments animating a large body of people may, from one viewpoint, appear as the material that gives the manipulator of opinion his opportunity. From another viewpoint, they may appear as forces that demand some mode of common action and which leaders may slightly deflect, but cannot resist, let alone create. In a country such as Britain, where class feelings are so ancient and deeply founded, it is hardly implausible to suggest that quite apart from what rational self-interest may dictate and leaders may try to impose, the sense of class irresistibly demands political expression.

Like the elitist and unlike the Socialist, the pluralist plays down ideology or social philosophy as a bond of unity in a party and as a source of program and policy. But unlike the elitist and like the Socialist, the pluralist finds the origin of party policies in the demands and wishes of ordinary voters. His conception of democracy too is not individualist and, like the Socialist, he stresses the fact that these demands and goals originate in and are shared by members of groups. The Socialist, like the pluralist and unlike the elitist, finds that the basic initiative comes from groups. In contrast with both elitist and pluralist, however, the Socialist makes a large claim for ideology; party purpose, even after allowing for the in-

---

[2] *Human Nature and Politics* (London, 1920), p. xvii.

[3] Joseph A. Schumpeter, *Capitalism, Socialism and Democracy*, 2nd ed. (New York, 1947), pp. 256–64.

evitable deflections of tactics, personal idiosyncrasy, and the pressure of circumstance, flows fundamentally from a distinctive party perspective on society, economy, and polity.

LABOUR AND THE NEW PRESSURE POLITICS

The Labour Party has its great place in the history of British Socialism. But it also has a place in the history of British pressure politics. Knowing what the party later became, one may be tempted to read its later into its earlier character, and so to give undue prominence to Socialist influences during its first years. In trying to characterize the party as a political formation at that time, it is helpful to look at it as part of the new pattern of politics that emerged between the Third Reform Act and the First World War.

The key element in this new pattern was the organized interest group based on an occupational stratum of what had become a highly industrialized economy. A few examples may be mentioned. As previously observed, the railway politics of the late nineteenth century had been much affected by the rise of nationwide associations of manufacturers and traders. In general, employers were developing organizations not only for economic purposes, but also for political action. In the last twenty years of the century, trade associations began to appear in substantial numbers and in 1898 the Employers Parliamentary Council, an interindustry organization for representing business interests before Parliament and Government, was set up,[4] although British business did not find lasting and effective agents of political action until the establishment of the Federation of British Industries and the National Union of Manufacturers during the First World War. From its beginnings in 1870, the National Union of Teachers,[5] the agent chiefly of the elementary school teachers, took to pressure politics, as did the associations of their more genteel competitors from the secondary schools. The ancient landed interest itself gradually turned to organized political action, landowners taking the lead in the first

[4] Frank Bealey and Henry Pelling, *Labour and Politics 1900–1906 : A History of the Labour Representation Committee* (London, 1958), p. 13; S. E. Finer, "The Federation of British Industries," *Political Studies*, Vol. IV, No. 1 (February, 1956), p. 61.

[5] See Asher Tropp, *The School Teachers : The Growth of the Teaching Profession in England and Wales from 1800 to the Present Day* (New York, 1957).

phase, which began with the founding of the Central Chamber of Agriculture in 1865,[6] while farmers took the initiative in the second phase with the organization of the National Farmers Union in 1908.[7]

This is not the place to relate the political history of these bodies. It will be touched on only to note the many similarities with the political behavior of trade unions. The Parliamentary Committee of the T.U.C. on behalf of organized labor as a whole, as well as individual unions on behalf of their respective memberships, sought to influence ministers and M.P.'s by standard lobbying techniques, backing up their powers of persuasion with meetings calculated to affect public opinion and with attempts to pledge candidates to the support of desired measures. So also did these other organized groups of producers. Moreover, other interest groups sought some sort of direct representation in Parliament. Economic strata, such as landowners and businessmen, which consisted of persons with wealth and social position, enjoyed direct representation simply from the presence in Parliament of "interested" M.P.'s who themselves owned land or engaged in business. For this reason there was less need for these groups to turn to organization for the purpose of influencing Westminster and Whitehall or winning representation. Still, both the Central Chamber of Agriculture and the Employers Parliamentary Council had members in the House who helped with legislative matters.

Organizations of the less-advantaged groups in the economy, however, turned most readily to the new methods and pushed them farther. For instance, they sought direct representation by sponsored M.P.'s—members who were ready to advocate the views of the organization in the House and who in turn received a subsidy for their election expenses and perhaps also, as in the case of trade union M.P.'s, maintenance while they were in Parliament. While the best-known examples are the sponsored M.P.'s of trade unions during their Lib–Lab phase, the N.U.T. also successfully used this device and it was imitated in the plans of the Farmers Union.

A further extension of the new pressure politics was the attempt to turn a number of "interested" M.P.'s into a bloc that would act

[6] See Alfred H. H. Matthews, *Fifty Years of Agricultural Politics: The History of the Central Chamber of Agriculture 1865–1915* (London, 1915).
[7] See Peter Self and Herbert J. Storing, *The State and the Farmer* (London, 1962).

independently of the two major parties on questions of direct interest to the outside organization. In 1900 the teachers achieved
this on a modest scale with their three sponsored M.P.'s, two
Liberals and one Conservative. The Central Chamber of Agriculture attempted something of the sort in its establishment of a
bipartisan agricultural committee in the House. The Farmers
Union similarly hoped to create from its pledged and sponsored
M.P.'s a bloc that could manipulate the balance of power on
agricultural issues before the House and, while no "direct representatives of the Union" were elected until 1922, some sixty-eight
M.P.'s pledged to support the N.F.U. program were returned in
1910.[8]

Likewise, during the Lib–Lab phase of trade union politics,
which began with the election of MacDonald and Burt in 1874,
the relationship of Labour members with the Liberal Party consisted in "a system by which you cordially cooperate with your
friends, whilst reserving to yourself, should need arise, your own
independence of action."[9] The Lib–Labs attempted to act in uni-
son, an effort that was promoted by the Parliamentary Committee
of the T.U.C. that met with them to discuss parliamentary action,
and by such actions as the formation in 1899 of a group of eight
Lib–Lab M.P.'s "to watch closely the agenda paper of the House
of Commons, in order to be prepared when labour questions were
likely to be under discussion."[1] Indeed, they showed their independence not only on labor questions, but also at times on such
"political" questions as the South African war.

The sectionalism of the trade union movement, however, impaired their cohesion. In 1894 the Webbs, referring to the trade
union movement, wrote :

the basis of the association of these million and a half wage-earners
is primarily sectional in its nature. They come together, and contribute their pence, for the defence of their interests as Boilermakers,
Miners, Cotton-spinners, and not directly for the advancement of the
whole working class. . . . The vague general Collectivism . . . [of the
salaried officers of the unions] has hitherto got translated into practical
proposals only in so far as it can be expressed in projects for the
advantage of a particular trade.

[8] *Ibid.*, pp. 42–3.
[9] Henry Broadhurst, as quoted in Bealey and Pelling, *op. cit.*, p. 188.
[1] T.U.C. *Report* 1899, quoted in Bealey and Pelling, *op. cit.*, p. 185.

As a result, they continued, the question whether it was possible to "counteract the fundamental sectionalism of Trade Union organisation" and "to render the Trade Union world . . . an effective political force in the State" was "the most momentous question of contemporary politics."[2]

At the same time, the pull of party was strong and the Lib–Labs sat as Liberals and usually voted with the main body of the party. The organized agricultural interest was also confronted with that problem. In spite of their efforts to lift agricultural questions above party politics, both the C.C.A. and the N.F.U. found their representatives almost entirely among Conservatives on whom the demands of party usually overrode the claims of the agricultural interest. Disappointment with the tactic of the independent bloc led some sections of the C.C.A. to press for a bolder initiative when in 1907–8 a fairly strong move was initiated to set up an Agricultural Party. The local chambers, it is said, welcomed the proposal, but the C.C.A.'s governing body, in which M.P.'s were numerous, killed it with amendments.[3]

The trade unions successfully achieved this further extension of pressure politics—which agriculture was unable to attempt—when they established and maintained the Labour Party. That event constituted not so much a change of goals as a change of tactics. The new tactics meant that the Labour M.P.'s would have a solidarity that the Lib–Labs had been unable to achieve. In particular, they were to be members not of either major party, but of a distinct group that had the power to make binding decisions on its own policy. As before, however, the goals were primarily defined by "the direct interests of labour."

During the period 1868–1914 Government and Parliament were subjected increasingly to pressures from organized producers groups. A principal channel of influence was the new kind of "interested" M.P., such direct representation taking various forms : 1) M.P.'s who were merely members of the outside organization; 2) M.P.'s who were sponsored and subsidized in varying degrees; 3) sponsored M.P.'s who formed a bloc acting more or less independently on questions of interest to the outside organization; 4) a bloc of M.P.'s, sponsored or not, acting as a pressure group within one of the major parties; and 5) finally, in the case of the Labour Party, sponsored M.P.'s separated from other parties

[2] *History of Trade Unionism,* new ed. (London, 1920), pp. 678–9.
[3] Matthews, *op. cit.,* p. 340.

and bound to a measure of common action in Parliament. The character of Parliament was being changed and, quite accurately, the manifesto of the Labour Representation Committee in 1906 said of it : "Landlords, employers, lawyers, brewers, and financiers are there in force" (from which it concluded rhetorically), "Why not Labour?" Recognizing the same trend in society as a whole, the N.F.U. asked with alarm in 1913 :

The question we propose to ask you is whether you think you are safe, at a time when every trade is combining AGAINST EVERY OTHER, in remaining outside your own Farmers' Union. Against every other, mind you. Every trade in the world is combined against yours. Dare you risk isolation?[4]

The purposes and modes of action of the trade unions in the political arena were in harmony with this general pattern of pressure politics. When some of them founded a party in 1900, they went a step beyond the tactics of pressure politics already established. One may, however, think of the party during its first decade and a half as a coalition which included a small Socialist wing, but consisted largely of organized producer groups with many similar interests. As Bealey and Pelling conclude, although the L.R.C. M.P.'s took the name of "Labour Party" after the election of 1906, they were still regarded by union leaders as "primarily a body representing the interests of organized labour—a pressure group on the floor of the House of Commons rather than a national political party with aspirations of governing the country."[5]

Forming the Coalition

"The Labour Party," Ernest Bevin once said, "has grown out of the bowels of the T.U.C."[6] The occasion for founding the party was provided by the vote in 1899 of that body, which represented organized labor as a whole. But the effective action toward this end was taken separately and over a period of years by the various organizations that joined the coalition. Among the unions, each made the decision largely in the light of its view of its own interests. The rationale of their joining together was the logic of logrolling. Thus, during the 1899 debate at the T.U.C. the Shop

---

[4] Quoted in Self and Storing, *op. cit.*, p. 41.
[5] *Op. cit.*, p. 282.
[6] 1935 *LPCR*, p. 180.

Assistants supported the new initiative because as a small union it could not get satisfactory legislative action by its own unaided efforts. On the other hand, the miners, who had long had representatives in Parliament, were opposed. The president of their Federation put their reasons bluntly to his members when he asked "why we as a Federation should be called upon to join an Association to find money, time or intellect to focus the weaknesses of other Trade Unionists to do what you are doing for yourselves, and have done for the last fourteen years."[7] Although the miners agreed on the need for greater labor representation and in 1901 set up a central parliamentary fund for their own candidates, they did not find it to their advantage to affiliate with the Labour Party until 1909.

The conditions that led each union to its decision often varied from one to another. Conventionally, of course, the Taff Vale decision is treated as the major cause of the growth that solidly established the new party. The grave threat it raised to the funds of the unions and so to a principal basis of their industrial action led many unions to seek through the L.R.C. the political strength to reverse the decision. Trade union membership in the party, which had only risen from 353,070 in 1900 to 455,450 in 1901, leaped to 847,315 in 1902, the year after Taff Vale. The decision was not responsible for the whole of this growth. The textile workers, for instance, who joined in 1903, were responding to a particular situation in Lancashire. But even here it was a similar threat, a local attack by the organized employers on the legal status of the unions, that led them to decide for direct parliamentary representation and affiliation with the L.R.C.[8] In short, as these instances illustrate, the strong sectionalism among the unions was being qualified by a similarity among their interests that made coalition easier and laid the foundation for the new tactic of solidarity in the House of Commons. The goals of the infant Labour Party reflected, on the whole, the interests of conventional trade unionism, the party seeking, above all, to protect the unions as industrial organizations and to promote a brand of social reform entirely compatible with capitalism and with the piecemeal social reform of the Radicals.

Such stress on the role of trade unions may seem to neglect

---

[7] *Miners Federation Annual Report, 1899,* quoted in Henry Pelling, *The Origins of the Labour Party 1880–1900* (London, 1954), pp. 205–6.

[8] Bealey and Pelling, *op. cit.,* p. 101.

unfairly the influence of Socialists and Socialism in these early years. For two decades before the party was launched in 1900, Socialists had been spreading their message and, especially through the Social Democratic Federation and Independent Labour Party, advocating an independent party based on the working class. Socialist societies were members of the coalition constituting the party, and in comparison with their tiny memberships provided a disproportionate number of party leaders and M.P.'s. But after a year the S.D.F. withdrew, while the Fabians, preferring the tactic of "permeation," assumed an attitude of "benevolent passivity" toward the party.[9] The party, moreover, studiously avoided committing itself to Socialism and, although Socialists, especially from the I.L.P., occupied positions of power, they did so only on condition that, whatever their hopes might be, they accept the limited objects of trade union politics.

The conference of 1900, for instance, was a remarkable success for the I.L.P. leaders, who won a surprising number of victories in the votes establishing the L.R.C. It would be a mistake, however, to regard this as evidence that the Socialists, or this Socialist group, had much power. As Pelling has pointed out, the victories of the I.L.P. resulted from the fact that on the main questions before the conference it took a central position between two other groups.[1] On the one hand the S.D.F. wanted the new party to commit itself to a Marxist program, while on the other a number of union officials and members wanted to keep it under the control of the Parliamentary Committee of the T.U.C. Between these two extremes ranged the bulk of the delegates—the Railwaymen, the Boot and Shoe Operatives, the Gasworkers, the two Dockers' Unions and probably the Engineers—and the views of those groups coincided with those of the I.L.P. Of the key resolution of the conference, advocating a distinct Labour Group in Parliament with its own whips and policy, Hardie said that it "represented a compromise upon reasonable and workable lines between the different sections."[2] Hardie was a man of missionary zeal, but, as this characterization suggests, his actual role at the conference was,

---

[9] Bealey and Pelling, *op. cit.*, p. 169.
[1] *Ibid.*, pp. 25–7.
[2] *Ibid.*, p. 28. The rival groups, according to Pelling, put "varying interpretations" on the resolution. "Even the term 'Whip,'" he writes, "was ambiguous, for both the Parliamentary Committee of the T.U.C. and the Miners Federation used it to describe anyone whom they deputed to influence the votes of M.P.'s on a particular issue."

in accord with the pluralist theory of leadership, very much that of the "broker" among groups who finds the formula that maximizes consent, if necessary at the expense of breadth and clarity.

THE ROLE OF CONFERENCE

In its methods and structure, the Labour Party, in the years before the First World War, continued to display the pluralistic democracy that had characterized it during its foundation. Unlike the Liberals and Conservatives, the party had not grown out of groups first formed in Parliament. On the contrary, it had been deliberately created as the instrument of an extra-parliamentary movement which, moreover, although highly organized and enjoying a certain "instinctive solidarity"[3] was strongly marked by sectionalism. In consequence, during its early years the structure of the party was so shaped as to give great weight to the extra-parliamentary organization and to pluralize the forces exerting influence within it.

The power of the annual conference over the parliamentary party was expected to be, and in fact was, far greater than that of the parallel bodies of either of the two major parties, even the Liberal Council at the height of Radicalism. One can get a sense of this relationship by comparing the decisions of the conference of 1907 with the subsequent action reported by the parliamentary party. That conference, which met January 24–6 in Belfast, passed some twenty-one resolutions dealing with government policy and requiring action by Labour M.P.'s.[4] These resolutions were divided about evenly between questions of what one may call social reform and questions directly concerned with trade union interests. The subjects of the social reform resolutions and the body to which the delegate moving them belonged were as follows: temperance legislation (the Executive); old age pensions (Amalgamated Society of Engineers); unemployment (London Trades Council); women's suffrage (Woolich T.C.; amendment by London T.C.); education (Gas Workers); national sanatoria; public ownership of monopolies; opposition to militarism; reduction of fee for naturalization. For the last four resolutions, which were passed without discussion and at the end of the conference, the speaker and organization were not reported.

[3] The phrase is the Webbs', *op. cit.*, p. 678.
[4] 1907 *LPCR*, pp. 43–63.

Resolutions directly bearing on trade union interests were : the eight-hour day (Ironfounders); amendment of trade union law to facilitate amalgamations (Carpenters); state insurance by employers for purposes of workmen's compensation (Shop Assistants); hours and conditions of work of shop workers (Shop Assistants); factory act amendment to reduce hours of paper mill workers (Paper Mill Workers); amendment of the truck act (Clothiers' Operatives); factory act amendment against sweating in the clothing trade (Clothiers' Operatives); industrial assurance legislation (Prudential Assurance Agents); wages of Government workers (Deptford Victualling Yard Workers' Protection League); postal grievances (The Fawcett Association, a post office workers' union); state provision of workshops, schools and pensions for the blind (League of the Blind). In nearly every case, the resolutions of the second category reflected a particular problem confronting the trade union to which the mover of the resolution belonged.

This brief enumeration itself indicates the very great extent to which the affiliated trade unions used the party, and specifically the party conference, to promote their sectional interests. In Parliament the unions had won their long struggle for sheer legality. In industry they were winning their battle for recognition by employers. They were still far from having won, however, that basic code of legislation protecting the interests of their workers in their conditions of employment, which was achieved in the next forty years. Hence, in its practical British way, each union, in the light of its particular needs, was making vigorous use of the new political instrument.

Their numerous and urgent demands, indeed, had caused misgivings among the party's leaders on the Executive and in Parliament. Many of the resolutions submitted to the conference had "instructed" the parliamentary party to take certain action "during the coming session." As previous experience had shown, the result when such resolutions were carried was that the interested organization expected immediate action by the parliamentary party. "The affiliated organisations," as Arthur Henderson explained to the conference, "after getting their resolutions carried, if they did not get them put into the shape of a Bill, were constantly sending letters of protest."[5] (The Liberal Council, it may be recalled,

[5] *Ibid.*, p. 50.

suffered from the same trouble as a consequence of the Newcastle Programme.) Yet in view of the limitations of time and opportunity in Parliament, it was impossible for the parliamentary party to carry out immediately and directly the will of the conference.

In response to this situation, the Executive submitted to the conference of 1907 a resolution defining the relation between conference decisions and parliamentary action. It read :

That resolutions instructing the Parliamentary Party as to their action in the House of Commons be taken as the opinions of the Conference, on the understanding that the time and method of giving effect to these instructions be left to the Party in the House, in conjunction with the National Executive.[6]

This resolution, one may note, fully acknowledged that conference could instruct M.P.'s. Nor was this denied by the spokesmen for the Executive—Hardie, Pete Curran, and Arthur Henderson. What the resolution gave to the leadership (that is, to the parliamentary party in cooperation with the Executive) was simply, in Hardie's words, the power to decide "which questions should have priority."[7]

Likewise, Philip Snowden, looking back on this time, recalled that "the party . . . was expected to take its directions from the resolutions of the Party Conference." He added immediately, however :

Fortunately it never quite worked out like that in practice. The men upon whom has devolved the practical task of carrying out a Party programme realise how much more difficult that is than passing resolutions in a Conference after a few minutes discussion.[8]

And, of course, the translation of will from conference to Parliament was not instantaneous and mechanical. Yet during this period the relationship was very close. Each year the National Executive Committee reviewed the various resolutions of the party conferences and from them put together a list of bills and motions which it wished the parliamentary party to support in the House. This list was then discussed with the Parliamentary Labour Party at the opening of each session and, as McKenzie says, was "normally adopted with only slight modifications." If successful in the ballot,

[6] *Ibid.*, p. 49.
[7] *Ibid.*, p. 49.
[8] *An Autobiography* (London, 1934), Vol. I, p. 218.

members were expected to put forward the party bills in the order of priority decided by the joint meeting.[9]

In Parliament, the Labour M.P.'s expressed themselves on a great many questions by speaking, voting, and other actions. The Speaker, recognizing them as a party, called upon them to speak on all questions debated by the House and, as a consequence, it was said that the parliamentary party "man for man, out-talked the average Liberal Member easily."[1] What concerns us, however, is the action they regarded as significant for the party and which, therefore, was reported in the annual parliamentary report or the quarterly circulars. Measured by this standard, the concerns of the parliamentary party corresponded closely to those of conference, a very heavy emphasis falling upon direct trade union interests. Indeed, on many matters there was an immediate relation to conference resolutions passed at the 1907 conference.[2] For example, the highest priority of the session was given to pressing the Government definitely to commit itself to old age pensions legislation. Also in accord with conference decisions of that year, the party introduced the Sweated Industries bill, the Unemployed Workmen bill, and the Coal Miners (eight-hour) bill; carried a resolution in favor of more drastic legislation regarding the closing of shops and the hours of shop assistants; and "brought constant pressure upon the Government"[3] with regard to the wages of workers for the government and for government contractors.

Some actions, of course, did not spring directly from the resolutions of the 1907 conference. These included a bill to restrict the use of British dockers as blacklegs in strikes abroad; pressure for the appointment of workmen as factory inspectors; a resolution in favor of equalizing the incidence of local property taxes among various areas in London; and an amendment brought forward during a debate on the House of Lords demanding its abolition. In introducing a compulsory weighing and measurements bill, the parliamentary party was promoting a measure that had been urged by the T.U.C. as early as 1892. In urging fresh legislation to limit the hours of railway workers, it was, according to the annual

---

[9] *British Political Parties : the Distribution of Power within the Conservative and Labour Parties* (London, 1955), p. 397.

[1] 1907 *LPCR*, pp. 47–8, quoting a Liberal M.P.

[2] See 1908 *LPCR*, "Parliamentary Report," pp. 43–8, and *Quarterly Circulars* Nos. 16 (April, 1907), 17 (July, 1907), and 18 (October, 1907).

[3] 1908 *LPCR*, p. 47.

report, "carrying out resolutions" of the railway workers union.[4]
Likewise, the Eight Hours bill for miners, although introduced by
the parliamentary party, had originated with the Miners Federation, not yet affiliated to Labour.[5] Moreover, while a bill to extend
to Scotland the Provision of Meals Act of 1906 did not originate
in a resolution of the 1907 conference, the original act itself had
been urged by conferences in 1905 and 1906.

Among the social reform questions that had been taken up by
the 1907 conference, old age pensions and unemployment were
given substantial attention by the party in Parliament. Only very
limited action, such as intervention in a debate, was taken on behalf of temperance, state provision for the blind, and woman
suffrage, while the last four social reform resolutions passed by the
conference found no reflection whatsoever in the reported activity
of the parliamentary party. On the other hand, the grievances of
the shop workers, clothing workers, postal workers, and government workers, as expressed at the conference, were given substantial attention and, although several conference resolutions in
this category were passed over, the greater part of the parliamentary party's efforts was concerned with questions of direct
interest to trade unions.

In the light of this evidence we may reassess the significance of
the resolution of 1907 defining the relation between conference
decisions and parliamentary action. No doubt the P.L.P. sometimes independently initiated policies that it would advocate in the
House. The impressive fact, however, is the very great extent to
which it acted in response to the initiative of extra-parliamentary
sources. This initiative might run directly from the trade unions to
the parliamentary party. But in most cases it was expressed through
a conference resolution. In relation to these initiatives, the parliamentary party had, as the resolution of 1907 granted, the power
to decide questions of priority. The main substance of its work,
nevertheless, was performed under the direction of conference.

PLURALISM IN STRUCTURE AND PURPOSE

According to A. L. Lowell, writing in 1908, the Labour Party
outside Parliament was "not a compact body." "It is hardly a fed-

---

[4] *Ibid.*, p. 45.
[5] *Ibid.*, p. 45, and see G. D. H. Cole, *British Working Class Politics 1832–
1914* (London, 1941), p. 193.

eration," he continued, "but rather an instrument for combining the political action of many independent organisations for a single purpose, that of electing representatives of Labour to the House of Commons."[6] Within the House, however, he said, it had made its representatives "a united party." A central parliamentary fund had been set up to pay a fraction of each candidate's election expenses and, especially, a salary of £200 a year if he were elected to Parliament. Lowell particularly stressed the fact that by the constitution of the party, moreover, candidates were obliged to "undertake to join the Parliamentary Labour Party, if elected" and to "agree to abide by the decisions of the Parliamentary Party in carrying out the aims of this Constitution."[7]

In practice the action of M.P.'s was not rigidly controlled, since, as Snowden recalls, differences of opinion led to the introduction in 1906 of a "conscience clause," which gave "freedom to members of the Party who felt a difficulty in accepting a majority decision either to abstain from voting, or even to go to the length of voting against the majority of the Party."[8] The party met every week during the session to decide what was to be its course of action in the House. Its officers also met daily.[9] But although Mac-Donald, as Secretary of the Executive Committee until 1911, exercised a considerable influence over the local organizations, in Parliament the party lacked the unifying influence of a leader in the traditional sense. And certainly, although the original conception of the party owed a good deal to the example of the Irish Nationalists, the Labour M.P.'s gave to no chief a loyalty approaching that given John Redmond by his followers in the House.[1] Each year the party elected a chairman for the coming session, five men (Hardie, Shackleton, Henderson, Barnes, and MacDonald) holding this position between 1906 and 1914. That none of these enjoyed the power of the traditional party leader

[6] *The Government of England*, new ed., with additional chapter (New York, 1924), Vol. II, pp. 39–40.

[7] 1907 *LPCR*, App. VI, Constitution, Art. III, Clauses 1 and 2.

[8] *Op. cit.*, Vol. I, pp. 134–5. According to Pelling, the conscience clause originated in February, 1907, when the P.L.P., confronted with a threat from Hardie that he would resign from the parliamentary party, voted to let him vote against party policy based on the conference resolution of 1907 opposing any women's suffrage on a property franchise. Henry Pelling, *A Short History of the Labour Party* (London, 1961), p. 21.

[9] Snowden, *op. cit.*, Vol. I, p. 133; McKenzie, *op. cit.*, p. 391.

[1] Snowden, *op. cit.*, Vol. I, p. 132.

proceeded from deliberate design as well as the natural flow of forces in the party.

The Labour Party [wrote Snowden], had always set its face against a permanent Chairman, and had insisted that the Sessional Chairman should not be regarded as the "Leader." It was considered undemocratic. The Party must not permit one man to dictate the policy of the Party. The Chairman was simply the mouthpiece of the Party, stating its decisions in the House of Commons.[2]

Dissension often arose within the party and not infrequently led members to take different paths toward the division lobbies. The issues dividing them were not only those on which Socialists and non-Socialists disagreed. There were also differences over religious education, women suffrage, and even such questions as whether children under sixteen should be legally prohibited to buy and smoke cigarettes.[3] In the sessions of 1906 and 1908, for instance, in about one quarter of the divisions, one or more Labour M.P.'s voted differently from the rest of their colleagues.[4]

If the P.L.P. was, as Lowell said, "a united party," this was true only if judged by the standards of party unity of the time. By British standards, the cohesion in voting of the Labour M.P.'s was not exceptional and fell well below its later achievement. In the 1906 session the index of party voting for the P.L.P. was 80.4 per

[2] *Op. cit.*, Vol. I, p. 218.

[3] See Division 241 *H.C. Deb.*, 1908.

[4] This conclusion and the data in the next paragraph are derived from a study I have made of party unity in the Conservative, Liberal, and Labour parties in the House of Commons during the sessions of 1906, 1908, and 1945. In this study I computed two measurements of party unity, the index of party voting and the coefficient of cohesion. The first I took from A. L. Lowell, who defined a party vote as one in which 90.0% or more of the members of a party voted on the same side of a question. See "The Influence of Party upon Legislation in England and America," *Annual Report*, American Historical Association, 1901. The second I took from Stuart Rice. See his "Behavior of Legislative Groups," repr. in John C. Wahlke and Heinz Eulau, *Legislative Behavior* (New York, 1959). Starting from the assumption that a 50–50 split in a party signifies zero cohesion, one calculates the coefficient of cohesion by dividing by 50 the difference between 50 and the percentage of party members voting on one side. Thus, when 90.0% of the members of a party are on one side, the CoC is 80.0%.

One further comment. To analyze every division in a session, as Lowell did, would involve vast drudgery. I have computed my data from a sample of 1 in every 10 divisions. I satisfied myself that this sampling procedure would give reliable results by trying it for sessions for which Lowell had analyzed all divisions.

cent as compared with exactly the same figure for the Conservatives (Liberal Unionists included) and 88.2 per cent for the Liberals (Irish Nationalists excluded). In 1908 Labour's index of party voting was 87.2 per cent, the Conservatives', 78.7 per cent; and the Liberals', 97.9 per cent. The figures for coefficients of cohesion tell the same story. For the 1906 session they are : Labour, 88.4 per cent; Conservatives, 89.8 per cent; and Liberals, 93.9 per cent. For the 1908 session : Labour, 92.8 per cent; Conservatives, 88.4 per cent; and Liberals, 95.0 per cent.

During this period before the First World War, the party refused to frame and adopt a "programme," although often urged to do so by its Socialist wing. But can its purposes be characterized in a general way? Its distinctive aims centered on the organizational interests of the unions, the conditions of employment of their members, and the immediate circumstances of the lives of their members and families—in short, "the interests of labour." That phrase had been used not only by the L.R.C. when it described its purposes in 1900, but also at the very start of the Lib–Lab phase of labor politics when the Labour Representation League announced its aims in 1869. And beneath the words there were important continuities of meaning. Like the Lib–Labs and the T.U.C. in those earlier years, the Labour Party gave first priority to defending the organizational interests of the unions. The effort to reverse Taff Vale is the principal example. Bills having been unsuccessfully introduced in 1903, 1904, and 1905, this demand was put at the head of the L.R.C., as of the T.U.C., manifesto in 1906 and was wholly satisfied when the Liberal Government, yielding readily to pressure from its own supporters as well as the Labour Party, substituted the Labour bill for its own rather milder version and Parliament enacted the Trade Disputes Act of 1906. Once political representation had been adopted as an aim by the unions, the protection of its power to field and finance candidates also became an organizational interest. Thus, after the Osborne decision of 1909 a major object of the party was to restore the legal status of the political levy, a demand which, subject to the provisions for a ballot and contracting out, was conceded in the Trade Union Act of 1913. Traditional also were the party's concerns with such questions as the Factory Acts and Workmen's Compensation.

Still, in spite of such important continuities, there had been a change in the legislative purposes of the trade union movement, as the austere Gladstonian Liberalism of union leaders in the early days of the T.U.C. had given way to advocacy of piecemeal social reform. Before the end of the century, the T.U.C. and the Lib–Labs had been won over to the cause of old age pensions and the eight hour day, and with these demands the Labour Party pressed forward. Other major measures of social reform that the party strongly supported and which were carried by Liberal Governments included the Wages Board Act of 1909, the Labour Exchanges Act of 1909, the Lloyd George budget of 1909, and the great act of 1911 establishing a system of compulsory health and unemployment insurance.

Interests and Ideology

One is tempted to say that these concerns of the Labour Party reflect nothing more than a straightforward, utilitarian politics of economic self-interest, untainted by ideology or social philosophy. But what an individual or organization takes to be its "interest" is not an immediate datum of experience. It results from an interpretation of that experience and in this interpretation some broader perspective—perhaps vague, perhaps ambiguous—plays an important part. The principal measures advocated by the Labour Party in these years could still be justified on the premises of Radicalism and were so conceived by the bulk of the party in Parliament and the country.[5] These measures consisted of state action not merely to eliminate conditions judged bad, but also to create conditions judged good, the state itself sometimes providing these conditions by means of services that might involve redistribution of wealth. Such intervention, however, was piecemeal : it aimed to correct particular grievances and was usually instigated by the pressure of some particular social group. It certainly constituted no attempt to assert governmental guidance of the economy as a whole or to change fundamentally its individualist and capitalist character.

The bulk of the party, in short, shared a general frame of thought and values within which it carried on its politics of interest, and this perspective could still be fitted into the ideology of Liberal Radicalism. Ramsay MacDonald may well have been exaggerating (for obvious tactical reasons), but it is notable that

[5] For the Radical conception of policy on contrast with the Socialist conception, see above, Ch. III, 79–82.

he could say, while negotiating the *entente* of 1906 with Herbert Gladstone, not only that the majority of the members of the L.R.C. had hitherto worked with the Liberals and wished to continue, but also that the L.R.C. candidates were "in almost every case earnest Liberals who [would] support a Liberal Government."[6]

And in fact the Labour M.P.'s did more than merely serve the immediate interests of trade unions. They also joined enthusiastically in support of the other Radical reforms of Campbell-Bannerman's and Asquith's great "New Deal" Governments. "The Labour Party," wrote Lowell in 1908, ". . . professes to be wholly independent of all other parties, but really agrees with, and is inclined to support, the Liberals on matters that do not touch the special interests of Labour."[7] In the 1906 and 1908 sessions, for instance, a majority of Labour M.P.'s voted with the Government tellers in 89.0% and 84.0% respectively of all divisions. This was not strange. On the whole, these Labour M.P.'s ardently shared the Liberal commitment to Free Trade, Nonconformity, and Home Rule. They adhered to the Radicals' anti-militarism and anti-imperialism and with them championed democracy against aristocracy. They sided with the Government in its effort to amend the Education Act of 1902 and in its equally futile effort for temperance reform. They could vote solidly against the Government in support of their own Unemployed Workmen bill.[8] They sought to exploit their tactic of solidarity by bargaining with the Government, as when in 1911 MacDonald promised Lloyd George that the party would support his National Insurance bill and in return obtained state payment of M.P.'s.[9] But they avoided broad challenges of the Liberal Party at the polls and in Parliament worked with them to bring about a reformist achievement that has been compared with 1832 and 1945. When the party did adopt Socialism, this represented not a shift from interest politics to ideological politics, but a basic change in ideology.

[6] Quoted in Philip P. Poirier, *The Advent of the British Labour Party* (New York, 1958) p. 186.

[7] *Op. cit.*, Vol. II, p. 41.

[8] Division 41 *H.C. Deb.*, 1908.

[9] Pelling, *Short History*, p. 27.

CHAPTER V

The Socialist Generation:
The Commitment

The Labour Party never ceased to be a coalition, but it also became something more. The party of the interwar years was a very different sort of political formation from the party of the Edwardian decade. One needs new language and concepts to characterize its principal features. These features appear if one examines the party's commitment to Socialism and its power structure.

In 1918 the party made the formal decisions that committed it to Socialism and a Socialist program. Thenceforth it was accepted and official usage to say that its ultimate aim was a new social order, "the Socialist Commonwealth." This change had been maturing over the years and particularly during wartime, as the readiness with which it was accepted by the party shows. What did the adoption of Socialism mean to the party?

When one asks that question, one wants to know, in the first place, the intellectual content of the commitment. During the generation after 1918 Labour produced a huge mass of party utterance—conference debates, party programs, parliamentary speeches, and the like. Reflected in it one finds, of course, special interests and various currents of opinion, as well as changing emphases of policy in response to changing circumstances. But one does not find merely a miscellany of ideas. Knitting together the pluralism of views, there is something that can be called an orthodoxy, a unified doctrine, even a system of thought, which not only pervades the party, but also, still more surprisingly, persists without fundamental change through the interwar period and into the years after 1945.

This change in purpose made the Labour Party a different kind of political formation—a radically different kind of "whole"—from a mere coalition. As a coalition the various groups in the party were joined by the logic of logrolling, fortified by wide similarities among their particular interests. The commitment to Socialism, however, meant that now all groups had the same object, the Socialist Commonwealth. As all traced their particular grievances to the same cause, the capitalist system, so all saw in a Socialist society the one and only remedy for those grievances.

Previously one group could conceive of its grievances being remedied although those of its allies were not. This is indeed the essence of the political tactics of social reform, tactics which proceed from the reformers' conception of the social and economic system. In the reformers' eyes, the system is such that particular conditions within it can be reformed without alteration of the system as a whole; hence the grievances of one group can be remedied while the grievances of others remain. For the Socialist, however, there is one grand and general cause of all basic grievances, the capitalist system, and the only permanent and thorough going remedy is the establishment of the Socialist Commonwealth. The grievance of one group can be remedied only by remedying the grievances of all. The groups suffering from these grievances—primarily the working class—now have a solidarity of interest quite lacking among aggrieved groups in the Radical universe of discourse and their party has a solidarity of purpose far transcending the bonds of unity of a mere reforming coalition.

BELIEFS AND VALUES

During the bitter controversy that broke out in the Labour Party in 1951, it was often asserted by the "revisionists" that Socialism is essentially a social ethic. It was said, for instance, that "socialism is about equality," seeking to create greater equality of opportunity and, especially, a much greater degree of equality of economic condition. Such values, ran the revisionist case, set the ends of Socialism; the particular means to these ends—for instance, public ownership, economic planning, and various social services—would change from one period to another, depending on circumstances and our knowledge of society.

But the commitment made by the party in 1918 was not merely

a commitment to a social ethic, a system of values. It was also the acceptance of a theory of society, a system of beliefs about how the main social forces actually operated and how they could be brought to operate differently. There were two facets of Socialist ideology, the ethical and the analytical, the normative and the existential, and they were inseparably linked in the new sense of purpose which the party acquired toward the end of the First World War and which was broadly shared by its various components in the next generation.

The Socialist system of values included a distinctive view of equality and liberty. But one gets at the heart of its ethical message with the concept of fellowship. "Socialism," wrote Bruce Glasier in 1919, "means not only the socialisation of wealth, but of our lives, our hearts—ourselves."

Socialism, in truth, consists, when finally resolved, not in getting at all, but in giving; not in being served, but in serving; not in selfishness, but in unselfishness; not in the desire to gain a place of bliss in this world for one's self and one's family (that is the individualist and capitalist aim), but in the desire to create an earthly paradise for all. . . . Yet it may be better simply to say with William Morris that Socialism is fellowship, and that fellowship is life, and the lack of fellowship is death. Fellowship is heaven and the lack of fellowship is hell.[1]

Glasier's words are not from a scholarly treatise and should not be analyzed as the utterances of a professional philosopher. Yet it would be an even greater mistake to dismiss them as rhetoric or mere conventional morality and fail to see their distinctive ethical tendency.[2] To ask for the "socialisation" of hearts, lives, and selves is to suggest a conception of the good life that bursts the bonds of even the qualified moral individualism of the advanced Radical reformer. The reformer will emphasize the positive duties of mu-

---

[1] *The Meaning of Socialism* (London, 1919), pp. 226 and 229–30.

[2] It is certainly incorrect to say that the social ethics of Labour's Socialism was derived from the Bible, as is implied in the common judgment that in Britain the Bible made more Socialists than Karl Marx. Socialists, such as Keir Hardie, did indeed use the Bible when expressing their ethical position, but they used it in a highly selective way. After all, the Bible was used for ultimate justification by all sides in these controversies, certainly by capitalists as well as Socialists. Liberals, Radicals, Conservatives, and indeed in their days Old Tories and Old Whigs had relied on some version of the Biblical message. Given the wide variety of moral positions that was thus derived from the Bible, one must also suppose some non-Biblical criterion of selection if one is to identify a certain social ethic with a Biblical source.

tual aid that individuals owe to one another. He is not a rugged individualist insisting solely on the negative obligation of men not to harm one another; he claims that men also have an obligation to create conditions which will enhance the ability of all to live and live well. To this extent in his ideal community there is a common will, a system of purpose and sentiment that is identical in each person. But at the same time this ideal community, although qualified by such a common will, is strongly individualist. For within the framework of the common will each man finds his own way to his unique vision of the good life and produces an achievement, moral and economic, attributable to himself alone.

A thoroughgoing moral collectivism would totally eliminate this essential residuum of private will and purely personal experience. In its ideal community there would be no private griefs and joys, no achievement that was purely personal. Selflessness would not be the self-sacrifice of the individualist who gives up an object of his own in order to help others realize their individual objects. On the contrary, the conflict and isolation of selves from which such self-sacrifice arises would be transcended and abolished in the new society. Each person's life would be selfless in the sense that his self and the common "self" of the community would be merged. Insofar as this community was a democracy, each member would have a share in the continuous reformulation of the communal purpose. But he would accept gladly such democratic decisions and his private will and personality would be merged in the comprehensive will of the community. There would be no problem of obedience, since the evolving will of the community would be his own evolving will. His heart, life, and self would be totally "socialized" and "democratized."

Now, we need not suppose that such a total—not to say totalitarian—moral collectivism was implied by the Socialist doctrine of fellowship. Yet it serves to define a position toward which Socialist ethics tended as it broke away from ethical individualism. A powerful stream of nineteenth and twentieth century thought, as Sheldon Wolin has observed, consisted in

the attempt to restate the value of community, that is, of the need for human beings to dwell in more intimate relationships with each other, to enjoy more affective ties, to experience some closer solidarity than the nature of urbanized and industrialized society seemed willing to grant.[3]

[3] *Politics and Vision* (Boston, 1960), pp. 363-4.

Socialism was a main current in this stream. In part, it consisted of a reaction against particular grievances, and Socialist parties in their practical political life were primarily concerned with remedying these. But Socialism also offered a vision of a new society where the self-development of each was not simply tolerated, nor simply supported by others, but integrally and internally related to the development of the community as a whole. It was on some such "earthly paradise for all" that the doctrine of fellowship fixed the utopian hopes of the British Labour Party.

This notion of the good life, this normative concept, was at the same time a fundamental principle of Socialist economics. For Socialists held that such solidarity was not only desirable, but also possible. Cooperation could take the place of competition and the public service motive the place of the profit motive precisely because men could live in fellowship. They could be brought to dispense with incentives—with "the desire to gain a place of bliss in this world for one's self and one's family"—because they could be brought to identify their own individual good and gain with the common welfare. Men would not need the sticks and carrots of the free market to allocate them to their proper places and manners of productive work because they would gladly accept the decisions of a democracy to which they fully belonged and which they fully controlled. Fellowship, in short, would be the social force that made the Socialist Commonwealth a viable society.

In 1924 Ramsay MacDonald told the party conference :

. . . the aim of Socialism is to get at the hearts of men, because we cannot survive unless we discover how to produce the *willing* workers and not merely the man who toils for reward. We have been too long thinking and speaking as though the spirit of artistic production was different in kind from the spirit required for manual production. Those of us who drank early from the refreshing springs which William Morris made to flow in a dull and deadening generation never held that heresy, and never will. Men live by their generosities, by their loyalties, not by their interest, and their self-regarding interests. And until somehow or other, by change of heart and condition, or both, we can put our industry on the footing of the willing gift of service, we shall have nothing but quarrels and the sacrifice of the common weal. It is the aim of getting our industry on that footing, that is the aim of the Socialist inspiration that gives us power in our Labour Movement.[4]

[4] 1924 *LPCR*, pp. 108–9.

The statement of this belief was not confined to ceremonial occasions, such as the opening of a party conference, but had been taken by the Socialist missionaries into literally millions of homes. A generation earlier, for instance, Robert Blatchford in *Merrie England* had observed that the critics of Socialism say that it is impossible because it would destroy "the incentive of gain." That men respond to this incentive, he continued, is not, however, a constant of human nature, but only "the state in which men live under a competitive commercial system."[5] And even in such a society one can see that there are more enduring and powerful motives on which a new society could be founded.

Look about you and see what men do for gain, and what for honour. Your volunteer force—does that exist for gain? Your lifeboat service, again—is *that* worked by the incentive of dirty dross? What will not a soldier do for a tiny bronze cross, not worth a crown piece? What will a husband endure for his wife's sake? a father for his children? a fanatic for his religion? But you do not believe that Socialism is to destroy all love, and all honour, and all duty and devotion, do you?

. . . Is there any community as united and as effective as a family? The family is the soundest, the strongest, and the happiest kind of society, and next to that is the tribe of families. And why? Because all the relations of family life are carried on in direct opposition to the principles of political economy and the survival of the fittest. A family is bound by ties of love and mutual helpfulness.[6]

The problem with which these men were dealing is obviously of central importance to Socialist theory and would be of crucial practical importance to the successful working of a Socialist society. The "incentive of gain" is the principal motor of capitalism. Socialists would abolish it because of its corrupting influence on human nature and social relations. In the Socialist Commonwealth men would enjoy, if not absolute economic equality, at least a far greater equality of condition than ever before. What then was to take the place of the old basis of motivation? How was cooperation, as a working system, to be substituted for competition? "The public service motive," "fellowship," "the spirit of artistic production"—in such phrases Socialists attempted to suggest the new moral basis of the new society, illustrating what they meant and supporting the plausibility of their expectations from their im-

[5] (London, 1894), p. 114.
[6] *Ibid.*, pp. 120 and 139.

mediate experience of the family, of merchant seamen, of civil servants, doctors, nurses, artists, inventors, and others who already acted from those higher motives on which the Socialist Commonwealth would depend. I do not mean to say that there was universal agreement among Socialists on a systematic social psychology. But that some such new culture and new morality would arise was central to the orthodoxy of the Labour Party.

Ideology and Program

Socialist theory included a view of the social forces that would make possible the new system of the cooperative commonwealth. It also provided an analysis of the source of the grievances that afflicted society and especially the working class. That source was the capitalist economic system. Capitalism was responsible for the waste and inefficiency of the modern economy, for setting man against man in the harsh egoism of the market place, for the oppressive inequality of worker and employer, rich and poor. Not individuals, certainly not human nature, but "the system" was at fault. Just how "the system" produced these evils was the subject of elaborate analysis. But all Socialists would agree that the root of the problem was the private ownership of the means of production, distribution, and exchange.

A social movement or political party may be consistent in its adherence to certain broad views of social forces and values, and yet highly adaptable in the programs and policies it espouses over the years. In the United States, for instance, the Democratic Party is sometimes thought to have a core of belief that runs back to Thomas Jefferson's "cherishment of the people," yet its stand on such a matter as government intervention in the economy has ranged over a wide spectrum. It is some such flexibility that the revisionists of the Labour Party in the 1950's wished to read into British Socialism. But the dominant ideology of the party during the interwar years hardly permits this reading. For the interwar Socialist critique of capitalism implied a quite specific and programmatic consequence : as private ownership of the means of production was the source of existing evils, so common ownership was the main structural reform on which the new cooperative and democratic order would be founded. There was some variety of opinion over the form that common ownership would take. When the Socialists first brought their resolutions into the

T.U.C. and the Labour Party they called for "nationalisation."[7] Rather later "socialisation" often came to be used, normally under the influence of Syndicalism, as a way of suggesting immediate control over industries and firms by the workers employed in them. Accommodation was also extended to the cooperative movement to include its mode of activities under common ownership. While embracing such variations, common ownership was stressed consistently, however, not merely as one among many features of the Socialist society, but as the basic and governing reform.

For this reason the party constitution adopted in 1918 could define the Socialist objective in the brief words of Clause 4 : The "full fruits of their industry" were to be secured to the workers by hand and by brain "upon the basis of the common ownership of the means of production,[8] and the best obtainable system of popular administration and control of each industry or service." The words echo those used by the I.L.P. when at its inaugural conference of 1893 it stated its object as "the collective ownership of all the means of production, distribution and exchange."

Similarly, in 1894 Blatchford had been able to write :

Practical Socialism is so simple that a child may understand it. It is a kind of national scheme of cooperation, managed by the State. Its programme consists, essentially, of one demand, that the land and other instruments of production shall be the common property of the people, and shall be used and governed by the people for the people.[9]

Ernest Bevin, in his campaign for the City Council of Bristol in 1909, declared :

. . . you will realise the chaos, misery and degradation brought upon us by the private ownership of the means of life. I claim that Socialism, which is the common ownership of these means, is the ONLY SOLUTION OF SUCH EVILS.[1]

And in 1933 Herbert Morrison wrote :

[7] For illustration, see below, pp. 164–73. Henry Pelling writes : "Socialists of the late nineteenth and early twentieth centuries have almost all been committed to the aim of public ownership, in one form or another, of 'the means of production, distribution, and exchange'; and except for Syndicalists, this has meant nationalisation in the first instance." *The Challenge of Socialism* (London, 1954), p. 291.

[8] The phrase "distribution and exchange" was added by conference in 1929. See 1929 *LPCR*, p. 206.

[9] *Op. cit.*, p. 100.

[1] Quoted in Alan Bullock, *The Life and Times of Ernest Bevin* (London, 1960), Vol. I, p. 21.

The vision of one Minister alone socialising two big industries in one year pleases me enormously. . . . Socialism for me is a policy for today and not for some indefinite day after tomorrow. . . . The function of Labour Governments in the future will rather be to secure the socialisation of industry after industry under a management which can be broadly relied upon to go on with its work.[2]

In 1937, nineteen years after the Labour Party's decision of 1918, Clement Attlee, the party's leader, proclaimed :

The evils that Capitalism brings differ in intensity in different countries but the root cause of the trouble once discerned, the remedy is seen to be the same by thoughtful men and women. The cause is private property; the remedy is public ownership.[3]

Attlee still expressed the ancient and orthodox meaning of Socialism when, as Prime Minister and Leader of a party that had just won a sweeping victory in a general election, he told the 1946 annual conference :

We . . . are resolved to carry out as rapidly and as energetically as we can the distinctive side of Labour's programme : our socialist policy, our policy of nationalisation.[4]

Writing in 1956, a group of revisionists of the Labour Party characterized the belief of the Socialist pioneers of the late nineteenth century in these words :

Although differing in their views on the exact shape of things to come, on their central message they were united—the economic system was wrong and had to be replaced by another and totally different one. Minor reforms to ease the sufferings of the victims of capitalism were all very well, but what was wanted was a new system which would have no victims at all. In setting this as their goal, socialists distinguished themselves from all other reform movements of the time.
On one point only did they agree with the defenders of the established order. They shared with them the idea of their being two, distinct, opposing and ultimately irreconcilable economic systems—capitalism and socialism. You could have the one or replace it by the other, but you could not mix the two.[5]

[2] *Socialisation and Transport* (London, 1933), p. 140.
[3] *The Labour Party in Perspective* (London, 1937), p. 15.
[4] Quoted in Herbert E. Weiner, *British Labour and Public Ownership* (London, 1960), p. 87.
[5] *Twentieth Century Socialism : the Economy of Tomorrow* (London, 1956), p. 12.

Having described "this simple conception," which once "dominated socialist thought," these writers went on to point out that it "has undoubtedly faded with the passing of time, and the theories which supported it have been sharply challenged by events." Nevertheless, "its influence," they observed, is by no means exhausted. "Like a ghost from the past it still haunts our thinking."[6]

There is no cause to quarrel with this analysis. But one will not understand the nature of the Labour Party of the previous generation, nor will one be able to make sense of the prolonged and violent ideological conflict that shook the party during the 1950's if one starts from the assumption that the "simple conception" was entertained only by pioneers of the early days and Left-wing extremists of a later time. The "ghost" haunted the party of the 1950's because it had been the soul of the party in the 1920's and 1930's.

If the implication of sudden and violent change is extracted from the term "revolution," it is correct to say that the meaning of Socialism to the Labour Party was a commitment to ultimate social revolution. At its foundation the party was, and during its later history it remained, massively devoted to parliamentary and democratic methods despite the efforts of Syndicalists, Communists, or others to divert it from the path of constitutionalism. This meant that it would also be gradualist, accomplishing its aims step by step, statute by statute. In Parliament, moreover, it fought to protect and to extend particular measures of social reform and at election times it knew how to put in the forefront of its appeal to the country promises of immediate material benefit. Moderate in these respects, the party was, however, utopian in its ultimate aspirations. It thought of itself not just as a party, but as "the Movement." The millenary emotions that animated large sections of the party were not fixed simply on the redress of grievances. They were matched on the intellectual plane by a vision of a radically new and different world, a vision that spokesmen articulated in their ideology of the Socialist Commonwealth.

During the interwar period and through the victory of 1945 such "system-thinking" informed the standard rhetoric of the party at conferences and in Parliament, in Socialist tracts, routine propaganda, and comprehensive statements of purpose. One could fully document this assertion only by intolerably voluminous ref-

[6] *Ibid.*, p. 15.

erences. But one can remind the reader of the flavor of these pronouncements.

Three comprehensive policy statements were drawn up between
the wars. In 1918 the first of these, *Labour and The New Social
Order*, proclaiming "the end of a civilisation," declared that "we
need to beware of patchwork . . . what has to be reconstructed . . .
is . . . society itself." In 1928 MacDonald wrote :

The Labour Party, unlike other parties, is not concerned with patch-
ing the rents in a bad system, but with transforming Capitalism into
Socialism . . . industry must be converted from a sordid struggle for
gain into a cooperative undertaking, carried on for the service of the
community and amenable to its control.

Stressing the same theme, *For Socialism and Peace* declared in 1934
that "the choice before the nation is either a vain attempt to patch
up the superstructure of a capitalist society in decay at its very
foundations, or a rapid advance to a socialist reconstruction of the
national life." The central structural feature of that reconstruction
was then clarified :

There is no halfway house between a society based on private ownership of the means of production with the profit of the few as the
measure of success, and a society where public ownership of those
means enables the resources of the nation to be deliberately planned
for attaining the maximum of general well being.

The rhetoric of fundamental reconstruction and of "system-
thinking" was carried over into the policy statements and conference speeches of wartime, if anything in even stronger form. In
1942 *The Old World and The New Society* announced "a crisis
in our civilisation as profound as that of the Reformation and the
French Revolution." Both at home and abroad, in economic depression and aggressive war, "all the major evils of the 'appeasement period,' " it said, "are directly traceable to the unregulated
operation of our economic system." It hailed the "new age" of "a
planned democracy" and re-emphasized the ancient orthodoxy
of Socialism : "Common ownership will alone secure that priority
of national over private need which assures the community the
power over its economic future." Although shorter and aimed
specifically at the election campaign of 1945, *Let Us Face The
Future* revealed its descent from this body of sentiments in the
general views in which its numerous and specific pledges were

embedded. Denouncing "the chaos of economic do-as-they-please anarchy" as responsible for war, exploitation, and depression, it proclaimed : "The Labour Party is a Socialist Party, and proud of it. Its ultimate purpose at home is the establishment of the Socialist Commonwealth of Great Britain."

The form itself of the party's comprehensive statements reflected its new and distinctive approach to the task of governing. As the structure and purpose of the Labour Party differed from those of the Liberals, so also did the manner in whch they framed their proposals. Unlike the Nottingham or Newcastle Programmes of the Liberals, these statements were not simply lists of particular reforms. They presented a broad analysis of the state of the nation, developing the Socialist view of its ills, of their causes, and of the new system that would set them right. The significance of this difference was recognized in the party. "May I remind you," said Ramsay MacDonald to the conference in 1928, ". . . that the production of a mere list of items of a programme, after the manner of the Newcastle Programme, was not the right way to go about the business." On the contrary, the Labour Party's program is "meaningless" unless you get the voters to see "that, for example, when you say 'pensions' . . . you convey to the minds of your audience not merely a money payment, but a new system of society which is going to do justice to the weak, the needy and the abandoned."[7]

THE BREAK WITH LIBERALISM

We have yet to ask the question why the Labour Party made the decision to adopt Socialism. What is the explanation of this event? If we can identify its causes, we may get some light on the more interesting question of what forces sustained the "orthodoxy" of the Labour Party in succeeding years.

One could begin with the actions and interactions of certain leaders. The principals were Lloyd George and Arthur Henderson. If any one moment is to be singled out as decisive, it surely is the maneuver by which in December, 1916, Asquith was ousted from the premiership and Lloyd George installed in his place. In preparing this coup and in forming his new Government, Lloyd George became deeply beholden to forces that would hardly toler-

[7] 1928 *LPCR*, pp. 196-7.

ate in any serious sense "an opening to the Left." His principal supporters in the attack on Asquith, for instance, included Bonar Law, Sir Edward Carson, Max Aitken, and Lord Northcliffe—to mention only a few of the inner core. The new Government, in which the Liberal–Conservative balance shifted sharply toward the Conservatives (fifteen Conservatives received ministerial posts as compared with ten under Asquith), was viewed with deep apprehension by Ernest Bevin, who found in it bitter enemies of the Labour Movement.[8] There was a similar shift to the Right in Lloyd George's majority in Parliament when the Liberals split between Asquith and Lloyd George, who now became heavily dependent upon his Conservative support.

This choice of allies by Lloyd George ultimately led to the breach with Arthur Henderson in August, 1917. In the "doormat incident," Henderson was excluded from a meeting of the Cabinet while it discussed his proposal (which Lloyd George at one time had favored) that British delegates be sent to the proposed International Socialist Congress in Stockholm.[9] His hand probably having been forced by other members of the Cabinet,[1] the Prime Minister then rejected the Stockholm proposal. With the Labour Party conference fully supporting the proposal, Henderson indignantly resigned from the Government.[2]

Although Labour remained in the Coalition, this incident marked a turning point in the history of the party. In the following months Henderson turned to the dual task of designing a new party organization and framing for the first time a party program. For help in both tasks he enlisted the aid of Sidney Webb, thereby giving to the views of the Fabian Society, which had long been in decline, a major influence on the future of the party. At the conferences of 1918 the party adopted the new constitution and the new program, *Labour and The New Social Order*, with virtu-

---

[8] According to Ralph Miliband, Bevin complained that "the Cabinet ... included some of Labour's bitterest enemies." *Parliamentary Socialism* (London, 1961), p. 52. Actually, of the five men Bevin singled out for attack at the party conference of 1917—Lloyd George, Lord Milner, Lord Rhondda, Lord Devonport, and Lord Derby—only the first two were members of the War Cabinet. See 1917 *LPCR*, pp. 96–7.

[9] David Lloyd George, *War Memoirs* (Boston, 1934), Vol. IV, p. 151.

[1] Henry Pelling, *A Short History of the Labour Party* (London, 1961), p. 41.

[2] See M. A. Hamilton, *Arthur Henderson* (London, 1938), p. 155; Stephen Graubard, *British Labour and the Russian Revolution* (Cambridge, Mass., 1956), pp. 23–35; and A. J. P. Taylor's lecture, "Lloyd George, His Rise and Fall" (Cambridge, Eng., 1961).

ally no dissent. "The Labour Party," wrote the American ambassador in January, 1918, "is already playing for supremacy."[3]

An explanation that stopped at this point would leave a great deal unexplained. We can hardly suppose that this major upheaval in the British party system was the result of the decisions and reactions of half a dozen men at the top of British politics. "Right up to 1914," writes Cole, "any attempt to commit the Labour Party to Socialism would have endangered trade union support."[4] Why then were the unions so ready to accept this sharp ideological shift to the Left in 1918? A clue to one possible explanation is given by the speech with which J. H. Thomas initiated the debate on Labour's new program at the conference of June, 1918. During the war, he emphasized, the Government did not entrust the conduct of the economy to private enterprise, but turned to state control. "The taking over of railways, mines and munitions factories and other controlled establishments during the war," he said, "really meant that in the considered judgment of the Government . . . the private ownership of these things in time of war was a danger to the State." In his view it followed that in time of peace private ownership was equally dangerous and state control equally desirable.[5]

This argument, often used by Socialists in the postwar years, rested on the fact that the war effort had involved vast and unprecedented extensions of state power over the economy. These included not only such interferences with the free market as price-fixing and allocation of materials, but also direct government management of the railways and coal mines. As a result of their experience with this wartime system, Stephen Graubard has concluded, "ordinary men and women understood that government control and intervention might mean a larger weekly wage, a more secure employment, and a greater number of social benefits."[6]

One may readily grant that wartime measures taught trade

---

[3] Quoted in Pelling, *Short History*, p. 42.

[4] *History of the Labour Party from 1914* (London, 1948), p. 53. Ben C. Roberts writes: ". . . it would have been impossible before the war to persuade a majority of the unions that State socialism was a desirable objective." *The Trade Union Congress, 1868–1921* (Cambridge, Mass., 1958), p. 305.

[5] 1918 *LPCR*, p. 43.

[6] "The World War: Labour's Teacher" (unpublished paper delivered before the American Historical Association, 1960).

unionists that large-scale state control was practicable as well as beneficial.[7] But to ask for greater state control, even including public ownership of mines and railways, is not the same as to adopt, as Labour did in 1918, the comprehensive ideology of Socialism. For Labour's decision did not consist only in a demand for the particular measures set forth in the program of 1918, multitudinous as they were, but also as I have argued in previous pages, in a commitment to a new system, a "new social order," indeed a "new civilisation." This ideological break with Liberalism was intimately related to the other major decision, the adoption of a new framework of organization. It is necessary to examine the interdependence and causal priority of these two decisions.

In its effect on the future relations of the Labour Party with the Liberals, the commitment to Socialism was crucial. It ruled out the old cooperative relation as well as any closer union of the two parties. Or to put the matter a little differently : the adoption of Socialism set the seal on the decision of 1900 to form a separate and independent political party. In spite of the words of 1900, Labour's independence in actual practice had been far from resolute. Cooperation with the Liberals had deeply qualified its proclaimed independence not only in Parliament, but also in the country. In view of the leaders' public adherence to independence, it is not strange that they felt obliged to conceal the *entente* of 1906 from the membership. Such electoral arrangements have often been the road to fusion. Nor did the agreement of 1906 mark a temporary and exceptional tactic. In practice, Labour continued to refrain from offering a broad electoral challenge to the Liberals during the prewar period.

It is hardly a universal law of political behavior that when two parties follow a tactic such as that represented by the *entente* of 1906, they must have in common some bond of ideology, or at least not be divided by opposing ideologies. Still, such cooperation is greatly facilitated if the allies belong to the same political tendency. MacDonald suggested as much when, in the 1906 nego-

[7] At the party conference of 1917, G. J. Wardle, who was chairman of the conference as well as chairman of the P.L.P. and N.E.C., said that the cure for profiteering is "the principles of ownership and control, so long advocated solely by the Labour Party." Referring to government intervention during the war, he then said that "progress in applying [these] principles has been remarkable." 1917 *LPCR*, p. 85.

tiations, he made his only slightly mendacious statement to Herbert Gladstone that the L.R.C. candidates could be regarded as "earnest Liberals." So long as Labour's purposes were simply those of trade union politics, framed in the broad terms of Radical ideology, the independence of the party was still seriously in doubt. Indeed, there remained the real possibility that it might become simply a wing of a more socialistic, though not Socialist, Liberal Party.

Conversely, while the adoption of Socialism did not create barriers to cooperation that in no conceivable circumstances could have been overcome, it raised these barriers far higher than they had ever been before. A debate that took place in the House of Commons in 1923 illustrates the point. Its subject was "The Failure of the Capitalist System" and the motion moved by Snowden on behalf of the party read as follows :

That in view of the failure of the capitalist system to adequately utilise and organise natural resources and productive power, or to provide the necessary standard of living for vast numbers of the population, and believing that the cause of this failure lies in the private ownership and control of the means of production and distribution, this House declares that legislative effort should be directed to the gradual supersession of the capitalist system by an industrial and social order based on the public ownership and democratic control of the instruments of production and distribution.[8]

The motion is quoted in full because it conveys succinctly the tone and temper of the debate that followed. Only Continental parliaments, we are commonly told, have been the scene of conflict between opposed ideologies, while the House of Commons sticks to immediate problems and practical solutions. Anyone who holds this view should consult *Hansard* for this debate. As an exercise in ideological thinking, it is by no means an unworthy echo of the great three-day clash between Jaurès and Clemenceau in the Chamber of Deputies in 1906. Nor, although the debate was initiated by Snowden and concluded by MacDonald, did the Labour side include only spokesmen of the I.L.P. Clynes and Henderson also spoke forcefully and in the same utopian vein. Both dissociated themselves and the Labour Party from mere reformism, emphasizing the essentially Socialist position that the evils they complained of were inherent in capitalism and could be

[8] 161 *H.C. Deb.* 2472 (20 March 1923). The debate was continued on 16 July 1923.

eliminated only by a change in the "system." Henderson in particular bore down hard on this point, which, after all, was the real issue of the debate. For the question was not whether there were injustices and faults that needed correction; all speakers, some with more, some with less sensitivity, admitted this point. The difference lay in the fact that, as Henderson said, the older parties thought these things were "not inherent in the system," while "the Labour party, on the other hand, is convinced that however much the capitalist system may be improved there are still formidable evils that cannot be eradicated, even if it were possible to reduce or mitigate their effects."[9]

During the course of the debate, Lloyd George remarked on the novel character of the confrontation of views. "In the old days," he said, "when there was discontent, you could blame your parties for it, but now you have to blame systems, and that is the danger."[1] It was not, however, only the Socialists who thought in terms of systems. Not the least remarkable aspect of the debate was the way in which the Socialist motion elicited the ideology of their opponents. One sees this in the amendment moved by a leading Liberal, Sir Alfred Mond :

[That] this House believing that the abolition of private interest in the means of production and distribution would impoverish the people and aggravate existing evils, is unalterably opposed to any scheme of legislation which would deprive the state of the benefits of individual initiative, and believing that far-reaching measures of social redress may be accomplished without over-turning the present basis of society, is resolved to prosecute proposals which, by removing the evil effects of monopoly and waste, will conduce to the well-being of the people.[2]

Declaring that the country was presented with "a clear issue between Individualism and Socialism,"[3] Mond deployed the old and familiar arguments for free enterprise and free trade that constituted the Liberal orthodoxy. With great concern, Lloyd George pointed to specific conditions that required amelioration. Yet he also kept his proposals within the terms of the amendment, interpreting these faults as "the evil effects of monopoly and waste." Neither proposed a breach with "the individualist system."

The Conservatives, incidentally, offered no amendment and al-

[9] 166 H.C. Deb. 1963 (16 July 1923).
[1] Ibid., 1948.
[2] 161 H.C. Deb. 2490 (20 March 1923).
[3] Ibid., 2505.

though they attacked Socialism and defended private ownership, they did not unanimously accept the Liberal orthodoxy. On the contrary, Leopold Amery held forth on the merits of protection and a strong native agriculture, of Empire development, and of State guidance of the economy.[4] Looking ahead a few years, it is interesting to note that, although the Conservatives had no orthodoxy to offer, Sir Alfred Mond soon deserted Free Trade and in 1929 joined Amery to found the Empire Economic Union. But that is a theme we shall take up in a later chapter.

Socialist ideals, Snowden had said, are going to be "the dividing lines in the future between the different parties."[5] The confrontation of this debate, which put the antagonism between Labour and the older parties on the plane of basic economic and political principles, illustrates how Labour's adoption of those ideals contributed to the lasting division of the two former allies on the Left.

ORGANIZATIONAL NECESSITY AND CLASS ANTAGONISM

The adoption of Socialism fitted in with and set the seal on the strategy of full-fledged independence. This is not the same as saying that it led to this strategy. Indeed, it is worth looking at what is roughly the reverse of that proposition and examining the reasons why the necessity for independence led to the adoption of Socialism.

The war was not a period of decline for the working class, certainly not for the organized working class. On the contrary, in power, status, and even material condition, trade unionists greatly benefited. Some have tried to explain the Labour Party's break with the Liberals as a fairly simple economic calculation : the Liberals had failed to represent the interests and remedy the grievances of the working class, and more specifically, the organized working class of the trade unions. Hence, it is said, disillusioned with the old cooperative strategy and the attempt to remedy their grievances within capitalism, the unions concluded that only a change in system would satisfy their needs. This has been an explanation which Socialists have stressed. In the debate of 1923, for instance, Snowden claimed that although there had been an improvement in the material condition of the working

[4] 166 H.C. Deb. 1998–2001.
[5] 161 H.C. Deb. 2473.

class between 1850 and 1874, the period 1874–1908 had witnessed
a relative and absolute decline.

There is indeed evidence of both a relative and absolute decline
in the condition of the working class before World War I. In 1910
real wages were substantially below what they had been in 1900,
and they did not begin to rise until 1914. Moreover, since the end
of the century the share of the national income going to wage-
earners had fallen considerably.[6] These material factors no doubt
contributed to the labor unrest that disturbed industrial relations
just before the outbreak of war and on which the Syndicalists
capitalized. But this turn toward direct action by some trade
unionists does not correlate with a shift toward Socialism in the
unions generally. They, as we have noted, remained hostile. Indeed, when judged in the light of what trade unions and the
Labour Party were demanding in the sphere of government action,
the tactic of cooperation had been remarkably successful. There
had been friction with Liberal Governments and delays in the
satisfaction of Labour's demands. But in sum the corpus of social
reform enacted in the half dozen years or so after 1906 constituted
an achievement that has often been compared with the results of
1832 and 1945. Not only did Liberal Governments and the Liberal
Party outside Parliament adopt proposals originating with Labour
and the unions; in important instances the Liberals took the initiative in conceiving and proposing basic measures. Hugh Dalton
recalls : "The Liberals, indeed, were making the running in those
years."[7]

The crucial shift in union opinion took place during the war.
This cannot be traced to a sharp deterioration in the material condition of the working class. On the contrary, it can be argued that
as a whole the working class was materially better off during the
war than before.[8] The most striking correlation, in actual fact,

[6] Ben C. Roberts, *op. cit.*, p. 233.
[7] *Call Back Yesterday* (London, 1953), p. 70.
[8] Although the cost of living rose faster than wages (Ben C. Roberts, *op.
cit.*, p. 287), on the other hand, an immense amount of overtime was worked
and many wives and daughters of working class households entered industry.
As a result, one historian is prompted to write, there was "a very marked
rise in the standard of living throughout the wage-earning classes." "Organized labour," he continues, "was determined that these standards should be
maintained after the war." D. C. Somervell, *British Politics Since 1900* (London, 1950), p. 108.

is with the immense rise in trade union membership since 1914. Henderson could respond aggressively to the "doormat incident" not only because the Liberals were split, but also because the growth of trade unionism at last provided the party with the means for a strategy of full-fledged independence. Moreover, the increase in organizational power of the unions did more than merely provide an opportunity for this strategy. It also virtually forced the Labour Party to adopt it and to break politically with the Liberals. The commitment to Socialism, in turn, can be regarded as a consequence of this breach. In other words, the adoption of the new ideology was not so much a cause as an effect of the hardly avoidable break with the Liberals.[9] Underlying this rupture were the divisive forces of the British class structure at the time.

The basic dynamic factor was the growth in trade union membership. Membership in unions affiliated with the T.U.C., one must recall, had grown very slowly in the past. By 1900, thirty-two years after the founding of the Congress, it had reached 1,250,000. By 1913 it had risen to only 2,232,446. Then with the war came a sudden and dramatic upsurge, in five years membership doubled, reaching 4,532,985 in 1918, the trend continuing upward to 6,505,482 in 1920.[1] Membership in the Labour Party had followed a roughly parallel course. From 375,931 in 1900, it had risen to just short of 1,000,000 in 1906 and stood at 1,612,147 in 1914. Then, nearly doubling, it reached 3,013,129 in 1918 and rose in the next two years to 4,359,807. Similarly, the local organization of the party grew hardly at all before the war. In 1908 there were 134 local bodies, either local associations or trades councils. By 1914 these had grown to only 158. As compared with this net increase of only 24 in six years, the number of local bodies grew by 102 between 1914 and 1917, reaching a total of 260 in the latter year.[2] This, it should be observed, was before the great increase in local

[9] Henderson explicitly reasoned along these lines, judging by G. D. H. Cole's reconstruction of his intentions. Cole writes : "His [i.e., Henderson's] study of the position had, however, convinced him, by 1917, that some sort of Socialist faith was the necessary basis for the consolidation of the Labour Party into an effective national force." Henderson, continues Cole, "turned naturally" to Fabian Socialism for "the new gospel which he needed to give substance to the Constitution that he had in mind." *Op. cit.*, p. 60.

[1] Roberts, *op. cit.*, p. 309.
[2] Cole, *op. cit.*, p. 50.

bodies that resulted from the new form of organization adopted in 1918.[3]

In short, as these figures show, the great growth in trade union membership was a necessary condition for the growth of the Labour Party which, its strength more efficiently mobilized by the new constitution, was able to field 361 candidates in the General Election of 1918, as compared with only 78 and 56 in the two elections of 1910. The results of the election of 1918 tell the same story of a major advance, constituting a qualitative change in the power position of the movement. Although the number of Labour M.P.'s returned was only 60, the total vote for Labour relative to that of other parties showed an immense increase. The percentage of total vote won by the Labour Party had shown only slight gains before the war : 5.4 in 1906, 8.1 in 1910 (January), and 7.7 in 1910 (December). Then, in the 1918 election, it rose to 23.9, continuing upward to reach 30.0 in 1922, when the party became the leading Opposition party in Parliament.

The *entente* with the Liberals, explicit in 1906 and tacit in 1910, had depended upon Labour's ability to put forward only a modest number of candidates. How could this relationship have been maintained when the immense growth in trade unionism meant that the party would present not a few score, but several hundred candidates? How could Labour have avoided a broad nationwide electoral challenge to the Liberals? One possibility would have been for the Liberals to have refrained from putting up candidates in scores, even hundreds of constituencies, in the expectation that Liberal voters would support the Labour candidate. Labour presumably would have done the same in some equivalent number of cases. But can one conceive of the middle and upper class personnel of the local Liberal associations abdicating in this manner and on such a scale in favor of working-class candidates? And if they had, the effect would have been not so much cooperation as fusion. Nominally, of course, the possibility of fusion was open under the formal organization of the local Liberal parties. Theoretically, trade unionists could have joined and, where they won a majority, have nominated whoever they pleased for Parliament. But in practice, as previous experience had shown, the middle- and upper-class leaders of the local caucuses would resist any such implementation, however logical, of the

[3] In 1918, under the new constitution, the number of local bodies rose to 398, of which 73 were trades councils and 325 political. Cole, *op. cit.*, p. 50.

theory of Radical democracy on which presumably their extra-parliamentary organization was founded.

These speculations are merely intended to direct attention to the fundamental and hardly obscure fact that in Edwardian and post-Edwardian Britain class antagonism drew a bold line through British politics. "In the world of Edwardian England," Alan Bullock writes, "an impassable gulf still separated the man in a cloth cap from the classes born and educated to conduct the affairs of State."[4] The middle- and upper-class leaders of local Liberal associations were happy to cultivate the votes of the working class. They would have them as members of the caucus so long as they did not try to assert a claim to leadership. They were even ready to go far toward recognizing the "interests of labour," as was shown when Liberal Councils welcomed measures of social reform introduced by their Governments at the instigation of Labour. They refused, however, to share their power.

This refusal goes back to the days of Lib–Lab politics. Hardie, MacDonald, and Henderson had all personally experienced it. The decline of the Labour Electoral Association resulted from its inability to get Liberal caucuses to adopt working-class (i.e., trade unionist) candidates, a failure that turned the thoughts of many labor leaders toward a separate party. Moreover, the *entente* established between the two parties by MacDonald and Gladstone was severely limited in scope and time. It depended, as we have seen, on the weakness of the Labour Party. It lasted, even in a tacit and attenuated form, only through the elections of 1910. Thereafter, as Cole has observed, the Liberal associations were not prepared to allow Labour men any further seats; indeed, they were disposed to reclaim seats which had been held by Lib–Labs. On the eve of the war, collaboration in the constituencies had virtually ceased to exist.[5]

This refusal by local Liberals to accept greater representation for the organized working class either by means of Lib–Lab or outright Labour candidates was recognized and lamented by some Liberal leaders.[6] But they themselves made no great effort to

---

[4] *The Life and Times of Ernest Bevin*, Vol. I, p. 27.
[5] Cole, *British Working Class Politics 1832–1914* (London, 1941), p. 224.
[6] In 1892 Herbert Gladstone admitted, "The long and short of it is that the constituencies, for social, financial and trade reasons are extremely slow to adopt Labour candidates." Quoted in Pelling, *The Origins of the Labour*

bring Labour men into the inner circle of power. Apart from
John Burns—and by 1906 his ties with organized labor were
tenuous—no trade unionist was given ministerial office before the
war and only minor posts were offered Shackleton and other
trade union officials.[7] The Liberal leaders in Westminster were
no more willing to share power at their level than the local Liberals were at theirs.

Trade unionists had good reason to regard the caucus as "a
middle class machine."[8] But one should not neglect the independent force of the demand among the organized working class
for a political instrument of their own. They too were class
conscious, and did not merely react to the middle-class rebuff;
they also were increasing, as trade unionism grew, their demand
for political power as a class. Some remarks of Ernest Bevin's to
a group of employers during the war reflect these sentiments.
The subject was industrial relations, not politics, but Bevin's
rugged language gave voice to this strong sense of separateness
in identity and destiny :

> I had to work at ten years of age while my employer's son went to
> the university until he was twenty. You have set out for me a different
> set of conditions. I was taught to bow to the squire and touch my
> hat to the parson; my employer's son was not. All these things have
> produced within me an intense hatred, a hatred which has caused me
> to organise for my fellows and direct my mind to a policy to give to
> my class a power to control their own destiny and labour.
>   . . . At present employers and employed are, too often, separated
> by something akin to a barrier of "caste." . . . The operatives are
> frequently regarded by employers as being of a different and inferior
> order. . . . So long as these views continue to exist they inevitably
> produce an intense class bitterness.[9]

In Edwardian and post-Edwardian Britain there was the normal
clash of interest between employers and employees. But one may

---

Party 1880–1900 (London, 1954), p. 237. In 1901 Gladstone, by now Liberal
Chief Whip, wrote : "I could come to terms with the leaders of the Labour
party. . . . The difficulty lies with the constituencies . . . and the unfortunate
necessity of providing funds." Quoted in Bealey and Pelling, Labour and
Politics 1900–1906 : A History of the Labour Representation Committee
(London, 1958), p. 131.
    [7] Roberts, op. cit., p. 242.
    [8] So characterized by Threlfall, the leader of the Labour Electoral Asso-
ciation, in 1894. Pelling, Origins of the Labour Party, p. 236.
    [9] Quoted in Bullock, op. cit., Vol. I, pp. 69 and 70.

doubt whether this clash alone would have sufficed to maintain the divorce between Liberals and trade unionists. After all, even when trade unionists had accepted Gladstonian economics, they found it impossible to win a place of equality in the Liberal Party. Throughout the generation before 1918, whether wages were high or low, the unions gaining or losing, government favorable or unfavorable, the nation at war or at peace, the strong sense of class—on both sides—powerfully reinforced the clash of interest, preventing any unity closer than a transient and limited collaboration. Given such a division of sentiments, it is hard to see how the powerful trade union movement, having reached the heights of power that it occupied in 1918, could have failed to break definitively with the Liberals and make its separate bid for political supremacy.

The adoption of Socialism as an ideology was functional to this choice of political independence. If the party was to pursue power independently, it needed a set of beliefs and values distinguishing it from other parties. For the sake of its own followers, present and prospective, the party had to articulate in its declaration of purpose the profound sense of difference—or if you like, alienation—that sprang from their consciousness of class. In 1918 there still were, to be sure, a few labor leaders who favored not a Socialist, but only a "trade union" party. Such a party championing traditional union interests and some broader social reforms might have been viable. But such a party purpose and program would have retained strong ideological links with the Radical wing of the Liberal Party. In the constituencies it would have made a sharp electoral challenge to the Liberals far more difficult. It could never have provided, as Socialism did, the intellectual basis for the missionary zeal that party activists displayed in the years ahead. One can only agree with the wisdom of Arthur Henderson when he concluded in 1917 that "some sort of Socialist faith was the necessary basis for the consolidation of the Labour Party into an effective national force."[1]

THE SOCIALIST VIEW OF CLASS

Yet to see why the strategy of independence required a distinctive party purpose is not to understand fully why that purpose

[1] Cole, *History of the Labour Party*, p. 60.

had to be the Socialism that I have described as Labour's "orthodoxy." The nature of British trade unionism—the way unions
ran their own affairs, their approach to relations with employers
and, of course, their previous political traditions—meant that
revolutionary alternatives were excluded and that the party program would be democratic, constitutional, and gradualist. It
would also, of course, include advocacy of "the interests of
labour." Moreover, the practices and sentiments of British trade
union life—all that is connoted by the word "solidarity"—meant
that party adherents would favor a vision of society that promised
a closer and more intimate community among men. No doubt
also their sense of alienation and class exclusion prepared them
to demand not merely amelioration, but a radical reconstruction
of the "system." All these elements were present in the Socialist
faith, deriving from both the I.L.P. and the Fabians, that was
adopted in 1918.

That there was such a "fit" between the needs of an independent
party and the Socialism it adopted in 1918 does not mean that
this ideology was merely an "efflux" or "echo" of those needs.
For decades British Socialism had been developed by intellectuals
of various persuasions. (Indeed, as we shall have occasion to remark, its great creative period came to an end about the time that
Labour made its choice of an ideology.) Those of the S.D.F.
elaborated a strongly Marxist and revolutionary theme, which
found and continued to find little response among the organized
workers. Moreover, the theories developed by I.L.P. and Fabian
intellectuals included elements that do not have the same immediate and direct "fit" with trade union experience and needs
as those elements previously mentioned. Such, for instance, was
the doctrine of "common ownership" that Socialist intellectuals,
following the old tradition of their creed, made central to the
British version. This doctrine was compatible with the trade union
value of "solidarity" and gratified the demand of the alienated
for a new "system." Other doctrines promising equal solidarity
and novelty were conceivable. But in a long series of pamphlets,
speeches, and books the philosophers and propagandists of Socialism had made common ownership the basis of the theory which
the Labour Party, like Arthur Henderson, found at hand, ready
for adoption, when it sought a faith that would enable it to
become "an effective national force." From this viewpoint,

Labour's adoption of Socialism was the product, on the one hand, of the necessities impelling the party toward independence and, on the other, of the alternatives offered by British political culture.

If we are looking for reasons that made Socialism appropriate to trade unionism as a political faith, we can hardly give more importance to any aspect of the ideology than to its conception of class. If the sense of class was as strong as I have contended it was, then the Socialist view of the working class as the foundation for a party that would lead the whole nation to Utopia was bound to meet with a powerful response among organized workers—once they reached for the power to rule. Here was a rationalization for the thrust for power that could hardly be bettered. It instilled pride and confidence in class, yet also promised to all men a society which, if it could be realized, would fulfill ancient ideals of British and indeed European civilization.

That British Socialism had such a conception of class may seem simply to reflect the fact that its intellectual founders had observed, and in some cases experienced, the fact of class division and even class conflict. I by no means deny this. There was, as I have emphasized in discussing the relations of the Liberals and the trade unions, a sense of separate class identity and a clash of classes in Britain. I would, however, also insist that once Labour had adopted Socialism, the sense of class among its adherents was still further heightened. Again, Socialist ideology did not merely reflect existing sentiments, it also added to and intensified them. From the conditions of their life and the old hierarchic values of British culture, workers derived a sense of being a social class. From trade unionism, they acquired a sense of being a separate economic class. Socialism provided a definition of the situation that endowed many of them with the further belief that they were also a separate political class.

The previous pages have raised the question of why the Labour Party adopted Socialism in 1918. They have suggested that the answer is to regard this decision as a consequence of the more basic decision to "play for supremacy" taken by the organized working class. The crucial decision, embodied in the new constitution and new frame of organization, was this thrust for power. The adoption of Socialism was incidental to this decision. Verbally the party had chosen "independence" as its foundation. But an independence that could aim at supremacy was made possible only by the great organizational strength of trade unionism reached by 1918. And once organized labor had achieved this position of power, its decision in favor of the new strategy was hardly a matter for deliberation and free choice.

It is against the background of these larger developments that one must view the particular events, such as the "doormat incident," which led to the decisions of 1918. The new balance of social forces gave Henderson the power and indeed the incentive to respond as he did. Even if the "doormat incident" had been patched up or had never taken place, one can hardly believe that Labour would not have chosen the new strategy of independence. Similarly, the experience of wartime Collectivism undoubtedly provided evidence to support arguments for state intervention. But the organized working class and its leaders did not merely infer that certain programs of amelioration of the existing system were now practicable. Indeed, they made quite the opposite inference, leaping to the conclusion that the whole system could and must be altered. Something more than the interests of labour, enlightened by the practical lessons of the war, was at work in their motives. A class—or more precisely, the organized section of a class—was asserting its claim to power.[2]

If this analysis of the decisions of 1918 is correct, it raises various interesting suggestions about the later history of the Labour Party. One is the possibility that if the thrust for power was the main driving force behind the adoption of Socialism, it might be expected that when and as power was won by organized labor, the concern with Socialist ideology would decline. We shall examine this possibility in Chapter VII.

[2] For this analysis, as applied specifically to the miners, see below, Ch. VI, pp. 164-70.

CHAPTER VI

The Socialist Generation:
The Power Structure

During the generation 1918–48, the Labour Party was an ideological and programmatic Socialist party based primarily upon the organized working class. Within these main conditioning forces of purpose and power, the party developed. They did not wholly or mechanically determine that development. The party had an organizational life with its own autonomy. Individuals and groups put forward new ideas and contested positions of influence. But these events occurred within the broad framework of Socialist purpose and trade union power.

ELITISM WITHIN CONSENSUS

It is from this perspective that one needs to look at the question of elitism in the party. In the interwar period the party acquired leadership in quite a new sense, as compared with prewar days. The most striking change was, in R. T. McKenzie's phrase, "the emergence of the Leader." Before the war the parliamentary party had elected a "chairman" at each session, the post, as we have seen, often changing hands. The choice of the title was deliberate, as it was the sense of the party, Snowden recalls, that "the Sessional Chairman should not be the 'Leader.' It was considered undemocratic. The party must not permit one man to dictate policy."[1] In practice, as we have observed, the parliamentary party acted very largely as the agent of the extra-

[1] *Autobiography*, Vol. I (London, 1934), p. 218.

parliamentary organization. While its chairman served as spokesman, he was in no position "to dictate policy." After the election of 1922, when Labour became the second largest party, there occurred a change in title, MacDonald being elected "Chairman and Leader" of the parliamentary party. Thereafter the leader of the parliamentary party came to be regarded as the leader not only in Parliament, but also in the country. The election manifesto of 1924, for instance, was signed by MacDonald as "Leader of the Labour Party."[2] Moreover, as in the older parties, there emerged alongside the Leader a small body of his chief lieutenants who would very probably occupy, and often had occupied, high Cabinet posts. This constituted the parliamentary leadership—for instance, the group that Dean McHenry, referring to the period 1922–31, called "The Big Five" : MacDonald, Snowden, Henderson, Thomas, and Clynes.[3] But what did the Leader and the parliamentary leadership actually do? What was their role in the internal power structure of the party and the Movement?

There are many functions that a party leader may perform. In the words just quoted, Snowden singled out the question of his influence over policy. If we take these words broadly, they pose the crucial question : How far does the Leader, or leadership, determine the ends the party pursues and the methods by which it pursues them? To what extent does he (or do they) have the power to shape the party purpose?

Looking at the Socialist generation as a whole, one is prompted to make two observations of basic fact. In the first place, the party's purpose—what I have called Labour's orthodoxy—was rarely called into question either by the leadership or by any substantial section of the party. Throughout this period there was a broad consensus in the party on ideology, program, and strategy. Hence, the question that the elitist hypothesis poses— that is, the question of power between leaders and party—hardly ever arose in a serious form. In the second place, however, when this question was raised by action of the leadership, it was met and mastered by a strong counterthrust from the trade unions. The identity of purpose running from the commitments of 1918 to the manifesto of 1945 consisted not only in a fidelity to Socialist ideology and gradualist strategy. It also involved a re-

[2] McKenzie, *British Political Parties* (London, 1955), p. 311.
[3] *The Labour Party in Transition : 1931–1938* (London, 1938), pp. 139–41.

markable similarity of detail among the many statements of party program. This similarity has been noted by more than one historian of the party. "*Labour and the New Social Order*," G. D. H. Cole wrote, ". . . is seen to contain in substance by far the greater part of what has been put forward in respect of home policy in subsequent Labour Programmes, and of the actual policy which the Labour Government of 1945 began vigorously to carry into effect."[4] Similarly, Henry Pelling has said : "*Labour and The New Social Order* . . . was of great importance because it formed the basis of Labour Party policy for over thirty years—in fact, until the general election of 1950."[5] To be sure, emphases were altered and in some instances items were deleted or added over the years, as we shall have occasion to observe. But the list of industries to be nationalized and the scheme of ameliorative reforms to be enacted changed very little. Moreover, the minor theme of Labour's orthodoxy, its "principles of socialist foreign policy," showed hardly less continuity. The faith in international organization and the rejection of balance of power politics can be traced in major party pronouncements from the *Memorandum on War Aims* of 1917 to *The International Post-War Settlement* of 1944, and remained strong even in the first years after World War II.

In the nineteenth and early twentieth centuries, Socialist thought in Britain, as well as in Europe generally, had engaged some of the liveliest minds of the time and produced some of the most imaginative criticisms of the social order. This period of growth came to an end about the time the Labour Party adopted its particular synthesis from the Socialist tradition. During the interwar years the party had its eloquent and humane advocates, such as Cole, Laski, and Tawney, but the seminal minds of the generation—a J. M. Keynes, for instance—were not among them. Reread today, the party pronouncements of the time have strongly Victorian overtones. Such continuity in purpose (such archaism, if that is not too severe) is especially striking in view of the enormous and critical changes taking place at the time in the British economy.

In any case, this consensus on purpose deeply qualified the

---

[4] *History of the Labour Party from 1914* (London, 1948), p. 56.
[5] *A Short History of the Labour Party* (London, 1961), p. 44.

new elitism as well as the old and continuing pluralism of the organization. Where all major elements, whether leaders or followers, whether Right or Left, were so much in agreement, serious questions of power were not raised. The decisions independently taken by leaders and the issues that arose between them and sections of the party did not, on the whole, touch the fundamentals of purpose. Similarly, the initiatives taken by groups within the party to maintain or alter items of program were only variations on an agreed design. Indeed, such a consensus, one may argue, was a necessary condition for the emergence of leadership. For now there was a corpus of principle and program whose acceptance by leaders could be taken for granted; they did not need continually to be instructed by the organization, but could be trusted with wide discretion in meeting the exigencies of prolonged and intense political combat. Likewise, the pluralistic democracy of the party, similarly conditioned by agreement on fundamentals, could continue without endangering party cohesion. The existence and function of such consensus need to be emphasized because it did not characterize the party in its early years, nor in the decade of crisis that supervened in the 1950's.

THE ROLE OF THE LEADER

When the Labour Party came on the scene, British constitutional practice had already endowed a Prime Minister with certain well-understood elements of authority and these, in turn, strengthened the position of a party Leader who, although in Opposition, was a potential Prime Minister. When, for instance, a party Leader was summoned by the monarch to accept the commission to form a Government, the Leader made his own decision whether to accept and, if he accepted, what persons to select for his Cabinet. In Cabinet meetings, while he might "take the voices" on a controverted question, he was not bound to accept the majority view: after all, he had the authority to secure the dismissal of any minister. Similarly, the decision on the resignation of the Government or a request for the dissolution of Parliament was his sole decision. In all these cases, of course, the Leader faced certain realities—the existence, for example, of colleagues with strong personal followings or with helpful executive skills. And in his decisions to accept office, form a Cabinet, resign, or dissolve he would usually choose to consult informally with colleagues. Constitutional norms, however, left him free to take these decisions by his sole authority and without consulting anyone (except the monarch), and certainly without seeking instructions from his party organization.

During the interwar period efforts were made from time to time in the Labour Party to restrict the Leader's exercise of these traditional prerogatives.[6] This aim could well be considered a logical deduction from the plain words of the party constitution, which could be taken to legitimize arrangements such as those that prevailed under the "caucus" system in the Australian Labour Party. On the whole, however, these efforts failed, and on the three occasions between 1924 and 1945 when a Labour Leader took office as Prime Minister his procedure in accepting the King's commission, making a Cabinet, presiding over it, and deciding on a dissolution was in accord with the usual practice.[7]

These are not unimportant decisions and the authority to make them endowed the Leader of the Labour Party with powers well beyond what he gained from the party constitution and Labour's official theory of its structure of authority. Yet a party Leader could exercise these powers and still not exert a decisive influence on his party's goals or strategy. British constitutional norms leave a great deal to circumstance and can fit quite different structures of effective power and influence. In assessing the effec-

[6] McKenzie discusses these efforts in detail. For instance, conference resolved in 1929 that the Cabinet should be selected by the Parliamentary Labour Party (McKenzie, op. cit., p. 315) and in 1932 that Ministers should be subject to decisions of the P.L.P. (p. 320). In 1933 a resolution was passed providing that a Labour Prime Minister, in forming his Cabinet, should consult with the Secretary of the Party and three M.P.'s elected to advise with him; that a Labour Prime Minister should be subject to majority decisions in the Cabinet; and that he should recommend the dissolution of Parliament only on the decision of the Cabinet confirmed by a meeting of the P.L.P. (p. 321).

[7] In 1924 MacDonald consulted with no one when deciding who was to hold what Cabinet office and ranged widely outside his party in making his ministerial selections. Again, in 1929, although when allocating offices he took counsel with Snowden, Thomas, Clynes, and Henderson, his decisions were subject to no outside instructions. Likewise in 1945 Attlee accepted the King's commission and chose his Cabinet on his sole authority. He did not follow the procedure envisaged by the conference resolution of 1933 (see above note 6) and comments: "I am quite sure that the method of the Australian Labour Party, whereby a number of members are elected by the Caucus and all that is left to the Prime Minister is to fit the pieces into a jigsaw puzzle as best he may, is quite wrong." As It Happened (London, 1954), p. 156.

tive power of the Leader of the Labour Party during the Socialist
generation the case of MacDonald is crucial, as it is obvious that
his influence over the party greatly exceeded that of any of his
successors—Henderson, Lansbury, and Attlee. If we can find
limits on his scope of decision, we shall have located the outer
boundaries of the Leader's power in that period.

On what questions of party purpose did MacDonald exercise
a determining influence? A major question that divided the party
in the 1920's and 1930's will illustrate both the extent and the
limits of his effective power. This was a question inherent in
the position of an ideological and programmatic party confronted
with the prospect of taking office while still in a minority. Should
it introduce "some bold Socialist measures"[8] which would lead
to its defeat, but which could then be made the basis of an appeal
to the country? Or should it attempt only those ameliorative
reforms which might be expected to win the support of Parliament and which would also help the party to show that it was
"fit to govern"? MacDonald's preference was clearly for the
latter alternative, and throughout his period of leadership he
had his way in spite of opposition from sections of the parliamentary and extra-parliamentary parties.

In 1924 this choice was weighed by the inner core of the
parliamentary leadership—MacDonald, Snowden, Thomas, Henderson, and Webb—who decided against the "extreme policy."[9]
Criticism of their choice was voiced while the party was in
office and in later years merged with the initiative taken by the
I.L.P. for *Socialism in Our Time*, the title of its 1927 policy
statement the principal proposal of which was for a "Living
Wage." What the I.L.P. demanded was not only that the party
adopt these proposals, but also that any future Labour Government, even though in a minority, should base its immediate policy
upon them, deliberately inviting defeat in order to make a further
appeal to the country. MacDonald and the parliamentary leaders
continued to prefer the tactic of 1924, which was implied by the
less restrictive program offered by them in *Labour and the Nation*.
At the conference of 1928, when this program was adopted, they
easily beat down the I.L.P. challenge[1] and again the 1929 Government embarked on the more prudent course.

[8] Snowden, *Autobiography*, Vol. II, pp. 595–6.
[9] *Ibid.*
[1] By a vote of 2,780,000 to 143,000.

Although in the long run the MacDonald tactic was designed to promote Labour's pursuit of supreme power, in the short run it qualified the policy of political independence by entailing, in effect, that the Government would introduce only those measures which a substantial body of Liberals would support. During MacDonald's day this choice of tactics involved the parliamentary leaders in a sharp, running controversy with important sections of the party in which the views of the leaders, whether in or out of office, were upheld by conference and accepted by the parliamentary party. For the sake of argument, let us grant the elitist case and agree that the Leader "imposed" his answer to this question upon the party. The essential point remains, however, that the controversy was over tactics and did not bring into question the fundamentals of Labour's orthodoxy. For all its militant language, the I.L.P. accepted the strategy of winning power and achieving Socialism by democratic, parliamentary means.[2] Moreover, in the context of Labour's received doctrine and program, there was nothing particularly radical about the content of the "Living Wage" proposals. If, therefore, we wish to cite this controversy as an example of the influence of the parliamentary elite, we must also recognize that it did not involve the fundamentals of the party's purpose and that the alternatives the leadership chose among fell well within the boundaries of the consensus on ends and means. Even in the era of Mac-Donaldism, and with regard to its major controversy, elitism in the Labour Party extended only to questions of tactics, not strategy, and involved variations on an agreed design in program, not fundamental alterations.

The limits imposed on the elite by the party consensus are seen even more clearly if we turn to the major instance when the Leader overstepped those limits. This was, of course, Mac-Donald's agreement to form a National Government in 1931. He and Snowden had not been able to carry the Cabinet with them in accepting the 10 per cent cut in unemployment benefits that the New York banks had made a condition of a loan to support

[2] Only during the last stages of its break with the Labour Party did the I.L.P. depart from this strategy when, at its conference of 1932, it called for "mass industrial action" as an additional means of winning power, along with democratic, parliamentary methods. Cole, *History of the Labour Party From 1914*, p. 276.

sterling.[3] For although a majority of the Cabinet favored acceptance, the minority who would resign was so substantial that
MacDonald concluded that he could no longer carry on the
Government.[4] A measure such as the proposed cuts struck at
the party's ancient commitment to the "interests of labour." The
General Council of the T.U.C. had firmly informed Snowden of
its opposition and the parliamentary party had on the whole
been strongly against.[5]

The party's ability to resist its Leader on this question of social
policy, however, was exceeded by the virtual unanimity of its
negative when MacDonald attempted to lead it into coalition. In
the Cabinet, for instance, while MacDonald was able to find
eleven of its twenty-one members who would follow him on the
unemployment cuts, he could bring along only three in support
of the National Government.[6] This is understandable. For if the
party had gone into a National Government, it would have meant
not only supporting an attack on the "interests of labour," but
also a major reversal of the basic commitment of 1918 to a
strategy of political independence.

"Evidence of practical unanimity in the Party is growing,"
wrote Hugh Dalton the day after MacDonald had informed his
astonished Cabinet of his decision to lead a National Government.
"Press estimates of J. R. M.'s Parliamentary following rapidly
falling. How ignorant of our Movement the enemy Press is!"[7]
The Press, and perhaps even the King, had expected a large
defection to MacDonald, who himself had thought that about
half the parliamentary party would follow him.[8] In the ensuing
general election MacDonald did attract many who otherwise

[3] Hugh Dalton, *Call Back Yesterday* (London, 1953), pp. 271–6; Harold
Nicholson, *King George The Fifth : His Life and Reign* (London, 1952),
pp. 460–4; Charles L. Mowat, *Britain Between the Wars, 1918–1940* (London,
1955), pp. 379–93.

[4] Mowat, *op. cit.*, pp. 392–3. But see Reginald Bassett, *1931* (London, 1938),
pp. 85–94.

[5] After recording in his diary the hostile reaction of the General Council
of the T.U.C. to Snowden's proposal to reduce the period during which
unemployment benefit would be paid, Dalton continues : "This is not the
kind of thing that *we* can do. Better keep the Party together in opposition
than break it up, and disappoint all the deep, simple hopes of our supporters."
Call Back Yesterday, pp. 269–70.

[6] Mowat, *op. cit.*, pp. 392–3.

[7] Dalton, *op. cit.*, pp. 271 and 274.

[8] Pelling, *A Short History of the Labour Party*, p. 68.

would have voted Labour, and the party's poll fell by two million as compared with 1929. But the organized party remained solid. Only three ministers—Snowden, Thomas, and Sankey— and a tiny handful of M.P.'s followed the leader, all of whom the N.E.C. duly expelled.[9] Not a single constituency organization or trade union budged.

Judging by the previous behavior of other British parties, such solidarity was unprecedented. For a decade MacDonald had enjoyed a vast ascendancy over the party in Parliament and in the country and Snowden and Thomas, his principal associates in the decision of 1931, had for years belonged to the innermost circle of the political elite. It is hard to believe that either of the older parties could have suffered such a defection among its leaders without being split from top to bottom. Indeed, the National Government tactic of which Neville Chamberlain was the "constructive engineer"[1] is reminiscent of a similar maneuver in which the Conservatives, by accepting the leadership of Lloyd George for a short while after World War I, helped enormously to widen the schism among Liberals and hasten the decline of that party. If a similar effect was indeed intended in 1931 by the Conservatives, like the "enemy Press" they showed themselves gravely ignorant of the "Movement."

The similarity of response among the various sections of the Movement—parliamentary party, General Council, and N.E.C., constituency organizations and trade unions—can be understood only in the light of Labour's deep-running commitment to the strategy of political independence. But the original organizing force, the trade unions, also came into play. During the days of crisis the General Council, and especially its dominating personality, Ernest Bevin, took critical initiatives in the disavowal of MacDonald and the settlement of a new political line.[2] Moreover, in succeeding years the center of leadership moved away

[9] On the 28th of September, 1931. *Ibid.*, p. 73.

[1] Keith Feiling, *The Life of Neville Chamberlain* (London, 1946), p. 193. While reporting Chamberlain's thoughts during the interparty consultations that preceded MacDonald's resignation and the formation of the National Government, Feiling records that Chamberlain realized "politically how urgent it was to get an all-party agreement and, tactically, how desirable to split the Labour Party."

[2] See Alan Bullock, *The Life and Times of Ernest Bevin* (London, 1960), Vol. I, p. 489.

from the small and weakened parliamentary party toward the trade unions. "The General Council of the T.U.C. under the leadership of Bevin and Citrine," writes Pelling, "abandoned its usual role of being the sheet-anchor of the party and instead moved in to take the helm."[3] The National Council of Labour, which represented the party and the unions, but on which the unions had a majority, laid down the outlines of policy.[4] Within these outlines the National Executive worked out detailed programs for a Labour Government. Under this new balance in the party elite, all elements of the party accepted without controversy the new statements of party program set forth in *For Socialism and Peace* (1934) and *Labour's Immediate Programme* (1937). These, however, although more precise and definite than *Labour and The Nation*, involved no fundamental innovations.

In the 1930's another threat to Labour's orthodoxy was raised, when members of the intellectual elite of the party attempted, particularly through the Socialist League, to commit the party to a United Front with the Communists or to a Popular Front with a broad range of representatives of other parties as well as the Communists. These efforts, however, which again endangered the strategy of political independence and at times also had strong anti-parliamentary overtones, were easily defeated, with the union leadership playing a major role.[5]

In the same period, the menace to peace of the Fascist powers raised the issue of sanctions. This prospect of a use of force in which Britain might take part created problems that were difficult for the party's anti-militarists and impossible for its pacifists. Again the unions, and especially Bevin, exerted a weighty influence on the major decisions, such as the repudiation of Lansbury's pacifism at the conference of 1935 and the acceptance of rearmament by the parliamentary party in 1937, by which the party adjusted to the new international situation.[6] Important as these adaptations were, they fell within the boundaries of Labour's internationalism,

---

[3] *Op. cit.*, p. 77.

[4] *Ibid.*, p. 79. See also Alan Bullock, *op. cit.*, Vol. I, p. 512.

[5] Pelling, *op. cit.*, p. 83.

[6] *Ibid.*, p. 84. Technically, the P.L.P. switched from voting against the Defence estimates to abstaining. Dalton, *The Fateful Years* (London, 1957), pp. 133–6.

in particular its long-standing commitment to collective security under the League.[7]

In short, although the union leadership "moved in to take the helm" after 1931, it used its influence to keep the party on the same broad course in domestic and foreign affairs on which it had embarked in 1918. The scope of the union elite in MacDonald's day was limited by the consensus on Labour's orthodoxy. Bevin himself enjoyed great personal influence thanks to his remarkable personal capacities as well as his position as head of one of the largest trade unions. But he was able to push the party only in directions in which it was already committed to move by long-standing commitments. His power was by no means dictatorial. In spite of his best efforts, we should recall, he was unable to secure the election of Arthur Greenwood as Leader in 1935.

PLURALISM WITHIN CONSENSUS

To speak of "pluralism within consensus" may seem curious, if not self-contradictory. If the various groups in the party were agreed on program and purpose, their activity in favor of some goal would be in harmony with the intentions of others : hence, whoever the spokesmen, the ends pursued were common to all and an apparent pluralism is swallowed up in an actual monism. Such indeed was very generally the case with the flourishing

---

[7] The acceptance of rearmament by the party in 1937 has been termed a "fundamental alteration in Labour policy" by Francis Williams in his *Ernest Bevin* (London, 1952), p. 189. No doubt this change, which Dalton and Bevin worked together to bring about, ran against strong anti-militarist emotions and old hopes for peace. But the party had long been committed to collective security under the League. Dalton argued that it was illogical to ask the Government to stand by collective security, yet refuse approval of the forces with which to carry out this policy. *The Fateful Years*, p. 138. Similarly, the resolution that Dalton moved at the Conference of 1936 defended rearmament in the name of collective security : "This Conference declares that the armed strength of the countries loyal to the League of Nations must be conditioned by the armed strength of the potential aggressors." His opponents did not deny Dalton's premise, but tried to contend, in Morrison's words, that "this Government's armaments policy is a purely competitive national armaments policy." *Ibid.*, p. 101. For the P.L.P. to abstain from voting against the Defence estimates, as Dalton finally persuaded it to do in 1937—which meant in effect accepting the need for rearmament—was not, therefore, a "fundamental alteration" of policy, but a logical adaptation of a long-standing party policy to the situation created by the rise of powerful aggressor nations.

pluralistic democracy of Labour during the Socialist generation.
Vast numbers of resolutions were moved at party conferences in
these years and normally were voted with unanimity. This was
quite natural, since they were for the most part restatements of
familiar declarations.

Yet the agreement on purpose was not wholly clear, detailed,
and unchanging. Occasionally new items were added to the
received program and old proposals were developed and adapted.
Sometimes new proposals were raised, briefly accepted, then dis-
carded. In these interactions the activity of groups was often
important. Even where an item of program was commonly accepted in the party, pressure from a group might greatly help
maintain it in a position of high priority. As with the elites, groups
within the party were limited and guided by the party consensus.
But in the maintenance of that consensus and in such development
as it underwent, group activity was a significant force.

Mines Nationalization to 1918

No single case is typical, but the proposal for the nationalization
of the coal mines will illustrate some aspects of the relationship
between group activity and Labour's orthodoxy. One can imagine
two quite opposite ways by which the proposal might have gotten
into the Labour program. One is to suppose that first came the
conversion of the party to Socialism and then the application of
the new ideology to the particular case of the coal industry. In
this case initiative and support would come not from a group
with any special interest, such as the miners, but from Socialists
with their broad concern for the whole society. A different possibility is that the proposal originated from the practical experience
of the miners. Taught by that experience that their desires for
better wages, shorter hours and safer and more healthful working
conditions could not be met under existing economic arrangements, they gradually concluded that private ownership was the
source of the difficulty and only some form of common ownership would provide remedies. In this case the initiative would come
from the miners who would continue to keep the proposal in
the forefront of the party's priorities.

The actual process by which miners and party became committed to mines nationalization combined both these possibilities.
Pressure from the miners played an important part in ensuring

that mines nationalization would be included in Labour's program. At the same time, the Socialist perspective provided a framework through which they interpreted their experience and identified the causes of, and remedies for, their grievances, while the common commitment to Socialism furnished continuing support for their demands within the party and the labor movement.

The idea that the mines should be nationalized was first put forward by Socialists, and it was Socialists who took the initiative in advocating it within the Miners Federation and the T.U.C. in the late nineteenth and early twentieth centuries. The doctrine of nationalization was, of course, part of their common stock of ideas, but the intellectual advocates of Socialism were not the first to apply the doctrine to the coal industry. In the Fabian essays of 1889, for instance, public ownership of the mines is not specifically mentioned.[8] In those days, as Sidney Webb later recalled,[9] the Fabians talked about nationalization only in general terms; their first publication specifically concerned with public ownership of the coal industry appears to have been a tract reprinting the nationalization bill submitted by the Miners Federation in 1913.[1] Nor was Hyndman more in the vanguard with specific proposals. In *England for All* (1881), while calling for public ownership of the railways, he advocated for the mines, as for factories and workshops generally, only "supervision" by the state and in *The Historical Basis of Socialism* (1883), mines nationalization is only implied.[2]

[8] It could be inferred that Fabians favored it. Annie Besant, while saying that the state would take over the great centralized industries, also commented: "All minerals would most properly be worked in this fashion." *Fabian Essays*, Jubilee ed. (London, 1948), p. 146.

[9] In his introduction to the 1920 reprint of the *Fabian Essays*.

[1] This was a Fabian pamphlet, "The Nationalisation of the Coal Supply," outlining a plan and making the case for public ownership, published in July, 1916, in *How to Pay For The War*. This pamphlet was the basis for the resolution moved at the party conference in 1917 by Robert Smillie. But by this time the miners and the labor movement generally were strongly committed to mines nationalization. The Fabians, in short, were important: 1) as a source of the general doctrine of nationalization and 2) as a source of more detailed proposals, once the idea of mines nationalization had been accepted by the miners.

[2] *England for All* (London, 1881), p. 107. In *The Historical Basis of Socialism* (London, 1883), p. 467, Hyndman wrote: "That the land, and with the land, mines, rivers, etc., will come under the control of the people we have already seen, nor is it reasonable to suppose that any compensation will be given to the land-holders, the fund-holders, or the railway or water

One of the first, if not the very first, to make specific mention of the mines as a proper object of nationalization was a man who was both a miner and a Socialist. In the July, 1887, issue of *The Miner*, Keir Hardie sharply criticized the Lib–Lab leadership of the time and in contrast outlined the kind of program he thought the Parliamentary Committee of the T.U.C. ought to have been supporting. Along with such measures as the eight hour day, working class housing, payment of M.P.'s, adult suffrage, free education, local option, and abolition of food taxes, his program called for immediate nationalization of land, railways, minerals, and mines.[3] Again it was by Socialist miners that the proposal was first brought forward within the trade union movement. At the T.U.C. of 1892, William Small and Robert Smillie, associates of Hardie in Scotland, moved a resolution in favor of mines nationalization which was passed unanimously and without debate.[4] In the Miners Federation the initiative was taken two years later by Tom Greenall, a young Socialist from Lancashire. Although the President of the Federation, Ben Pickard, was a stanch Liberal who had made his opposition clear at the start of the conference, Greenall's resolution that "the best interests of the nation will be served by the nationalization of the mines of the country" was passed after "a long and animated debate."[5]

The Socialist origin of the proposal needs to be stressed because in certain restricted cases nationalization was advocated on Liberal grounds. The nationalization of land and of minerals could be justified by Ricardian economics and, what was more important in the late nineteenth century, by the ideas of Henry George, whose *Progress and Poverty*, published in 1879, had great influence among Radicals. Similarly, a Liberal might accept the need for public ownership of the railways and canals because they were monopolies, as did Winston Churchill at one time when he was a Liberal.[6] But mines nationalization, as Arnot has observed, was "put forward in the early days as part and parcel of the general So-

---

share-holders. . . . In the end the entire power and means of production will belong to the State or its delegates, who will then be like the State itself, simply one great body of equal men organized in concert, with leaders chosen by themselves."

[3] Emrys Hughes, *Keir Hardie* (London, 1956), p. 37.

[4] T.U.C. *Report* 1892, p. 70.

[5] R. Page Arnot, *The Miners: Years of Struggle* (London, 1953), p. 128.

[6] Herbert E. Weiner, *British Labour and Public Ownership* (London, 1960), p. 6.

cialist programme, and not on the ground that mining was in a special position in relation to the British economy."[7]

The fact, however, that mines nationalization was recognized to be a Socialist proposal does not mean that its acceptance by union conferences marked their conversion from Liberalism. After 1892 the T.U.C. itself from time to time voted resolutions to this effect. Sometimes the resolution included a list, usually some combination of land, minerals, mines, railways, and canals; on occasion it called comprehensively for collective ownership of all the means of production.[8] But as we have already observed, the trade unions did not make their serious commitment to Socialism until World War I. Beginning in 1916, demands for nationalization came with a rush, covering many industries and embedded in a system of proposals for comprehensive reform of "the pre-war industrial stystem."[9]

Similarly, the Miners Federation after 1894 frequently expressed an opinion favorable to nationalization of the mines.[1] Their views on the organization of the economy, however, were much more accurately reflected in the words of Ben Pickard than in those of Keir Hardie. At the conference of 1894 when the question was first raised, Pickard declared :

I am not a mines nationaliser. I don't think that if the mines were nationalised the miners would be a penny better off than they are today. The crux of the whole question affecting miners is not as to

[7] Arnot, *op. cit.*, p. 132.

[8] For example, in 1893 the T.U.C. accepted an amendment that candidates who would receive financial assistance from a proposed election fund should pledge themselves "to support the principle of collective ownership and control of all the means of production and distribution." In 1894 Hardie secured the passage of an amendment calling for the nationalization of the means of production, distribution, and exchange. In 1895 an attempt to repudiate Hardie's amendment of the previous year was ruled out of order and a resolution was passed in favor of the nationalization of land, minerals, and railways. In 1896 a resolution was passed in favor of nationalization of land, mines, minerals, royalty rents, and railways, as well as the municipalization of water, artificial light, and tramways, it being understood that this resolution would take the place of Hardie's more comprehensive resolution of 1894. Thereafter nationalization resolutions are fairly common in the T.U.C.

[9] T.U.C. *Report* 1916, p. 250.

[1] For example, a resolution for nationalization of land, mines, and railways was passed in 1897; for nationalization of land, mines, minerals, and railways in 1902; for nationalization of production, distribution, and exchange in 1904 and 1905; for nationalization of mines and minerals in 1906. Arnot, *op. cit.*, pp. 128–9.

whom the mines belong, but as to how the coal should be sold which is produced in the mines and brought to the surface for public use.[2]

In view of the militancy, political as well as industrial, for which the miners were noted during the interwar years, we have to remind ourselves that they were among the stanchest supporters of Liberalism well into the first decade of this century. For this reason, when the Miners Federation finally affiliated with the party in 1909, many Socialists regarded this gain of adherents for the party as a grave setback for their hopes of converting Labour. Bernard Shaw later recalled:

I had said repeatedly, when the Miners Federation joined the Labour Party, and put money and an overwhelming card vote into it, Socialism would have to take a back place in the Party, and the term Socialist would come to mean no more than the term Christian after the Edict of Constantine.[3]

These fears proved to be groundless. In the years just before the war, the miners were turning away from their traditional Liberalism and toward Socialism.[4] As in the case of trade unionism generally,[5] this shift of sentiment and purpose among the miners coincided with their reaching a new peak of power and success. The Federation now included the hewers' trade unions in every coal field, wielded the largest single vote inside the T.U.C., and exercised a strong and growing influence on Government and Parliament.[6] Coal was an expanding industry, the number of miners in Great Britain increasing from 600,000 in 1891 to 1,000,000 in 1911, and output reaching its all-time peak of 287,000,-000 tons in 1913. The membership represented by the Federation, which had stood at 185,000 in 1894, had risen to nearly 600,000 in 1910.[7] Industrial militancy on the eve of the war had substantially pushed up wage rates and had helped win the Minimum Wage Age of 1912. The Federation, in Arnot's words, "had become a power in the land."[8]

[2] *Ibid.*, p. 128.
[3] *Ibid.*, p. 125.
[4] *Ibid.*
[5] See above, Ch. V, pp. 143–9.
[6] Arnot, *op. cit.*, p. 19.
[7] Arnot, *The Miners: A History of the Miners' Federation of Great Britain, 1889–1910* (London, 1949), pp. 305 and 393; Robert A. Brady, *Crisis in Britain* (Berkeley, 1950), p. 96.
[8] Arnot, *The Miners: Years of Struggle*, p. 19.

As the miners turned toward Socialism, the familiar resolution on mines nationalization began to be taken seriously. It was no longer a "pious hope," a mere "expression of opinion." In succeeding years the miners continued to keep the question before the T.U.C. and the Labour Party. In 1913, on the motion of Herbert Smith of the Miners Federation, the Labour Party conference voted without controversy to instruct Labour M.P.'s "to seize every opportunity to press forward . . . the Bill to Nationalise the Coal Mines."[9] In 1917 Robert Smillie, president of the Miners Federation, although not a member of the party's Executive, moved on its behalf a comprehensive resolution for mines nationalization based on a Fabian pamphlet of the preceding year.[1] This resolution was passed unanimously and without discussion. In the long series of resolutions for nationalization and socialization approved by the T.U.C. in 1918, the resolution pertaining to mines and minerals was moved in the name of the Miners Federation. The mover, J. Robinson, could tell delegates that "it is a very long while since we convinced ourselves that this step would be to a great advantage to us as miners in particular and to the general community."[2] Following a vote of the miners conference of the same year, a new and more elaborate bill, including provisions for joint control by workers and the state, was drawn up and introduced in Parliament.

By the latter years of the war there was no doubt of the miners' firm and serious support for public ownership of the mines and their ardent commitment to Socialism and the Labour Party. It was a foregone conclusion that Webb and his subcommittee would include the "immediate" nationalization of the mines in the program set forth in *Labour and The New Social Order* in 1918 and in the conference resolutions based on it.

In the process by which the Labour Party became committed to nationalization of the coal industry, the pressure of a powerful trade union was obviously an important force. At the same time, there was another and broader change taking place—the conversion of the trade unions to Socialism. It was upon this broad movement of sentiment and opinion that the success of the miners in

[9] 1913 *LPCR*, p. 109.
[1] "The Nationalisation of the Coal Supply," in *How To Win the War* (1916). 1917 *LPCR*, p. 117.
[2] T.U.C. *Report* 1918, p. 176.

winning the approval of the party for mines nationalization depended. Both group pressure and a general change of ideology in
the movement were necessary conditions for the result.

Mines Nationalization 1918–46

During the interwar years, both forces continued to condition
the party's attitude toward this question. Indeed, they were
strengthened by the state of the industry, which after the short
postwar boom fell into a chronic slump. Whether Socialists were
moved by considerations of equity for the miners or of efficiency
for the national economy, the necessity to nationalize the industry
was in their eyes only more and more clearly demonstrated. At
the same time, reductions in wages enforced by lock-outs, as in
1921 and 1926, along with unemployment, which in 1932 reached
34 per cent of the labor force in the industry, sharpened the
miners' militancy which, along with claims for relief of their
immediate grievances, focused intensely on the demand for public
ownership.

In 1919 the threat of strike action by the miners in support of
their demands for not only higher wages and shorter hours, but
also nationalization, secured the appointment of the Sankey Commission. But when, in spite of the majority report in favor of
public ownership, the Government refused to nationalize the
mines, the miners were unable to win the support of the T.U.C. for
"direct action" to enforce their demand and could only join with
the T.U.C. and Labour Party in the "Mines For the Nation"
campaign of political education. From the propaganda used in this
campaign the miners' representatives drew that stock of arguments, which they persistently repeated at subsequent party
conferences. The demand for nationalization, the former general
secretary of the Miners Federation, Frank Hodges, wrote in 1924,
"has now a peculiar and special place in the general ideology of the
Labour Movement. . . . It is now generally accepted that the first
task of industrial reconstruction which would follow the advent
of a Labour Government, *based upon a majority vote*, would be
to nationalise mines and minerals."[3] The proposal was, of course,
included in the broad policy statements *Labour and The Nation*
(1928) and *For Socialism and Peace* (1934) and in *Labour's Immediate Programme* (1937).

[3] *Book of the Labour Party* (1925), pp. 3–4.

Throughout World War II the miners continued to urge nationalization as a means of meeting the wartime problems of the industry. With the support of the General Council of the T.U.C., the Labour Party—whose principal leaders were now members of the Churchill Government—refused to press the demand at that time. But in the manifesto of 1945 coal was put at the head of the list of industries to be taken into public ownership and by July, 1946, the Coal Industry Nationalisation Bill had been enacted. By this time not only the Labour Party, but also by far the larger part of parliamentary and informed public opinion had accepted the necessity for public ownership and the bill went through the House with hardly more than token opposition.[4] Over the years, however, pressure from the miners had kept this demand in the forefront of the party's priorities. "It would have been unthinkable," Roy Jenkins has said, "at any time since 1918 for a programme to have been put forward for a majority Labour Government which did not include a proposal for giving miners the change of ownership which they had been demanding so passionately and for so long."[5] Indeed, the demand for nationalization voiced by the miners and their union had by 1945 become "so irresistible that no government, whatever its political convictions, could have allowed matters to continue as they were under private ownership."[6]

Iron and Steel Nationalization

While coal was the first industry to be nationalized by Attlee's Government, iron and steel was the last, a difference in timing that reflected a difference in party priorities. As in the case of coal, both the attitude of the industry's union and the party's general commitment to public ownership had been major factors in determining that nationalization of iron and steel should have a place, although a lower place, in Labour's priorities. The initia-

[4] "Support for the principle of public ownership of the mines is now very wide, extending probably to two and a half of the three parties." *Economist*, August 18, 1945, p. 220. "The owners have been given every encouragement to put the industry on a rational basis; they have failed to do so. . . . The necessity for nationalisation is generally accepted." *Economist*, November 17, 1945, p. 712.

[5] *Pursuit of Progress* (London, 1953), p. 71.

[6] William A. Robson, *Nationalized Industry and Public Ownership* (Toronto, 1960), p. 31.

tive had been taken by the Iron and Steel Trades Confederation, an amalgamation of unions in the industry formed at the end of World War I. At the T.U.C. of 1931, it successfully moved a resolution proposing that the industry be brought under the control of public utility corporations which would ensure that it would be nationally planned and efficiently organized. At the party conference a month later, a general resolution on Trade Policy moved by the Executive declared that "the most important basic industries" (in which iron and steel was included) should be reorganized in the form of public utilities, as proposed by the Iron and Steel Trades Confederation scheme. From the debate at both meetings it is clear that the union, although committed to public control, had not yet made up its mind about public ownership.[7] The party Executive accordingly tried to keep open its options. On the one hand, its resolution referred to "public utilities on the basis of National Ownership"; on the other hand, the mover allowed that at least for a transitional period the public utility form might not involve public ownership.[8] This was not the main focus of the debate which, at the party conference as at the T.U.C., centered on workers' control. An I.L.P. delegate, however, did ask for a more definite commitment to nationalization. When this delicate Socialist nerve was touched, the Executive instantly responded. "The question of public ownership and control was never at stake," its spokesman assured the conference; and "a form of words" would be found which "completely" covered the objection.[9]

In the following years, as the world depression deepened, this ambiguous initiative was merged in the rising concern of both party and trade unions with the broad problem of reorganizing Britain's economy. In the early 1930's the principles of nationalization as an instrument of planning and control were worked out in some detail and embodied in schemes for individual industries, of which iron and steel was one.[1]

[7] At the T.U.C. the resolution did not specify public ownership, nor was the question raised in the debate. At the party conference, Walker of I.S.T.C. objected to the words "public ownership," preferring the term "public utility," and stated that the public utility form might or might not involve public ownership. 1931 *LPCR*, p. 200.

[8] 1931 *LPCR*, p. 197.

[9] *Ibid.*, p. 204.

[1] See the general report, entitled "The Public Control and Regulation of Industry and Trade," adopted by the T.U.C. in 1932. T.U.C. *Report* 1932, pp. 206–19.

Both party and T.U.C. cooperated in this work, but the accepted protocol left with the unions the principal initiative and a power approaching that of veto. Starting with the I.S.T.C. proposal of 1931, the Economic Committee of the General Council developed a scheme which was presented to the T.U.C. in 1934 as a "Report on the Socialisation of the Iron and Steel Industry,"[2] and which clearly provided for public ownership.[3] Only now that union approval had been given did the party again turn its attention to the question. At the conference of 1934, a proposal for nationalization of iron and steel was included in the new statement of party program, *For Socialism and Peace*. This proposal was based on the T.U.C. scheme, and in resisting amendment by conference the Executive spokesman emphasized that since both the union and the T.U.C. had accepted the proposal in its existing form, the party ought not to make alterations.[4]

The nationalization of iron and steel, one could now fairly say, was part of Labour's "program."[5] This did not mean, however, that within the party and T.U.C. it enjoyed the continuous and urgent advocacy that was given to the nationalization of coal. While iron and steel nationalization was made a pledge of the election manifesto of 1935, it was omitted from *Labour's Immediate Programme* of 1937. In 1944 the T.U.C.'s *Interim Report on Post-War Reconstruction* included iron and steel in the long list of industries to be nationalized. And Dalton—against the wishes of some members of the N.E.C.'s Policy Committee—slipped an approving reference into his report on full employment.[6] On the

[2] T.U.C. *Report* 1934, pp. 189–205.
[3] The plan had been drawn up in the first instance by I.S.T.C., James Walker having a large hand. Later there had been discussion and agreement with the Policy Committee of the N.E.C. and the Economic Committee of the General Council of the T.U.C. Dalton, *The Fateful Years*, pp. 53n, 73n.
[4] The Socialist League had offered an amendment providing that there be direct representation of workers through the union on the Iron and Steel Corporation and that the chairman of the corporation be a minister. Asking conference to reject the amendment, James Walker, also a member of the N.E.C., said : "I am asking you on behalf of the Executive to reject this amendment, first of all for the reason that what we are asking you to adopt today is the plan that was passed, without amendment, by the Trades Union Congress at Weymouth this year." 1934 *LPCR*, p. 201.
[5] In the formal sense that, as required by Clause V of the Party Constitution, it had been approved by a majority of not less than two thirds of the conference and in the more important sense that it had gone through the mill of trade union and party inquiry and approval.
[6] Dalton, *The Fateful Years*, p. 422.

other hand, from 1934 to 1944 there had been no serious reference to the matter at either the party conference or T.U.C.

CONFERENCE AND MANIFESTO

It is in the light of this history that one needs to examine the process by which nationalization of iron and steel came to be included in *Let Us Face The Future*, the party manifesto for the 1945 general election. The events are particularly interesting as they suggest the extent, and at the same time the limits, of the influence on policy that the party conference could exert during the Socialist generation.

At the conference of 1944, postponed from June to December because of the invasion, a main piece of business was the discussion of several reports on postwar policy. One, entitled "Full Employment and Financial Policy," had been drafted by Hugh Dalton and approved by the executive "with only a few small amendments."[7] The adoption of this report along with a summarizing resolution was moved by Emanuel Shinwell.[8] To this resolution Ian Mikardo, on behalf of the Reading Trades Council and Labour Party, moved an amendment that would commit the party to including in its election manifesto a list of industries to be taken into public ownership—"land, large-scale building, heavy industry, and all forms of banking, transport, and fuel and power."[9] The Mikardo amendment had been composited from twenty-two resolutions which sprang from a concern, voiced at previous conferences, that the party make such specific pledges. Although the Executive asked Mikardo not to press his amendment to a vote, he persisted and the conference, its Socialist nerve touched as in 1931, supported him so overwhelmingly that there was no call for a card vote.[1]

In this instance of successful insurgency, the initiative had been taken by a delegate who was not yet an M.P., member of the Executive or recognized leader of the Left. Such occasions, however, when the "rank and file" beats "the platform," are not too hard to find in the history of Labour Party conferences. The important question is : what effect did this formal decision of conference have on policy? In particular, were the pledges of the

7 *Ibid.*
8 1944 *LPCR*, p. 160.

9 *Ibid.*, p. 163.
1 *Ibid.*, p. 168.

manifesto of 1945, because of the Mikardo amendment, significantly different from what they would otherwise have been?

That the amendment specifically mentioned land, the Bank of England, transport, and fuel and power was a matter of no great consequence. These were long-standing items of party program that the Executive had reaffirmed in recent policy reports[2] and which in any case would have appeared in the manifesto. On the other hand, there was, in spite of the Mikardo amendment, virtually no chance that the joint stock banks or building industry would be listed in the manifesto as candidates for public ownership. In the past, the nationalization of joint stock banks, as well as the Bank of England, had been voted by conference, a proposal that had briefly been accepted by the Executive. But the leading party authorities on finance, first Snowden and then Dalton, had opposed it, and during the previous ten years, statements of policy had proposed only "control."[3] Public ownership for the building industry had enjoyed even less support, the Executive having easily defeated an attempt at the 1943 conference to include a proposal for public ownership of "the building and civil engineering trades" in its resolution on postwar housing and town planning.[4] Accordingly, *Let Us Face The Future* promised, with regard to the joint

[2] On transport, fuel, and power, see 1944 *LPCR*, pp. 158 and 171. On the Bank of England, see Dalton's report, cited above p. 174, n. 7, and "The Labour Party and The Future" in 1943 *LPCR*, p. 4. On land, see "The Labour Party and the Future" and N.E.C. Resolution on Housing and Town Planning, 1943 *LPCR*, pp. 202 and 205.

[3] In 1928 conference approved a supplement to *Labour and The Nation* that provided for public ownership of the Bank of England. In the debate both Snowden and Dalton declared their opposition to nationalization of joint stock banks. 1928 *LPCR*, pp. 232, 236. In 1932, on the initiative of an I.L.P. spokesman, conference beat the platform by so amending a resolution for nationalization of the Bank of England as to include joint stock banks. 1932 *LPCR*, pp. 188, 194. And in 1933 Dalton, for the N.E.C., presented a scheme for carrying out this resolution. 1933 *LPCR*, pp. 171-4; Dalton, *The Fateful Years*, p. 45.

According to a party brochure of 1935, however, while the Bank of England was to be nationalized, commercial banking would be subject only to "control." *Labour's Financial Policy* (1935), p. 15. The manifesto for the general election of 1935 vaguely proposed public ownership for "banking." Dalton, *The Fateful Years*, p. 73. *Labour's Immediate Programme* (1937) proposed nationalization only for the Bank of England, as did Dalton's report on Full Employment in 1944.

[4] 1943 *LPCR*, pp. 202-205. At the 1944 conference another N.E.C. resolution on the same subject would only go so far as to promise that "a directly employed national building organization" would be created "where the public interest demands."

stock banks, only to "harmonise" their operations with industrial needs and, with regard to the building industry, only to take "drastic action" to ensure its efficiency.

The case of iron and steel—which everyone understood was the meaning of "heavy industry" in Mikardo's amendment—was intermediate : the prospects of its being included in the manifesto were neither fully assured nor entirely hopeless. In this situation the influence of a conference vote might be determining. Hugh Dalton's memoirs give us a glimpse of what happened.

Early in 1945 the N.E.C. appointed a small campaign committee to take charge of preparations for the coming election.[5] Morrison was put in the chair, his primary duty being to draft a policy declaration. "This I did," he recalls, "and gave it the title of 'Let Us Face The Future.' "[6] The committee gave Morrison "plenty of elbow room," but on April 11th, according to Dalton, there was "a row."

> Morrison proposed, supported by Greenwood, to back down on iron and steel, and leave it out of the Policy Declaration. He had been lunching, he said, with some friends of ours in the City, who had told him that it was too ambitious to talk of any Public Board "owning" this complicated and troublesome industry. I strongly resisted this, and won. I said that, if iron and steel was dropped, I should refuse to speak in support of the Policy Declaration at Conference, and then Morrison and Greenwood could explain to the delegates why this item, which had been enthusiastically adopted by Conference only last December, had now vanished.[7]

The threat to appeal to the forthcoming conference was Dalton's weapon; the fact that conference had strongly and recently made its mind known put this weapon in his hand. In short, the insurgency of conference in December was very probably responsible for the heavy commitment that the manifesto's declaration in favor of "public ownership of iron and steel" imposed on the Labour Government. Yet, we must immediately observe, con-

[5] The Campaign subcommittee consisted of Herbert Morrison (Chairman), C. R. Attlee, Ellen Wilkinson, Arthur Greenwood, Hugh Dalton, Tom Williamson, H. J. Laski, Mrs. B. Ayrton Gould, and W. W. Henderson (Secretary). This was "a strong and representative sub-committee," as it included the chairmen of the Policy, International, Organisation, Finance, and Press and Publicity subcommittees of the N.E.C. 1945 *LPCR*, p. 15.

[6] *Herbert Morrison : An Autobiography* (London, 1960), p. 232.

[7] Dalton, *The Fateful Years*, p. 432–433.

ference had this influence only with regard to an item that had long since gone through the mill of trade union and party inquiry and approval. Formally, the Mikardo amendment also made nationalization of building and banking items of the party "program." Operationally, this aspect of the conference decision was meaningless. Conference exerted influence only with regard to an item which, although not enjoying a high priority, had been at least on the margin of Labour's orthodoxy.

Moreover, the decision of conference had influence only on the condition that it find a weighty advocate among the party elite. Once the draft had gone through the N.E.C. and had been published, there was little real opportunity to change it. Having been sent out to unions, local parties, and other affiliated organizations in April, the statement was the basis for a three-day discussion at the conference which met at Blackpool, May 21–25. Conference debated and approved the statement section by section, but its procedure did not permit amendments to be offered. To be sure, resolutions were moved and some were passed against the advice of the platform. But, although the Executive said that it would "take account of" any resolutions passed,[8] they were not considered to be amendments to the manifesto, which emerged from conference and went to the public in exactly the form given it by the N.E.C. The crucial and only moment for bringing to bear the influence of conference had been seized and utilized by Dalton in February.[9]

Conference took seriously the ultimate authority over program with which the party constitution endowed it. Leaders and rank and file delegates alike accepted this premise of party action. Over the years, however, the constitution had acquired a complex gloss, a system of expectations that defined and legitimized the role of

[8] 1945 *LPCR*, p. 103.
[9] Dalton himself stresses the importance of his "obstinacy." Referring to the Cabinet discussions in 1947 of Morrison's proposal for a system of control over iron and steel that fell short of nationalization, and which the Cabinet finally rejected, Dalton writes: ". . . Gordon Walker was emphasizing to George Brown two nights ago—Morrison's P.P.S. [Parliamentary Private Secretary] to mine—that this whole trouble was my fault, owing to my obstinacy on the National Executive and its Policy Committee. It was my fault that iron and steel was in our programme at all at the last election." "This was quite true," he concludes, "as I have related elsewhere"—and he gives a reference to the "row" in 1945 which has been reported above. Dalton, *High Tide and After: Memoirs 1945-1960* (London, 1962), p. 251.

conference and other elements of the party in the making of policy. As the history of the iron and steel proposal illustrates, this gloss legitimized a degree of pluralism not specified in the constitution. In particular, it included great deference to the wishes of a trade union in matters concerning its industry. The initiative in bringing the proposal for public ownership of iron and steel before the movement was exercised by I.S.T.C. But this special role of the union was not simply the product of group pressure. It was clearly part of the accepted protocol of decision-making in the party. Once, however, the proposal had been included in Labour's orthodoxy, it could be legitimately advocated by party members in general.

The previous analysis of party decisions does not by any means suffice as a complete description of this complex system of expectations with which the constitution had been glossed. One must attempt to ascertain some of these premises of party action, however, if one is to say when conflict did or did not arise between conference and leadership. The plain words of the Mikardo amendment, for instance, stipulated that the election manifesto was to include the building industry and all banks as candidates for public ownership. Yet it is quite clear that conference did not feel that it had been "defeated" or "overridden" when they were omitted. At the 1945 conference, during the debate on that section of the manifesto pertaining to nationalization, a resolution in almost the same terms as the Mikardo amendment was moved. After the reply by Shinwell, speaking for the N.E.C., however, the resolution was withdrawn without fuss or objection.[1] More interesting is the reaction of Mikardo himself to the omission of these two items. Immediately after Morrison introduced the draft, Mikardo welcomed it as "a good and workmanlike job," the result of "a successful partnership between the decisions of the last Conference and the results of studying just how much work is involved in controlling Britain's economy and nationalising Britain's industry and just how much of that work we can expect to do in our first five years of power."[2] Mikardo's opinion expressed in a letter to the author also shows his lack of concern over the omissions. "Of course, I wasn't . . . much disturbed by the fact that some points covered by my resolution were not included in *Let Us Face The Future*. When one defeats the N.E.C. one is quite happy with a 90 per cent victory!"

[1] 1945 *LPCR*, pp. 134 and 138.   [2] 1945 *LPCR*, p. 92.

A PROGRAMMATIC PARTY IN POWER

Elitist and pluralist theory direct attention to important features of the structure of power of the Labour Party between 1918 and 1945. The roles of leaders and of groups, however, were limited and guided by a consensus within the party on both broad principles and items of program. In this sense the behavior of the party was a function not of the independent decisions of leaders or of the pressure of groups and balancing of interests, but of a widely shared programmatic commitment.

What shall we say of the party after the election of 1945, when for the first time it won a majority in Parliament and a full five-year lease on office? One can readily see different possibilities. The attempt to plan the economy might well intensify group pressures that ran contrary to the party's programmatic commitments. Similarly, the complex and changing actualities of home and foreign affairs, one might think, would often oblige Labour ministers to make decisions on major matters that were not anticipated by the party program and which could not sensibly be referred for decision to the party conference. In view of these highly plausible questions, does the model of the programmatic party give us much help in understanding the behavior of the Attlee Governments of 1945–51? Does program explain the basic decisions of these years?

When we examine the legislative record of the Government, the answer is emphatically "yes." The statutes in which it embodied its purposes of social and economic reconstruction were derived directly and by deliberate intent from the party program. The framing and carrying out of these statutes were, of course, affected by the advice of experts, the suggestions of civil servants, the demands of interest groups, and the personal preferences of ministers. But the main fact remains : to an extent unprecedented in British political history the legislation of a Government was dictated by a party program.

In the first place, the legislation of the Government was deliberately based upon the pledges of the manifesto of 1945. "It was on the basis of this policy document," Herbert Morrison has written, "that the majority Labour Government set about shaping both its legislative programme and its work of administration."[8]

[8] *Government and Parliament* (London, 1954), p. 222.

The Future Legislation Committee, of which he was chairman, had the task of deciding what bills would be introduced during each session. It acted on the assumption, Morrison relates, "that subject to unforeseen circumstances we would seek to implement the legislative aspects of *Let Us Face The Future* within the lifetime of a single Parliament."[4]

How well the Government succeeded one can readily see by going through the Public General Acts of 1945–50 and comparing the promises of the manifesto with the major statutes put on the books. It is no great exaggeration to say that for every paragraph of pledges one finds a corresponding statute. The items are familiar, but it is well briefly to recall the principal ones in order to have a sense of the magnitude of the accomplishment.

In the manifesto Labour promised to bring under public ownership the Bank of England, the fuel and power industries, inland transport (by road, rail, air, and canal), and the iron and steel industry. This it did in seven statutes : the Bank of England Act of 1946, the Coal Industry Nationalisation Act of 1946, the Civil Aviation Act of 1946, the Electricity Act of 1947, the Transport Act of 1947, the Gas Act of 1948, and the Iron and Steel Act of 1949.

In fulfilling the pledge of "great national programmes" of social services, the Government consolidated and extended the social insurance scheme by the National Insurance Act of 1946, which provided sickness, unemployment, and retirement benefits as well as maternity grants, widows' pensions, and death grants, and by the Industrial Injuries Act of the same year. The National Assistance Act of 1946 covered the destitute not provided for, or not adequately provided for, by national insurance. The National Health Service Act of 1946 nationalized almost all hospitals and set up a free and comprehensive medical service. In seeking to carry out its promises with regard to housing—the goal was "a good standard of accommodation for every family in this island"—the Government enacted important legislation, such as the Rent Control Act of 1949 and the Housing Acts of 1946 and

---

[4] *Ibid.*, p. 224. When opening the second reading debate on the Bank of England Bill, the first nationalization measure of the Attlee Government, Hugh Dalton began : "I hold in my hand a document entitled 'Let Us Face the Future, a Declaration of Labour Policy for the Consideration of the Nation.' The nation considered it and having done so elected this House of Commons. We have an unchallengeable popular mandate to carry out all that is contained in this document." Dalton, *High Tide and After*, p. 40.

1949. The Children Act of 1948 helped fulfill the pledge of "better child welfare services."

Corresponding to the party's pledge of a "radical solution" to the problems of land acquisition and land use, the Town and Country Planning Act of 1947 nationalized development value, restricting the owner's interest in land to its existing use and transferring to the state the exclusive right to financial benefit from the development of land. To the farmers Labour promised "stable markets" and a "fair return" : by the Agriculture Act of 1947 it established a system of "assured markets and guaranteed prices." A first step toward the promised "supervision of monopolies and cartels" and prohibition of "anti-social restrictive practices" was taken by the passage of the Monopolies and Restrictive Practices (Inquiry and Control) Act of 1948.

In line with long-standing party policy, the manifesto advocated "taxation which bears less heavily on the lower-income groups" and Labour's Chancellors maintained from wartime, and in some respects sharpened, a steeply progressive scheme of income taxation. To the list of major legislation one should also add the Supplies and Services (Transitional Powers) Act of 1945, which contained many of the wide powers over the economy that the Government had exercised during the war and which gave it, in Morrison's words, "appropriate authority for the economic planning and control which we regarded as essential if we were to achieve a successful transition from war to peace."[5]

Pledges of legislation were not the sole content of the manifesto. Its first and major pledge of full employment—"Jobs For All"—was understood to depend both upon structural reforms achieved through legislation and upon administrative and fiscal policies. The manifesto also gave attention to international affairs. But much as it stressed the importance of keeping the peace, its proposals in foreign policy were few—and its hopes rosy—by far the greater part of the program being concerned with home affairs.

If promises and performance in the field of legislation are compared, Attlee was fully justified in claiming, when he went to the country in February, 1950, that his Government "had carried out the programme which we had put forward at the last General Election."[6] But the Government not only performed

[5] *Government and Parliament*, p. 225.
[6] *As It Happened* (London, 1954), p. 193.

what the party pledged; it also did not go substantially beyond those pledges. One can find important statutes that cannot be traced back to the manifesto—for instance, the Criminal Justice Act of 1948—but they are few. With regard to the Government's legislative record, the manifesto was not only imperative, it was also conclusive.[7]

Herbert Morrison called this record "the most extensive and significant legislative programme in the history of our great Parliament."[8] He could also have said that never before had a Government's actual record of law-making been previously laid out before the country in such completeness and detail by a party seeking office at a general election. Even in the days when Radical influence ran strongly in the Liberal Party, its electoral promises were a far less complete and accurate guide to its Government's actual legislative efforts. As we have seen in Chapter II, the great reforming Government that came to power in 1906 committed itself to a number of important measures—especially those in the field of social reform—which its spokesmen had not anticipated during the election.

Origins of the Program

Labour ministers felt that they were entitled, indeed obliged, to carry out the pledges which their party had made at the election and for which the voters, by sending Labour to Westminster with a majority, had given the Government a mandate. But how did these pledges achieve this status? Who or what made them a program that would be binding on a Labour Government? While the party constitution (by Clause V) gave conference the authority to decide what proposals should be included in "the Party Programme," it provided that the N.E.C. and Executive Committee of the P.L.P. should jointly decide which items from that program should be included in the manifesto for a general election. Binding pledges, in short, were to be determined by the

---

[7] Dalton clearly held that the Government and P.L.P. were confined to the proposals in the manifesto. Referring to the dispute in the Cabinet in 1947 over Morrison's "hybrid" scheme for iron and steel, he writes : ". . . I was quite sure throughout that the Parliamentary Party would never accept it. Nor were they under any obligation to do so, for it was not what was in our election programme, nor in earlier conference declarations on iron and steel." *High Tide and After*, p. 249.

[8] *Government and Parliament*, p. 76.

parliamentary and extra-parliamentary authorities. If there was conflict between leaders and followers or between conference and P.L.P., this requirement of joint determination would be very important. But in a party as fundamentally at one as Labour in 1945, it was superfluous—and in the actual procedure by which the manifesto was authorized was not followed. The P.L.P. as such was not brought into the process by which the manifesto was prepared and approved, and Labour's election pledges acquired their authority exclusively by the action of the extra-parliamentary party.

As we have seen, it was the N.E.C. and its campaign subcommittee that initially drew up and approved the manifesto. Similarly, the debate at conference made it quite clear that the statement was not merely advisory to the parliamentary leadership, but was to be an authoritative control on their action if they won office. Introducing *Let Us Face The Future* for the N.E.C., Morrison called it "Labour's Five-Year Plan" of legislative and administrative work.[9] That these, but only these, promises would be binding on the party was explicit in his warning to candidates that "the Labour Government is not going to meet promises not authorized by the party program."[1] Closing the debate, the conference chairman, Ellen Wilkinson, asked delegates to vote their approval of the manifesto "as a declaration of policy on which we shall go forward to victory at the General Election."[2]

Drawn up and submitted by the N.E.C. and approved by conference, the statement was called "our Election Manifesto" by Attlee,[3] "an election manifesto and programme" by Morrison,[4] "the document on which we fought the last election" by the N.E.C.,[5] and the Labour Party's "main declaration of policy" by the principal students of the election of 1945.[6] Not endorsement by the Leader, by candidates, or by the parliamentary party gave it this status, but the action of the N.E.C. and the annual conference. The point is worth stressing because of the radical difference from Conservative procedure. Moreover, as we have seen,

[9] 1945 *LPCR*, p. 89.
[1] *Ibid.*, p. 91.
[2] *Ibid.*, p. 144.
[3] *Op. cit.*, p. 162.
[4] *Government and Parliament*, p. 222.
[5] 1946 *LPCR*, p. 114.
[6] R. B. McCallum and Alison Readman, *The British General Election of 1945* (London, 1947), p. 47.

such authority was never claimed or exercised by the representative assembly of the Liberal Party of Victorian and Edwardian days, even at the height of Radical influence. Not only in its Socialist purpose, but in its conception of democratic politics, the Labour Party showed itself to be a distinctive type of political formation.

Party Cohesion

As wholeheartedly as their leaders, the parliamentary rank and file accepted the manifesto and the legislative program based on it. Recalling the triumphs of the early days of the Attlee Government, Hugh Dalton exclaimed nostalgically, "Yes, we were all in step then!"[7] With the help of a study of voting in the House during the 1945–6 session, one can put this impression in quantitative terms. Twenty-nine divisions, a sample of one in every ten, were examined. All twenty-nine were party votes in the sense that 90 per cent or more of Labour M.P.'s taking part voted on the same side and, since the Government put on the whips in every case, this meant that all votes were party votes for the Government position. The coefficient of cohesion gives a more exact measurement. In twenty-eight divisions, since there was no cross-voting whatsoever by Labour M.P.'s, this coefficient was 100 per cent.[8] For the whole sample the coefficient of cohesion was slightly more than 99.9 per cent. Tables 6.1 and 6.2 are based on a sample of one in ten divisions.

TABLE 6.1

Party Unity, Session 1945–6

All Divisions*

Index of Party Voting		Coefficient of Cohesion
Labour	100	99.9
Conservatives	95.9	99.0

* The sample for 1945–6 consists of 29 divisions, private bills being excluded.

[7] *High Tide and After*, p. 47.
[8] The exception was the division on the second reading of the Bretton Woods Agreement Bill, when 4 Labour M.P.'s voted against the Government position, 297 voting in favor of it.

Whip Divisions

(A division is counted as a whip division for a party only when that party puts on its whips.)

Index of Party Voting		Coefficient of Cohesion
Labour	100	99.9 (Whips on in 29 of 29 divisions)
Conservatives	100	99.7 (Whips on in 21 of 29 divisions)

TABLE 6.2

Comparison of Party Unity of Liberal Party (Session of 1906) and Labour Party (Session of 1945–6)

All Divisions*

Index of Party Voting		Coefficient of Cohesion
Liberals (1906)	88.2	93.9
Labour (1945–6)	100.0	99.9

Whip Divisions

Index of Party Voting		Coefficient of Cohesion
Liberals (1906)	95.7	96.8 (Whips on in 47 of 51 divisions)
Labour (1945–6)	100	99.9 (Whips on in 29 of 29 divisions)

* The sample for 1906 consists of 51 divisions, of which 1 was on a private bill.

Throughout the life of Attlee's Governments, party cohesion in the division lobbies continued to be virtually perfect. This does not mean there was no dissension. Even during that "annus mirabilis," as Dalton calls 1946, there were at times rebellious mutterings among some backbenchers. At first centering on foreign and defense policy, dissent was fed during the later years of Attlee's regime by disagreements that raised fundamental questions regarding the meaning of Socialism. But that is a story we shall consider in another chapter. With regard to the massive legislative program proceeding from the manifesto of 1945, and with the exception of Cabinet doubts that delayed the introduction of the bill nationalizing iron and steel, agreement in the party at all levels was monolithic.

No doubt many factors played a part in producing and maintaining such unity. In controlling individuals and small groups of dissidents, the large formal powers of discipline with which the party constitution and standing orders endowed party organs were useful. In five individual cases the N.E.C. exercised its authority to expel members from the party and, although the P.L.P. suspended its standing orders—which among other things required M.P.'s not to vote contrary to the decision of the party meeting— the right to withdraw the whip was retained and exercised in such "extreme cases."[9] Leaders were strengthened by their control over the avenues of advancement toward and up the ministerial ladder and such impulses toward rebellion as might exist were powerfully restrained by the prospect that mutiny might help the Tories. But if one imagines these forces removed from the situation and consults the known wishes of M.P.'s, it is obvious that the great bulk of them would have similarly supported the program of *Let Us Face The Future*.

However one analyzes the party—as leaders and followers, as parliamentary and extra-parliamentary, as trade unions and constituency organizations—one finds the same unity of purpose. During the war the main thrust in preparing a program for postwar reconstruction had come from the leaders, and already in 1943 a policy statement submitted by the N.E.C. to conference, entitled "The Labour Party and the Future," embodied the principal proposals of the manifesto of 1945 and, indeed, under much the same headings.[1] Conference had approved this statement as it did the manifesto, and in its *Interim Report on Post-War Reconstruction* of 1944, the T.U.C. had expressed its support for substantially the same proposals. The cohesion on these basic measures of reconstruction that prevailed in the party within parliament and outside parliament under Attlee's regime was essentially the product of the consensus on purpose which had reigned in the party for many years and had been given comprehensive expression in

[9] The expression is Morrison's (*Government and Parliament*, p. 129). The expulsions by the N.E.C., which took place in 1948 and 1949, included four M.P.'s who had deviated to the Left (John Platts-Mills, Konni Zilliacus, L. J. Solley, and Lester Hutchison) and one who had deviated to the Right (Alfred Edwards).

[1] 1943 *LPCR*, p. 4.

the election program of 1945. Thanks to this consensus, and within its limits, the party could act effectively, harmoniously, and coherently. In this sense Attlee's Governments were the culmination of the Labour Party of the Socialist generation. It remained to be seen how the party would behave when it could no longer rely upon such consensus.

"This federal hybrid," R. H. S. Crossman has said of the Labour Party's constitution, "with its ambiguous division of powers, is as unworkable as the constitution of the United States; and here, as there, the test of a leader is whether he can make it work."[2] The comment is just, but it attributes too much to the powers of a leader. The Labour Party, as a party both ideological and internally democratic, worked effectively when and because its various, sprawling parts were united by a strong sense of common purpose. The disruption of that consensus produced a decade of crisis.

[2] *New Statesman and Nation* (June 21, 1961), p. 1010.

CHAPTER VII

Old Ideals
and the New Social Order

For more than a decade after the Attlee Government, the Labour Party was racked by bitter dissension. For a time the conflict centered on Bevanism. But this fierce struggle over the succession, which exploded in public with Bevan's resignation from the Cabinet in April, 1951, and was terminated only with the election of Gaitskell as leader in December, 1955, simply exacerbated and dramatized a fundamental conflict over the purpose of the party. The Labour Party has always been boisterously pluralistic and prone to public quarrels between Left and Right. But the prolonged struggle of the 1950's brought to an end the long-sustained consensus within which the quarrels of the Socialist generation had been contained. It divided the party at every level over the meaning of Socialism in both domestic and foreign affairs. In this sense the crisis was unique and not comparable to the periods of rough passage in the interwar years.

The peculiarities of this crisis depended upon certain traits of the party, especially its commitment to ideology and its democratic structure. In examining this relationship, we must also consider certain features of the contemporary British political system, in particular the new and greater political role of the organized producers groups of a modern economy. The power of these groups was a major force compelling the party to adapt its purposes. In turn this adaptation of party purpose affected the political system, greatly promoting the rise of a new group politics.

The critical period was 1947–50. Labour made its postwar plans, assumed office, and embarked on its tasks of reconstruction with a robust faith that the old orthodoxies would guide it to the Socialist Commonwealth and "A World of Progress and Peace" (the title of the next to last section of *Let Us Face The Future*, which dealt with foreign policy). By the last year of Attlee's regime the party had suffered shocks of experience in both domestic and foreign affairs that had caused the needle of party purpose to swing sharply from its ancient orientation. One might call this a process of decision-making. Certainly, critical choices were made in a brave and intelligent effort to master circumstances. The story of the Government's actions was not a story of drift and inability to choose. Yet the outcome was so little foreseen or intended by the Government, the party, or any leading person that "decision" is a misnomer if applied to the events as a whole from which the new party purpose began to emerge. "Policy determination" describes this process better than "policy decision." Forces with which the old orthodoxies of the party could not cope were shaping British politics.

In this period of British foreign policy the rosy hopes that Labour had entertained of easy and fruitful cooperation with the Soviet Union were dashed by events. But the shock was not merely to the belief that "Left can talk to Left." Where Stalinist Russia was concerned "negotiation" did not resolve conflicts, and the United Nations, confronted by Soviet intransigence and belligerency, could not in fact perform its function of collective security. A Labour Government, therefore, found itself compelled to resort to the detested tactics of balance of power, backed up by military force and directed to the service of vital national interests. These realities challenged fundamentals of Labour's orthodoxy in international affairs, reluctant as many sectors of the party were to admit it and to draw the necessary conclusions for the modification of party outlook.

On both foreign and domestic affairs, the party outlook was affected, and in each sphere—by a curious symmetry—the same period was the turning point. In this account I shall be concerned only with the details of the determination of domestic policy.

ECONOMIC PLANNING AFTER THE WAR

The central change was a shift away from the old commitment to the Socialist Commonwealth and toward an acceptance of the

Welfare State and Managed Economy as the basic structure of policy within which the party would pursue its aims. We can get a closer and sharper view of this change if we will follow the development of the Government's conception of economic planning. For this shift in the way Labour approached its economic task was no minor matter. The old Socialist theory of how the economy could and should operate had been an expression of the party's fundamental ethical and social vision. The term "planning" was not widely adopted by British Socialists until the 1930's. But the essential idea had been expounded when they proposed public administration under democratic control as a substitute for the market as the controlling mechanism of the economy.[1] Public ownership was advocated on various grounds : to equalize wealth, to eliminate the political power of private wealth, to promote democracy in industrial life. But the principal case for it was the need for public control of the economy. In this sense, nationalization and economic planning were logically interdependent in Socialist thought. Of his policy when he took office in 1945, Attlee has said : " "Fundamental nationalisation had got to go ahead because it fell in with the planning, the essential planning of the country."[2] If the faith in economic planning, as Socialists conceived it, could be undermined, the case for nationalization would lose a major support in Labour's ideology. That, in a nutshell, is what happened as a result of the experience of Attlee's Governments.

While British Socialists had always been committed to the general concept of a planned economy, they inherited from the Coalition Government two new systems of technique. One, which was derived from the ideas of Keynes, had been given practical application in wartime fiscal policies, beginning with Kingsley-Wood's budget of 1941, and was being developed as the method

---

[1] For "the individualist system of capitalist production, based on the private ownership and competitive administration of land and capital" (Webb had written in 1918 in *Labour and The New Social Order*), the Labour Party would build up a social order based on "a deliberately planned cooperation in production and distribution" (pp. 3 and 4). A major goal was "a healthy equality of material circumstances." The essential means to such equality, however, was a radical reconstruction of the economic system in which public administration under democratic control took the place of the blind forces of the free market.

[2] Francis Williams, *A Prime Minister Remembers : The War and Post-war Memoirs of The Rt. Hon. Earl Attlee* (London, 1961), p. 88.

of national income analysis.[3] The other, which had been worked out by civil servants as they confronted and coped with the emergencies of the war effort, consisted in a system of quantitative planning utilizing physical controls. Both systems had been used during Britain's vast mobilization of resources for total war, but the overwhelming emphasis in that effort had been on the system of physical planning. The main economic decisions were made in the course of framing quantitative programs which were then carried out by means of physical controls. The central program was the manpower budget, which stated how the total labor force was to be allocated among the chief industries and the fighting services, the principal control consisting of comprehensive powers of industrial conscription and labor direction.[4] The White Papers on national income and expenditure continued to be published from 1941, and financial budgets based on them helped restrain inflation. But the steep decline in the importance of finance was reflected in the fact that for much of the war the Chancellor of the Exchequer was not in the War Cabinet.

In its first years, the Labour Government continued to emphasize physical planning. Certain of the wartime physical controls were surrendered, but in order to implement their quantitative programs, the Government retained a network of controls that included building licensing, import licensing, production controls, materials allocation, price controls on many producers' and consumers' goods, and consumer rationing. The use of physical controls was guided by a series of quantitative programs, or economic "budgets," as had been done during the war. These programs might be concerned with particular problems, such as the balance of payments, investment, or critical resources that were in short supply. The two programs in terms of which the economy

[3] See Richard Stone, "The Use and Development of National Income and Expenditure Estimates," in D. N. Chester, ed., *Lessons of the British War Economy* (Cambridge, Eng., 1951), and E. F. John, "The Recent Use of Social Accounting in the United Kingdom," in E. Lindsay, ed., *Income and Wealth* (Cambridge, Eng., 1961).

[4] See W. K. Hancock and M. M. Gowing, *British War Economy* (London, 1949), Ch. XV, "Manpower." The manpower budget, the authors write, "was, in fact, the only method the War Cabinet ever possessed of determining the balance of the whole war economy by a central and direct allocation of physical resources among the various sectors. . . . At the end of the war, the manpower budgets were the main force in determining every part of the war effort from the numbers of R.A.F. heavy bombers raiding Germany to the size of the clothing ration" (p. 452).

as a whole was analyzed, however, were the budget for national income and expenditure and the budget for manpower.[5] Of these, by far the greater reliance was placed upon the manpower budget. The Government, Attlee told the House in February, 1946, approached the task of working out a plan for dealing with the economic situation "in what is really a new way of attacking the problem. We attacked it from the point of view of manpower rather than of finance—our human resources rather than our financial resources."[6] Accordingly, the *Economic Survey for 1947* laid out the lines of action for the year by first setting forth the economic "objectives" and then listing, industry by industry, the distribution of manpower needed to achieve these objectives.[7] The broad powers of labor direction that had been used in carrying out the manpower programs of wartime had been surrendered, except for arrangements to maintain the existing labor force in coal and agriculture. The Government hoped, however, that it would be able to bring about the desired distribution of labor by various devices, including its controls over material factors, the improvement of conditions in undermanned industries, and not least by the voluntary cooperation of workers and employers.[8]

In 1947—that "annus horrendus" of the Labour Government, as Dalton calls it—inflationary pressures severely strained the British economy, finally obliging the Government to take sharp countermeasures that it maintained in the following years as part of a continuing concern with the problem of "too much money chasing too few goods." In analyzing the reasons for the Government's failure to meet this problem promptly, one may criticize the form of planning organization adopted by Labour in those early years, in particular the failure to integrate the

---

[5] *Economic Survey for 1947* (Cmd. 7046), p. 6.

[6] 419 *H.C. Deb.* 1957.

[7] Paras. 118 and 128.

[8] See the remarks of Cripps when explaining how the "plan" was to be carried out. 434 *H.C. Deb.* 969. There was also more than a hint of a wages policy in Cripps' remarks that, for instance, ". . . the undermanned industries, the less pleasant and heavier industries, must have their conditions improved, so that they become less unattractive"; and that ". . . stress is laid upon the need for having some incentive element throughout the wages structure which will be an inducement to a higher rate of productivity," *ibid.*, 993–4.

Treasury closely with the rest of the planning machinery.[9] Many have tried to find a personal scapegoat in Hugh Dalton who, as Chancellor, has been criticized for not using fiscal policy (not to mention monetary policy) with sufficient vigor.

For the present analysis, the important point is that the conception of economic planning generally shared by the Government, and indeed the party, implied for both the Treasury and finance a secondary role. The Government recognized the danger of inflation, but its conception of planning led to a distinctive way of perceiving the problem and the possible remedies. In essence, the remedy was to hold down prices by direct controls while manpower was built up to the point at which production would eliminate the disparity between supply and demand.[1] Dalton, who thought of planning in the same terms as other ministers concerned with economic affairs, shared this analysis. As one of the ministers charged with preparing the *Economic Survey for 1947*, he considered "our two principal economic anxieties over the next few years" to be "our balance of external payments" and "our production for the home market."[2] These problems were to be met primarily by getting more labor into the export trades and into production for the home market. The principal need in his view was to close "the manpower gap" and, accordingly, in Cabinet he fought to get a reduction in the manpower used by the Armed Services and defense industries.[3] In meeting the problem of inflation, so conceived, finance had its part to play, but it was clearly secondary.

Dalton's budgets of 1945, 1946, and April, 1947, do show remarkably little evidence of being influenced by the new and de-

[9] Hugh Dalton, *Tide and After : Memoirs 1945–1960* (London, 1962), p. 187.

[1] This "manpower-production" analysis of the inflationary problem was expressed, for instance, in the *Statement on the Economic Considerations affecting relations between Employers and Workers* (Cmd. 7018) issued by the Government in January, 1947. Recognizing the inflationary pressure, its solution was to increase production while holding prices and costs steady. The key to increased production was to man up the essential industries, as well as to maintain full employment and raise output per worker. The biggest problem was considered to be the "almost universal shortage of manpower." Similarly, the report of the N.E.C. entitled *Labour for Higher Production*, presented to the party conference in May, 1947, stressed the need to increase output. "In Britain today," Morrison said when presenting it to conference, "the battle for Socialism is the battle for production" (p. 137).

[2] *Op. cit.*, p. 195.

[3] *Ibid.*, pp. 193, 198.

veloping techniques of national income analysis.[4] For this approach
to fiscal policy, his personal views were no doubt in part responsible. He was (one might infer from his memoirs) more interested
in the social than the economic consequences of financial and
monetary policy. Certainly, the cheap money policy with its
promise of "the euthanasia of the rentier" was very much a personal policy.[5] Also, the massive economic dislocations of the immediate postwar period no doubt would have required a high
degree of physical planning by any Government. At the same time,
we must note that the Government's conception of economic planning, with its de-emphasis of money and finance and its preference
for dealing with physical resources, drew strong support from the
ancient Socialist faith in public administration rather than the
market.[6] If we wonder why a Socialist did not take up wholeheartedly the national income approach, it may be instructive to
recall that Keynesian theory, from which this approach derived,
was intended by its author to save capitalism.

The Shift to Economic Management

Between 1947 and 1950 the Labour Government's approach to
economic affairs was radically transformed. At the heart of this
transformation was the shift from the manpower budget to the
financial budget as the principal means of guiding the economy.
This change did not occur suddenly; nor did it coincide with the
succession of Cripps to Dalton as Chancellor of the Exchequer
and to Morrison as the minister principally in charge of economic

[4] In his April 1947 budget speech, for instance, he did consider the danger
of inflation and the worsening balance of payments. But unlike later Chancellors—and indeed, unlike wartime Chancellors—he made no effort to estimate
how far savings would cover investment and to propose specific steps for
closing the "inflationary gap," nor did he examine systematically the interdependence of investment, consumption, and the foreign balance and fit his
budgetary proposals into the resulting analysis. As a Conservative backbencher, A. C. M. Spearman, said in the budget debate, Dalton did not
consider "the vital matter," namely the need for "balancing total national
production and expenditure," 436 H.C. Deb. 372 (15 April 1947).
[5] High Tide and After, p. 182.
[6] As expressed, for instance, by Tom Sargant, when moving a Keep Left
resolution at the 1947 party conference : "Socialist economics mean seeing
and dealing with our problems as a whole in real physical terms, with all
the money-juggling, all the manoeuvres for private profit, all the waste of
duplicated effort, cut down to a minimum." 1947 LPCR, p. 138.

affairs. The first stage was the rise, and after some delay the acceptance by the Government of the "disinflationary" analysis of Britain's economic problems, which involved a major emphasis on the national income approach as the framework for dealing with these problems. The second stage was the withering away of the manpower budget and with it much of the reliance upon physical planning and control.

The principal theme of the disinflationary analysis was that the root of the trouble was not a manpower shortage, but suppressed inflation, which prevented the movement of labor to basic industries, depleted inventories, diverted resources from export manufacture, and wasted dollar assets on unessential imports. Hence, it was said, the remedy was a vigorous budget surplus. To this advice some joined a further plea for decontrol and greater reliance upon the market, appropriately conditioned by fiscal policy. The sequence in which this analysis arose and spread through the political community seems to have been : academic economists; then economic journalists; then Members of Parliament, especially the Opposition; and finally the Government.[7] While the small surplus of Dalton's April budget briefly stilled some critics, the attack mounted during the spring and summer.

---

[7] As late as January, 1947, Lionel Robbins had written that "exaggerated stress has been laid upon the danger of inflation arising from an excessive volume of spending," and emphasized instead the manpower shortage. *Lloyd's Bank Review*, p. 26. Perhaps the first statement of the disinflationary thesis was a letter by Professor Hubert Henderson in the London *Times* for February 26th in which he asserted that Britain was suffering not from an overall shortage, but a maldistribution, of manpower which arose from "a huge excess of purchasing power" (p. 5).

In an editorial of March 1st, the *Economist* took up this theme and developed the case for "a little deflation" (p. 309). After Dalton's April budget the *Economist*, like the *Times*, relaxed its criticism, but certain academic economists, among them Robbins, Henderson, and Harrod, continued the attack. In Parliament, Conservative spokesmen showed no great foresight. In the March 10, 1947, economic debate, however, the disinflationary analysis was picked up from recent comment in the press, among others by Sir Robert Boothby and Clement Davies. In debates of the spring and summer this theme became common.

The term "disinflation," incidentally, appears to have been first used by the *Economist* in an article entitled "A Dis-Inflationary Budget" in its issue of March 22nd. Earlier, this journal had expressed the need for a new word which would refer to the need for measures to deal with suppressed inflation but which would be free of the unpleasant connotations of "deflation" (March 8, 1947, p. 314).

At last, in deed, if not words,[8] the Government admitted the force of the disinflationary prescription when in the fall it drastically cut expenditure on defense and investment, both public and private, and in Dalton's supplementary budget of November sharply increased a wide range of taxes bearing on all classes. It is worth noting, however, that Dalton increased neither income tax nor surtax.

This autumn budget, as one economist later put it, "largely set the pattern for 1948 and subsequent years."[9] Dalton's budget did set the pattern in the sense that it brought in a large surplus—so unexpectedly large indeed that Cripps in his budget of 1948 found it necessary to make only a few changes in taxation. Far more readily than Dalton, however, Cripps admitted the strength of the disinflationary analysis, stressing the distorting effect of inflationary pressures on planning generally and on the distribution of manpower in particular. Of greatest importance for the future pattern of policy was his reiterated premise that the budget must be considered from the viewpoint of its function in the economy as a whole,[1] and his explicit use of the categories of national income analysis in examining the economic problem and deciding what the content of the budget should be.[2]

The Decline of Physical Planning

In this manner, then, the disinflationary analysis made its way from the thoughts of academic economists into the policies of

[8] In the economic debate of August 6th–8th, 1947, Attlee admitted that "it may be we have tried to do too much in a short time." 440 H.C. Deb. 1489. But Dalton, when introducing his supplementary budget in November, said that its purpose was merely to reinforce still further "our budgetary defences" against inflation and resulted from the imports cuts and export increases of recent months. 444 H.C. Deb. 391.

[9] I. D. M. Little, "Fiscal Policy," in G. D. N. Worswick and P. H. Ady, The British Economy 1945–1950 (London, 1952), p. 172.

[1] By taking the Economic Survey and the budget proposals together as the subject of a single debate, Cripps gave special emphasis to this approach to planning. 449 H.C. Deb. 37 (April 6, 1948). "The new task of the Chancellor of the Exchequer," said Cripps, "is not merely to balance the Budget; it is a much wider one—to match our resources against our needs so that the main features of our economy may be worked out for the benefit of the community as a whole." 449 H.C. Deb. 57.

[2] See 449 H.C. Deb. 46, where Cripps refers to the various claims on resources under the headings of public consumption, public and private investment, and private consumption.

Government. But this does not mean that the Government beat a sudden retreat from its original conception of economic planning. On the contrary, during 1947 it also considerably strengthened physical planning, tightening up certain quantitative programs and physical controls. Such a response to the crisis had been strongly urged on the Government by a group of critics within the party who sharply opposed the disinflationary school and who looked to stronger and more centralized physical planning for the solution to Britain's economic problems.

Typical of this view were the opinions of the Keep Left M.P.'s, a group of Labour backbenchers who, agreeing on "the need for a more drastic Socialist policy,"[3] had begun meeting early in 1947.[4] Critical of both the Government's foreign and economic policy, the group in April, 1947, published its views in *Keep Left*, a *New Statesman* pamphlet.[5] After demanding more centralized planning machinery with power to override the autonomy of government departments, the writers declared that in winning "the Battle of Production" the "major strategic operation" was the deployment of manpower—"to get the men to the right jobs." To achieve this object, they proposed such measures as controls to direct materials, and hence labor, to essential industries; negative direction of labor to withhold replacements from inessential trades; and differential real wages in the form of more consumers' goods and lower taxes to attract workers to essential jobs. Looking at the larger needs of economic reconstruction, they strongly supported nationalization for "every industry which has a hold over our economy or which cannot be made efficient in private hands."[6] They did not even mention the budget and fiscal policy. In short, whether they were dealing with the immediate economic problem or the broad questions of reconstruction, the Keep Left Socialists consistently drew the implications of Labour's ancient orthodoxy.[7]

[3] *Keep Left*, by a Group of Members of Parliament (May, 1947).

[4] The leading academic advocate of this view was Dr. Thomas Balogh. See, for instance, his article, "Britain's Economic Problem," *Quarterly Journal of Economics* (February, 1949).

[5] Written by R. H. S. Crossman, Michael Foot, and Ian Mikardo and signed by twelve other Labour M.P.'s.

[6] Specifically mentioned were heavy chemicals, insurance, iron and steel, motor vehicles, and electrical components.

[7] With regard to foreign policy, the writers opposed the "Fulton policy" of an Anglo–American alliance against Russia which would demand large British forces at home and in the Middle East. Britain should not take sides between the U.S. and the U.S.S.R.: "Collective security against Com-

In its response to the crisis of 1947, the Labour Government did not deliberately make a decision to shift from physical planning to primary reliance upon the global controls of fiscal policy. Rather it compromised, adopting measures suggested by its critics on both the Right and the Left. Disinflation, but not decontrol, was added to a strengthened physical planning.[8] National income analysis was given new and greater importance, but the manpower budget continued in a prominent role. The case for physical planning had been weakened, but its future had not yet been determined. If physical planning had proved to be effective, it is possible that this compromise would have been continued, or even that the Government might have moved toward greater reliance on quantitative programs. For this to have happened, certain conditions would have been necessary : in particular, as we shall see, conditions relating to the motivation of the workers. But if these conditions had been present, the system of planning proposed by Keep Left Socialists would have worked as well as the system of economic management finally adopted.

In the next two or three years, however, the balance in the compromise tipped steadily against physical planning. The central reason was the failure of manpower planning. Major manpower targets for 1948, as for 1947, were badly missed and the debate on manpower planning of March, 1949, was said to mark the end of the idea that such planning could be an effective way of influencing the economy.[9] By 1950 the manpower budget was no longer operational[1] and Cripps, in his budget speech of that year, could

---

munism is a betrayal of Socialist principles." For further expression of the Keep Left economic policy, see the debate on the economic situation of August 6th–8th, 1947.

[8] Export licensing, which had been given up at the end of the war, was reintroduced. The existing controls on imports were used to make heavy cuts in imports from the Western Hemisphere and to accomplish a massive diversion of imports to non-dollar areas. A number of trade and payments agreements quickened the tendency toward bilateralism. At home, investment programing of both public and private investment was tightened up and used to reduce capital expenditure; a modest measure of labor direction was reimposed. A further favorable factor was demobilization which, at an increased tempo, not only had its effects on expenditure at home and abroad, but also added to the labor force available for industry.

[9] *Economist*, April 2, 1949, p. 623.

[1] The "broad picture of the national economy" was drawn by the *Economic Survey for 1948* "in terms of man-power and the national income" (p. 41). Its industry-by-industry budget for the current year was called "tentative," but the labor forces proposed for critical industries (coal, agri-

call the financial budget ". . . the most important control and the most powerful instrument for influencing economic policy which is available to the Government."[2] That "new way" which Attlee had claimed for Labour when in February, 1946, he described how the Government was attacking the economic problem from the viewpoint of "our human resources rather than our financial resources" had veered off in quite the opposite direction. Even the economic emergencies brought on by the Korean war did not result in the reinstatement of manpower budgeting and Gaitskell, in his budget speech of April, 1951, made explicit and elaborate use of national income analysis in deciding how the budget was to fulfill its threefold task of preventing the aggravation of inflation by money demand; discouraging the use of labor and materials for home consumption and less essential investment rather than defense and export industries; and allowing for the fact that the expected price rises would hit the low and fixed income groups hardest.[3]

By the last years of the Attlee Government a quite definite "choice" had been made among the alternative types of economic planning. The significance of the "decision" should be briefly emphasized. The Government did retain some important forms of physical planning, particularly with regard to investment and imports.[4] But more and more it had turned away from direct control by public administration and toward indirect control by manipulation of the market. From physical planning it turned to economic management. This approach to planning is quite compatible with private ownership, competition, and profit-seeking. Indeed, it depends upon a general pursuit of economic self-interest.[5] From

culture and textiles), were "targets in the full sense" (pp. 41, 43). The *Economic Survey for 1949* showed that some of the main targets had been missed. Coal aimed at an increase of 32,000 men and achieved only 8,000; cotton at an increase of 58,000 and achieved only 20,000; agriculture at 55,000 and achieved 36,000 (p. 31). The *Economic Survey for 1950* continued the industry-by-industry table, but called its end-of-year figures merely forecasts of changes "which it is expected will take place" (p. 30).

[2] 474 *H.C. Deb.* 40 (18 April 1948).

[3] 486 *H.C. Deb.* 826–867.

[4] For the changes, see Samuel H. Beer, *Treasury Control: The Coordination of Financial and Economic Policy in Great Britain*, 2nd ed. (Oxford, 1957), Ch. III, "The Coordination of Economic Policy," esp. pp. 79–93.

[5] "Every economic system devised for ordinary human beings," wrote W. Arthur Lewis in a Fabian study published in 1949, "must have self-

the viewpoint of economic planning, in consequence, it makes public ownership superfluous and the whole Socialist conception of the cooperative economy sustained by the public service motive irrelevant.

Why had the Government made this "choice"? What were the forces influencing this process of policy determination?

TRADE UNIONS VERSUS PLANNED ECONOMY

The principal cause, I shall argue, was the resistance of trade unions to government control over the movement and compensation of labor. A system of physical planning that expresses its objectives in quantitative programs must be able to include manpower in these programs, especially the manpower needed in industries of critical importance to the economy at any particular time. If these manpower programs cannot be carried out, some more relaxed method of planning will have to be adopted. In Britain between 1947 and 1950, the attitude of the unions obliged the planners gradually to move to this conclusion.

No doubt there were other forces that contributed to the result. The personal preferences of some ministers, for instance, may have played a role. On the whole, however, it is not fruitful to look for villains or heroes or for a conflict between true and false Socialists among party leaders. The personal policies of Dalton, as we have seen, were not of major importance in determining the role of the budget in planning while he was Chancellor. He held a thoroughly Socialist conception of economic planning which was widely shared in the Government and which only under the pressure of circumstance and the disinflationary criticism did he reluctantly modify. Similarly, the personal views of Cripps do not account for the change in the general method of planning

---

interest as its driving force." *The Principles of Economic Planning*, p. 7. This study of Lewis' reflects the new direction Labour was taking and shows how attitudes toward planning were linked with conceptions of fundamental Socialist values. Lewis stressed that planning must rely on self-interest and should be carried out largely through the budget, other forms of control being relegated to a subsidiary position. At the same time, he held that the distinctive value at which Socialism aims is equality (not, as with earlier Socialists, fellowship). "Socialism," he wrote, "is about equality" (p. 10).

between 1947 and 1950. His devotion to Socialism was incontestable and his preferences, it appears, were for physical planning.[6] That he should have presided over this critical transformation points up sharply the fact that it was not ministerial or party preferences that were controlling, but rather the circumstances with which planners were obliged to cope.

Among the circumstances that made physical planning difficult were certain characteristics of British government. To be successful, physical planning would have required—as the Keep Left critics fully recognized in criticizing "the autonomy of departments"—a high degree of centralized coordination and control in the machinery of government. There would have had to be some central department or agency with the power to direct and command other departments in accord with a unified and consistent system of plans.[7] But in Britain "Cabinet democracy"—the phrase is Herbert Morrison's—means that no single minister can be given final, overriding authority over others responsible for departments. Similarly, the relation of command and obedience is foreign to the habits and spirit of the Civil Service, particularly members of the Administrative Class, when one department is dealing with another. No more than ministers do departments—not even the Treasury—order one another about. Likewise, in the economy there were pluralistic forces other than those rising from the trade unions that put a drag on the efforts of planners to program quantitatively the various sectors of activity. Business and professional sectors, as we shall later have occasion to note, had and used very considerable leverage against government control.

[6] In *Democracy Alive* (London, 1946), Cripps had declared that planning and control on the wartime model would be necessary for full employment (p. 19). His wartime experience as Minister of Aircraft Production and President of the Board of Trade had familiarized him with the immense apparatus of quotas, rationing, and controls used by these ministries. See Calvin Cooke, *The Life of Richard Stafford Cripps* (London, 1957), p. 334. When Cripps first informed the House in February, 1947, of the Government's intention to create the Central Economic Planning Staff, he described it as "a joint Planning staff, somewhat on the lines of the procedure that was so successfully developed during the war." 434 *H.C. Deb.* 470 (10 March 1947). Moreover, S. C. Leslie, former head of the Information Unit of the Treasury, relates how in late 1947 or early 1948 Cripps sent him a description of planning in Czechoslovakia that involved detailed targets of production, and added the comment that this showed what Britain should also do. Author's conversation with Leslie, February 9, 1959.

[7] See discussion in Beer, *op. cit.*, Ch. III.

Yet the labor force, because of its size, its human character, and its high degree of organization, remained the central factor. Observers, Socialist and non-Socialist, had recognized the problem before Labour took power in 1945. If the government was to attempt to fulfill quantitative programs, they pointed out, it would have to have the means to secure the right distribution of manpower. Two possible means were labor direction and a wages policy. "Planned production," Barbara Wootton, for instance, had written, "implies either compulsory industrial direction or a planned wage structure."[8] If collective bargaining was to be retained as the means by which wages and conditions were determined, then labor direction would be necessary to get workers in the right jobs. On the other hand, if collective bargaining could be eliminated, state wage-fixing would serve to attract workers voluntarily to where the plan showed they were needed.

This problem raises basic questions not only of economic planning, but also of Socialist theory. The role of trade unions in a planned economy is obviously of central importance for the theory of Socialism. It has been said that since the organized workers will feel a much greater sense of identity with a Socialist than a non-Socialist government, the general problem of labor discipline will be greatly eased.[9] This is not only a question of industrial peace—strikes, for instance, will appear as harmful to the workers' own government—but also of the new requirements that Socialist planning will impose on unions and workers. If democratic control is to take the place of market forces, then directly or indirectly, by labor direction or a wages policy, government must control wage-fixing and the movement of labor from one employment to another. But insofar as the workers are committed to the Socialist vision of a cooperative society ruled by fellowship, they will accept these innovations. Admittedly, this means that the traditional functions of their unions will have to be radically adapted. Under capitalism the unions have developed an industrial purpose centering on hard-won rights of collective bargaining. This industrial purpose must be modified to meet the needs of the planned economy which, as political organizations, they have brought into being. Sincere Socialists presumably will be ready for this change of attitude and purpose.

[8] *Freedom Under Planning* (Chapel Hill, 1945), p. 118.
[9] Joseph A. Schumpeter, *Capitalism, Socialism and Democracy*, 2nd ed. (New York, 1947), pp. 210–12.

Union Resistance to a Wages Policy

During the war, the unions had resolutely resisted wage-fixing by the state, accepting instead industrial conscription and labor direction. While they refused to surrender collective bargaining, they did agree to a ban on strikes and to compulsory arbitration. The Government, in turn, pursued a policy of "fair shares" that included consumer rationing, heavy profits taxation, subsidies on food and clothing, and price controls. As a result of this wartime bargain, the unions did not take advantage of the scarcity of labor to push up wage rates excessively. In general, wartime planning enjoyed substantial success both in controlling the distribution of manpower and in restraining inflationary pressures, whether from excessive demand or wage raises.[1]

The Labour Government, as we have seen, continued from wartime the method of physical planning, the main quantitative program being the manpower budget. Labor direction having been given up, how were these targets to be realized? The logical alternative, a wages policy, had been sternly ruled out by the T.U.C.,[2] and the Government repeatedly denied that it had any intention of interfering with free collective bargaining. Yet even these denials suggest that from an early date planners had a secret hankering for what the unions had forbidden.[3]

As the economic situation darkened, critics demanded a wages policy which would not only restrain "wage-push" inflation, but

[1] Ben C. Roberts, *National Wages Policy in War and Peace* (London, 1958), Ch. 2, "British Wage Policy in Wartime."

[2] In a reply of the General Council in 1943 to an inquiry from Sir William Beveridge, asking them for their attitudes toward a wage-price spiral under full employment and toward measures to secure adequate labor mobility. See Roberts, *op. cit.*, p. 54.

[3] In the manpower debate of February, 1946, for instance, Morrison, then minister in charge of economic affairs, declared that the Government was nowhere near the point of telling employers to raise wages or trade unions not to ask for increases. Yet he also said that, as for a wages policy, no final statement could be made at the time on this "complex and difficult subject," but looking forward hopefully, thought that perhaps in time there might be sufficient information, which was generally accepted, to ensure "that arguments about wages are circumscribed within certain elastic considerations." 419 *H.C. Deb.* 2115 and 2118 (27 February 1946). Conservative spokesmen had pressed the point that it was not possible to have a planned economy without a wages policy. See, for instance, the remarks of Norman Bower in the same debate, *ibid.*, 1991–2.

also provide incentives in the form of differential rates to draw workers to the undermanned industries.[4] Both types of wages policy, but particularly the latter, would involve interference with collective bargaining and both were opposed on the whole by the unions.[5] The Government, it seems clear, wished to get a wages policy for manpower distribution as well as disinflation,[6] and one might suppose that given its strong parliamentary position, not to mention its wide legal authority under powers of delegated legislation, it could readily have imposed its solution. The Government realized, however, that a wages policy, regardless of its legal status, could not succeed unless it enjoyed the cooperation of the unions. As ministers in their definitions of "democratic planning" repeatedly declared, "the execution of the economic plan must be much more a matter for co-operation between the Government, industry and the people, than of rigid application by the State of controls and compulsions."[7] These negotiations (and "negotiation" rather than merely "consultation" is the correct term) were carried on with labor representatives in the National Joint Advisory Council, directly with the General Council of the T.U.C., and individually with union leaders. In the fall of 1947 union consent was won to a modest measure of labor direction.[8] But

[4] For example, *Economist*, on January 25th, 1947 (p. 129), and Nicholas Kaldor, who in a letter in the *Times* of February 25th urged the Government not only to bring in more foreign labor and cut the armed forces, but also to restrict employment in unessential industry and to reshape the systems and relative scales of wage payments.

[5] See, for instance, the remarks of Arthur Deakin at the party conference in May, 1947 *LPCR*, p. 144.

[6] At the party conference of May, 1947, Dalton, after explaining for the N.E.C. that there were only two ways of altering the distribution of labor, declared that "in the view of the National Executive the balance of argument lies in favour of seeking to do it . . . by seeking to arrange and to facilitate relative inducements and advantages for the undermanned industries" (pp. 151-2). The mineworkers, who would have benefited from a wages policy, offered a resolution to this general effect. Deakin of the Transport and General Workers expressed strong opposition, saying, "The people I represent are not prepared to play second fiddle" (p. 144). The N.E.C. accepted the mineworkers' resolution, while sharply criticizing a resolution implying some form of Labour direction that had been offered from the Keep Left group (pp. 137-8).

[7] *Economic Survey for 1947*, p. 9.

[8] Under a Control of Engagements Order which went into effect in October, 1947, it was made compulsory for all workers seeking employment and all employers seeking workers to do so through the machinery of the employment exchanges. The worker was to be given a wide choice among

two months of negotiations with the General Council in the latter part of the year produced no concessions on a wages policy.[9]

The Wage Restraint Bargain of 1948

In the early months of 1948 a bargain was finally struck. This bargain was remarkable as much for the way in which it was reached as for its content and results. The principal negotiators were three—the Government, organized labor, and organized capital. The bargain was not itself embodied in any legislative instrument such as a statute or statutory order. Yet it achieved a regulation of an important aspect of the British economy that no such legislative instrument by itself could have done. Indeed, one may think of it as a kind of extra-governmental legislation. It was effective in the sense that the regulation of behavior stipulated by it remained in force for the better part of three years and greatly assisted the Government in its efforts to maintain economic equilibrium. In content, however, it was not the differential wages policy for which planners had hoped, but in essence a wages policy aimed primarily at disinflation—in short, a policy of wage restraint.

The negotiations were complex and protracted, but the main outlines can be briefly sketched. Unable to reach a satisfactory agreement with the unions, the Government early in 1948 took a new and public initiative. Stressing the dangers of inflation, especially to the foreign balance, it issued a statement conceived by Cripps, but presented under Attlee's name, which made a broad case against any rise in incomes.[1] While profits were mentioned, the main items concerned wages. Wage increases were opposed, including increases to maintain traditional differentials among various trades or to meet anything less than a marked rise in the cost of living. Exceptions were permissible only if necessary to attract workers to undermanned industries or if in a particular industry there had been a rise in productivity. The ensuing

---

available jobs on essential work. If he refused any of the proffered jobs, a direction compelling him to take essential work could be issued by the Minister. During 1948 only twenty-nine directions were issued.

[9] "Interim Report on the Economic Situation," issued by General Council, December, 1947; T.U.C. *Report* 1948, p. 289.

[1] *Statement on Personal Incomes, Costs and Prices,* Cmd. 7321. Presented to Parliament February 4, 1948. 446 *H.C. Deb.* 1821. Calvin Cooke in his biography of Cripps, *op. cit.,* indicates that Cripps was primarily responsible for the statement (p. 367).

negotiations with the Crisis Committee of the General Council
produced the demand from labor that if the unions were to accept
the new policy, the Government should act "not only to stabilize
but to reduce profits and prices."[2] Cripps thereupon communicated
to business a request for a general reduction in both profits and
prices.

In his relations with business, Cripps dealt directly with the peak
organizations, the Federation of British Industries, National Union
of Manufacturers, and Associated British Chambers of Commerce.
Concerting their action by means of a small committee, these three
organizations communicated Cripps' requests to their respective
memberships and in turn informed Cripps of the business position.[3]
Members of Parliament with connections in the business world
were also used to express its views in the House and to serve on
delegations to ministers.[4] Through these intermediaries the business
world had by late March agreed to a broad acceptance of a policy
of voluntary dividend limitation. Over the next three years, this
agreement, although there were exceptions and some attempts at
renegotiation, was honored by business. With regard to prices,
however, the Government was less successful. In February the
Board of Trade, carying out Cripps' policy, put ceilings on all
goods under price control on the basis of prices prevailing in the
previous two months. Further efforts to tighten and extend price
control, however, were relaxed in April, owing, it appears, to
pressure from business.[5]

Whether the limitation on dividends involved sums large enough
to make any substantial reduction of inflationary pressures may
be questioned. Clearly, however, it had a psychological effect

---

[2] V. L. Allen, *Trade Unions and the Government* (London, 1960), p. 286.
[3] Federation of British Industries, *Annual Report*, 1948, pp. 9–10.
[4] For instance, when Cripps reported his request for a reduction in prices
and profits in the House and hinted at statutory dividend limitation, Oliver
Lyttleton, chairman of Associated Electrical Industries, Ltd., and a Conservative frontbencher, assured the Government that if it would ask for
voluntary dividend limitation, business would cooperate—as proved to be
the case. Among other M.P.'s connected with the negotiations on behalf of
business were Sir Peter Bennett, a large motor manufacturer, chairman of
Joseph Lucas, Ltd., a director of Imperial Chemical Industries, and a past
president of the Federation of British Industries, and Sir Patrick Hannon,
president of the National Union of Manufacturers. Both served on a delegation to Cripps. See also Bennett's role as a representative of business
when he reported the F.B.I.'s proposals to the House. 449 *H.C. Deb.* 201
(April 7, 1948).
[5] *Economist*, April 24, 1948, p. 683.

in inducing unions to accept the restraints asked of them.[6] As before, labor would not agree to those aspects of the incomes policy which involved the creation of new differentials to influence the distribution of manpower.[7] Far from accepting new differentials, the unions insisted on retaining the right to press for wage increases needed to maintain the traditional differentials among various trades, as well as the right to demand raises for workers receiving unduly low pay.[8]

With these qualifications, which made the incomes policy essentially a policy of wage restraint, the unions gave their agreement. As a *quid pro quo* they asked and received, in addition to profits reduction, two other measures. One was the Special Contribution, a "once and for all" capital levy that Cripps included in his budget of 1948 and which was expected to realize 50 million pounds in that fiscal year. The other was the continuation of subsidies to hold the line on food prices, a policy that resulted in a very substantial increase of their cost beyond the figure at which Cripps had proposed to hold them.[9]

As in its relations with business, the Government dealt directly with representatives of the peak organization of labor. For the most part this meant the General Council, possibly as represented by a delegation or subcommittee. The bargain was not concluded, however, by the sole action of the General Council. On March 24th a conference was called in London, consisting of the members of the executive bodies of the unions affiliated with the T.U.C. In the qualified form in which the General Council had accepted it, the incomes policy was put to this body, discussed and approved by a majority in the proportion of five to two. At the annual

[6] The General Council conditioned its qualified acceptance of the White Paper on a reduction in prices and profits. *Economist*, February 28, 1948, p. 336.

[7] Similarly, when in September, 1947, a letter was sent out by the Ministry of Labour to bodies engaged in wage negotiations, calling their attention to the need for wage restraint and for differentials in favor of undermanned industries, a delegation from the General Council visited the Prime Minister and the Minister of Labour and obtained the ministers' disavowal of the letter. T.U.C. *Report* 1948, p. 289. See also Allen, *op. cit.*, pp. 284 and 290.

[8] *Economist*, February 28, 1948, p. 336.

[9] In 1947 Cripps proposed to hold food subsidies to 400 million pounds. In fiscal 1948–49 they actually ran to 485 million pounds, the Government breaking through the ceiling in order to restrain wage demands. That food subsidies were considered a *quid pro quo* is implied by the December, 1947 report of the General Council, in which it considers the subsidies in the context of the problem of wages and profits. See T.U.C. *Report* 1948, p. 289.

meeting of the Congress in September, wage restraint was, of course, accepted overwhelmingly.

This triangular bargain between government, labor, and capital lasted until the latter part of 1950. In that year the devaluation of 1949 led to price increases which finally broke up the bargain. By the spring of 1950 the alliance of the Government and General Council was being disrupted by the action of individual unions and, at the Congress of September, although the Prime Minister personally added his plea to that of the General Council, a resolution opposing wage restraint was passed. From late that year wages began sharply to rise and in the same period businesses relaxed their limitation of dividends.[1] The urgent, indeed desperate, efforts of the Government during its last months in power to reach a new bargain with the unions were unavailing.

Judged by any reasonable standard of governmental achievement in such matters, the policy of wage restraint was a success.[2] The unions did not exploit to the full their powers of collective bargaining under conditions of full employment and labor shortage. They would not, however, accept that sort of wages policy which would have enabled the planners to achieve their targets. As a result, "the much vaunted manpower planning of the Labour Government was reduced to a farce,"[3] and the method of physical planning gradually gave way to the more relaxed approach of "economic management."

THE NEW BALANCE OF POWER

Three aspects of this remarkable bargain between government, labor, and capital are of particular interest. One, the purposive aspect, is the response of the unions to the Government's efforts to plan the economy, in which they revealed what they would and would not do. The process also throws light on the power struc-

[1] On the movement of wages, see Roberts, op. cit., p. 60. On the rise in dividends, see Economist, December 23, 1950, p. 1160.

[2] Weekly wage rates, which had risen by 8% in 1946 and 5% in 1947, rose only 4% in 1948 and in 1949 went up only 1½ to 2%, no increase taking place in such important industries as coal, engineering, and railways. Economist, February 4, 1950, p. 291. In 1950, the year when the bargain finally broke down, the index of weekly wage rates remained the same from January through September. Abstract of Statistics (London, 1952), Table 141.

[3] Roberts, op. cit., p. 63.

ture of postwar Britain, illustrating the vast power of organized producers groups—in this instance particularly the power of labor —in the determination of the pattern of government policy. These three aspects, policy, power, and purpose, are interrelated. The pattern of policy—specifically the broad attempt to plan and control the economy—meant, of course, an extension of government power over the behavior of those engaged in production. At the same time, the need for their cooperation, if the planning effort was to succeed, gave organized producers groups a strong position from which to bargain. And this position of power in turn shaped in no small measure the purposes to which labor was committed. This abstract way of stating the analysis will be more helpful if we will pursue the question of why the unions would not accept effective control, direct or indirect, over the distribution of manpower.

The immediate answer is that such control would vitally infringe on traditional purposes of the unions as industrial organizations. Labor direction would mean that workers could not reap the advantages of a superior bargaining position when labor in their industry was in short supply. As Lord Dukeston, former head of the General and Municipal Workers, said when explaining to the party conference of 1947 why the trade unions would not accept a policy of direction : "For the first time in history those who do the manual work are in short supply." Hence, he continued, planning must start "with the knowledge that attraction, and not coercion or direction, is the method we are going to apply."[4] On the other hand, a differential wages policy would cut the heart out of collective bargaining, its function in wage-fixing. As the next speaker, Arthur Deakin, General Secretary of the Transport Workers, put it : "Under no circumstances will we accept the position that the responsibility for the fixation of wages and the regulation of conditions of employment is one for the Government."[5]

These are the familiar attitudes of labor organizations, and indeed of economic actors generally, in the capitalist free market. But they are radically incompatible with the type of economic planning which was attempted by Britain's Socialist government and which would be necessary in the Socialist Commonwealth. Here was a union movement which, for more than a generation,

[4] 1947 *LPCR*, pp. 143-4.
[5] *Ibid.*, p. 144.

had steadfastly supported the Socialist vision of a new order, where cooperation would supersede competition and the motive of public service that of profit and gain. When the opportunity for putting this purpose into practice was presented, they refused to adapt their behavior to its requirements.

It is too easy to be condescending about the response of the unions and simply accuse them of hypocrisy in failing to live up to their Socialist pretensions. In the first place, their acceptance of wage restraint did involve an important adaptation of their traditional behavior. The bargain of 1948, both in procedure and content, was a major innovation in the relations between government and unions, when compared with the patterns of the interwar and earlier periods. Such bargaining was a type of behavior inherent in the conditions of the Welfare State and Managed Economy and, while that system was not itself the Socialist Commonwealth, it was a political and economic order very different from nineteenth-century capitalism.

Moreover, in trying to understand why the unions and their members accepted something less than "full-blooded" Socialism, we must consider the immense changes that had affected their position since the interwar years. The most obvious was the improvement in the material welfare of the working class, especially their relative welfare when compared with that of other classes.[6] This general line of argument has been used by those who would explain the decline of Socialist ideology in the working class because of the "affluence" of Britain in the 1950's.[7] While

[6] "The working class now takes about 22% more consumer goods and services than before the war. After allowance for a 5% increase in population, the per capita improvement in their standard of living is on the order of 17%, apart from changes in the commodity composition and possibly the quality of their consumption. Middle class consumption is of the order of 18% below that of prewar, while that of the wealthy appears to be about 42% less than in 1938." Finley Weaver, "Taxation and Redistribution in the United Kingdom," *The Review of Economics and Statistics* (August, 1950), pp. 210–11.

The change in *relative* welfare dating from the war years (not merely 1945) was perceived and emphasized by Labour spokesmen. At the conference of 1947, for instance, Herbert Morrison, when illustrating the fact that "we have got far more of the actual substance of social and economic equality than ever before," pointed out that "90 per cent of our people who have the lower incomes command 67 per cent of our total national purchasing power today as compared with 55 per cent before the war. That is, their share has risen by one fifth in a few years." 1947 *LPCR*, p. 136.

[7] See, for instance, C. A. R. Crosland, "The Future of the Left," *Encounter* (March, 1960).

Britain in the late 1940's was by no means "affluent," the relative improvement in the material conditions of the working class, which had already begun during the war, may help explain the weakening of Socialist commitment.

But we should also recall the extent to which not merely a demand for greater equality in material conditions, but also a thrust for greater equality in power motivated the original commitment of the unions to Socialism. For if the material conditions of their members had been improved by the late 1940's, the power position of the unions had been unrecognizably transformed. The power won by the unions when the Labour Party in 1940 joined the wartime Coalition and in 1945 formed its first majority Government was only one element in this change. In addition, a system of consultation, formal and informal, had grown up which brought the unions into such continuous and intimate contact with ministers and civil servants throughout the executive branch of government as to give the spokesmen of the organized working class a direct and influential voice in virtually all fields of policy. This system, which burgeoned during the war and continued during the postwar years, gave the unions a position of power quite independent of which party was in office. No matter what the political complexion of ministers or the Government, union spokesmen always had access. This new position of power was not merely a result of administrative arrangements giving access, but was a function of the new demands that government was making on society as the pattern of policy expanded into economic planning.[8]

Consultation with organized producers groups has a long history in Britain. It became increasingly common as, from the latter part of the nineteenth century, government began to intervene in various sectors of the economy and as organizations representing businessmen, farmers, and workers were formed. These groups, as we have seen, often sought direct representation in Parliament through interested M.P.'s. They also sent deputations to ministers to present their arguments for or against a piece of legislation or some administrative practice. During World War I a closer form of contact arose, when the need for wide control over the economy led the Government to set up a system of committees associating representatives of such organizations

[8] See below, Ch. XII.

directly with the administrative machine.[9] Although this system of consultation was abruptly dismantled after the war, contact between industry and government, as we shall have occasion to observe, was often close when Conservative Governments were engaged in important phases of making and executing policy.[1] Under the political and economic conditions of the interwar years, however, the position of the trade unions was so weak that, as Allen has written, "the Government was able to ignore their direct representations and they had no alternative to using the Parliamentary Labour Party as a means of contact with the Government."[2]

THE NEW SOCIAL CONTRACT

Total war transformed the position of the unions. Manpower became the ultimate scarce resource on whose mobilization the extent of the war effort depended and on whose allocation the system of wartime planning was based. The cooperation of the unions and their members was indispensable—and was given unstintingly. Yet labor did not accept these heavy burdens without receiving and indeed demanding major concessions from other groups in the society.[3] R. M. Titmuss has described the "revolution in social policy" that took place after the full fury of the war was loosed on Britain in the spring and summer of 1940.[4] Ministers and civil servants who had found certain extensions of the social services "financially impossible" during peacetime and the early part of the war now accepted them and put them into effect. Generally, among the public there was a mood of introspection and self-criticism which led to broad agreement that, after the war, Britain must become "a more generous society in which all ele-

[9] See Allen, *op. cit.*, pp. 29–30.
[1] See below, Ch. X.
[2] *Op. cit.*, p. 24.
[3] For instance, when describing the "political" background of the appointment in June, 1941 of the committee that produced the Beveridge Report on social security, Lord Beveridge notes that "the General Council of the Trades Union Congress for some time had been pressing the Government for a comprehensive review of social insurance." *Power and Influence* (London, 1953), p. 296. Assessing its influence, he concludes that "The Congress had been largely responsible for securing the establishment of the Committee" (p. 300). And later : "The commissioning of the inquiry through which it [the Beveridge Report] came to birth was due to the driving force of the Trades Union Congress" (p. 317).
[4] *Problems of Social Policy* (London, 1950), pp. 506–9.

ments more fully recognize their obligations to one another."[5] In effect, this meant that steps were to be taken to remedy the insecurities and deprivations from which the working class had suffered during the interwar years.

At least as important as the new social policy of "fair shares" was the new position of authority in the state acquired by the trade unions. The entry of the Labour Party into the Churchill Government, of course, put trade unionists—of whom Ernest Bevin was the most eminent—directly in the seats of highest political power. Moreover, and in great part at the instigation of Bevin, unions were given open and easy access to all departments. In particular, at every level and in most spheres of policy their representatives were included on committees directly associated with the administrative machine; the number of Government committees with trade union representation, which had been only 1 in 1931–32 increased to 12 in 1939, and to 60 by 1948–49.[6]

But mere representation on committees, or even the opportunity to consult with high civil servants and ministers, was not the essential advance. The important thing was the change in attitude, on which the unions had strenuously insisted. From the 1930's Ernest Bevin and Walter Citrine had worked to convert the T.U.C. from dreams of overthrowing capitalism or from a mere "guerrilla war" tactic of extorting piecemeal concessions to a policy of demanding a voice in making industrial and social policy. The outbreak of war presented them with the opportunity to achieve their aim. As Citrine reported to the T.U.C. in 1940, its leaders sought during the war "to widen the ambit and influence" of the unions, insisting on a degree of consultation with Governments and with departments that would enable the movement "to shape the life of the nation."[7]

---

[5] *Ibid.* See also *Times* editorials of July 1, 1940 and August 31, 1940, entitled "The New Europe" and "The Moral of Tyneside." "By the end of the Second World War," Titmuss writes, "the Government had, through the agency of newly established or existing services, assumed and developed a measure of direct concern for the health and well-being of the population which, by contrast with the role of Government in the nineteen thirties, was little short of remarkable." *Op. cit.*, p. 506.

[6] Allen, *op. cit.*, pp. 32–4.

[7] T.U.C. *Report* 1940, pp. 229–31, 271. Donald F. MacDonald writes that according to Citrine the trade union movement expected to emerge from the war more powerful than ever and would not be content with merely being consulted, but would insist on sharing with the Government the responsibility for policy making in economic and social matters. *The State and the Trade Unions* (London, 1960), p. 120.

Ernest Bevin put the point bluntly in his union's journal shortly after the war began. Trade unionists would not sit on any committee if invited as an act of patronage; ministers and departments would have to cease treating them with a scarcely veiled contempt. The support of the trade unions could be won only if the established powers accepted the principle of equality. And by this he meant "Equality not merely in the economic sense, but in conception and in the attitude of mind of those in power. . . ."[8] As in his earliest days, the question of power was central to Bevin's mode of thought and the new arrangements of 1940 meant a new position of power for the unions. As a result, on a broad range of social and economic questions, the Government consulted and, if necessary, negotiated with representatives of the organized working class. The significance of this vast change was caught by the *Times* correspondent when, in replying to the traditional vote of thanks to the press at the T.U.C. of 1945, he said :

You have no longer any need to thunder; you have only to whisper and Ministers tremble and Field-Marshals bend their knees. How very far away are those days when a few top-hatted, frock-coated gentlemen made a promenade of Government offices in Whitehall respectfully carrying resolutions passed by Congress, leaving them at the door, extremely happy if they saw a permanent secretary, and most handsomely flattered if by accident they stumbled across a Minister.[9]

The changes in the pattern of policy caused by the war, particularly the urgent extension of economic mobilization and control in 1940, provided the basis on which the new power of the organized working class was founded. After the war this new position was sustained by the continuation of economic planning in one form or another, and the process of bargaining from which the policy of wage restraint emerged in 1948 illustrates how it enabled the unions to shape and influence Government programs. Nor did their power vanish when the Conservatives took office, for although less favorable to planning than Labour, they too were obliged to manage the economy. Writing in 1960, Allen concluded that although certain tensions and differences of opinion had arisen, these constituted only "small, perhaps temporary, changes in the relationship between trade unions and Government. The

[8] Quoted in Roberts, *op. cit.*, p. 30.
[9] Quoted in Allan Flanders, *Trade Unions* (London, 1952), p. 64.

system of direct communication which was established by Ernest Bevin in 1940 remained basically unaltered."[1]

Writing of the significance of the plans for postwar reconstruction prepared by the Coalition Government, Hancock and Gowing have called them one part of "an implied contract between the Government and the people."[2] On their side, the people refused none of the sacrifices necessary to win the war. On its side, the Government prepared for "the restoration and improvement of the nation's well-being when the war had been won." One gets a better understanding of the meaning of this change in attitude and intentions on the part of Government if one looks at it not merely as a bargain between Government and people, but rather as a major readjustment in the relations between classes. After all, the principal beneficiaries of the proposed postwar plans, as of the wartime policy of "fair shares," were the working class. For the upper and middle classes the new policies meant on the whole fewer privileges and heavier burdens. Moreover, the middle and upper classes not only agreed to a more generous sharing of material advantage; they also accepted a wider sharing of power, as the organized working class was brought into a new position of participation in the political system.

The critical moment in the forging of this new "social contract" was not 1945, but 1940. The major readjustment resulted not from a shift in the electoral balance of power, but from a shift in the balance of economic power. In a limited, but important sense, the old syndicalist thesis was vindicated. For it was initially not by their votes, but by their control over instrumentalities necessary to carrying out vital national purposes that the organized working class raised themselves from their old position of exclusion and inferiority. The Labour victory of 1945[3] and the consequent adaptation of Conservative policy were later phases of this general process, as was the intense competition of the 1950's between the two parties in their bidding for the votes of a populace conditioned to the Welfare State. If, however, we are to understand the de-

---

[1] *Op. cit.*, p. 74.

[2] *The British War Economy*, p. 541.

[3] According to A. D. Lindsay, "the really big thing" about the Labour victory was not the resulting legislation, but the fact that "the struggle for power between the old English governing class and the new active and rising elements in English politics has at last been settled . . . the calm assumption that the governing of England was their particular business has been shattered." *Virginia Quarterly Review*, Vol 22, No. 2 (Spring, 1946), p. 258.

cline of ideology not only in the ranks of the Labour movement, but also in British politics generally, we must give the major role to the new balance of power between classes that was achieved during the war and lasted into the postwar period. It did not mean that class distinctions vanished from British life. But it did immensely reduce one of the most galling aspects of the British class system—namely, that inheritance from feudalism which made class not merely a social and economic distinction, but also a political distinction between those who govern and those who are governed. Not all members of the working class, one hardly needs say, resented this discrimination. But vast numbers, located principally in the unions, did resent it, and from their resentment had flowed the ideological alienation expressed in the Labour Party's commitment to Socialism. The new position of the organized working class in the Welfare State and Managed Economy undercut the grounds for this alienation and prepared the scene for a new and far less doctrinaire kind of politics.

CHAPTER VIII

In Search of Purpose

What would be the Labour Party's response to the experience of the Labour Government?

Perhaps the question itself seems odd. The obviously sensible thing, it may appear, was for the party to adapt to the realities of governing and at the same time to attempt to give them coherent direction. The utopian vision of the Socialist pioneers had proved to be unrealistic. Yet the possibilities of a humanized capitalism had proved to be more promising than they had anticipated. A Welfare State and Managed Economy were being constructed and by 1950 the main outlines of the structure had appeared. Was it not the proper task of the Labour Party to welcome this achievement and to develop from such of its old ethical principles as were relevant a new social philosophy that would lend guidance to the new pattern of policy?

This argument for adaptation was strengthened by the party's electoral problem, which became more and more acute in the following years. The decline marked by the elections of 1950 and 1951 came as a shock. But far more disturbing were the routs of 1955 and 1959. In four successive general elections, Labour received a steadily declining percentage of the vote given the two major parties. Such a record of defeat was unique in its history. Earlier in that history, Labour's vote had sometimes fallen off—as in 1931. But normally such decline was followed by recovery, if not victory—as in 1935. So, taking the long view, one could always argue that the party's fortunes were on the upgrade. This was not the case in the 1950's. Labour's cause became increasingly unpopular and the doctrine of nationalization, along with the

TABLE 8.1

Per Cent of Major Two-Party Vote 1945–59[1]

	Conservatives	Labour
1945	45.2	54.8
1950	48.4	51.6
1951	49.6	50.4
1955	51.8	48.2
1959	52.9	47.1

party's working-class image, was one of the principal reasons.[2] Not only partisan expediency, but also respect for the voters' judgment might well seem to imply that the party ought to cast aside much of its ancient ideological baggage. British politics, moreover, had itself recently provided an example of how a political party might adapt old views to new governmental and electoral realities. While in opposition following their crushing defeat in 1945, the Conservatives, after a brief period of confusion and incoherence, had rapidly adjusted their policies to a major acceptance of the Welfare State and Managed Economy, including the principal reforms that the Labour Government had introduced. At least in part due to this readiness to bow to the wishes of the democracy, the Conservatives at succeeding elections made another of their trend-reversing recoveries of popularity.

Such adaptation may seem not only rational, but also typical. In a democratic two-party system, it is often said, competition for votes will force the policies of the two parties toward one another. If at any moment of time the two parties do have a distinctively "Left" and "Right" orientation, their efforts to maximize electoral support will tend to bring about a convergence of policy on a centrist position. And it is true that in the 1950's one can fairly claim to detect such a tendency in British politics and to find the party of the Right extending its appeal to groups on its Left and the party of the Left extending its appeal to groups on its

[1] We are concerned in this chapter with the struggle within the Labour party that took place mainly in the 1950's. For comparison, however, it is interesting to note the percent of the two party vote received in the general election of 1964 : Conservatives 49.6%, Labour 50.4%.

[2] Surveys of public opinion showed that while in 1949 27% of the public favored further nationalization, by 1960 this figure had fallen to 11%. Among Labour supporters the decline had been from 60% to 21%. See Mark Abrams and Richard Rose, *Must Labour Lose?* (London, 1960), Tabs. 18 and 20, pp. 35 and 37.

Right. But in the case of the Labour Party (we shall consider the Conservatives later) there were also powerful forces working against this tendency.

FUNDAMENTALISM VERSUS REVISIONISM

One faction, the revisionists, did advocate a degree of adaptation of policy in view of the governmental and electoral problems confronting the party. But accepting the revisionist case meant altering the fundamentals of Socialism as it had been conceived during the Socialist generation. And a large part of the party was not ready to tolerate this revolution in belief and sentiment. As a result, for more than a decade the party was torn by dissension between revisionists and fundamentalists, a conflict that divided the party at every level over the meaning of Socialism, not only in domestic, but also in foreign affairs. Before looking at the general features of this conflict it will be helpful to sketch some of the principal events and to identify its main phases.

Fundamentalist Attack

The main phases in the conflict were marked by the general elections of 1951, 1955, and 1959. As an election approached, the party would paper over the cracks with a compromise program and close ranks against the common enemy. Defeat, however, would open the way for a new onslaught by one faction, or by both. Well before the electoral setbacks of 1950 and 1951, however, the experience of the Labour Government in domestic and foreign affairs had raised the doubts that swelled into the fierce controversy of later years. Beginning in July, 1949, for instance, a series of conferences was held by leading intellectuals to consider these doubts and attempt to resolve them. From these meetings resulted the *New Fabian Essays*, published early in 1952. Although the essays showed how deeply the old orthodoxies had been shaken, and the principal propositions of later revisionist doctrine can be found in some of the contributions, they expressed no coherent new doctrine. Even those writers who were most acutely aware of the inadequacies of public ownership could find reasons to call for "a large-scale extension of nationalisation."[3]

[3] *New Fabian Essays* (New York, 1952), pp. 66 and 81.

In its pronouncements prepared for the elections of 1950 and 1951, the party showed similar hesitancy. Directly in charge of policy statements and programs was Herbert Morrison, who not only held the posts of Lord President of the Council and Leader of the House in the Government, but also served as chairman of the N.E.C. subcommittee on policy from 1946 to 1952. His aim was consolidation.[4] In statements of program he wished to avoid another "list" of industries to be taken into public ownership and to state merely "criteria" which would guide a future Labour Government. At first, although the documents he fathered expressed a new recognition of the virtues of competition and private enterprise,[5] he was unable to have his way completely on public ownership; and the manifesto of 1950 included a strange medley of nationalization proposals.[6] The height of Morrison's influence on program was reached when, his hand strengthened by Labour's poor showing at the polls in 1950 and by evidence of the unpopularity of nationalization, he was able to secure the omission of a "list" from the policy statement of August, 1950 and from the manifesto of 1951.

After the defeat of 1951 the conflict entered a new and fiercer phase. Now those who clung most strenuously to the old orthodoxies had in Aneurin Bevan a redoubtable chief among the parliamentary leaders. For more than five years the party was torn by the "Bevanite" controversy. To term this phase of the conflict "Bevanite" is correct in so far as this phase was, in R. T. McKenzie's phrase, "a ferocious struggle for the succession."[7] Personal rivalries were indeed intense, at first primarily between Bevan and Morrison and then increasingly between Bevan and Gaitskell, as Gaitskell gained on Morrison as the leader of revisionism and as a contender for the succession to Attlee. But the controversy within

[4] See, for example, his comments in *Government and Parliament* (London, 1954), pp. 221-2.

[5] See *Labour Believes in Britain* (1949) and *Let Us Win Through Together*, the manifesto of 1950, as well as the policy statement, *Labour and The New Society* (August, 1950).

[6] To be nationalized were sugar refining, beet sugar manufacturing and cement. To be examined as likely candidates for nationalization were the chemical industry, water, fruit and vegetable marketing and meat wholesaling. Industrial assurance was initially put down for nationalization, but the objections of the Cooperative movement led to this being changed to "mutualization."

[7] R. T. McKenzie, "Policy Decision in Opposition: A Rejoinder," *Political Studies*, Vol. V, No. 2 (June, 1957), p. 178.

the party did not begin with Bevanism, nor did it end with the reconciliation between Bevan and Gaitskell accomplished in 1957. The struggle over the succession was given its power to arouse wide and deep antagonism by the continuing ideological division in the party.

Two factions had fairly clearly emerged. The Bevanites were led by a strong representation from the political, trade union, and intellectual elites of the party. Although Bevan was incontestably chief, he had able lieutenants in the parliamentary party, such as Wilson, Crossman, Driberg, Mikardo, and Barbara Castle, who usually were also members of the N.E.C. Moreover, he found strong support among the trade unions, including the three large organizations of the engineers, the shop and distributive workers, and the railwaymen.[8] Among the constituency parties, the Bevanite following was much stronger than in the parliamentary party, but even among Labour M.P.'s Bevan could count on a solid core of about a quarter of the parliamentary party which, when the issue was favorable, could be raised to almost half.[9]

In Parliament the opposing faction was led initially by Morrison and then increasingly by Gaitskell; Attlee inclined toward them, but frequently played the "broker" between the factions.[1]

[8] Between 1950 and 1955, total membership of the party ranged from 5.9 million to 6.5 million. Party membership of the three unions in round numbers was : Amalgamated Engineers Union, 590,000/635,000; Union of Shop Distributive and Allied Workers, 370,000; National Union of Railwaymen, 365,000/295,000.

[9] For instance, at its meeting of February 23rd, 1954, the P.L.P. agreed by a majority of only 113 to 109 to support the European Defense Community ("German rearmament"); a contrary amendment offered by Harold Wilson lost by the even narrower vote of 109 to 111.

[1] For example, in March 1955, over the question of Bevan's expulsion from the party. In the debate on the Government's White Paper approving manufacture of the H-bomb, Bevan had openly challenged Attlee's position and, along with sixty-two Labour M.P.'s, disregarded a three-line whip by abstaining from voting for the party amendment to the Government motion. By a vote of 9–4, Attlee obtained a recommendation from the Parliamentary Committee that the P.L.P. withdraw the whip from Bevan. With some reluctance Attlee put this recommendation to the party meeting, where it carried 141–112. Then, seeing the dangers not only of an even more bitter public split but also of resignations from the N.E.C., he did not support Morrison and Gaitskell in their effort to get the N.E.C. to expel Bevan from the party, but rather offered a compromise by which a subcommittee of the N.E.C. would interview Bevan and report back. Bevan seized this opportunity and offered promises of good behavior, which were accepted by the N.E.C.

This Morrison-Gaitskell faction enjoyed the support of most ex-ministers[2] and in the trade union world was stoutly supported, not to say egged on, by the Deakin-Lawther-Williamson axis with its command of about one third of the votes at the party conference and at the T.U.C.[3]

From 1951 to 1955 the strategic initiative was taken largely by the Bevanite faction. The Morrison-Gaitskell faction, of course, often made the first step in proposing a line of action. But its position consisted essentially in a defense of the policies and commitments of the Labour Government. Thus, for instance, while it resisted denationalization of steel and road haulage and proposed their return to public ownership, it accepted proposals for further measures of public ownership principally because of the need to compromise with the Bevanites. Similarly, in foreign affairs, it defended, against Bevan, the massive rearmament program that the Conservatives had inherited from the Labour Government and agreed to "German rearmament," which in principle Labour had accepted when in office.[4] Likewise, its acceptance of the decision to make the H-bomb can be viewed as the logical implication of the Labour Government's acceptance of atomic weapons.

Against this policy of consolidation the Bevanites launched a broad attack, taking issue on questions of both domestic and foreign affairs. Bevan had resigned over the question of charges

[2] Among them, however, a group of "mediators" sometimes appeared. In March 1952, for instance, Bevan and fifty-six Labour M.P.'s did not follow a party decision to vote for a Labour amendment to the Government's defense motion and to abstain on the main motion. Instead they abstained on the vote on the Labour amendment and voted against the Government motion. In the party meeting Attlee's motion that the rebels be censured was defeated 162–73, largely owing to the efforts of a group of ex-ministers including George Strauss, John Strachey and Kenneth Younger and supported by some eighty Labour M.P.'s. Their compromise, which consisted in the reimposition of Standing Orders, was then accepted.

[3] The party membership of the three unions between 1950 and 1955 was, in round numbers: National Union of Mineworkers, 650,000/675,000; Transport and General Workers Union, 830,000/1,000,000; National Union of General and Municipal Workers, 400,000/650,000.

[4] In February 1951, Attlee, while still Prime Minister, had approved of a West German contribution to European defense, with the proviso that "the arrangements must be such that German units are integrated in the defense forces in a way which would preclude the emergence again of a German military menace." 1954 LPCR, p. 23. In its statement approving of E.D.C., the N.E.C. referred to this previous declaration of the leader of the party. Ibid. See also Leon Epstein, "Cohesion of British Parliamentary Parties," American Political Science Review, Vol. L, No. 2 (June 1956), pp. 369–70.

for National Health Service prescriptions, but broadened his ground to include opposition to the rearmament program and reaffirmation of the old beliefs in public ownership. At the Morecambe conference of 1952, the need for a new program similar to that of 1945 was affirmed with all the old familiar rhetoric in a resolution that instructed the N.E.C. "to draw up a list of the key and major industries to be taken into public ownership" by a future Labour Government during a five-year period in office.[5] Bevan had made clear what such a new program meant to him when he assured conference that there was no other way "to achieve our socialist purposes which would not lead us through the old hard agony of public ownership."[6] Although the N.E.C. had found it discreet to accept the resolution, the Morrison-Gaitskell leadership went down that road only as far as they were pushed. In the process by which the new policy statement, *Challenge to Britain*, was drawn up, the Bevanites on the N.E.C. and at conference fought doggedly for their position and, although consistently outvoted, obtained numerous concessions. The peak of Bevanite influence in both the parliamentary and extra-parliamentary party was reached in 1954 during the conflict over "German rearmament." In the parliamentary party the policy survived by a margin of only two votes[7] and at conference only the last-minute switch of the woodworkers, who were joined by a few other small unions, saved it from defeat.[8]

Revisionist Counterattack

With Gaitskell's election as leader in December, 1955, a new phase of "rethinking" was inaugurated, the strategic initiative now being taken by the revisionists. The policy of consolidation that the majority faction had supported in the previous phase had implied a basic revision of the old orthodoxies. At the same time, certain individuals and groups had attempted to give this inchoate revisionism a coherent doctrine and to formulate a new statement of the meaning of Socialism.[9] After the defeat of 1955 and with

[5] 1952 *LPCR*, p. 91.
[6] *Ibid.*, p. 83.
[7] See above, p. 221, n. 9.
[8] The vote was 3,270,000 to 3,022,000. 1954 *LPCR*, p. 108.
[9] For instance, Hugh Gaitskell's pamphlet *Socialism and Nationalisation*, written in 1953 and published by the Fabian Society in 1956 (as Fabian Tract 300) and his article "The Economic Aims of the Labour Party," *Political Quarterly*, Vol. XXIV, No. 1 (January–March, 1953).

Gaitskell as leader, this effort was pushed forward. Comprehensive and well-considered statements of the revisionist view were produced, among them Socialist Union's *Twentieth Century Socialism* (1956) and C. A. R. Crosland's *The Future of British Socialism* (1957). At the same time, the party organization embarked on a far more elaborate process of program-making than had been previously attempted. A series of nine policy studies were prepared by subcommittees of the N.E.C., which were assisted by a large number of co-opted members, representing expert knowledge, important interest groups within the party, and different doctrinal points of view.[1] At the conferences of 1956, 1957, and 1958 these studies were considered and approved, and in late 1958 the party published *The Future Labour Offers You*, a comprehensive program that became the source of the manifesto for the election of 1959.

Not all the new ideas were warmly welcomed by conference. *Industry and Society*, which dealt with the future role of public ownership, had an especially rough passage in 1957 and although it won by a vote of 5,383,000 to 1,442,000, the critical remarks of Frank Cousins, head of the transport workers, suggested that so far as his personal opinion was concerned the union's million votes might just as well have been cast against the new proposals.[2] Still, on balance Gaitskell's views were accepted and the conflict with Bevan was stilled when, at the 1957 conference, having been appointed Shadow Foreign Secretary by Gaitskell, Bevan pleaded with great effect the platform's case against unilateral surrender of the British deterrent.[3] The party went into the campaign of 1959 in good heart and fought the election with energy and apparent unity at all levels.

But again the peace of the party was shattered on the morrow of defeat. Both factions took the initiative and had at one another with unparalleled virulence. Gaitskell attacked fundamentalism head-on by proposing to amend the ancient formula of Clause IV of the constitution, which defines the party's objectives as including "the common ownership of the means of production, distribution and exchange." Any hope he had of changing these

---

[1] The pamphlets were : *Personal Freedom; Homes of the Future; Towards Equality; Public Enterprise; Industry and Society; National Superannuation; Learning to Live; Prosper the Plough; Plan for Progress.*
[2] 1957 LPCR, p. 143.   [3] *Ibid.*, pp. 179–83.

words soon had to be abandoned and even a compromise, by which a lengthy revisionist version of the party's purpose would be added to Clause IV, was given up in favor of a mere recommendation to conference that this statement be accepted as "a valuable expression of the aims of the Labour party in the second half of the 20th century."[4] Yet this mild proposal itself aroused substantial opposition, the critical vote being 2,310,000 to 4,153,000.[5]

Some such modification of Clause IV as Gaitskell proposed, one may well think, was nothing more than the logical implication of the policies—especially those expressed in *Industry and Society* —that he had successfully espoused in recent years. But revisionism and fundamentalism did not only divide Labourites against one another. In many instances, it seems, these two currents of opinion also divided individuals against themselves. As well as a struggle of groups, the conflict was a *crise de conscience* throughout the party. The N.E.C., although it had supported Gaitskell's new line of policy, would not amend Clause IV and, in the face of wide opposition in constituency parties and trade unions and anticipating the reaction of the coming conference, retreated from its compromise position. The party's "principles" were, if anything, even more ambiguous after than before this abortive effort at clarification. "Labour politics," commented one observer, "are becoming the art of impossible verbal contortionism."[6]

The same conference that recorded this rejection of revisionism also administered to the leader of the party one of the most stinging defeats in Labour's history when the defense policy proposed by the N.E.C. was defeated by the proponents of unilateralism. The question of nuclear weapons had increasingly occupied the attention of the party, in no small part because of the activity of the Campaign for Nuclear Disarmament, which had been founded in 1958 and whose views were pressed within the party by the Victory for Socialism group. Initially accepting the need for an independent British deterrent, the official party policy had gradually moved toward the unilateralist position. The proposal of a unilateral and temporary suspension of tests gave way in 1959

[4] 1960 *LPCR*, p. 13.
[5] *Ibid.*, p. 221.   [6] *Economist*, March 19, 1960, p. 1079.

to the idea of the "non-nuclear club"[7] and in 1960, as the unilateralist campaign within the party made rapid and evident headway, this position was abandoned when the N.E.C. proposed
that Britain unilaterally give up its independent deterrent.[8] This
made the issue at the Scarborough conference of 1960 essentially
"neutralism" rather than "unilateralism," since the principal object of the opposition's attack was the N.E.C.'s willingness to
cooperate with the American deterrent in NATO by permitting
American use of British bases.

The hard core of the opposition on foreign policy was much
the same as that on domestic policy.[9] Among the large trade unions
it included the railwaymen and the transport workers who, under
Frank Cousins, had swung toward fundamentalism; and among the
leading politicians were Michael Foot, Barbara Castle, Tom Driberg, and Ian Mikardo (with Harold Wilson and R. H. S. Crossman playing for compromise). And, indeed, in winning support
for their case the champions of unilateralism, like the champions
of "full-blooded socialism," were fundamentalist, appealing to
premises and sentiments inherited from the Socialist Generation.
The old hostility to power politics was strongly marked. Rather
than military force organized in an alliance to maintain the balance
of power, they proposed negotiation; and moral suasion, along with
a strengthened United Nations, was set forth as the means to
preserve the peace.[1] Defeated at conference by small majorities,
the Gaitskellite faction organized its counterattack in an intra-

---

[7] *Disarmament and Nuclear War : The Next Step.* A joint statement by
the N.E.C. and General Council of the T.U.C., it was published June 24,
1959. The proposal was that Britain negotiate with other powers than the
U.S. and U.S.S.R. an agreement "not to test, manufacture or possess" nuclear
weapons.

[8] In a statement issued in July 1960, by the N.E.C. and General Council
of the T.U.C. on foreign policy and defense. See 1960 *LPCR*, p. 14.

[9] In his study of resolutions submitted to the Labour conference from
1955 to 1960, Dr. Richard Rose found that "support for CND and for Clause
4 and, alternatively, for Crosland's revisionist ideas and for NATO have
shown a very high degree of correlation." From a personal communication
to the author.

[1] The hostility to power politics and the adherence to supranationalism
come out strongly in the motion of the Amalgamated Engineering Union
and the speech of its mover. "The only defence for Britain," declared the
motion, "is for the settlement of international differences by negotiations
and a spirit of toleration between the nations and an understanding that
countries with different social systems can and must live with each other."
1960 *LPCR*, p. 176. Against this faith in negotiation, the proponents of

party movement called the Campaign of Democratic Socialism and, succeeding in winning over certain large unions, such as the Union of Shop, Distributive, and Allied Workers and the Amalgamated Engineering Union, as well as many constituency parties, was able to reverse the previous year's decisions at the conference of 1961, although not without still further concessions.[2]

Stalemate

Looking at the Labour Party during this decade, little seems to change. With almost compulsive iteration, the same battles are fruitlessly fought out again and again through the same cycle of renewed confrontation, bitter strife, and temporary and indecisive compromise. Personal factors and special historical circumstances affect the conflict : for instance, Bevan's personal ambition and remarkable powers of leadership, or the unique problems presented by nuclear weapons. Yet in the behavior of the party there is remarkable continuity of pattern.

In the first place, the basic conflict over party purpose continued throughout. Particular questions arose, such as an item of program or a choice among persons for some office. These questions were perceived and fought out, however, from the perspective of two opposing conceptions of the meaning of Socialism which, from time to time, precipitated fairly well-defined factions. The party structure for debate and decision-making was highly responsive to the initiatives of the factions, and more than adequately performed its role as a means of communication. But as a means of making lasting and clear-cut decisions, that structure was a failure.

NATO called on the other "principle" of Labour foreign policy, collective security under international auspices (see Sam Watson's speech, *ibid.*, p. 171). The A.E.U. speaker, however, did not find that NATO fitted Labour's conception of supranationalism. "If we really believe in world peace," he said, "can NATO provide the answer? If you think it can, you are not with me. I think the only answer is the collective strengthening of the United Nations and possibly some reorganization of the regional pacts that tend to disrupt peace and interfere with the spirit of tolerance" (*ibid.*, p. 177).

[2] In particular, the proposal that Britain cooperate with the American deterrent in NATO by providing bases was qualified by the proviso that Britain "must remain free to decide according to the circumstances whether or not any particular project should be accepted and under what conditions." 1961 *LPCR*, p. 8.

When a question was formulated and brought to a vote in one of the party's forums of decision, the revisionists usually had the better of the contest. To this extent, observers were justified in speaking of the "transformation" of the party.[3] Yet these victories of revisionism were neither clear-cut nor permanent. One could never say with perfect assurance that the party had surrendered its old goal of the Socialist Commonwealth in favor of the Welfare State and the Managed Economy. And once the electoral pressure for unity had passed, the struggle was reopened.

Yet in spite of this prolonged conflict over principle, exacerbated by personal ambition and no little malice, the party hung together. From time to time a "party within a party" appeared. Yet Labour did not split, often as that eventuality was forecast. No set of leaders and followers broke off to form a new organization, or to form an alliance with the Liberals or Communists. In the House, although there were often sharp exchanges among party members, and on occasion substantial abstentions on party votes, cross-voting was negligible and party unity in the division lobbies could hardly have been higher. At election times, candidates and party workers did acknowledge a common program and a common leadership. In crucial aspects of behavior, in short, the party, for all the dissidence, retained much of its ancient solidarity.

The Labour Party of 1951–61 was not the Labour Party of the Socialist Generation. Yet these special features of the decade of conflict can only be understood in the light of the characteristics the party had inherited from the earlier period; in particular, its democratic structure, its commitment to ideology, and its class character.

FOLLOWERS AND LEADERS

What model of the party's power structure best fits the facts of the period 1951–61? Elitist theory suggests a general approach. Basically the conflict is seen as an interaction between "leaders" and "followers." The leaders are those who hold, or expect to hold, high political office, and the followers are those who, as members of the mass organization, perform tasks of electioneering

[3] See, for instance, Gerhard Loewenberg, "The Transformation of British Labour Party Policy since 1945," *Journal of Politics*, Vol. XXI, No. 1 (May, 1959), pp. 234–57.

in the localities. The leaders tend to be moderate, the followers militant. There are various reasons why the two groups differ in their views of the party purpose. In general, one might try to relate the differences to different functions in the party. The leaders, it could be said, will be more sensitive to the need for appealing to marginal voters—after all, it is they who will or will not enjoy office—and more aware of the difficulties of carrying out large promises, since they will be the ones with the responsibility. The followers, on the other hand, lacking the motivation that comes from the anticipation of office, will be more likely to be partisans with utopian hopes.[4] In any case, conflict is normal, and possibly inherent, in a mass party with a representative form of organization.

A further step in the development of this approach is the suggestion that in such conflicts the leadership normally has its way. The parliamentary chiefs (so the hypothesis would run) enjoy a dominating influence in the party. This is because of the usual technical and psychological reasons of elitist theory and, in the British case, especially because of the authority that gravitates to the parliamentary leaders of a party from the British constitution and two-party system which make them the prospective chiefs of a future Government. Such influence makes the leadership a true elite, that is, a body of men who can impose their views on the mass of their followers. Thus, for instance, while the leadership must make some allowance for the views expressed by their followers at the annual conference of the party, they can on the whole control those views or, if need be, disregard them.

This latter view need not detain us long. For the story of the 1950's is certainly not the story of an elite imposing its views upon the mass. If it had been, those years would not have been so deeply troubled a decade. There was indeed a group of moderate leaders who tried to win acceptance of their views from the mass membership of the party. They usually could muster a majority for their side in the various forums of decision—the P.L.P., the

---

[4] "The voluntary and amateur nature of these associations," Leon Epstein has written, "ensures that they attract zealots in the party cause, and particularly so at the local leadership level, where there are many routine political chores which only the devoted are likely to perform. Principles, not professional careers, are what matter here." "British M.P.'s and their Local Parties: The Suez Case," *American Political Science Review*, Vol. LIV (1960), p. 385.

N.E.C., and the conference. But they certainly were not able to impose their views on the party as a whole. The fundamentalists were usually outvoted, but this led, at best, only to a lull in the conflict, not a termination. And far from being able to disregard the opinions of the militants, the revisionist leadership, even when in a majority, normally made substantial concessions to their views.

The general proposition that the conflict was essentially between leaders and followers deserves more attention. A specific form is sometimes given this view in the crude assertion that the parliamentary leadership plus "the unions" dominate the party and that, in particular, the leadership depends upon the block vote of the unions at conference to steamroller the militant demands of the constituency parties. Plainly, this version does not conform to the facts, since in the 1951–61 period the unions were substantially divided. One gets rather closer to the facts, however, with the proposition that usually in the Labour Party the parliamentary leadership plus the leadership of the larger trade unions are able to overpower the militant element among the followers. During Attlee's regime and for some time thereafter— so this interpretation would run—the parliamentary chiefs along with the heads of the three largest unions (Deakin of the transport workers, Williamson of the municipal workers, and Lawther of the mineworkers) constituted "the leadership" of the party. They were substantially in agreement on their moderate views of the party purpose, but confronted, however, a militant opposition strongly based in the constituency parties and including several unions, the larger being the engineers, the shop and distributive workers, and the railwaymen. In the higher echelons of the party —the P.L.P. and the N.E.C.—the "leadership" was safely in control. Its main confrontations with the militants took place at the party conference, where the "followers" were heavily represented. The Big Three among the unions, however, cast about one third of the votes at conference. Thanks to this huge block of support, the "leadership" had such an initial advantage in any contest (it needed to win in addition only about one fifth of the votes) that it rarely was defeated. In this way, some observers would conclude, the big unions kept conference in the hands of "the leadership" and the combination among the political and industrial chiefs maintained Labour as a "responsible," i.e., moderate, party.

The essential error of this model is its attempt to identify the contesting groups as leaders and followers. In fact, the party was not split, so to speak, horizontally between upper and lower echelons, but vertically between two sets of leaders and followers. At every level there was conflict—from Shadow Cabinet through N.E.C. and conference to individual constituency parties and trade unions.

The leader-follower model presupposes a unified leadership. And in Bevanite days, for instance, the Parliamentary Committee was, to be sure, preponderately moderate. But whether he was at any particular moment a member of the Parliamentary Committee, Aneurin Bevan was at all times a major parliamentary leader and, as we have seen, he had able co-adjutors in the political, intellectual, and industrial elites of the party. This leader-follower model of the conflict is also misleading in that it obscures the difficulties that the moderate leadership had with the P.L.P. and exaggerates the opposition they met among constituency parties. The hard core of Bevanite M.P.'s, to be sure, included only about one fifth to one quarter of Labour M.P.'s, while rather more than half of the constituency delegates usually followed the Bevanite lead at conference. But on a favorable issue the Bevanite faction in the P.L.P. could raise its support perilously close to a majority and, even when in a minority, could force concessions from the moderate leadership.[5] Nor did the constituency parties constitute a solid mass of militants.[6] On the contrary, within individual parties, as in the party as a whole, there was a division of opinion, some-

[5] When, for instance, the Conservative Government's motion approving German rearmament under the Paris Agreement came before the House in November 1954, the logical thing for the P.L.P. to do would have been to vote in favor, since the policy had been approved by votes of both the parliamentary and extra-parliamentary organizations. The threat of the Bevanites and others to vote against the Agreement, however, obliged the moderate leadership to compromise by making abstention the party line in order to avoid public display of a wide split within the party. One Labour M.P., Jock McGovern, did vote for the Government motion, showing thereby that he had "the courage of Mr. Attlee's convictions." See Leon Epstein, "Cohesion of British Parliamentary Parties," *American Political Science Review*, Vol. L, No. 2 (June, 1956), pp. 369–71.

[6] At the 1953 conference, for instance, a resolution proposing public ownership for twelve industries concerned with engineering and shipbuilding was moved by the Foundry Workers and seconded by the A.E.U. It was defeated by a vote of 4,499,000 to 1,797,000. 1953 *LPCR*, p. 128. At least half the minority votes came from trade unions, so no more than 900,000 could have been cast by constituency delegates. Since, however, the constituency parties were entitled to a vote of 1,291,000, some 400,000, or about a third of the constituency party vote, must have been cast for the moderate position and against the resolution.

times fairly well-defined as factions that had acknowledged leaders and consistent supporters, and which contended for the support of those who were committed to neither side, or who in a real sense belonged to both, responding to the old utopian appeals and yet accepting men and measures of the moderate wing. In short, what one found in the local party was not a platoon of the extremist army, but a battleground, which in little reproduced the struggle that was rending the party as a whole.[7]

The conflict did not consist in a struggle between elites but in the clash of two currents of opinion, each running strongly throughout the party. During the Bevanite period the conflict was exacerbated by "a ferocious struggle for the succession." But the clash of opinion had already begun before Bevan made his bid for power ("We welcomed him into our ranks," commented one leader of Keep Left) and it rose to new heights of intensity after Bevan had made his peace with Gaitskell in 1957. The initiative in conducting the conflict was not monopolized by the leadership of the respective factions, but was widely diffused in the various sectors and at the various levels of the party. And the way to an expression of these initiatives was opened and kept open by the democratic procedures of the party—not only at conference, but in the N.E.C., P.L.P., and Parliamentary Committee as well. A defeat for one side, even if layered over with compromise, did not settle the issue. It was always possible and legitimate to reopen the controversy.

[7] In a comprehensive study of resolutions submitted to conference over the five years 1955–59, Dr. Richard Rose has put this matter of the attitudes of the constituency policies into perspective. Classifying the resolutions as Non-Partisan, Partisan, Right, and Left, he defined the last category, "Left-wing Labour," as statements "calling for a radical transformation of the domestic mixed economy welfare state, or of the existing system of international relations, in order to make the breakthrough to the Socialist society." Of all resolutions from trade unions and other affiliated societies, as well as constituency parties, during these five years, about one third fell into this category. There was, however, no significant variation in the scores of the constituency parties alone as compared with trade unions. The resolutions of each constituency party were also examined, each party being classified according to the per cent of extremist resolutions it submitted. In this classification only 18% of the parties fell under the category of "high extremism" by submitting resolutions of which half or more could be called "Leftwing Labour." Those with average extremism—i.e., 25% to 50% of their resolutions were Leftwing—made up 35% of all parties studied. The low and no extremism categories included 47%. "The Political Ideas of English Party Activists," American Political Science Review, Vol. LVI, No. 2 (June, 1962), pp. 360–71.

The Role of Conference

What was the role of conference? Specifically, was conference the "final authority" in determining the party's purpose? In 1959–60 this question, in some circles, excited as much passion as the substantive issues. In the first place, it should be observed, no one doubted the full authority of conference to determine the party program from which the manifesto, binding on M.P.'s and any future Labour Government, would be selected. The question came on whether the conference could change a policy to which the parliamentary party had been pledged by the manifesto, namely Britain's commitment to NATO.[8] The refusal of the P.L.P. to accept the "neutralist" decisions of the 1960 conference showed that conference was not the "final authority" in this sense.

On the other hand, in this instance, as generally throughout this period, the balance of opinion at conference exerted a very great influence on the policy of the parliamentary party. As we have observed, from 1958 to 1961, the Gaitskellite leadership had moved toward the position of its opponents, so much so that by the 1961 conference its policy was almost indistinguishable from that of Frank Cousins and the original policy of the Campaign for Nuclear Disarmament.[9] To be sure, the influence of conference was exercised largely by anticipation, as the moderate leadership made such adjustments in its views as were necessary to avoid defeats at conference.[1] This made it no less influential, although

[8] "We have always realized," said the manifesto, *Britain Belongs to You*, "that power is required to make the rule of law effective. That is why during the period of east-west deadlock we have stood resolutely by our defensive alliances and contributed our share to western defence through NATO."

[9] Commenting on these facts, David Marquand wrote: "The real point is that the balance of power in the Labour Party proved to be such that the leadership could maintain its position only by making significant concessions to its critics." "Passion and Politics," *Encounter*, Vol. XXVII, No. 6 (December, 1961), p. 3.

[1] Martin Harrison writes: ". . . normally the N.E.C. is careful to prepare its victories. It makes sure that its fate is no longer in the balance long before Conference meets, making promises and concessions if need be." *Trade Unions and the Labour Party Since 1945* (London, 1960), p. 196. Similarly, Saul Rose, a former member of the central party staff, has said: ". . . estimates of the feeling within the Party and probable Conference reactions play a considerable part in shaping proposals made by the N.E.C. . . . Results are not guaranteed: it is not very exceptional for the N.E.C.

it does make that influence far harder to measure. Nor was it
strange that conference should be heeded. It assembled representatives of the main resources of the party : its political, industrial,
and intellectual leaders; bureaucrats, M.P.'s, activists, and money-
givers. Quite apart from formal provisions of the party constitution and the powerful democratic "myth" of the Labour Movement, such an assemblage would have great weight in the party.

IDEOLOGY VERSUS DEMOCRACY

The nonelitist, democratic structure of the party perpetuated
the conflict without being able to settle it. Why this failure of
the democratic method? We will get some light on this question if
we will look at the task the decision-making structure of the party
was being asked to perform.

A major political party will be at least a coalition of interest
groups. Sometimes it will be united by nothing beyond these
ties and some broad and perhaps confused tendencies in social
outlook. Nor need such loose bonds of belief prevent it from
being at times the agent of notable deeds. Since 1918 the Labour
Party, however, has claimed to be much more. When it became
a Socialist party at that time, it committed itself to an ideology—
that is, to a comprehensive social philosophy with definite implications for program. The program was carried out by the Attlee
Government; the social philosophy was called into question by
the Government's experience : hence the conflict between those
who championed the old meaning of Socialism and those who
tried to formulate a new meaning. But even in this struggle over
major beliefs, the contestants, whether fundamentalist or revisionist, agreed on a basic premise. All accepted the necessity for a
social philosophy with programmatic consequences. The opposing
sides were at swords' points with regard to their respective ideologies, but they were united in their ideologism.

When, for instance, the authors of the *New Fabian Essays*
held their meetings, beginning in 1949, they found themselves
opposed on many points. But on "the nature of the main problem"
they were agreed. What the party needed was not "merely new

---

to be defeated at conference or be obliged to make concessions." "Policy
Decision in Opposition," *Political Studies*, Vol. IV, No. 2 (June, 1956), pp.
131-2.

expedients" or "new planks in an election programme," but "a new analysis of the political, economic and social scene as a basis for reformulating socialist principles."[2] This, one need not emphasize, is a tall order : to work out with regard to a particular nation "a new analysis of the political, economic and social scene" in order to derive the principles that will guide a great political party. But on this premise, later fundamentalists and revisionists—R. H. S. Crossman along with C. A. R. Crosland, Ian Mikardo along with Roy Jenkins—were at one.

Again, in 1956 at the start of the Gaitskellite phase of rethinking, Socialist Union, a revisionist group, similarly grounded its case for "twentieth century socialism." While "traditional theories of socialism" were no longer adequate, it would be a mistake to follow the advice of "empiricists" who are "content to deal with immediate problems as they arise. On the contrary, "some new vision must now be sought" which would provide a "philosophical substitute appropriate to the mid-twentieth century."[3] With no less devotion to the need for vision and theory, fundamentalists scorned the products of Gaitskellite rethinking. One of the policy statements issuing from it, for instance, was described by them as a "pathetic document" whose many vices sprang from its authors not having "a theory of society," but only "a set of ad hoc responses to particular abuses." "This is what happens," it was concluded despairingly, "when a party surrenders its soul to the empiricists."[4]

The crisis in the party was, in the first place, the product of the confrontation of old Socialist commitments with new social and political realities. One can understand this prolonged and bitter conflict only if one sees it against the background of the party's commitments during the Socialist Generation. If Labour had been merely a coalition in which the Socialist wing was only one among many elements, if it had been a party united only by some broad tendencies in social outlook, its response would have been different and the process of adaptation very much easier. But Labour was a party in which commitment to a specific Socialist orthodoxy had for years given it, in R.H.S. Crossman's words, "a central myth,"

---

[2] *Op. cit.,* p. xi.
[3] *Twentieth Century Socialism* (London, 1956), pp. 14, 16, 17.
[4] *New Statesman and Nation,* June 23, 1956, in a review of *Personal Freedom.*

"a structure of ideological loyalty."[5] When these beliefs were challenged by revisionism, the resulting conflict was bound to be severe.

But the conflict was not simply between ideologues and empiricists. The question was not simply, "Shall we give up ideology?" Empiricists there no doubt were—those who were "content to deal with immediate problems as they came up." But empiricists were disparaged by revisionists and fundamentalists alike. This ideologism of the two factions, their compelling idea that Labour must have a unifying idea, gave the struggle much of its peculiar character. It meant, in the first place, that great effort and serious attention would be devoted to "rethinking." For fundamentalists this meant reaffirming the old orthodoxies and injecting them into new programs for advance toward the Socialist Commonwealth. Revisionists undertook the more difficult task of framing a new orthodoxy. For although they were ready to adapt to what they regarded as social and political realities, they did not advocate mere adaptation. On the contrary, they sought to construct a new theoretical analysis and prescription that would not only win votes and enable the party to govern, but also give it a new "agreement on its principles."[6] Like the fundamentalists they too believed that Labour was united by an idea.

Revisionist Ideology

The conflict over what this idea was raised major questions of ideology. In their continual quarrels over program, revisionists and fundamentalists normally joined issue on the question of public ownership : What further industries should be specified for nationalization? Or, more generally, was public ownership to be extended until private ownership became no longer the rule, but the exception? At times it seemed that an inordinate amount of attention was devoted to this question. That would indeed be the revisionists' opinion. For their contention was precisely that public ownership was merely one of various means to Socialist goals. In the old orthodoxy for which the fundamentalists spoke, however, public ownership was of central signifi-

[5] "On Political Neuroses," *Encounter*, Vol. II, No. 5 (May, 1954), p. 67.
[6] Rita Hinden in Abrams and Rose, *op. cit.*, p. 117.

cance. It was an indispensable condition and a major expression of a radically transformed economy, society, and culture.

In the fundamentalist view, only by means of public ownership could the market be dethroned and public administration established as the central means of control over the economy. But for the revisionists the market rather than public administration would be the principal controlling mechanism. Admittedly, this market would be conditioned by heavily progressive taxation and massive welfare services and manipulated by broad controls, largely fiscal and monetary. Otherwise, however, competition among separate units would determine the allocation of resources, human and material.

This conflict over economic theory involved vital differences in social and ethical outlook and in the quality of life that revisionist and fundamentalist, respectively, thought Socialism could and should achieve. Where the market rules, there self-interest is the dynamic of behavior. The revisionists were ready to accept this implication. Indeed, one might better say, they started from it as a premise : "every economic system devised for ordinary human beings," wrote Arthur Lewis, "must have self-interest as its driving force."[7] In revisionist thinking and in the party documents that reflected it, there was during the 1950's a growing emphasis not only upon the private sector of the economy and the mechanisms of the market, but also upon the incentives of gain and competition.[8]

The revisionists, to be sure, wished to reduce the scale of existing pecuniary differentials in the name of Socialist equality. Yet they also expected that the dynamic of the future society would enlist the support of other egoistic motives : the desire for prestige, power, status, "esteem for success" and "recognition of ability."[9] It may be that no social system can function effectively unless it does enlist such motives. In this sense the revisionist an-

[7] See Ch. VII, p. 199, n. 5.

[8] This was markedly the case during the Gaitskellite period of rethinking, as, for instance, in the party pamphlet on equality and freedom, *Twentieth Century Socialism*, and Gaitskell's pamphlet on nationalization. All place much reliance upon the commercial motives of capitalism among both workers and managers, in the public as well as the private sector.

[9] "Esteem for success" and "recognition of ability" were some of the incentives on which the authors of *Twentieth Century Socialism* relied in addition to differences in income. *Towards Equality*, a party pamphlet published in 1956, recognized the desire for prestige and power as motives that would be utilized in a Socialist society.

alysis and prescription may well have been correct. Whether correct or not, revisionism attacked Socialist ideology at its heart—the doctrine of fellowship. For in this doctrine Socialism had not rejected merely commercialism and capitalism, but something more fundamental—moral egoism.

Fellowship referred not only to a motive—selfless service—but also to the standard of social evaluation on which the culture of a classless society would be founded. It might well be questioned how far that society could be classless in which egoistic incentives played as large a part as allowed them by revisionist social theory. Differences in prestige and esteem—the principal marks of a class system—would remain as incentives to individual ambition. In the ensuing struggle in the marketplace and other arenas of social competition, the mechanisms of success would not be the same as under capitalism. The effects of inheritance would be largely eliminated and disparities in income and wealth greatly reduced. Equality of opportunity in education and in promotion in industry would be established. And presumably the general social ethic would be such as to lead the members of the community to accept as right and proper these restrictions on the older forms of privilege and self-aggrandizement. But social hierarchy would remain and might well be strengthened because social status would now be firmly based on social function.

It is not my purpose to elaborate a critique of revisionism, but only to show that far from being merely a set of *ad hoc* responses to governmental and electoral problems it consisted of a body of doctrine—fairly coherent doctrine—and that these ideas challenged many of the fundamentals of Labour's old orthodoxies. Each faction of the party, in short, had an ideology and each sought to commit Labour to its ideological position. Yet, although the balance of advantage in program-making lay with the revisionists, the party was unable to make a clear-cut decision.

In repeated attempts to restate Labour's purpose, whether as principle or program, the outcome was compromise. From the perspective of other types of politics, that was hardly unnatural and should have been the likely road to a settlement. What could be more familiarly "political" than compromise in which each side makes concessions to the other, or, if concessions cannot be traded, each side is mollified by ambiguities open to rival interpretations? But the compulsive ideologism of Labour ruled out this sort of politics and the unity which was achieved from time to time was only temporary.

In 1960, after nearly ten years of fierce controversy, a prominent revisionist could write: "Unity in the Party can never be re-created by a series of uneasy compromises; the trouble goes too deep for that." Labour, she granted, had worked in unity during the previous election. "But all the time, beneath this façade of unity, there lurked conflicts of principle which were never resolved. . . . No political party can be effective without some underlying agreement on its principles; it is that which ultimately determines whether it speaks with one voice."[1] The ideologism shared by the revisionist with the fundamentalist is evident in this analysis, which assumes that not only Labour but also any political party must be united on principle and must speak with one voice to be "effective." But the analysis is nonetheless correct as applied to Labour, for if this assumption is widely shared in a party, then indeed that party will not be able to find lasting unity in compromise.

"Democracy" characterizes a type of power structure and "ideology" a type of group purpose. The two principles are not easily combined in the organization of a single political formation. Democracy multiplies the chances and opportunities of dissent and so limits the extent to which an identity of views can be achieved. Usually, therefore, the decisions it produces are heavy with compromise among divergent interests and opinions. Ideology, on the other hand, spurns compromise and in a high degree demands an identity of views and unanimity of purpose. In a democratic context this demand is likely to lead to continual controversy and an inability to make lasting decisions. For effective action, some more authoritarian and elitist form of rule would seem to be the appropriate companion of the commitment to ideology. Yet Labour had chosen to be both ideological and democratic and, given the special circumstances of the Socialist Generation, when the party was pervaded by substantial consensus on the Socialist orthodoxies, the party was able to make the combination work. The loss of this consensus revealed the natural antipathy of the two principles of organization.

[1] Rita Hinden in Abrams and Rose, *op. cit.,* p. 117.

CLASS AND GROUP POLITICS

In spite of the prolonged and intense conflict over purpose, the party did not split. There is more than one reason for this. But when one is trying to assess the influences that held the party together through this decade, one cannot neglect the role of the trade unions. I have not made them, I trust, the *deus ex machina* that explains everything the party has done and not done. The solidarity of their support, however, has incontestably been a major restraint on the party's fissiparous tendencies. How deep this sentiment runs has been remarked by Martin Harrison in his study of the unions and the party during the postwar period. "No one who has worked among active trade unionists," he has said, "could fail to be aware of how often affiliation with Labour is taken as a natural and undiscussed part of union life. The association between union membership and Labour voting is assumed to be automatic."[2] This sense of identification is reflected in the union conferences where Labour policies that "arouse furious debate outside" are accepted without question.[3] Although controversy between unions and within unions was bitter over questions of party purpose, the alliance retained its vitality. There was never any real prospect that any union would leave the party over these political differences. If its leaders had made the attempt, their rank and file would not have followed them.[4] Nor had this solidarity with the party been merely a matter of refraining from separation. Throughout the decade of conflict, as generally in the postwar period, the unions maintained their massive financial contributions to the party, which received more than half its total income from them.[5] Without access to a substantial fraction of this money—to put the matter very bluntly—it would have been utterly suicidal for any section of the political wing of the party to break off.

To put the point in the terms used in our account of the party during the interwar period, one can say that the organized working class continued to adhere to its strategy of political independence adopted in 1918. Even though the old consensus on the meaning of Socialism had been disrupted, the consciousness of

[2] *Trade Unions and the Labour Party Since 1945* (London, 1960), p. 18.
[3] *Ibid.*, p. 158.
[4] *Ibid.*, p. 345.   [5] *Ibid.*, pp. 99–100.

class persisted. For those who were trying to modernize the party's image, this was a distressing fact, but nonetheless a fact. Actually, of course, the working class, now as in the past, was by no means solid in its support of Labour, and the Conservatives continued to draw a very substantial working-class vote—on average in the postwar period of about one third of that vote.[6] But overwhelmingly, Labour's supporters identified it as the party that was supported by the working class and which stood for the working class.[7]

Class relations had vastly changed from the days when economic insecurity and political exclusion had isolated the mass of the manual workers from the rest of British society. Their great material grievances had been largely remedied by welfarism and full employment and their passionate thrust for power mollified by quasi-corporatism and the general acceptance of organized labor as a full and legitimate member of the political community. With this change in economic and political relations, as many observers have commented, the old hostilities of class conflict relaxed. They did not vanish : the language of class still came quite naturally to the lips of Labour supporters.

Moreover, within the broad framework of the Welfare State and Managed Economy there remained important questions of "more" and "less" that involved the economic and social interests of groups in the working class : higher benefits for old age pensioners, heavier subsidies for tenants of state housing, equal pay for women workers, improvements in pay and conditions for shop and factory workers, wider educational opportunities for children of the less well-to-do, more generous provisions for Health Service patients, greater consideration for the farm workers and the "small farmer."[8] On these goals, fundamentalists and revisionists alike could agree. From such promises, party managers could hope to make electoral gains. During the 1950's such appeals to interest groups constituted a very large component of those compromise programs on which the party periodically managed to unite. Increasingly, Labour's electoral effort was directed toward winning votes by a politics of group interest.

[6] See, for instance, Richard Rose's table averaging out surveys of the class basis of Conservative and Labour votes during the postwar period in Abrams and Rose, *op. cit.*, p. 76.

[7] *Ibid.*, see tables, pp. 20 and 15.

[8] These examples of group appeals are taken from the 1958 statement, *The Future Labour Offers You.*

Indeed, the policy statement in which the Gaitskellite period of rethinking culminated, *Your Personal Guide to The Future Labour Offers You*, was conveniently thumb-indexed with references to "Your Home," "Your Job," "Education," "Health," "Age Without Fear," and so on, as if to enable tenants, workers, patients, and other groups to turn directly to the promises beamed to them. Putting the matter in a historical perspective, one could say that, broadened in scope, the "interests of labour," which had given the party its purpose at its foundation, continued to provide it with goals of policy when its ideological commitment was obscured and enfeebled.

Compared with the interwar years, British politics in the 1950's showed a great decline in class antagonism. At the same time, the issues between the parties became much less ideological. To a great degree the questions dividing them became marginal, statistical, quantitative : questions of "more" or "less" rather than great social theories in conflict. Correspondingly, general elections consisted less of pitched battles between opposing social philosophies than of small raids on interest groups. As class and ideological contours faded, groups appeared as more prominent features of the political scene.

Comparatively considered in a historical view, these generalizations are correct. Yet they should not be allowed to conceal other features. The ideological urge, though confused and weakened, was by no means extinguished in Labour. In its determinations of domestic and foreign policy, old ideological currents helped shape the party's position. Labour still had a conception of purpose and an order of priorities readily distinguishable from those of the Conservatives. Such comparisons, however, can be more intelligibly made after we have taken a look at the Conservative Party.

PART THREE

The Conservative Party

CHAPTER IX

Disraelian Conservatism

Tory Democracy involves both a conception of authority and a conception of purpose, an idea of how power ought to be distributed and an idea of the objects which power should serve. In Chapter III we examined the first aspect of Tory Democracy; the primary task of the following chapters is to compare the Tory image of political organization with the actual behavior of the Conservative Party, asking how far image and reality coincide. Yet the question of power cannot be isolated from the question of purpose. As in our study of the Labour Party, we shall also be obliged to ask what purposes the Conservative Party has served, what broad policies it has used the power of the state to promote. Our concern will be mainly with the Conservative Party of the years after World War II, but we shall also take a briefer look at the party during the period from 1867 to World War I and during the interwar years.

POWER STRUCTURE : TORY AND SOCIALIST MODELS

Central to Toryism in its democratic and pre-democratic phases is the notion of the independent authority of government. "A British government . . . is an independent body which on taking office assumes the responsibility of leading and directing Parliament and the nation in accordance with its own judgement and convictions."[1] Amery's words echo a view that not only runs back through the nineteenth century—Salisbury, Disraeli, Peel—but

[1] Quoted above, Ch. III, p. 96.

also, as we have seen, derives from the basic Tudor conception of statesmanship. This notion of independent authority is not simply a view of the basis of the legitimacy of governmental decisions— the idea, for instance, that the authority of government decisions derives from inherent powers of the Crown as well as from the will of the people.[2] It is also a practical rule of how decisions should be made if government is to be effective. In the view of this Tory sociology, self-government in the Radical or Socialist sense is impossible, or, so far as it is possible, leads to the triumph of selfish interests and to general ineffectiveness. But this does not mean that in the Tory view the independence of the Government is absolute. There is room and need for listening to grievances, taking advice, and winning acquiescence : thus the Cabinet "parleys" with Parliament and the nation, as once the Monarch did with the estates of the realm. In the democratic framework, moreover, the Government may be removed from power by the electorate. If the Tory version of the Constitution is followed, its successor, however, will have the same powers of independent decision-making. In this way the modern electorate, as Burke said of the House of Commons, is a control on government, but does not itself govern.

A similar conception of authority informs the Conservative Party's official theory of party leadership. Party policy is determined by the Leader. He will in practice consult with groups and leading individuals within the party and indeed will receive advice from party organs. But final decisions are exclusively his to make. His authority, moreover, is subject not only to the influence of such parleys but also to the final sanction of removal. The subtle protocol governing these palace revolutions, as well as the initial choice of a Leader, is a subject better learned from the history of the party than from any explicit rules of organization.[3] The broad similarity with the Tory conception of constitutional authority remains : The Leader is expected to lead. If he is removed, his successor is endowed with the same wide authority.

These views of the necessary power of leaders, whether in Government, party, or indeed any sphere where a social order

[2] Discussed by Harry Eckstein in *Patterns of Government*, Beer and Ulam, eds., 2nd ed. (New York, 1962), esp. pp. 75–80.

[3] The standard study is R. T. McKenzie, *British Political Parties* (New York, 1955), Chs. II and III.

must be created and maintained, descend from a body of political thought of great antiquity. This body of thought stresses the importance of strong government and includes a view of the nature of the governing process and of the personal qualities that governors must have if government is to be strong and effective. It does not disdain the need for foresight in those who govern or for a tradition to guide them. But it is deeply suspicious of attempts to subject the process of governing to an explicit and comprehensive social philosophy from which imperative programs are derived. It would rather trust men of the governing class to do "what is necessary" in any particular set of circumstances. As the nature of governing requires wide discretion for the governors, the capacities of the governing class justify their independent authority. In this manner, the ideas of independent authority, class rule, non-programmatic decisions, and strong government are logically related in a coherent body of political thought.

How do these ideas fit with the way power has actually been distributed in and used by the Conservative Party?

To this wide-ranging question spokesmen and intellectuals of the Labour Party, during the Socialist Generation, had a reply that is equally far-ranging and no less impressive for being familiar. Its key is, of course, class analysis, and its main theme is that the Conservatives have represented capitalism and the interests of the capitalist class. This interpretation has been stated with elaborations of greater or less sophistication. For the sake of having a coherent and sharply stated account, I shall, on the whole, follow the version offered by Harold Laski in 1938.

"A party," he wrote, "is essentially what is implied in the economic interests of its supporters."[4] The Conservatives, accordingly, have been a party of the capitalist class. While in the early nineteenth century they were particularly partial to landed wealth and the Liberals to industrial and commercial wealth, both parties accepted capitalism, differing only over "the precise manner in which the capitalist system should be run." Britain had "for all effective purposes, a single party in control of the state," although it was "divided, no doubt, into two wings."[5] In the twentieth

---

[4] *Parliamentary Government in England* (New York, 1938), p. 63.
[5] *Ibid.*, pp. 70, 72.

century this division was ended when the rise of Labour and the decline of the Liberals made the Conservatives the party of the unified interests of the capitalist class. Now the two major parties were divided on "fundamentals," Labour standing for "socialization" and the Conservatives for "a faith in the private ownership of the means of production."[6]

According to this Socialist view, the Conservatives have indeed stood for class rule, representing and being controlled by "the governing class." The important fact about this class, however, was not any special capacity for governing, but its position as the possessing class. The "main governmental apparatus," wrote Laski, "is in the hands of those who have been themselves successful in acquisition. It is they who determine what the state shall do with its power."[7] Many people who are not themselves capitalists have supported Conservatives. These are not, however, the supporters to whom the party is significantly responsive. The economic types who have predominated in the party's inner councils and whose interests it has mainly represented have been the great aristocrat, the landowner, the rentier, the businessman.[8] This is not to say that the governing class and the leaders of the Conservative party consciously act from mere economic self-interest. As much as any men, they are guided by conceptions of justice and of economic feasibility, but between these conceptions and the interests of capitalists there is substantial coincidence. Although not recognizing it, Conservatives are as committed to an ideology as any Socialist is.

Nor is there any need for Conservatives to inquire seriously into their party purpose and the principles by which they govern. That hostility to theory and to program on which they pride themselves is compatible with and indeed functional to their task. This task is not radically to reform society in the light of a social ideal, but to maintain the status quo. Their party history, therefore, has not been notable for great programs of legislation and their leaders have typically regarded administration as the main concern of government. Not any inherent quality of the governing process, but rather this commitment to maintaining the capitalist system

---

[6] *Ibid.*, p. 13. More recently in a brief but penetrating study Peter Shore has characterized the Conservatives as "a class party, historically concerned with the defence of property interests." *The Real Nature of Conservatism* (London, 1952).

[7] *Op. cit.*, p. 27.   [8] *Ibid.*, p. 62.

accounts for the Conservative preference for non-programmatic decisions.[9]

In view of the foregoing, the "independent authority" that Conservatives have claimed their leaders exercise needs to be severely scrutinized. The party and its leaders may well have acted independently of the wishes—or at any rate what the Socialist considers the needs—of the great mass of the electorate and even of the party rank and file. The judgment of these leaders, however, has ranged little beyond the interests and opinions of their well-to-do supporters. In Laski's opinion, it was no more likely that the Conservatives would adopt measures which would alienate businessmen than that Labour would act contrary to the interests of the trade unions.[1] For the Conservatives, as for Labour, "the area, in fact, within which each is free to manoeuvre is drawn fairly rigidly for it by the economic character of the support upon which it relies."[2]

At times, admittedly, Conservatives have been responsible for measures of social and political reform. Socialists meet these facts with a theory of "concessions," which is of crucial importance for their interpretation. The basic mechanism is simple electoral necessity. When Conservative Governments have enacted social reforms—factory regulation, mines safety, restriction of hours of labor, establishment of minimum wages and taxation of the well to do to pay for education, public health, and social amenities[3]—their purpose in essence has been to win or keep votes. They may have given in, after initial resistance, to a demand that originated with some section of the working class. Or perhaps the party through its more astute leaders took the initiative in the tactic of "catching votes." Thus, for instance, competition with Liberals for electoral support is viewed as having led Disraeli and Derby to introduce the measure that became the Reform Act of 1867. Similarly, Conservative extension of some aspects of Labour's reforms is taken to be the result of the party's precarious political position in the 1950's.

In such broadening of the theory of concessions, one must note, there is danger to the class analysis. For the farther it is admitted

[9] Peter Shore writes that "it is a distinguishing feature of Conservatism that it has no social goals to achieve, no major changes to make. It follows from this, and experience demonstrates the truth, that Conservative Governments are seldom memorable for their legislation; they are almost wholly concerned with administration." *Op. cit.*, p. 13.

[1] *Op. cit.*, pp. 63–4.

[2] *Ibid.*, p. 64. [3] *Ibid.*, p. 30.

that party competition can lead Conservatives to trench on capitalist interests, the smaller is the role attributable to those interests in dictating the policies of the party. The Socialist, therefore, will say that there is some "limit" beyond which Conservatives will not carry the tactic of concessions lest these impair the "fundamentals" of capitalism. In any case, he argues that reform measures carried by Conservatives do not reflect the Conservative outlook in the same sense as measures favoring the interests of the capitalist class and the maintenance of the capitalist system. When Conservatives claim that such reforms are in accord with their traditional concern for "the condition of the people," this is dismissed as "Disraelian make-believe." To argue otherwise—to admit that Conservatives could freely act to favor the interests of the working class, particularly if this imposed burdens on or harmed the interests of the property-owner—would be a break with the theory of economic class on which the whole analysis rests.

The theory of concessions is used not only to explain Conservative behavior, but also the behavior of many who, according to the Socialist analysis, ought to be supporters of the Labour Party. In the age of democracy the Conservatives have continued to receive a massive working-class vote. Laski explained this largely on the basis of concessions which the period of capitalist expansion made possible, but which the economic decline of the interwar years must halt.[4] A long continuation of Conservative social reform and of working-class Toryism clearly confronts the Socialist analysis with its most difficult problems of explanation.

To our comprehensive question this Socialist interpretation offers a comprehensive answer, suggesting important continuities in purpose and power structure that might be found in the Conservatism of the last hundred years or so. Yet we may not assume that the question has a comprehensive answer, whether Socialist or non-Socialist. It is possible that the question itself is unreal. George Kitson Clark has remarked that "principles except in their vaguest forms have little to do with the history of Parties." "Perhaps," he continues, "parties are only the chance creations of past accidents and present need, helped out by continuous organization and invested with an unreal unity, an imaginary consistency with the past, and an illusory belief that they inherit its ideals."[5] Such skepticism must remind us that although there has been at all times

[4] *Ibid.*, pp. 30–1.
[5] *Peel and the Conservative Party* (London, 1929), p. 214.

since the late 1830's a political formation known as "The Conservative Party," further continuities beyond the name may be negligible. Although Conservatives of recent years have often called on
Disraeli to sanction their actions, the party that he led greatly
differs from that of Macmillan and Home in principles, organization, and social basis. Perhaps what we shall find behind the façade
of a common name is only a series of interest-group alliances,
which change in character from one generation to the next and
become in time wholly unlike their more distant predecessors.
Skeptical pluralism, not class analysis, Socialist or Conservative,
may have the last word.

CONSERVATISM AND CLASS

The Socialist would not doubt and the Tory could not deny
that in the generation before World War I members of the governing class monopolized the positions of leadership in the Conservative Party and in Conservative Governments. The fact of
class rule and the attitudes of the governing class have been summarized by R. C. K. Ensor. Writing of the two Conservative
leaders, Balfour and Lansdowne, at the time of the Liberal Government of 1906, he remarked : "They belonged to, they led in,
and they felt themselves charged with, the fortunes of a small
privileged class; which for centuries had exercised a sort of collective kingship, and at the bottom of its thinking instinctively
believed that it had a divine right to do so." In their view Britain
owed her greatness to patrician rule and her system of government
had worked successfully because the personnel of parliaments and
cabinets had remained upper class, the function of the lower orders
being limited to "giving a popular *imprimatur* to the system by
helping to choose which of two aristocratic parties should hold
office." Tory Democracy, as put forward by Disraeli, did not
depart from this view. And although the extension of the franchise
had led to the entrance of some "middle-class upstarts" into Parliament on the Liberal side, the governing families had rallied successfully and maintained their position in alliance with "the ablest
of the upstart leaders," Joseph Chamberlain.[6]

There is more than a shade of Radical animus in this characterization. But the fact of class rule in this period is too plain to

[6] *England 1870–1914* (Oxford, 1936), pp. 387–8.

occasion debate. The only interesting questions are quantitative. Although members of the working class had the vote from 1867, no son of a manual worker or artisan sat in the Cabinet until John Burns was named in 1906; indeed, apart from this case and Arthur Henderson's brief membership during the war, there was no further instance until the Labour Government of 1924.[7] While in this sense it took more than half a century after the arrival of democracy for the working class to win representation in the highest positions, the aristocracy continued to preponderate in spite of successive extensions of the suffrage. Defining "aristocrat" as the son of a man with a hereditary title, Laski found that 64 per cent of all Cabinet members between 1832 and 1866 were aristocratic. For 1867–84 the figure was 60 per cent; for 1884–1905 it was 58 per cent. Only in 1906–16 are aristocrats outnumbered by sons of "other persons," the aristocratic element still comprising, however, 49 per cent of Cabinet members.[8]

As one would expect, this nonaristocratic element constituted a smaller proportion of Conservative than of Liberal Cabinets, the contrast between the two parties becoming quite marked in the early twentieth century. While in Disraeli's Cabinet of 1874 aristocrats had numbered 10 out of 17 and in Balfour's Cabinet of 1902, 12 out of 23, in Asquith's Cabinet of 1908 there were only 6 aristocrats in a total of 20. The nonaristocratic element, to be sure, was almost without exception upper middle class. As Laski's data show, Cabinet members before World War I in the vast majority had been educated at the great public schools and Oxford and Cambridge and for the most part were men of independent means not looking to a vocation for their livelihood.[9]

From the time of Disraeli to World War I, the leaders of the Conservative Party continued to be drawn with few exceptions from a very small number of families of high social position, wealth, and, quite often, long public service. The character of the

[7] W. L. Guttsman, "The Changing Social Structure of the British Political Elite, 1886–1935," *British Journal of Sociology*, Vol. II, No. 2 (June 1951), p. 125.

[8] "The Personnel of The English Cabinet, 1801–1924," *American Political Science Review*, Vol. XXII, No. 1 (February, 1928), pp. 12–31. Using a narrower definition of "aristocrat"—all those descended from a holder of an hereditary title in the grandparent generation—W. L. Guttsman shows that the per cent of aristocrats among Cabinet members for 1868–1880 was 54%; for 1885–1902, 55%; and for 1906–1914, 34%. *The British Political Elite* (London, 1963), p. 78.

[9] *Ibid.*, pp. 22–3.

economic interests with which the Conservative Party was associated, however, did change significantly from what it had been
in mid-Victorian days. As compared with the landowning interest,
financial, industrial, and commercial wealth greatly increased its
representation in the party. The change in the sources of income
of Conservative M.P.'s is a useful index of this shift. In the House
of Commons elected in 1865, for instance, 199 Conservative M.P.'s
were landowners, while 112 were connected with finance, industry,
and commerce. By 1892 the proportion had changed to 163 landowners in contrast with 298 interested in finance, industry, and
commerce.[1] Britain was, of course, rapidly industrializing and the
greater representation of the new forms of capital among Conservatives was in part simply a reflection of this change in the
character of the economy. But there were also significant shifts in
the economic support enjoyed by the two parties. Finance, industry, and commerce, which in the early years after the First Reform Act had found representation almost exclusively among
Liberals, moved over to the Conservatives.[2] At the same time, but
especially after 1884, that section of the landed interest which had
been Liberal also turned Conservative.[3] While the Liberals in
early Victorian days had preponderantly enjoyed the support of
industrial capital, they had also retained a strong representation
from the landed interest, coinciding on the whole with their
wing of Whig aristocrats. In the latter part of the century, however, the Conservatives gained from both economic sectors.

There were, in short, two movements. Wealth, whether "old"
or "new," was amalgamating its support around Conservatism.
More important, the wealth associated with Conservatism was increasingly financial, commercial, and industrial. Accordingly,
businessmen greatly increased among Conservative M.P.'s. Their
representation, however, did not rise in Conservative cabinets,

[1] W. Ivor Jennings, *Parliament* (Cambridge, Eng., 1939), Tab. II, p. 38.
This table lists the "interests" of M.P.'s in various parliaments. The figures
refer to interests, not to members, so a member with several interests is
included several times. Jennings' table is based on the research of J. A.
Thomas, published in his *House of Commons 1832–1901* (Cardiff, 1939).

[2] Jennings, *op. cit.*, p. 39.

[3] In 1865 Liberal M.P.'s had included 237 landowners and 344 connected
with finance, industry, and commerce. By 1892 not only had the landed interest shrunk to 51, but the number of M.P.'s with an interest in finance,
industry, and commerce had also fallen, to 297—and this at a time when
the representatives of new wealth were greatly increasing among Conservative M.P.'s. See Jennings, *op. cit.*, Tab. II.

which typically consisted of a large majority of aristocratic landowners joined by a small number of lawyers and still fewer businessmen.[4]

The political support of the Conservatives also was transformed.
After 1832 they had enjoyed a wide following among the new
middle-class electorate, whose enfranchisement they had bitterly
resisted for decades. Like their hardly less aristocratic competitors
on the Liberal side, they benefited from that "deference" cele-
brated by Bagehot in his account of British politics on the eve
of the Reform Act of 1867.[5] Yet on the whole they had not done
well at the polls, particularly since the breakup of the party in
1846, and not since the general election of 1841 had they returned
with a majority in the House of Commons. Disraeli's bold gamble
of 1867 failed to reverse the balance. For not only were the Conservatives defeated in 1868; even when they won a majority in the
House of Commons in 1874 it was on a lower national poll than
that of the Liberals. The split in the Liberal Party, however,
marked the revival of Conservative fortunes. From 1886 to 1900,
although the parties were fairly evenly matched, the Conservatives
won a majority of the two-party vote in four successive general
elections (Table 9.1).

These victories would have been impossible without massive
support from "the lower orders." Confirming Disraeli's perception of the Tory working man, a large section of the urban working class voted Conservative. When A. L. Lowell recorded his
impressions of British politics in 1908, he was speaking of both
parties, but, as he observed, his comments on the deferential nature
of the working-class voter were "far more true of the Conservative, than of the Liberal, party." "The fact is," he observed, "that
the upper classes in England rule today, not by means of political
privileges which they retain, but by the sufferance of the great
mass of the people and as trustees for its benefit."[6] Stressing the
function of social status in securing this support, he reported that

the sentiment of deference, or snobbishness, becomes, if anything,
stronger as the social scale descends. The workingman, when not pro-

---

[4] Guttsman, "The Changing Social Structure of the British Political Elite,"
loc. cit., Tab. VI, p. 128. See also Guttsman, The British Political Elite,
Ch. IV.
[5] See especially the Introduction to the second edition of The English
Constitution (1872).
[6] The Government of England (New York, 1924), Vol. II, pp. 508 and 513.

TABLE 9.1

General Elections, 1874–1900
(United Kingdom, including Ireland)

	Vote (in millions)		Conservative % of two-party vote
	Conservatives	Liberals	
1874	.69	.76	48
1880	.88	1.10	44
1885	1.90	2.20	46
1886	1.00*	1.60†	38
	1.40†	1.20*	54
1892	2.00†	1.90	53
1895	1.80†	1.70	51
1900	1.70†	1.50‡	53

Source: *Constitutional Year Book 1910* (London, 1910), p. 241.
* Not including Liberal Unionists.
† Including Liberal Unionists.
‡ Including Labour Party.

voked by an acute grievance to vote for a trade union candidate, prefers a man with a title, and thus the latest extensions of the franchise have rather strengthened than weakened the hold of the governing class upon public life.[7]

Lowell's summary, while more bland than Ensor's, does not differ from it in essentials, or indeed from the comments of many other observers at the time.

THE NEW PARTY ORGANIZATION

"I believe," said Disraeli, "the wider the popular suffrage, the more powerful would be the natural aristocracy."[8] Over a period of time the election results confirmed his insight. If economic class tended to divide the nation, what we may call political class tended to unite it. In spite of a democratic suffrage—indeed partly because of it, as Disraeli had foreseen—government continued to

[7] *Ibid.*, p. 508. The final assertion in this passage seems exaggerated, but it is supported by Laski's figures on the proportion of aristocrats in the Cabinet. The sharpest decline occurred after 1832, and while the decline continued into the twentieth century, it is less steep after 1867. In the 34 years from 1832 to 1866 the drop was 9%, but in the 38 years from 1867 to 1905 the drop was only 6%.

[8] Quoted in Asa Briggs, *Victorian People* (Chicago, 1955), p. 278.

be shaped by the "natural political hierarchy" of the nation.[9] The task of mobilizing this growing electorate for Conservative purposes, however, was not entrusted entirely to the traditional institutions of "the natural political hierarchy," and in the years after 1867 party organization outside Parliament was developed on a large and increasing scale. The Conservatives were at least equal to, and probably on the whole in advance of, the Liberals in building the new machinery. But again, as in their conduct of the national Government itself, they adapted the new forms to Tory principles of authority and leadership.

In constructing the new party organization, Toryism again showed its power to adopt the new without surrendering essentials of the old. The forms used—such as the local association, the national federation, and the annual conference—were much the same as those used by the Liberals. These forms derive from the principle of voluntary association, whose origins go back to the Protestant sects of the Reformation. As expressions of voluntarism and individualism they are radically in opposition to Tory authoritarianism and hierarchy. As employed by the Radicals they were intended to produce an agency that would offset the aristocratic elements in Liberalism and put the direction of the party and its policy in the hands of the membership at large. And in actuality, as we have seen, the N.L.F. and its conference did enjoy a degree of authority that was converted into influence strong enough significantly to affect the behavior of its parliamentary leaders.[1] Although the forms of party organization used by the Conservatives were similar, their intended purpose and their actual effect were quite different. As in the theory and practice of Tory Democracy, the principles of hierarchy and voluntarism were coherently combined. The result was a party organization that mobilized a large rank-and-file membership and at the same time strengthened party leadership and indeed the effective power of the Government.

The generation after 1867 saw a steep rise in party unity in the House of Commons among both Conservatives and Liberals (Table 9.2). This gain in party unity clearly strengthened the hands of party leaders in Parliament: the more dependable their majority,

[9] The phrase is Leslie Stephen's. See "On the Choice of Representatives by Popular Constituencies," *Essays on Reform*, n.a. (London, 1867), p. 101. Stephen thought that the system of caucuses in American politics was a necessary substitute for the "natural political hierarchy" of Britain, where even in every little constituency one found "recognized leaders" of the parties who enjoyed "the instinctive respect" of their followers.

[1] See above, Ch. II, pp. 54–61.

TABLE 9.2

Party Unity 1860–1908
(Measured by coefficients of cohesion)

Year		Liberals	Conservatives
1860			
	All Divisions	59.8	57.3
	Whip Divisions	58.9	63.0
1871			
	All Divisions	71.7	76.2
	Whip Divisions	75.5	74.0
1881			
	All Divisions	82.0	82.9
	Whip Divisions	83.2	87.9
1894			
	All Divisions	86.9	94.1
	Whip Divisions	89.8	97.9
1899			
	All Divisions	84.3	94.2
	Whip Divisions	82.5	97.7
1906			
	All Divisions	93.2	89.8
	Whip Divisions	96.8	91.0
1908			
	All Divisions	95.0	88.4
	Whip Divisions	94.9	88.3

In this table, "Whip Divisions" are those divisions in which the Government put on the whips, whether or not the Opposition also did.

Sources: A. L. Lowell, "The Influence of Party Upon Legislation in England and America," *Annual Report*, American Historical Association (1901); data supplied by Dr. Hugh Berrington relating to 1894 and 1899; Russell Jones, "Party Voting in the English House of Commons" (unpublished M.A. thesis, University of Chicago, 1933); author's study of the sessions of 1906 and 1908 (see Ch. IV, p. 122, n. 4).

the greater the chances that their legislative proposals would be enacted and their administrative measures approved; the more solid their ranks when in Opposition, the more effectively they could harass the Government.[2] The causes of this development,

[2] Conceivably, the rise in party unity might have resulted from a greater willingness of leaders after 1867 to compromise with their followers in Parliament. This was not the case, as we shall see when we consider the question of the independence of decision-making by Conservative leaders. See below, pp. 264–6.

however, were not simple. Generally in the country, as well as in Parliament, partisanship was intensified in the later years of the century as a period of reform at home and adventure abroad followed the quiescent years of mid-century. Much of this renewed interest in party politics centered on the new issues that the Radicals were bringing forward through the medium of the Liberal Party. Also, as we have seen, the complexion of the social and economic interests associated with the two parties was changing. As the Conservatives became more and more the party of both old and new wealth, middle-class elements and their Lib–Lab working-class allies became more influential among the Liberals. This new alignment of interests between the parties, expressed in new issues raised by them, could be expected to lead to greater partisanship in both Parliament and the country.

The spread of party organization outside Parliament fed on this growing partisanship. At the same time, however, party organization reacted on the situation to raise party voting among the electors and in the House of Commons. "The caucus," H. J. Hanham has remarked, "opened the way to the practice of modern electorates, which vote more or less automatically for the candidate of the party association, and against independents of any sort."[3] Of course, the caucus did not by itself create party voting in country or Parliament, but it is easy to see why over time it had a substantial effect. A well-organized local association that continually propagandizes and electioneers for the party and its candidates will tend to increase party voting among the electorate. When the party candidates backed by the local association must have the approval of the leadership—a condition which had been established in the Conservative Party by 1874[4]—the chances of independent or unapproved candidates will be reduced. The tendency of such party voting among the electorate, therefore, will be to defeat unreliable men and discourage potential rebels among those elected. Thus, given an economic and social environment that works in the same direction, party organization can be an important means by which party unity in the legislature is increased.

Liberal as well as Conservative leaders benefited from these

[3] *Elections and Party Management : Politics in the Time of Disraeli and Gladstone* (London, 1959), p. 143. With regard to the Liberals in 1885, he goes on to say, "This was not a problem of the immediate future."

[4] Barry McGill, *Parliamentary Parties 1868–1885* (unpublished Ph.D. thesis, Harvard University, 1953), p. 199.

effects, and party unity rose on both sides of the House. But the new party organization affected the power structures of the two parties quite differently. Liberal leaders could thank the N.L.F. and the local associations for help in creating the party unity that made it easier to get their programs through Parliament. At the same time, they had continually to confront, and often to compromise with, the efforts of the Federation to influence what that program would be. The National Union of Conservative and Constitutional Associations had no such immodest pretensions. "The National Union was organized," explained one of its founders, "rather as . . . a handmaid to the party, than to usurp the functions of party leadership."[5]

The different functions of the two extra-parliamentary organizations are suggested by the manner in which they were formed. The N.L.F. was very much a rebel movement against the "Whig" element in the party and was built upon a pre-existing organizational base created by the Radical pressure groups of the time. Characteristically, the impulse to the formation of a federation of Conservative associations came from the top. Founded in 1867 by a group of young Conservative politicians who were in the habit of assisting the party managers, the organization that became the National Union enjoyed from the start the approval of the party Leader.[6] Disraeli fully recognized the need for more broadly based local associations that could mobilize the larger electorate created by the Reform Act of 1867, and with Disraeli's strong support John E. Gorst worked to set up Conservative organizations, especially in the towns. Disraeli did doubt, however, the wisdom of separate Conservative workingmen's associations, which had been the plan of the original founders of the National Union, and after 1874 these bodies tended to become clubs, while the National Union became the federation of the new and enlarged local associations of the type fostered by Gorst. By various reforms the National Union achieved a representative form of organization and after 1885 began to debate and pass resolutions relating to questions of public policy. It did not, however, claim any powers of control over party policy or over the party bureaucracy and, except for the brief period when Randolph Churchill used it in

[5] Henry Cecil Raikes at the conference of 1873. Quoted in McKenzie, *op. cit.*, p. 146.

[6] For this account of the origins of the National Union I am mainly indebted to Hanham, *op. cit.*

his conflict with Salisbury, it was content with its role as an electioneering body, subordinate to the parliamentary leadership.[7]

Thus, in contrast with their opposite numbers on the Liberal side, the Conservative chiefs enjoyed the advantages that the new party organization brought to party leadership, but without having at the same time to trouble themselves greatly with its opinions. Advice, which would keep the leader in touch with his followers in the country, was welcome. But, as the political thought of Toryism implied and as the Chief Whip bluntly told the conference in 1906, "The party could stand many things, but it would not, in his judgment ever stand a caucus. (Cheers) The policy of the party must be initiated by its leader. . . ."[8]

In the generation after 1867 formal organization developed into a large and elaborate structure outside Parliament. It imposed, however, few burdens on the Conservative leaders. When, for instance, Lowell looked at the Conservative conference in the early years of this century, he found it a body of "no political weight." "Some great nobleman presides," he wrote, "and one of the party leaders usually addresses a public meeting in the evening; but statesmen of the first rank take no part in the regular proceedings." "The action of the conference," Lowell concluded, "is not fettered; it is ignored."[9]

That the Conservative conference did not trouble party leaders as much as did the Liberal meetings was undoubtedly true. But Lowell, in his anxiety to show that extra-parliamentary organizations were—and were bound to be—"shams," unduly depreciated the concern that important members and the Leader himself attached to the conference. The meeting at Sheffield in 1903, for instance, just after Joseph Chamberlain had opened up the explosive question of Imperial Preference, was not by any means treated with disdain by all Conservative politicians of weight. On the contrary, some showed themselves to be deeply engaged in its discussions. "I can still see Hugh Cecil passionately waving his long arms about," L. S. Amery later recalled, "as he shouted above the hubbub of dissent that if Conservatives adopted protection he

[7] Lowell in his *Government of England* and McKenzie in his *British Political Parties* amply document the docility of the extra-parliamentary organization in contrast with the fears of Ostrogorski that it would become a powerful "caucus." See the latter's *The Organization of Political Parties* (London, 1901), Vol. I, pp. 590–627.

[8] Quoted in McKenzie, *op. cit.*, p. 184.

[9] *The Government of England*, Vol. I, p. 577.

would have nothing to do with such an apostate party."[1] More-over, on that occasion Balfour himself showed his concern with conference in the pains he took to pacify its emotions and manage its opinions. Addressing the delegates the evening after they assembled, fully prepared to approve Chamberlain's proposals, he expounded what was in effect a compromise position, both criticizing and defending Free Trade and going so far as to declare in favor of retaliatory tariffs.[2] By this act of concession and management and by his implicit appeal to their loyalty to him, he held the delegates in line.

In the House of Commons, according to Lowell's description, the organization of the two major parties had hardly changed from what it had been in the early years of the nineteenth century. The Whips and the two front benches were still the main elements, although on the side of the opposition a "Shadow Cabinet" had emerged.[3] From time to time a party meeting might be held to select a leader in the House in those rare cases where it found itself in Opposition without a chief. Conservative M.P.'s sometimes formed committees expressing their concern with some aspect of policy, such as agriculture, or even with a wider perspective such as that of F. E. Smith's Social Reform Committee.[4] There was, however, nothing to compare with today's 1922 Committee, with its elaborate system of subcommittees and close consultation between leaders and backbenchers.

TORY SOCIAL REFORM

"The golden age of the private M.P." was brought to an end in 1867. In the following decades the development of party in the broadest sense laid a new foundation for the "oligarchic tradition" —or to use a kinder phrase, the Tory conception of statesmanship —and by the opening decade of the twentieth century, party whips, although used more sparingly when the party was in Opposition than at present, could produce results comparable to the monolithic unity of recent times (Tables 9.3 and 9.4). How

[1] *My Political Life* (London, 1953), Vol. I, pp. 259–60.
[2] *Ibid*.
[3] Jennings, *op. cit.*, pp. 71–2.
[4] This committee was active in the years just before 1914, and had subcommittees on such subjects as poor law reform, education, industrial relations, and health. On the whole, its views were those of Tory Democracy.

did the Conservative leadership use its opportunities? Did its decisions result from the exercise of "independent judgment"? What
purposes did its policy serve and what were these purposes said
to be?

TABLE 9.3

Party Unity : Whip Divisions 1881–1945
(Measured by coefficients of cohesion)

Year		Liberals	Conservatives
1881			
	Govt. Whips	83.2	87.9
	Party Whips	83.2	98.6
1894			
	Govt. Whips	89.8	97.9
	Party Whips	89.8	99.8
1899			
	Govt. Whips	82.5	97.7
	Party Whips	99.4	97.7
1906			
	Govt. Whips	96.8	91.0
	Party Whips	96.8	98.0
1908			
	Govt. Whips	94.9	88.3
	Party Whips	94.9	99.3
			Labour
1945–46			
	Govt. Whips	99.9	99.0
	Party Whips	99.9	99.7

Divisions indicated by "Govt. Whips" include any division in which the
Government of the day put on its whips, whether or not the Opposition did
likewise. Under "Party Whips" a division is counted as a whip division for
a party only if that party put on its whips. Sources: See above, Table 9.2.

Disraeli's Government of 1874 was Tory in both senses of the
word : it was a time of strong government and its policies were
rationalized by distinctively Tory purposes. The great program of
social reform enacted in the session of 1875 will serve for illustration. A mere listing of the principal measures is impressive evidence of vigor and originality. The Public Health Act of 1875

TABLE 9.4

Increase in Whipping 1881–1945

(% of divisions in a session when a party
put on its whips)

Party Forming the Government

Year	Liberals	Conservatives
1836	48.9	
1850	68.3	
1860	66.9	
1871	82.1	
1881	96.6	
1883	78.2	
1890		79.7
1894	90.2	
1899		85.7
1903		86.5
1906	92.2	
1908	95.7	

	Labour	
1945	100	

Party in Opposition

Year	Liberals	Conservatives
1881		6.1
1883		3.8
1894		16.6
1899	13.5	
1903	16.0	
1906		29.4
1908		42.6
1945		72.4

Sources: See above, Table 9.2.

secured the establishment of sanitary authorities throughout the country and remained until 1936 the key statute in the field. The Artisan's Dwelling Act, a milestone in legislation on the housing problem, introduced the clearance scheme, a new procedure under which local authorities had slums pulled down and whole areas reconstructed, the new buildings being devoted to the use of workers. The Sale of Food and Drugs Act was the first comprehensive measure on the subject and remained the principal statute until 1928. An Agricultural Holdings Act was the first to compensate displaced tenants for agricultural improvements. The Land Transfer Act laid down the general lines on which the subject of land registration was thereafter treated in England. The Merchant Shipping Act provided for the safety and protection of seamen, large powers being given the Board of Trade to detain unsafe ships.

Two major acts, which Disraeli told the Queen were the most important labor laws that had yet been passed during her reign,[5] concerned trade unions and the rights of workingmen. The Conspiracy and Protection of Property Act firmly extended legal protection to the right to strike and the Employers' and Workmen's Act reformed the law governing breach of contract, making it much less unfavorable to the employee. "The Conservative Party," the miner and Lib–Lab M.P. Alexander MacDonald told his constituents, "have done more for the working classes in five years than the Liberals have in fifty."[6]

Conceivably these measures could have simply resulted from pressure politics, organized campaigns in the country leading the Government to accept the demands of interested groups in the hope of winning their votes. Such forces and considerations were certainly not absent. The Merchant Shipping Act, for instance, clearly owed a great deal to the long campaign conducted by the Radical M.P. Samuel Plimsoll; at one point only the agitation set up by his supporters prevented the Government, pressured by shipowners as well as reformers, from dropping the question entirely.[7] Similarly, protection of the right to strike and reform of the Master and Servant Acts had been sought by the trade unions, the Parliamentary Committee of the T.U.C. having carried on an intensive agitation in recent years. There were, however, major reforms that did not come before Parliament with the support of an organized bloc of voters. The Artisan's Dwelling Act originated with Disraeli's brilliant Home Secretary, Richard Cross, and the President of the Local Government Board, Sclater Booth; the ideas of the Radical mayor of Birmingham, Joseph Chamberlain, also

[5] W. F. Monypenny and G. E. Buckle, *The Life of Benjamin Disraeli, Earl of Beaconsfield*, rev. ed. in 2 vols. (London, 1929), Vol. II, p. 712.
[6] *Ibid.*, p. 709.   [7] *Ibid.*, pp. 723-7.

proved useful when the legislation was being shaped.[8] The Public Health Act may be credited for its conception to a civil servant, Sir John Simon, medical officer to the Local Government Board and a pioneer in sanitation.[9]

With regard to the latter two measures, and indeed throughout, Disraeli's role was crucial. He took pains to study the labor laws question before taking office; in 1874 he appointed the Royal Commission in pursuance of whose report Cross introduced his bills on the subject; and he gave Cross the support needed to win the Cabinet's assent to these proposals.[1] Moreover, he had long seen and urged on his party the need for Tory social reform. As early as 1864 he had used the phrase "Sanitas sanitatum, omnia sanitas," which Randolph Churchill later seized on as expressing the "scheme of social progress and reform" of Tory democracy.[2] In later speeches he had defended and developed what the Liberals in ridicule called his "policy of sewage."

Yet although he had indicated the general subjects of his concern —as in his Crystal Palace Speech of 1872[3]—he had not committed himself to a program of specific reforms. Indeed, his election address of 1874—the closest thing to a party manifesto that the politics of the time produced—made only a brief and glancing reference to his continuing concern, whether in or out of office, with "all measures calculated to improve the condition of the people."[4] "There was," writes one biographer and contemporary, "no special measure which he had received a mandate to carry

---

[8] J. L. Garvin, *Life of Joseph Chamberlain* (London, 1932), Vol. I, p. 195.

[9] W. M. Frazer, *History of Public Health 1834-1934* (London, 1950), p. 120. Frazer also notes that the Act grew out of the report of the Royal Commission on the sanitary condition of England and Wales, 1869-1871. The Commission had been appointed by Disraeli at the prompting of the British Medical Association and the Social Science Association. *Ibid.*, p. 115.

[1] Monypenny and Buckle, *op. cit.*, Vol. II, pp. 711-12.

[2] In his article in the *Fortnightly Review* for May, 1883. Quoted in Winston Churchill, *Life of Lord Randolph Churchill* (London, 1906), p. 250.

[3] The generality of his remarks on the subject illustrates the extent to which he left himself a free hand. Of his policy he said : "It involves the state of the dwellings of the people, the moral consequences of which are not less considerable than the physical. It involves their enjoyment of some of the chief elements of nature—air, light and water. It involves the regulation of their industry, the inspection of their toil. It involves the purity of their provisions, and it touches upon all the means by which you may wean them from habits of excess and brutality." Quoted in Monypenny and Buckle, *op. cit.*, Vol. II, p. 530.

[4] *Annual Register, 1874,* p. 6.

through, no detailed policy which he had advocated which the country was enabling him to execute."[5] In this sense, bound by no program, he took office with a wide authority that he and his colleagues then used to embody the general ideas of his commitment in particular measures.

Disraeli's Principles

That such concern with "the condition of the people" would help Conservatives at the polls Disraeli was the last to deny. From his "Young England" days he had argued that his party must champion social reform if it was to survive and rule. He had also, however, contended that reform was a proper function for Conservatives and had tried to state his case for it from a distinctively Tory perspective.

It is sometimes said that conservatism, whether of the British or any other variety, has no "utopia" and produces no conceptions of an ideal society such as those worked up by ideologues of individualism or collectivism.[6] Disraeli's thought is a good test of this thesis. He did not, it hardly needs be said, develop a set of ideas comparable in system to the work of the classical economists or of the Socialists, whether Marxian or Fabian. As is typical with conservatives, he frequently expressed his distrust of abstract theory and of "programme." Yet in what he said and wrote, one finds a powerful design for certain crucial elements in the social and political order. Bizarre as some of his earlier sallies were and opportunistic as some of his later utterances had to be, his thought displayed on these points notable consistency and provided an intellectual and moral foundation for government policy then and later. As his principal biographers said of his social reforms: "The aspirations of *Sybil* and 'Young England,' the doctrines in which Disraeli had 'educated' his party for thirty years, the prin-

[5] J. A. Froude, *Lord Beaconsfield* (London, 1890), p. 237.
[6] T. E. Utley, for instance, writes that "there is no such thing as 'the Tory Society,' and the phrase ought never to be permitted to be used." *The Conservatives and the Critics* (London, 1956), p. 12. For a brilliant analysis of Conservatism in general as lacking an ideal of "any specific form of social organization" and as being essentially a "positional" ideology that typically arises as a defense of established institutions against a fundamental challenge, see Samuel P. Huntington, "Conservatism as an Ideology," *American Political Science Review*, Vol. II, No. 2 (June, 1957), pp. 454–73.

ciples laid down in the great speeches of 1872, were translated into legislative form; it was Tory democracy in action."[7]

I am not thinking of the specific institutions in whose defense he spoke (for instance, the "territorial constitution" of his case for the Corn Laws, or "the Empire of England" of his Crystal Palace speech, or even of the Monarchy, House of Lords, and established Church) but rather of the larger perspective from which he viewed society. Like Burke, another outsider called on to say what many felt—although in neither imagery nor conception by any means Burke's equal—he drew on the ancient legacy of Toryism, conceiving authority as hierarchic, society as organic, and the social ethic as traditional rather than rational. A major theme was class rule. Precisely who belonged to the governing class might be unclear. In *Sybil* it is "the aristocracy," especially "the new generation of the aristocracy," whose "hearts," as Egremont assures Sybil, "are open to the responsibility of their position. . . . They are the natural leaders of the people, Sybil; believe me, they are the only ones."[8] Or more broadly, the governing class might be "the gentlemen of England." These, as he told the House in 1848, are "the proper leaders of the people. If they are not the leaders of the people, I do not see why there should be gentlemen."[9] In any case, Britain had her "natural leaders"—and they their party, the Tories—to whom "the people" looked for guidance and governance.

Moreover, if in Disraeli's thought the ideal social order was hierarchic, it was also organic in the sense that its respective classes were joined together by powerful ties of positive mutual obligation. The "natural leaders" enjoy the trust of "the people" because, and only so long as, they recognize "the responsibility of their position." This responsibility had its hard, pragmatic rationale : "the palace is not safe, when the cottage is not happy."[1] But these long-run pragmatic considerations coincide with immediate ethical ones : the "duty" of the propertied and privileged orders to have a concern for "the condition of the people." "When I

---

[7] Monypenny and Buckle, *op. cit.*, Vol. II, p. 709.

[8] Benjamin Disraeli, *Sybil* (London, 1881), pp. 319–20.

[9] Quoted in R. J. White, ed., *The Conservative Tradition* (London, 1950), p. 164.

[1] Disraeli in 1848. Quoted in Monypenny and Buckle, *op. cit.*, Vol. II, p. 709.

know," said one of Disraeli's characters, "that evidence exists in
our Parliament of a state of demoralisation in the once happy population of this land, which is not equalled in the most barbarous
countries . . . I cannot help suspecting that this has arisen because
property has been permitted to be created and held without the
performance of its duties."[2]

Disraeli's assertion was ethical : the governing class ought to
care for the welfare and happiness of the people. It was also psychological : they could recognize and act for the interests of
others and not merely of themselves, displaying, if necessary, that
"self-sacrifice" to which, according to Disraeli, Liberal egoism was
averse.[3] There is here not only a denial of the utilitarian proposition that "every man is the best judge of his own interests." There
is also the complementary assertion that certain persons are better
judges of the interests of others and worthy of being entrusted
with their protection.

But Disraeli's case was also emphatically political. Fundamental
to it was the assertion that the fulfillment of the duties of the
"natural leaders" was a matter not only for individual and voluntary charity, but also for action by the state. According to his
Tory interpretation of history, it had been above all the Monarchy
that in earlier days had performed these paternal functions. Now
he called upon the Tory party acting through the "public institutions" of the nation to reassert this old concern. When state
power was in the hands of a governing class that fully recognized
its responsibilities, then and only then the "two nations" would be
one. This one nation would be composed of a variety of interests
and classes, and Disraeli showed continuing concern with the need
for a balancing of such forces. But such mechanisms alone would
not protect the national interest. The common good could not be
trusted automatically to flow from self-regulating processes. In
domestic as in foreign affairs, the power of the state guided by the
wisdom of men was essential.

In Disraeli's version of Tory Democracy a conception of authority was joined with a distinctive conception of purpose. One
finds not only the familiar Tory ideas of independent authority,
class rule, non-programmatic decisions, and strong government,
but also a view of the kind of social order that such a political

[2] White, op. cit., p. 214.
[3] See, for instance, his comparison of "popular principles" and "liberal
opinions" in a speech of 1847, quoted in White, op. cit., pp. 225–6.

system would serve. It would be highly pluralistic and inequality of condition would march alongside inequality of power. The nation would have, as the young Disraeli said in words echoing the rhetoric of the sixteenth century, "that free order and that natural gradation of ranks which are but a type and image of the economy of the universe."[4] But each class, rank, and interest would enjoy security of status. If necessary, this security would be guaranteed by law and backed by state power. "The rich and the powerful will not find difficulty under any circumstances in maintaining their rights," Disraeli wrote to the first meeting of the National Union, "but the privileges of the people can only be defended and secured by national institutions."[5] All classes were equal before the law, but the law must consider their "variety" and accordingly guarantee the rights appropriate to their different aims and conditions. Inequality and security are combined in this distinctively Tory conception of purpose. With pithy simplicity, Richard Oastler had expressed the ideal in his definition of Toryism as "a place for everything and everything in its place."[6]

In its emphasis on security as well as inequality, Toryism displayed a fundamental opposition to Liberalism, whose doctrine of self-help expressed a quite different conception of the good life. For the doctrine of self-help reflected not merely the ideal of social mobility and the theory of laissez faire. It was also an ethic of individuality whose main concern was with what each person does with his creative and innovating powers. By these powers the individual gives a moral law to himself and develops his potentialities. Only in such creative self-development does he realize his "worth as a human being." To follow tradition, to imitate one's "betters," to let others choose one's plan of life for oneself brings into play none of "the distinctive endowment of a human being," nor any faculty but "the ape-like one of imitation."[7] So far, therefore, as the state or society interferes with the liberty necessary for these creative activities of the individual, there is plainly an ethical loss.

For the Tory, on the other hand, to follow tradition, to imitate

---

[4] *The Runnymede Letters* (London, 1885), p. 51. Letter to Mr. Thomas Attwood.

[5] Quoted in White, *op. cit.*, p. 26.

[6] *Dictionary of National Biography*, Sidney Lee, ed. (New York, 1895), Vol. XLI, p. 295.

[7] See John Stuart Mill's *On Liberty*, especially Ch. 3, from which these phrases are quoted.

one's forefathers, to look for moral guidance to the models of classical literature and the Christian religion was natural, pious, and wise. Essential to the well-being of the nation, as Disraeli once said, was "a love of country and home, fostered by traditionary manners and consecrated by customs that embalm ancestral deeds."[8] Liberty was, of course, important and deserved the protection of the law. But liberty consisted not of a single set of conditions in which all men were equally interested, but of the many particular and traditional liberties of the various sorts and conditions of men. Not the innovations of creative individuality, but the continuities inspired by "traditionary manners" constituted the liberty that the law and the state must foster. Judged from this perspective, interference by the pressure of custom, by the moral suasion of natural leaders, by the preaching of the priesthood, and even by the force of law did not impair liberty, but on the contrary was the means by which these established liberties were maintained. To be sure, Tory doctrine was never so medieval as to commit itself to some fixed and unchanging pattern of social relationships and behavior. And, moreover, the doctrine of self-help was revised by Liberals of later days to allow for positive state intervention. Yet Liberal and Tory approached social problems from quite different perspectives. In the twentieth century, the Tory valuation of security found new and urgent relevance.

In this discussion I have not meant to give the impression that Disraeli was consumed by an interest in social problems or that he envisioned the Welfare State. On the contrary, as Prime Minister, he gave far more attention to foreign affairs and to Empire. Nor could his social reforms, at a time when the civil service numbered some 50,000 and income tax was only 3d. in the pound,[9] have an impact on society in any sense comparable to the role and effect of state intervention in recent decades. Disraeli himself, we should remember, was adamant on the point that, desirable as social reform might be, it was not to lead to new taxes. Yet in what he did and said later Conservatives could find a rationale for a distinctively Tory policy in domestic affairs. Certainly the Disraelian precedent could justify R. A. Butler when in 1947 he told the House that "We are not frightened at the use of the State. A good

---

[8] *The Runnymede Letters*, p. 51.
[9] See Herman Finer, *The British Civil Service* (London, 1937), p. 24, and *Annual Register*, 1874, p. 4.

Tory has never been in history afraid of the use of the State."[1] It could lend a color of legitimacy to this declaration of Anthony Eden at the party conference that approved the *Industrial Charter* in 1947 :

We are not the Party of unbridled, brutal capitalism, and never have been. Although we believe in personal responsibility and personal initiative in business, we are not the political children of the laissez-faire school. We opposed them decade after decade.[2]

Perhaps even some shred of justification may be extracted from Disraeli for the words of Harold Macmillan when in 1936 he declared that "Toryism has always been a form of paternal Socialism."[3]

CONSERVATIVE INERTIA

But if the Socialist reading of Conservative history is shaken by Disraeli's social reforms, the disturbance is only transitory. Admittedly, just as Tory democracy had had distinguished advocates before Disraeli, so also it found champions after him. In immediately succeeding years the most notable was, no doubt, Randolph Churchill. "But," as the admirers of Disraeli who wrote *One Nation* sadly remarked in 1950, "Lord Randolph did not live to assume Elijah's mantle, and inertia settled on the Tory Party."[4] From that time until the interwar years, the record of Conservative advocacy of social reform, whether in power or in Opposition, runs very thin. Consider, for instance, the achievement of ten years of Conservative Government from 1895 to 1905. The Workmen's Compensation Act of 1897 established the principle—which incidentally the Fourth Party had championed—that employers were liable to pay compensation to workers or their dependents in case of industrial accidents, its provisions being broadened three years later to include agricultural workers. The Factories and Workshops Act of 1901 improved and brought up to date the law relating to factories and workshops. The Education Act of

[1] 434 *H.C. Deb.* 1247 (10 March 1947).
[2] 1947 *CPCR*, p. 42.
[3] Interview in London *Star*, June 25, 1936. Quoted in Harvey Glickman, "The Toryness of English Conservatism," *Journal of British Studies*, Vol. I, No. 1 (November, 1961), p. 137.
[4] Iain MacLeod and Angus Maude, eds., *One Nation : A Tory Approach to Social Problems* (London, 1950), p. 14.

1902, a measure of great importance, put the national system of "provided" and "voluntary" schools on a permanent basis under local education authorities and gave these authorities the power to provide for secondary and technical schools. The Shops Act of 1904 authorized local authorities to shorten the working day of shop workers. The Unemployed Workmen Act of 1905 marked an important break from the tradition of the Poor Law, establishing an administrative structure of local committees separate from that of the Poor Law and authorized to establish labor exchanges, assist in emigration, and perform other functions.

Two or three of these measures were of major importance. But altogether this work of a decade of Conservative rule hardly compares with the work of the single session of 1875. Although Joseph Chamberlain had joined the Cabinet on the assumption that he would enjoy Conservative support for his "unauthorized program" of labor legislation,[5] the only measure of importance whose enactment he was able to secure was his scheme of workmen's compensation. In the following years of Liberal rule, the Conservatives exempted certain measures of social reform—notably the Trades Disputes Act of 1906 and the Old Age Pensions Act of 1908—from the "policy of selective slaughter" by which the Lords were used to decimate Radical reforms of education, plural voting, licensing laws, and land holding. When Lloyd George's great Insurance bill came before the Parliament, however, after a brief initial period of seeming acceptance, the party threw itself into violent, futile, and reactionary resistance.

In the party there continued to be persons, sometimes of weight, who gave voice to the demands of Tory Democracy. In the country, as the public was abundantly informed by trade unionists and social investigators, there was no lack of problems to which the Disraelian formulae could have been found relevant. That the Conservatives did not choose to act is most readily explained on simple electoral grounds. In imperialism (including in this not only the question of Empire but also of union with Ireland) the party had found a cause with a mighty appeal to the voter. Indeed, only from the election of 1886, at which Gladstone raised the "cry" of Home Rule, did the party win those majorities of the popular vote which had eluded even Disraeli. Social reform, one might infer, was a theme Conservatives could be induced forcefully to support only when defeat left it no other way of winning power.

[5] Garvin, op. cit., Vol. II, p. 618.

To be sure, the party did suffer defeats between Disraeli's death and 1914, notably the rout of 1906. If one asks whether there were special conditions of the period that might account for its failure to respond with the Disraelian tactic of "vote-catching," the changing composition of the economic interests associated with the party suggests an answer that some Conservatives themselves are ready to accept. As the party increasingly won the support of businessmen, they had—according to two Tory Democrats of the present day—"a profound effect on the party, purging it of most of its Tory philosophy and indoctrinating it with that peculiar blend of whiggery and laissez faire Liberalism which still colors the speeches of some of its leaders."[6]

The accession of Bonar Law, the wealthy iron merchant (and one might add, North American) to the party leadership in 1911, can be taken as an expression of this shift in the social base and political attitude of the party. His opinions were certainly not those of Tory Democracy. As his biographer notes, Bonar Law "personally believed that, for the Conservatives, social reform was not on the whole a profitable line to pursue."[7] These sentiments came bluntly to the surface when, in response to Asquith's question whether the Conservatives would repeal the National Insurance Act of 1911, he "replied by giving a nod and saying 'certainly.'"[8] Subsequently he qualified his position in a skillfully worded letter to the press, in which "repeal" was replaced by the more ambiguous "amend."[9]

Conservative attitudes toward the Health Insurance bill are worth examining as evidence of the increased influence of "business Liberalism" in the party. As Law's reply indicates, Conservative opposition not only hardened during the parliamentary battle, but also continued after the bill had been enacted. Their attack stressed the burdens that would be imposed on all three contributors to the scheme.[1] Direct taxation, it was said, was for the first time being imposed on the working classes. The state contribution,

[6] Roy Lewis and Angus Maude, *The English Middle Classes* (London, 1947), p. 74.

[7] Robert Blake, *The Unknown Prime Minister : The Life and Times of Andrew Bonar Law 1858–1923* (London, 1955), p. 140.

[8] 34 *H.C. Deb.* 35 (14 February 1912).

[9] Blake, *op. cit.*, p. 140.

[1] For this account of Conservative attitudes toward the bill, I am indebted to John S. Saloma III, "British Conservatism and the Welfare State" (unpublished Ph.D. thesis, Harvard University, 1961).

moreover, would add a heavy burden to be borne largely by tax-payers and rate-payers. The heaviest criticism, however, was directed against the contribution levied on employers. In attempting to cope with the resulting increase in the cost of production, it was said, employers could cut employment and workers' benefits, or they could raise prices—which under free trade would mean pricing themselves out of the market. Or, finally, they could reduce the "already bare margin of profit"—in which case the burden would fall wholly on the ordinary shareholder.

But Conservatives not only opposed the scheme, some also offered an alternative. Bonar Law, to be sure, refused to commit the party to any definite proposal, contenting himself with the pledge of "drastic amendment." But leading M.P.'s, strongly supported by the extra-parliamentary party, proposed the alternative of a voluntary scheme, aided by state subsidies. Their case was decked out in that rhetoric of mid-Victorian Liberalism which Disraeli and his friends had found chilling and un-Tory. Compulsion, it was said, not only meant state interference in the form of innumerable regulations enforced by an army of officials, but also brought under the scheme those who were "not really insurable," or who were "too improvident or too lazy to insure even though they can afford it."[2] The result, it was said, was to reduce benefits and penalize the majority in order to help the "least deserving." Moreover, a voluntary system had the merit of promoting thrift and self-reliance. No doubt many people would fail to make any provision for sickness but, on the other hand, the voluntary system "would let people free to make it in their own way." No Victorian ideologue of laissez faire could have spoken more strongly than Lord Robert Cecil when he told the House during the third reading debate :

. . . I have a fanatical belief in individual freedom. I believe it is a vital thing for this country, and I believe it is the cornerstone upon which our prosperity and our existence is built, and, for my part, I believe that the civic qualities of self-control, self-reliance, and self-respect depend upon individual liberty and the freedom and independence of the people of this country. . . . For these reasons I am strongly opposed to a compulsory scheme.[3]

The argument that an influx of businessmen raised the influence

---

[2] *Campaign Guide : 1914,* quoted in *ibid.,* p. 339.
[3] 32 *H.C. Deb.* 1476–7 (6 December 1911).

of "whiggery and laissez faire Liberalism" in the Conservative Party during the generation before World War I is persuasive, but it needs some qualification. In the first place, such influence did not take the form simply of a reflection of industrial and commercial interests. As Cecil's use of the strenuous doctrine of self-help illustrates, it also brought with it much of the ideology of Victorian Liberalism. This ideology was not merely a theory of political economy. It also embodied a moral philosophy that drew on one of the most important currents of thought since the Reformation—the current of modern liberalism. In its individualism, voluntarism, and rationalism, as in its anti-authoritarian distrust of the state, this Liberal perspective was sharply opposed to the ancient tenets of Toryism. Over the centuries, however, Tory thought and Tory practice had accepted and absorbed elements of these opposing ideas. The special influence of Victorian Liberalism that one finds in the years before 1914, therefore, is only one phase in a long-continuing process.

This is not to say, however, that the Conservative Party was either gradually becoming the Liberal Party in doctrine or that it was in the process of being wholly liberalized. That was not the manner in which Toryism responded to the rise of liberal thought. On the contrary, within the Conservative Party, distinctively Tory perspectives remained strong. If we are looking for continuity in the history of the party between 1867 and 1914, therefore, we will not find it in a single perspective or outlook on domestic policy. On these matters there were at least two "currents of opinion" within the party—the Tory and the Liberal. In statements of party purpose one or the other might be strengthened by the exigencies of party competition, the nature of particular issues, the views of certain leaders, or the movement of interests within the party.

To be so equipped with more than one system of guidance, one might think, should heighten that adaptability for which the Conservative Party is rightly famed. One cannot help thinking of the contrast with the Liberals, dogmatically committed to Free Trade, and with Labour, dogmatically committed to nationalization. Yet the mere possession of such resources of adaptation does not necessarily entail a mechanism ensuring that in any particular instance the party will make the wise or prudent choice. The behavior of the Conservative Party in the years just before World War I illustrates the point, not without overtones of tragedy. The party of authority turned a blind eye to the arming of the Ulster Volunteers, and some of the party's leading members lent their favor to an effort that brought Britain to the verge of civil war. By opposing the moderate welfarism of Lloyd George, whether in the form of his 1909 budget or his act of 1911, the Conservatives heightened existing tendencies toward class war and won no electoral advantage for themselves. Rather more Disraelian "make-believe" would have been to the advantage of both the party and the nation.

CHAPTER X

The Reassertion of
State Power

The interwar period is not a time on which Conservatives usually look back with pride. Recalling appeasement abroad and unemployment at home, one must grant that these were leaden years. And for most of the time, Conservatives had the power and responsibilities of office. Yet there were redeeming features, for some of which the party and its leaders may take credit. When combating the Labour Party's picture of the "gloomy Thirties" Conservatives often emphasize how the Disraelian tradition of social reform was revived and contributions were made to the creation of the Welfare State. The contention is just. Nevertheless, during the interwar years, social reform remained, as it always had been, a secondary concern of Conservatism. Far more notable were the steps taken by Conservatives toward the Managed Economy. In their reassertion of state power over the operation of the economic system as a whole, they not only broke with fundamentals of British policy in the previous hundred years, but also created many patterns of government action which, in spite of important modifications, have been followed since that time. In this respect British Conservatism was an innovating force. And what it did was in harmony with what Tories like to call the Tory tradition. "If we ask the true meaning of those years," a sensitive and learned Tory has written, ". . . we find that the older conflict of party has been almost destroyed, that the wheel has turned back two centuries, and that under conditions far changed from the Elizabethan the main activities of the state are being nationalised. . . ."[1]

[1] Keith Feiling, *The Life of Neville Chamberlain* (London, 1946), p. 200.

FOUNDING THE MANAGED ECONOMY

The Labour Party has talked a great deal more about planning and control of the economy than has the Conservative Party. Historically, however, it was the National Government, nominally a coalition, but in fact almost entirely dominated by its Conservative ministers and their ideas, that laid the foundations of the Managed Economy. We can see this contribution by looking back on events in the 1930's from the perspective of recent years. After World War II, as we have seen, British Governments possessed two systems for controlling the economy : Keynesian methods of national income analysis and wartime methods of quantitative programming and control. In their efforts to manage, or to plan, the economy, both Labour and Conservative Governments, with differing emphases, have picked and chosen among the instruments put at their disposal by these two methods. Yet both methods presuppose the work of the National Government. Neither could be used with any degree of effectiveness if Britain were tied down to the gold standard or free trade. Both presuppose that government has assumed a responsibility for general guidance of the economy as a whole.

One can trace the continuities between earlier and later phases of economic control in specific instruments of government action, finding instances of postwar practice that go back for their precedent to innovations of the National Government : for example, a managed currency, devaluation, bilateral trade agreements, tariffs, import quotas, subsidies, deficiency payments, controls on location of industry. Judged by later practice, the way such instruments were used by the National Government may seem crude and timid. Its attempt to achieve recovery by restrictionism may well have been wrong-headed. In major contrast with postwar Governments, of course, it had not learned from Keynes what an immensely powerful and flexible instrument for conditioning the economy the budget can be. Yet whether one thinks of the general reassertion of state power or of certain specific instruments and programs of state intervention, the continuities are significant. For the past two decades or so, both parties have accepted a general framework of collectivism consisting of the Welfare State and the Managed Economy. British Conservatism has played a part in the construction of both, but above all in setting the nation on the course of economic management.

The critical period was 1931–35. During these years, after the abandonment of the gold standard, the Government laid down the main lines of its economic policy. Its three main aspects were 1) monetary expansion, 2) mercantilism, and 3) industrial and agricultural rationalization. The most prominent element was, no doubt, the break with free trade and the turn to protection. The erection of tariffs, however, was only one in a complex of related policies dealing with economic affairs in their foreign, imperial, and domestic aspects. Protection was joined with imperial preference. Tariffs were used in bargaining with other governments and, indirectly, with foreign business organizations, such as the continental steel cartel. They were also a critical instrument employed by the government in its attempt to bring about the reorganization and rationalization of home industry and agriculture. "How false is the suggestion," said the moving spirit of the new policy, Neville Chamberlain, "that this is a safety-first government destitute of new ideas, and how in fact it is continually introducing changes of a really revolutionary character."[2] Whether or not "revolutionary" is the right word, it is fair to say that government decisions of these years endowed Britain with a pattern of economic policy that was comprehensive and radically different from that of previous generations.

How were these decisions made? The question involves both the manner in which they were made and the forces that made them. Our previous discussion suggests various approaches to the question. It will be helpful to sketch some of them briefly. One possibility is that the critical decisions were essentially "ad hoc" and "empirical." That is to say, each decision was taken not as the result of a general plan or program that had been thought out well in advance, nor did it derive from distinctively Conservative principles or doctrine. On the contrary, as the full force of the Great Depression beat upon the British economy in 1931, the National Government merely did what was "obvious" and "inevitable" in the circumstances. When it abandoned free trade, for instance, public opinion in general was rapidly moving toward this conclusion. Sooner or later any Government of any party or parties

[2] *Ibid.*, p. 229.

would have been obliged to take this step. The fact that Conservatives were the principal agents was not significant.

A variation on this theme would be the view that, although what the National Government did was "obvious" and "inevitable," the doctrinaire commitment to free trade among Labourites and Liberals prevented those parties from seeing betimes the need for the new policy. Conservatives, therefore, became its authors, not because they were prepared with ideas or programs, but simply because they were the nonideological, nonprogrammatic party.

Quite different would be an interpretation that one might derive from Socialist views. Its general line would be to find in the policies of the National Government merely the response of capitalism and capitalist interests to a deep economic crisis. What the National Government did was indeed "obvious," not, however, from the point of view of the workers, but from that of the business interests which constituted the controlling element in its social base. So long as the gold standard and free trade favored the activities of these interests, the Conservative Party had championed them. When those principles of policy were no longer in this sense useful, the Conservatives turned toward economic nationalism with appropriate imperial modifications and toward a home policy of promoting cartels, restricting production, raising prices, and reducing the workers' share of the national income. The important forces, therefore, were not party ideas or Government decisions, but the interests and influence of the British business community.

In contrast with any of these views would be an interpretation which held that the Conservative Party as such made the major contribution to the new policy. It might be argued, for instance, that the old Conservative inclination toward protection and imperial preference prepared it, as other parties were not prepared, to seize this opportunity to reverse what had been for generations a fundamental of British economic policy. Moreover, a still more basic current of opinion in the party—the Tory tradition of state power—greatly eased for Conservatives their acceptance of the government's assumption of large new responsibilities. To be sure, business interests welcomed protection and Conservative domestic social policy was by no means aimed at abolishing or reducing economic inequality. Yet there were aspects of policy that businessmen themselves had to be made to accept, and Conservative social reform, while not egalitarian, maintained a decent minimum in spite of the economic stringencies of the time. In this sense, then, the basic decisions were party decisions. Not that the party conference dictated them. They were made according to the independent judgment of Conservative leaders acting in the light of the economic situation and of certain broad party traditions.

The Gold Standard and Monetary Expansion

The abandonment of the gold standard was certainly an "ad hoc" decision. In the past Britain had gone off gold when faced with acute difficulties, but only for brief periods. Even in 1919, when this step had been taken to avoid a trade depression on the morrow of victory and peace, the restoration of the gold standard had been the recognized aim of the Government, endorsed "by nearly all persons of authority" and dominating "the outlook of the Treasury and the Bank of England."[3] Some were critical of the return to gold in 1925, but as the financial crisis deepened in the spring and summer of 1931, even these critics were not prepared to reverse that decision and the major excuse given for the formation of the National Government was the preservation of the gold standard.

The economies in government expenditure accomplished by the National Government, however, did not sufficiently restore foreign confidence in sterling; in the face of the continuing drain, Britain was obliged to go off gold only a month after the formation of the new Government. The deflationary remedies, in which not only Conservative leaders but nearly all authorities believed, had been tried and had failed. In view of this fact, opinion in the government and outside was as agreed on the need to abandon the gold standard as it had been on the need to preserve it a few weeks previously. Philip Snowden, who had been as rigidly devoted to gold as any banker in the City, was the Chancellor of the Exchequer who presided over this great reversal. In the following year, in a logical next step, the Exchange Equalisation Account was established to stabilize the external value of the pound and Britain was launched on a long course of exchange control.

The abandonment of gold having severed the link between British and world price levels, a policy of monetary expansion was

[3] A. C. Pigou, as quoted in A. J. Youngson, *The British Economy, 1920–1957* (Cambridge, Mass., 1960), p. 231.

now feasible. Bank Rate, which had been fairly high in the 1920's and had been raised to 6 per cent in 1931, was reduced to 2 per cent in 1932, where it stayed until 1939.[4] In a step of great importance toward lowering interest rates, Neville Chamberlain, now Chancellor of the Exchequer, managed a conversion of more than a quarter of the national debt from a 5 per cent to a 3.5 per cent basis.

How great an effect the cheap money policy had on Britain's gradual but steady recovery during the next few years has been disputed by economists. At the time, some authoritative opinion followed Keynes, who as a member of the Macmillan Committee had advocated low interest rates to stimulate borrowing and employment. The Government's original motive, however, appears to have been not so much one of promoting recovery as of reducing debt charges and so was in line with the deflationary policy of its first few years. In time great virtues came to be attributed to cheap money and by 1936 Chamberlain was saying that along with the tariff it was one of "the two main pillars" of the Government's policy for recovery.[5] But monetary expansion, conceived as a means of stimulating economic activity, can no more be traced to long-run plans of Conservative leaders than it can be imputed to a distinctive current of opinion in party doctrine.

Origins of Tariff Reform

Quite different were the origins of the complex of policies that were built on the return to protection. Its cornerstone was the Import Duties Act of 1932. Neville Chamberlain saw this measure as bringing to fruition the "great campaign in favor of Imperial preference and tariff reform" that his father had launched twenty-nine years before. Its proposals, he said when presenting the bill to the House in February, 1932, were "the direct and legitimate descendants" of Joseph Chamberlain's conceptions.[6] Indeed, the intellectual ancestry of the bill antedates those conceptions and the agitation of the Tariff Reform League. In the late 1870's the need

[4] Youngson, *op. cit.*, p. 90; C. L. Mowat, *Britain Between the Wars, 1918–1940* (London, 1955), p. 456.

[5] Feiling, *op. cit.*, p. 283. "Cheap money had saved interest charges of £40 millions and underpinned the building of 1¼ million houses." So Feiling summarized Chamberlain's view.

[6] *Ibid.*, p. 205.

for protection against foreign competition had already been voiced and the cry of "fair trade" raised by business interests; some spokesmen of the new demands even then saw them as part of a policy of imperial preference and self-sufficiency.[7]

The immediate stimulus was trade depression, which brought to an end a long period of vigorous and unchallenged economic expansion. In the same years, and partly in response to the same conditions, the first Socialist groups were being formed. From this time there are many parallels between the development of the two movements, on the one hand Socialism and on the other hand tariff reform—or mercantilism, as one may call it, to suggest its ramifications beyond mere protection. Each found supporters in a complex of interest groups, produced intellectuals to refine its doctrines, expressed its demands in promotional pressure groups, lodged itself in a party, and ultimately in some substantial degree embodied its ideas in public policy.

The similarity in the development of the two movements is real, but not comprehensive. While fair trade resolutions were passed by Conservative conferences from the latter part of the nineteenth century, the party remained divided on tariff reform even into the 1920's. Certain economic interests associated with the party long remained committed to free trade, as Baldwin learned in 1923 from the expostulations of some Conservatives on behalf of the Lancashire cotton industry.[8] Moreover, the leaders of the party, even though on the whole personally favorable to protection, believed that it was a vote-losing cause and therefore refrained from publicly committing themselves to it at election times, even pledging themselves, as in 1922, 1924, and 1929 against a general tariff. As a result, there was no Conservative document —comparable to the comprehensive statements of purpose inaugurated by Labour in 1918—which systematically stated the case for tariff reform, enjoyed the approval of the party conference, and was generally accepted as expressing the long-run in-

[7] R. B. McDowell, *British Conservatism, 1832–1914* (London, 1959), p. 153; Sir Ivor Jennings, *Party Politics*, Vol. III, *The Appeal to the People* (Cambridge, Eng., 1962), p. 368.

[8] Sir Charles Petrie, *The Life and Letters of Austen Chamberlain* (London, 1939), pp. 236–7; R. T. McKenzie, *British Political Parties* (New York, 1955), p. 114. Immediately after the war the opposition to protection included major Conservative leaders, such as Lord Salisbury, Lord Derby, Lord Northcliffe and Lords Robert and Hugh Cecil. Beaverbrook, *The Decline and Fall of Lloyd George* (London, 1963), p. 16.

tentions of the party. But this does not mean that tariff reform did not have an elaborate and respectable intellectual foundation. Like Socialism, it was a powerful current of thought, growing in force in the early twentieth century, and like Socialism it has made a major contribution to the pattern of policy of the contemporary Welfare State and Managed Economy.

Although Joseph Chamberlain's campaign to commit the party and to convert the country had failed, the doctrines of protection and imperial preference had become strongly lodged in the party, providing a broad intellectual approach to Britain's economic problems. But for leaders and followers in a party—even though in a majority—to accept such an approach to public questions is far from having a program of government action to which the party's parliamentary power is pledged. Did the Conservative Party ever acquire such a program? How and by whom were its positions on tariff reform framed?

The Tory model of decision-making suggests that such decisions are made by the leadership, especially the Leader, as a matter of their "independent judgment" of what is in the national interest. In 1923 Baldwin followed a course that is almost a caricature of the Tory model. Only recently installed as Prime Minister and party Leader, he was confronted by mounting unemployment. At the same time, he felt that he was bound by the recent pledge of his predecessor, Bonar Law, not to introduce protection, and that he could free the party and his Government from this restraint only by a new appeal to the country. Yet in the fall of 1923 after "some private thinking," he concluded that protection was the only remedy for the economic problem.[9]

This decision was independently his own and not the result of pressure from his protectionist colleagues. Political considerations, however, were by no means absent from his deliberations. The party was still sorely embittered by the struggle that had led to the breakup of the Coalition the year before, and Baldwin saw in protection a device for healing the wounds because of its appeal to former Coalitionists such as Austen Chamberlain and Lord Birkenhead. Moreover, he seems also to have feared that Lloyd George was himself on the verge of raising a cry for protection

[9] On these events, see Feiling, op. cit., p. 108; G. M. Young, Stanley Baldwin (London, 1952), pp. 65–7; L. S. Amery, My Political Life, Vol. II, War and Peace, 1914–1929 (London, 1953), pp. 279–80.

as a means of restoring his political fortunes and winning back his Conservative friends of Coalition days.[1]

In any case, the decision, as Baldwin's biographer remarks, was "a bold stroke"[2] in view of the fact that the issue had been dormant for ten years, the country had not been prepared by an educative campaign, party spokesmen were untrained for the debate, and, not least important, a number of his Cabinet colleagues were free traders. Baldwin, however, had his way. When he first publicly announced his decision (this took place before the party's annual conference, which received his declaration with "great enthusiasm"[3]) he was obliged by the dissentients among the leaders to speak only for himself. Also when he had decided to dissolve, he took care to make sure that he had the agreement of his colleagues to the policy to be included in his election address. Otherwise, the appeal to the country in both its timing and in its content reflected Baldwin's decisions.[4]

A resounding defeat such as that suffered by the Conservatives in 1923 might well make any political leader wary of excessive reliance upon his "independent judgment." Baldwin's slow and tortuous approach to the vital decisions of 1931 is the reverse image of his bold, not to say rash, behavior eight years earlier, and conceivably reflects his reading of the hard lesson of that disaster. After 1923, like Conservative leaders on many other occasions, he adapted the policy of his party and Government to what appeared to be the wishes of the electorate, regardless of his own and most of his followers' opinions of the merits of the question at issue. To these electoral considerations was added a further factor—the leadership itself was still divided on the merits of tariff reform. A free trade faction, though weakening, persisted among the party chiefs and had the redoubtable Churchill as its principal spokesman from the time of his appointment as Chancellor of the Exchequer in 1924 until his resignation from the

---

[1] So asserted by Baldwin in Amery, *op. cit.*, and accepted by Neville Chamberlain in Feiling, *op. cit.*, and by Winston Churchill in Amery, *op. cit.*, Vol. III, *The Unforgiving Years, 1929–1940* (London, 1955), p. 510

[2] Young, *op. cit.*

[3] Amery, *op. cit.*, Vol. II, p. 282.

[4] The Cabinet was divided on timing and there was much discussion of the question after Baldwin revealed his plans at a meeting on October 23rd. Yet Baldwin had already by October 10th thought of an "immediate dissolution" (Feiling, *op. cit.*, p. 108).

Shadow Cabinet in January, 1931, over the question of India.[5] In consequence, although there was some nibbling at free trade under Baldwin's regime from 1924 to 1929, the Government as represented by its Prime Minister and the party as represented by its Leader remained pledged not to embark on any large-scale program of tariff reform.

Yet if Baldwin yielded to the electorate and compromised in order to hold the allegiance of powerful lieutenants, he showed firmness toward other sorts of pressure. In the late twenties, the extra-parliamentary organization turned with growing fervor toward tariff reform, which also enjoyed the support of the majority, perhaps the vast majority, of Conservative M.P.'s. By 1929 280 Conservative M.P.'s belonged to the Empire Industries Association, an organization formed in 1924 to propagandize for protection and imperial preference.[6] Yet, as Amery sadly wrote of this period, "the Government had done nothing for the causes which the rank and file of its supporters cared about."[7]

Moreover, the business interests that wanted protection were no more successful than the party in changing the course of Government policy. The case of the iron and steel industry is illustrative. In the election of 1924, while adapting his policy to the free trade sentiments of voters, Baldwin nevertheless promised to provide protection for particular industries under the Safeguarding of Industries Act of 1921. Under this act the Government was empowered to impose discriminating duties on specific imports from a country that was judged guilty of methods of unfair competition, such as dumping, the duties being imposed at the discretion of the Board of Trade upon application by the manufacturers concerned and after an inquiry.

When the iron and steel industry made application, however, it was refused even the ordinary inquiry.[8] The Government did not deny that British manufacturers were severely pressed by unfair foreign competition—"long hours, low wages and depreciated currencies"—but held that to safeguard an industry of such magnitude would inevitably lead to conflict with the pledge against

[5] *Ibid.*, p. 184.
[6] Sir Henry Page Croft, *My Life of Strife* (London, 1948), p. 181. Amery, *op. cit.* Vol. II, p. 291, Vol. III, p. 24.
[7] Amery, *op. cit.*, Vol. II, p. 498.
[8] Viscount Swinton (Philip Cunliffe-Lister), *I Remember* (London, 1948), pp. 36–7; Amery, *op. cit.*, Vol. II, pp. 479, 493–4.

a general tariff.[9] Pressure continued from members of the Cabinet, from the party within and without Parliament (the Whips at one point reporting M.P.'s in "a state of open mutiny"[1]), and from both the iron and steel companies and their workers, only to meet with continued refusal. This decision had been accepted by the Cabinet[2] but there is no doubt that it conformed to the views of Baldwin,[3] who, we may recall, was himself the owner of shares in the family iron and steel business worth a quarter of a million pounds.[4]

ADOPTION OF "THE GREAT POLICY"

After the election of 1929 the Conservative Party went into opposition, committed by the repeated statements of its Leader and by the practice of his Government against any policy of general tariffs. By the early months of 1931 the Leader and his lieutenants had not only agreed on such a policy but had drafted a detailed scheme which, with minor modification, became the Import Duties Act of 1932. While we need not try to make a comprehensive analysis of this decision, it will be relevant to our concerns to identify the roles of the Conservative leadership, the business community, and the party in and out of Parliament.

The initiative in framing the program came from the leadership : not from the Leader, however, but from Neville Chamberlain, who, all accounts agree, was "the moving spirit" in preparing what he called "the great policy." Already in the first weeks after the election of 1929 he was writing of "my plan," which he described as one which was "to make tariffs or custom duties only a part of a larger Imperial trade policy." And within the next few months he had set to work on the details, making "enquiry with experts into the possibilities both rural and industrial, and agreements between home and Dominion producers."[5] Late in 1929, at Chamberlain's instigation, the Leader set up a new piece of party machinery, the Conservative Research Department, which proved to be of immense importance in both the immediate and more distant future. As chairman Chamberlain directed its work

[9] Swinton, *op. cit.*, p. 37.
[1] Amery, *op. cit.*, Vol. II, p. 495.
[2] Swinton, *op. cit.*, p. 37.
[3] Amery, *op. cit.*, Vol. III, pp. 493-4, 496.
[4] Young, *op. cit.*, p. 121.
[5] Feiling, *op. cit.*, p. 173.

in various fields of policy, including tariff reform. Among political leaders, however, the immediate responsibility for working
out a program of protection and imperial preference was entrusted
to a subcommittee of the Shadow Cabinet, of which, at Chamberlain's and Baldwin's request, Cunliffe-Lister (later Lord Swinton),
who had been President of the Board of Trade in Baldwin's second
Government, was chairman. Assisted by the experts of the Research Department, this committee took charge of "all work in
connection with the tariff." "We . . . worked for eighteen
months," recalled its chairman. "We received a mass of evidence
from many trades and industries, and produced a report covering
the whole structure and operation of a general tariff."[6] By the
early months of 1931 "a complete tariff scheme" had been worked
out, "ready to be rushed through Parliament at a moment's
notice."[7]

To be sure, when the National Government embarked on framing the Import Duties bill a Cabinet committee was formally
charged with drafting the measure. The principal function of
this "make-believe inquiry," however, was to arrange temporary
concessions intended to retain certain Liberal support, particularly that of Walter Runciman, a wavering free trader who was
President of the Board of Trade.[8] In fact, the basis for the tariff
legislation of the National Government, including both the
Abnormal Importations Act of 1931 and the Import Duties Act
of 1932, was provided by the detailed proposals of the Cunliffe-
Lister committee.[9] Few British Governments have taken office
equipped with such thorough and programmatic preparation for
a major innovation in public policy. For a party often identified
with *ad hoc* empiricism—not to say "muddling through"—in its
decision-making, the Conservatives in this instance showed a remarkable degree of systematic forethought.

If the initiative and basic conceptions had come from political
leaders, advice was sought not only from the experts of the Research Department but also from the business community. Business opinion, as we have seen, had not always been united in support of tariff reform. During the late twenties and after the onset

[6] Swinton, *op. cit.*, p. 38.
[7] Amery, *op. cit.*, Vol. III, p. 22.
[8] *Ibid.*, p. 76.
[9] Feiling, *op. cit.*, p. 202; Amery, *op. cit.*, Vol. III, p. 79.

of the depression in 1929, however, it became more and more protectionist. In August 1930, for instance, the Associated Chambers of Commerce adopted a strong report in favor of safeguarding and in October the Federation of British Industries found that 96 per cent of its constituent bodies supported protection and the widest possible extension of imperial preference. Even more indicative of the movement of business opinion, a number of leading bankers and businessmen, meeting at Hambro's Bank in July, resolved in favor of a general tariff and imperial preference. For the first time in its history, Amery comments, the "City" had reconsidered and reversed that fundamental position which it had maintained "ever since the famous declaration of the London merchants for Free Trade in 1820."[1]

How did these currents of opinion gain access to the process of policy-making? Amery has described one system of connections in which he, a former minister and a member of the Shadow Cabinet, played an important role. Immediately after the defeat of 1929, he took action toward "getting together the business world in support of a concrete, soundly based programme."[2] With the aid of Lord Melchett (the former Alfred Mond), who by now had turned away from free trade and from Liberalism,[3] he assembled a number of leading businessmen and launched the Empire Economic Union. As a propaganda organization, this body did little, but its research committee produced a number of policy studies which, according to the testimony of Amery, who was its chairman, had considerable influence on the National Government.[4] Its sources were both individual businessmen and the representatives of business organizations, such as the Federation of British Industries and the National Union of Manufacturers.

Through Amery's committee such business opinion and advice had access to the party committee under Cunliffe-Lister. Indeed, with regard to tariff reform, according to Amery, his committee "agreed upon the general principles with the Federation of British Industries" and left only "the framing of a detailed tariff scheme" to the party committee.[5] While Amery may have been guilty of some exaggeration on this point, the general relationship of businessmen and their organizations with Conservative leaders that

[1] Amery, *op. cit.*, Vol. III, p. 31.
[2] *Ibid.*, p. 19.
[3] See above, Ch. V, p. 142.
[4] Amery, *op. cit.*, Vol. III, pp. 20-2.
[5] *Ibid.*, p. 21.

he describes has its parallel on other occasions. When parties frame policies in opposition without a civil service to advise them, they often turn for advice, as Professor Finer has observed, to special interest groups. "This is true of both parties. But whereas the hard core of supplicants and supporters of the Labour Party are the trade unions, those of the Conservative Party are firms and trade associations."[6]

In such a manner, then, certain party leaders, working with the party's research staff and taking counsel with outside interests, framed the program for carrying out "the great policy." But to frame a program is not the same as adopting it as a commitment that the parliamentary forces of the party will carry out if given power. And indeed, throughout much of the time that the new policy was busily being prepared by Conservatives, the party itself remained publicly bound by Baldwin's pledges against protection. According to ancient party protocol, the party could be committed only by its Leader. How did Baldwin come to make the decision, whose content had been prepared by his colleagues?

The crucial months were from September 1930 to March 1931. By the early autumn of 1930 Baldwin had already made advances, though few and ambiguous, toward the full protectionist position, which involved not only a general tariff, but also those duties on food necessary to make possible substantial preference for the Dominions. Baldwin's principal concession had been to propose that any food duties agreed at the coming Imperial Conference, due to meet in October, would be subject to a referendum. This compromise, which had been acclaimed by a meeting of the Council of the National Union, had been Baldwin's response to a gloomy report of party unrest from the chief agent, and it had been accepted by Baldwin at a private meeting with Beaverbrook, whose campaign for "Empire Free Trade" was making substantial headway.[7] It is a question, however, whether Baldwin intended this proposal as anything more than a means of playing for time. However that may be, Neville Chamberlain, it is certain, thought it an unfortunate pledge that should be got rid of as soon as possible.[8]

[6] S. E. Finer, "The Political Power of Private Capital," Pt. II, *Sociological Review*, new ser., Vol. IV, No. 1 (July, 1956), p. 6.

[7] Feiling, *op. cit.*, p. 177; Amery, *op. cit.*, Vol. III, pp. 24–5.

[8] Feiling, *op. cit.*, p. 177.

The opportunity to suppress the referendum proposal was presented in the autumn by increasing dissatisfaction with Baldwin in the party. "The suggestion that a change in the leadership was desirable," reported the chief agent in September, "has grown from a faint whisper to a loud and continuous rumbling."[9] In October a letter (in form from Baldwin to Chamberlain, actually drafted by Chamberlain and approved by the Shadow Cabinet in spite of Churchill's strong dissent) was released to the press. In it Baldwin definitely and strongly declared for Imperial preference, at the same time implying the possibility of food duties.[1] The referendum was now dead. And while this declaration did not head off the party meeting that Baldwin's opponents desired, it did help him defeat a vote of no confidence at a gathering of Conservative M.P.'s, peers, and candidates by a vote of 462 for Baldwin to 116 opposed.[2]

Further intensified by Baldwin's support of dominion status for India, opposition to his leadership continued to mount within the party. In February 1931, the chief agent reported that it was doubtful whether the party could win the next election without a change in leadership and frankly stated that "it would be in the interests of the Party that the Leader should reconsider his position." All except one of the principal figures in the party leadership agreed that Baldwin "would have to resign," a judgment that Baldwin himself briefly shared.[3] While his position was strengthened by a victory over a Beaverbrook candidate at a by-election on which national attention had been focused, he subsequently accepted a "peace protocol" with Beaverbrook in which the latter's policy was accepted. Through the intermediation of Chamberlain, an exchange of letters was arranged toward the end of March in which Baldwin made it clear that

the Conservative Party's policy included the protection of British agriculture by duties on foreign food stuffs, quotas, or prohibitions, as might be most convenient, as well as the protection of manufacture and Empire Preference.[4]

[9] Amery, *op. cit.*, Vol. III, p. 36.
[1] *Ibid.*, p. 37; Feiling, *op. cit.*, p. 181.
[2] Feiling, *op. cit.*, p. 182; Avery, *op. cit.*, Vol. III, p. 36; R. T. McKenzie, *op. cit.*, p. 137.
[3] Feiling, *op. cit.*, p. 120, p. 185; Amery, *op. cit.*, Vol. III, p. 38; Young, *op. cit.*, p. 120.
[4] Amery, *op. cit.*, Vol. III, p. 40.

At last the party was committed to the policy for which the Cunliffe-Lister subcommittee was preparing a detailed program. Not least among the forces that had been pressing for this solution was the party in Parliament, where, according to Amery, the Empire Industries Association exercised "decisive influence."[5]

In making the decisions that led to this final commitment, Baldwin was clearly influenced by pressure from colleagues, the party, and the press "lords," especially Beaverbrook. But one cannot think of his behavior as merely a yielding and passive response. Threats of open revolt within the party at least hastened his decisions at critical times. Yet we must remember that in those same days he was adamantly resisting pressure which came from much the same sources and aimed at making him reverse his policy toward India. Moreover, now as always, Baldwin was convinced of the merits of tariff reform and held back only on grounds of political expediency. By the time he publicly declared for the full policy, Churchill had left the Shadow Cabinet and, what was probably far more important in Baldwin's calculations, major sections of public opinion had moved strongly toward protection. Not only businessmen and banks, but also the T.U.C. itself was looking hopefully in this direction,[6] and sections of the Liberal leadership, later to become National Liberals, were wavering. Indeed, by the fall of 1931 Churchill too had given up the old cause. For all the complaints of Baldwin's inertia and indecisiveness that the memoirs of the period record, the actual outcome in the spring of 1931 left not only Baldwin, but also the Conservatives, in an immensely strong political position in the country. Churchill, we may recall, judged him "the ablest party manager the Conservatives have ever had."[7]

INDUSTRIAL REORGANIZATION

Protection for home industry and agriculture was, of course, indispensable to the policy of Imperial preference by which it was hoped, through the medium of mutual concessions on the part of the home country and the Dominions, to create larger

[5] Amery, *op. cit.*, Vol. II, p. 291; Vol. III, p. 80.
[6] See Report on Imperial Preference by The Economic Committee, T.U.C. *Report* 1930, pp. 208–17.
[7] Winston S. Churchill, *The Second World War : The Gathering Storm* (London, 1948), p. 33.

markets for the exports of Great Britain and so to revive her economy. The power to impose tariffs was also used by the National Government in bargaining with foreign countries; between 1932 and 1935 some seventeen bilateral trade agreements were concluded, under which Britain gave quotas for the importation of such products as meat and butter in return for concessions for British exports. This mercantilist policy, moreover, was linked with a domestic economic policy aiming at the reorganization of industry and agriculture. The link was the power to grant—or deny—protection. Such discretionary power, wrote Chamberlain on the eve of his introduction of the Import Duties bill,

> does provide us with such a lever as has never been possessed before by any government for inducing or, if you like, forcing industry to set its house in order. I have in my mind particularly iron and steel, and cotton; and my belief in the advantages of protection is not so fanatical as to close my eyes to the vital importance of a thorough reorganisation of such industries as these, if they are even to keep their heads above water in the future.[8]

The more distant origins of this policy are to be found in certain economic and intellectual developments of the late nineteenth century. Already in the nineties, as we have observed,[9] the rise of industrial combinations and of trade associations showed the trend away from the individualist and polycentric economy of previous decades. On the eve of World War I, while the partnership and the private company still flourished, modern corporate forms had triumphed in banking, transport, public utilities, and much of industry. These forms, with refinements such as the holding company, opened up a new order of magnitude in private enterprise. The limited liability company not only made possible the concentration of a vast capital drawn from many investors, but also greatly facilitated expansion and amalgamation. By 1914 the giant corporation with bureaucratic organization and a professional management largely divorced from ownership was a familiar feature of the economy.[1] After the war, in industry and commerce generally (although there were notable exceptions such as coal), amalgamation and the growth of great new units went ahead rapidly, as did fusion among banks. By 1935 the de-

[8] Feiling, op. cit., p. 203.
[9] See above, Ch. III, p. 74.
[1] Sir John Clapham, An Economic History of Modern Britain (London, 1938), Vol. III, p. 289.

gree of concentration in many branches of industry was formidable.[2]

The growth of trade associations was intimately connected with the rise of economic concentration. Associations among firms to fix prices and regulate output, to represent employers in relations with trade unions, and to advocate business interests before Parliament existed in mid-Victorian times.[3] But most of these were local rather than national and, moreover, only in the last twenty years of the century did trade associations begin to appear in significant numbers.

As the scope of enterprise grew and production tended to become not only more specialised—a fact which encourages association between firms using the same machinery and processes—but also concentrated in relatively larger firms, control over both prices and output, or both, became possible by agreement between independent concerns.[4]

Thus the changing structure of industry provided conditions necessary for the development of trade associations, while the motives to form them derived from the rise of trade unions and the growing intervention of the state, as well as from the more specific economic conditions which made attractive such activities as the regulation of prices and output. Already by 1914 many of the great joint-stock amalgamations, as well as enterprises of other forms, worked in an extended framework of association. During World War I government action further stimulated these developments. Associations, often formed at the direct instigation of government, performed important functions providing expert advice on questions relating to their trades and at times serving as instruments of government control.[5]

[2] Taking "control" to signify the ownership of half the capital or voting power of a company, Leak and Maizels calculated the percentage of all employees in a trade who were employed by the three largest business units in 1935. On this basis, the index of concentration was—to give a few examples—for railways, 83%; petroleum, 82%; wrought iron and steel tubes, 71%; sugar and glucose, 71%; chemicals, 48%; engineering and vehicles, 43%; textiles, 23%. H. Leak and A. Maizels, "The Structure of British Industry," *Journal of the Royal Statistical Society*, Vol. CVIII, Pts. I–II (1945), pp. 142–99.

[3] Clapham, *op. cit.*, pp. 303, 315; W. H. B. Court, *A Concise Economic History of Britain from 1750 to the Present Time* (London, 1954), p. 214.

[4] Political and Economic Planning, *Industrial Trade Associations* (London, 1957), p. 4.

[5] *Ibid.*, pp. 11–13.

Against this background of growing concentration and association, there arose the rationalization movement of the late 1920's. This movement was not only a further development of previous tendencies, consisting in the formation of larger units through amalgamation and the use of trade associations to spread technical knowledge and eliminate inefficient, high-cost firms.[6] It also had a theoretical aspect, a conscious doctrine setting forth a justification of these developments in terms of the public interest. Although this doctrine had its advocates among intellectuals, it was peculiarly the product of the business community. One of its most prominent champions was Sir Alfred Mond (later Lord Melchett), who had himself presided over the formation of one of the largest amalgamations when Imperial Chemicals Industries, Ltd., of which he became chairman, was formed in 1926. With fervor he could write of the promise of rationalization :

Modern mergers are not created for the purposes of creating monopolies or for inflating prices. They are created for the purpose of realizing the best economic results which both capital and labor will share to the best advantage. They enable varieties of industries to form an insurance against fluctuations of markets and prices in individual products. . . . Amalgamations mean progress, economy, strength, prosperity.[7]

Rationalization, whether achieved by amalgamation or by agreement among separate firms, would tend to free industry from control by the impersonal forces of the market and open the way to conscious control of prices and output—in short, to "industrial self-government." On this level of discussion, the pragmatic arguments premised on the need for greater efficiency were strengthened by more general considerations of political and social theory. As we have seen, the new pluralism of twentieth-century thought legitimized an important role for functional groups, in particular the organized vocational bodies of a modern industrial economy.[8] Nor did Conservative publicists and politicians fail to see the similarities between this rising collectivism and elements of the Tory tradition. "In place of the extreme rivalry of the nineteenth century," wrote Sir Arthur Bryant, "industry is returning to the ancient medieval practice of cooperation and mutual agree-

---

[6] *Ibid.*, pp. 19-20; Youngson, *op. cit.*, pp. 226-8.
[7] *Industry and Politics* (London, 1927), p. 217.
[8] See above, Ch. III, pp. 73-9.

ment."[9] In 1934, when offering his proposals for "economic planning" and "industrial self-government," Harold Macmillan looked to "that organic conception of society which was the distinct contribution of medieval thought" as a counterweight to "individualism and *laissez-faire*."[1] And generally in these years, Keith Feiling, Tory historian and philosopher, found that "the wheel has turned back two centuries, and that under conditions far changed from the Elizabethan the main activities of the state are being nationalised."[2]

As an activity of the business community, rationalization made some progress. No antitrust movement on the American model arose to demand that amalgamations be prevented or broken up. Government inquiries, on the contrary, looked with favor on the trend.[3] In the highest Conservative circles, rationalization found ardent friends, a leading advocate being Cunliffe-Lister,[4] who, as we have seen, later served as chairman of the subcommittee of the Shadow Cabinet that worked up the tariff reform proposals of "the great policy." Yet even in industries with a high degree of concentration it was not easy to get all firms to reach agreement on a voluntary basis. Only with the arrival of protection in 1932 was the indispensable "lever" put into the Government's hands and a deliberate policy of using it to promote industrial reorganization adopted.

There is no need to describe in detail the particular schemes in industry and agriculture promoted by the National Government during the next few years. In his authoritative study, Arthur F. Lucas has identified four types of industrial controls supported by government in the mid-1930's: control of prices and output with reorganization to curtail productive capacity; unification through combination; concentration of sales through a central agency; and

[9] *The Spirit of Conservatism* (London, 1929), p. 103.
[1] *Reconstruction: A Plea for A National Policy* (London, 1934), pp. 127–8.
[2] *Op. cit.*, p. 200.
[3] Particularly the Committee on Trusts of 1919 and the Balfour Committee on Industry of 1924–29. See P.E.P., *Industrial Trade Associations*, pp. 17–20, and Youngson, *op. cit.*, pp. 225–28.
[4] As President of the Board of Trade, for instance, he introduced the Companies bill of 1928 that facilitated the amalgamation of firms by permitting corporations to force a dissenting minority among shareholders of 10% or less to consent to a merger. See also his comments made with reference to the Balfour Committee Report, quoted in P.E.P., *Industrial Trade Associations*, p. 21.

regulation of prices and output by associations.[5] Carried to an extreme, this line of policy could have established in Britain a "corporate state" directed from the center by a comprehensive planning organization. Although pressed, particularly by certain "progressive" Tories, to move farther in this direction, the Government was as reluctant to devolve large compulsory powers on industry as it was to assume the tasks of central planning.[6] The resulting changes, however, were of very considerable importance to the structure of industry and its relations with government. Associations among producers were greatly encouraged and were brought into regular contact with government. In this structure of "quasi-corporatism," the relationship was neither one of business pressure groups dictating to government nor of government agencies planning the activities of business. Decisions were made, rather, in a process of bargaining and negotiation.

For the sake of illustration, we may again look at iron and steel. The industry, as we have observed, had long sought a protective tariff and in 1932 a committee, representing 70 per cent of total iron and steel production, made application to the Import Duties Advisory Committee. The Committee's report, however, made the duties conditional upon the reorganization of the industry. Far from leaping at this opportunity to form a cartel with the Government's blessing, the industry held back and not until February 1934 was a new association, The British Iron and Steel Federation, established with powers of coordination over some twenty-seven affiliated associations representing the various sections of the industry.[7]

The tariff having been made permanent, the Federation discharged its responsibilities for price-fixing, controlling competition, subsidizing high-cost producers, and reviewing the development plans of individual firms under the broad supervision of the

---

[5] *Industrial Reconstruction and the Control of Competition* (London, 1937).

[6] See, for instance, a debate in the House on "improving the economic system," April 3rd, 1935, in which progressive Tories, such as Hugh Molson and Harold Macmillan, made a case for more government planning and specifically asked for legislation giving industries powers of self-government. 300 *H.C. Deb.* 377ff.

[7] G. C. Allen, *British Industries and Their Organization*, 3rd ed. (London, 1951), pp. 109–12; Duncan Burn, *The Structure of British Industry*, Vol. I (London, 1958), pp. 285–97.

Import Duties Advisory Committee. "From this time on," writes Allen, "questions of economic policy in the industry were settled by political negotiation rather than by market pressures which, of course, had been relieved by the monopoly powers conferred."[8] The outcome was not always a clear-cut victory for the Government. In 1935, for instance, it did intervene effectively (whether wisely is not our concern) with a major decision of one of the larger companies. Richard Thomas and Company, which had plants in South Wales, wished to build a new strip mill in Lincolnshire. Because of the unemployment problem in South Wales, however, the Government, itself subject to pressure from trade unions and public opinion, induced the company not to leave that region but to set up at Ebbw Vale. On the other hand, the industry as a whole made little progress toward one of the principal objects of rationalization, the reduction of costs. The British iron and steel industry remained a high-cost industry—even with a 33.3 per cent tariff foreign producers could make profitable sales in Birmingham. "The supervision of the I.D.A.C.," concludes one economic historian, "made pathetically little difference."[9]

While industry did not acquire full powers of self-government, the broad changes in the pattern of policy made by the National Government added new features to the power structure of British politics. Group consultation had been on the rise for many years. But it is not too much to say that the scale and nature of state intervention under the National Government founded a system of quasi-corporatism in which industry and government were brought into regular and continuous contact. Labor at this time had not yet achieved such governmental "recognition." In the early forties, however, trade unions, as we have seen, won a similar position in this informal but effective scheme of functional representation.[1]

THE DEVELOPMENT OF PARTY PURPOSE

It can be amply confirmed from the annals of the National Government that the world of business enjoys intimate and influential contact with the governing circles of the Conservative

---

[8] Allen, *op. cit.*, p. 112.
[9] Youngson, *op. cit.*, p. 106.   [1] See above, Ch. VII, pp. 211–16.

Party. But to insist on this proposition is not, however, to adopt
the model of decision-making that would have us hear in the
voice of Conservatism only an echo of the dictates of businessmen. The adoption of protection would seem to be a particularly
promising case to illustrate that model, but the facts do not fit.
If the model is to be accepted, we ought to find, for instance, a
correlation between authoritative party decisions and the movement of business opinion. Protectionist sentiment in business circles rose steadily in the 1920's, veered sharply upward after
1929, and reached virtual unanimity by the time the National
Government took office. But Conservative policy followed a very
different course. If we try to think of the adoption of "the great
policy" as a response to business pressure after 1929, it becomes a
puzzle why Conservative policy turned toward protection in the
fall of 1923, when business opinion was divided, then turned away
in the late 1920's, maintaining its resistance to growing business
pressure. Obviously, other considerations, not the least of which
were the electoral calculations of the Leader, must be weighed if
we are to assess properly the influences determining the course of
Conservative policy. To assume that we can merely read it off
as a reflex of business demands will simply mislead research. The
Conservative Party as a formation that seeks (among other things)
to win and hold power within a democratic political system may
well take action that does not coincide with, and may at times
affront, the wishes of even a section of the political community as
closely allied with Conservatism as the business world.

It can be very persuasively argued that the dominant and lasting motif of Conservative behavior is precisely this will to power—
and nothing more. The economic policy of the National Government suggests, however, that the Conservative Party is also the
vehicle of concepts of purpose that can strongly affect its use
of power. The party was prepared and directed in the task of
framing and putting into effect the neo-mercantilism of the
1930's by the currents of opinion set in motion within it by
Joseph Chamberlain. That this cause found lodging in the party
was, in turn, at least made easier by the fact that within the
memory of men Conservatism had been the home of protection.
Nor, speaking more generally, is it fanciful to find in the Tory
tradition of a pluralistic society ordered and protected by a
paternal state, a set of values and beliefs that legitimized for many

Conservatives the growing collectivism that interwar Conservatism tolerated and in part created.[2] A party may have its own political culture, inherited from different historical moments—and quite possibly, in the case of an old party, internally inconsistent—which from the resources of a distant past provides principles of action in a new situation. The older Tory traditions of mercantilism and of state authority, as well as protectionist and imperialist currents of opinion of more recent origin, prepared Conservatism to make its innovations in the 1930's.

Electoral calculations, party tradition, and the pressure of interest all played their part. Yet there is also one further element of the utmost importance. This was the periodic redefinition of purpose by the Conservative Party as an organization endowed with a role by the conventions of party government. These conventions gave it a general role : under appropriate conditions, to accept the responsibility for governing the country. To discharge this responsibility it needed to translate such principles as it derived from party tradition into programs and policies related to the changing circumstances of the time. This redefinition of organizational purpose could not be a mere deduction from party principles, no more than it was a mere response to the pressure of interests or a mere reflection of the party will to power. In Conservative structure the task of expressing in such concrete form some conception of the common good was vested mainly in the leadership. At a moment in the nineteenth century, as we have seen, Disraeli almost singlehandedly performed the task. In the case of "the great policy," the central figure was Neville Chamberlain. But he was also assisted by institutional structures, such as committees of the Shadow Cabinet and the Research Department.

In any organization, the function of setting objectives is performed in the context of many limiting and guiding forces. That does not mean that we can reduce this creative function to a mere reflex of these forces. Similarly, in the case of the Conservative Party in this time, as an organization with the role of governing, it framed policy under the influence of these forces, but also went beyond them. Neville Chamberlain did not simply repeat mechanically the proposals of his father. Or again, when he saw in protection a "lever" for forcing the reorganization of

<hr/>

[2] See Harvey Glickman, "The Toryness of English Conservatism," *Journal of British Studies*, No. 1 (November, 1961).

industry he was expressing an element of program that was no mere accommodation to the wishes of business. Not all political formations that call themselves parties have this capacity for creative redefinition of purpose. They may be too loosely structured or too rigidly fixed in their orientation by traditionalism or ideology. The general importance of this particular study of decision-making by the Conservatives is to show that at times party can perform this function and can in this sense be an independent force for the definition of the common good.

CHAPTER XI

The New Conservatism

The will to power of British Conservatism again showed itself in the years after 1945. The defeat of that year had been crushing and unexpected; the Conservative percentage of the major two-party vote, which had been 57 per cent at the last general election in 1935, fell to 45 per cent, and the number of seats in the House, which had been 423 in 1935, fell to 215.[1] Yet in a feat unprecedented in British political history, at each of the four succeeding general elections the party increased its share of the major two-party vote and from 1951 remained in power with growing majorities in the House. It almost seemed as if that "pendulum" on which writers on British politics had so long depended for a regular alternation of parties in power had ceased to swing against Conservatism.

These happy fruits did not drop into the Conservative lap by accident. The party busied itself furiously to win them, making major adaptations in tactics, organization, and, not least, policy and program. By 1950 it had accepted the basic framework of the Welfare State and Managed Economy that Labour was administering and, in the following years, the Conservative scheme of social and economic priorities was so close to those of Labour's public declarations at election time that the policies of the two parties could seem to be well on the way toward convergence. But if the results of policy-making by the two parties bore great similarities, the processes by which their policies were made remained very different. A commitment to both democracy and ideology as principles of party organization long impaired Labour's ability to make up its mind. The opposite principles greatly facilitated Conservative adaptation. A varied tradition supplied

---

[1] In these totals I include Liberal Nationals with Conservatives.

resources to legitimize the new departures in policy, while strong leadership enabled the party to read and act quickly on the lesson of the new electoral realities. In this sense, the "New Conservatism" was a product of the old.

But was so much flexibility compatible with the survival of anything distinctively Conservative? Bidding for the votes of consumers' groups in the narrowly divided electorate and bargaining for the cooperation of organized producers, Conservative Governments in the 1950's displayed their traditional will to win and hold on to office. But what else? In 1958 a leading authority on British parties could write:

The "objective aims" may be of greater or lesser importance in providing the basis of association and the motive force for the activity of a particular party.

But there is little doubt that it is the "collective pursuit of power" which is of overriding importance. It is obvious too that during the pursuit of power, and after it has been achieved, parties mould and adapt their principles under the innumerable pressures brought to bear by organised groups of citizens who operate for the most part outside the party system. . . . There can be no doubt that pressure groups, taken together, are a far more important channel of communication than parties for the transmission of political ideas from the mass of the citizenry to their rulers.[2]

If the pluralist model has ever sufficed as the framework for a comprehensive analysis of British politics, the 1950's would seem to be the time.

In the following pages we shall examine the Conservative Party of the postwar years, keeping in mind the models suggested by pluralist as well as Tory and Socialist thought. We shall look at it first during the period of adaptation in the late 1940's. We shall then turn to the behavior of the Conservative Government during the early 1950's—the period of policy convergence and strong group politics—and conclude with an examination of the new priorities that seem to emerge in the late 1950's and early 1960's.

TORY ADAPTATION : THE ISSUES

To infer what a party will actually do with power merely from what it says while in opposition is always a chancy business. In Britain, however, the practices of modern party government re-

[2] R. T. McKenzie, *Political Quarterly*, Vol. XXIX, No. 1 (January-March, 1958), pp. 8–10.

duce the hazards of such an inquiry in comparison with other countries with a looser party system. In the present case, the verbal transformation of Conservative purpose in the late forties was matched by the deeds of Conservative Governments in the early fifties. Indeed, in significant respects, those policies carried the party still farther along the road of adaptation, as Conservative leaders in power continued to respond to forces that had directed their reaction to the defeat of 1945. The essence of that reaction had been their acceptance of the vast Welfare State expenditure established by Labour, together with the sharply progressive taxation by which it was financed.[3] To say this is not to depreciate the thought that went into the redesigning of Conservative policies, nor to deny that Conservatives modified certain aspects of the Welfare State and Managed Economy which they inherited from Labour. These modifications, however, took place within the basic pattern of policy established by Labour, and that pattern of policy presupposed a new and vast financial commitment by the state.

The Conservatives, for instance, made some changes in the National Health Service. They accepted, however, a total N.H.S. expenditure of 402 million pounds in the financial year 1952–53 —a staggering increase over the amount foreseen by its proponents during the war—and of even larger amounts in later years. Or to take a broader question, let us examine the commitment to full employment. In the campaign of 1945 Churchill was ready to pledge on behalf of his Government only "a high and stable level of employment" as "one" of its primary aims.[4] By 1950, according to the manifesto published under his name, he regarded "the maintenance of full employment as the first aim of a Conservative Government."[5] Not long thereafter a Conservative Chancellor proved that he and his colleagues could will the fiscal policy necessary to meet that pledge in the fullest sense. As the Korean boom subsided, unemployment in Great Britain rose from 303,000 at the end of 1951 to 399,000 at the end of 1952.[6] The latter figure was only 1.7 per cent of the total working population, and in the

[3] "It is on the weight of taxation," wrote R. A. Butler in 1949, "that the clash between Conservative and Socialist policies is the sharpest." *Political Quarterly*, Vol. XX, No. 4 (October-December, 1949), p. 320.

[4] *Mr. Churchill's Declaration of Policy to The Electors*, p. 6.

[5] *This Is the Road : The Conservative and Unionist Party's Policy* (January, 1950), p. 8.

[6] *Economic Survey for 1953* (Cmd. 8800), pp. 41-2.

face of sharp reproaches from some backbenchers for his failure to cut government expenditures,[7] Butler made substantial tax concessions in his 1953 budget in order to stimulate economic activity. "For the first time in the history of this country," said one M.P., echoing a comment of the *Economist*, a Chancellor had "taken the lesson which we were taught by the late Maynard Keynes to heart" and in a time of slack, instead of drawing in, had "deliberately stimulated demand. . . . This is in fact very nearly deficit budgeting."[8] Generally, under Mr. Churchill's Conservative Government, as under Labour, the full employment pledge meant in effect holding unemployment down to 1 or 2 per cent.

In order to identify the change in Conservative policy after 1945 it is not enough to say that the party accepted the Welfare State. That term has both broader and narrower definitions. It means at least a system of social services involving some redistribution of income and providing benefits for individuals, primarily to meet the needs of unemployment, sickness, and old age.[9] In the light of this meaning, Conservatives of the interwar period had accepted and contributed to the growth of the Welfare State. Moreover, they had adjusted to the "new social contract" of wartime.[1] In March, 1943, for instance, Churchill had outlined what he called his "Four Year Plan" for peacetime. It included a national health service; extension of the social insurance system covering unemployment, sickness, and old age; a scheme of family allowances; and a major revision of education, later embodied in the Education Act of 1944. In the campaign of 1945 this "Four Year Plan," although left rather vague,[2] was emphasized by the Leader and other party spokesmen. By the end of the war there was, in short, as Churchill told the House, a "great mass of social legislation" to which "the leading men in both the principal parties" were pledged.[3]

But crucial questions remained unanswered. What priority

---

[7] See, for instance, the remarks of Sir Herbert Williams, 514 *H.C. Deb.* 75 (16 April 1953).

[8] 514 *H.C. Deb.* 709 (20 April 1953).

[9] It comes closer to popular usage, in addition, to include not only state-financed education and a subsidized housing program, but also a commitment to full employment.

[1] See above, Ch. VII, p. 212.

[2] R. B. McCallum and Alison Readman, *The British General Election of 1945* (London, 1947), p. 52.

[3] 406 *H.C. Deb.* 35 (29 November 1944).

would these measures be given by a Conservative Cabinet confronted with the economic conditions of the postwar world?
More important, how rapidly and generously would the financial
implications of the "Plan" be met if the Conservatives won in
1945? The Coalition Government's cool reception of the Beveridge
Report in 1943 had given some clue. The Government motion
"welcoming" the report was noncommittal.[4] The grounds for
that restraint were essentially financial and during the debate,
the Chancellor of the Exchequer, Kingsley Wood, and the Lord
President of the Council, Sir John Anderson, developed these
considerations, harping on the need to wait and see what the
financial and economic situation would be after the war before
any commitment could be made.[5] This position had been defined
by Churchill himself in a Cabinet note two days before the debate.
While approving the Beveridge approach to social security, he
declared: "We cannot however initiate the legislation now or
commit ourselves to the expenditure involved." The objections
were political (it would not be proper to commit a future Government) and financial (it was impossible to tell what conditions
would be after the war or how the expenditure on social insurance would fit in with other government expenditures).[6]

Churchill was at least keeping a free hand,[7] as he continued to
do through the campaign of 1945. Ralph Assheton, his appointee
as chairman of the party organization from 1944 to 1946, exerted
himself strenuously to restrain promises of welfare benefits for
fear of the burdens they would impose on industry.[8] Other Conservatives were more decisive and outspoken. During the Beveridge
debate, for instance, Sir Herbert Williams called the document "a
very bad report." His main objection was to the huge cost it
would involve and the consequent burden of taxation which, he

---

[4] See Herbert Morrison, *An Autobiography* (London, 1960), p. 229, and
Lord Beveridge, *Power and Influence* (London, 1953), p. 324.

[5] 386 *H.C. Deb.* 1826–30 and 1657–8 (16 February 1943).

[6] Winston S. Churchill, *The Second World War: The Hinge of Fate*
(Boston, 1950), pp. 959–60.

[7] Lady Beveridge avers that the Government's intent was "to torpedo the
Report." Lady Janet Beveridge, *Beveridge and His Plan* (London, 1954), p.
151. Attlee, on the other hand, thought Churchill engineered the delay in the
hope of having the Beveridge Report "to put through as an act of his
Government" when he had become "the first post-war Prime Minister."
Francis Williams, *A Prime Minister Remembers: The War and Post-war
Memoirs of the Rt. Hon. Earl Attlee* (London, 1961), p. 57.

[8] Author's private information.

predicted, would reduce capital investment and lead to unemployment.[9]

While Sir Herbert did not lack allies on the Conservative side, his views were opposed by fellow partisans who were equally outspoken. These were principally members of the Tory Reform Group that had recently been formed with the immediate object of "encouraging the Government to take constructive action on the lines of the Beveridge Report,"[1] and which was joined by some forty Conservative M.P.'s, its most prominent member being Quintin Hogg (later briefly Lord Hailsham). While the Tory Reformers did not feel able to vote against the Government and in favor of the hostile amendment supported by the bulk of unofficial Labour and Liberal members,[2] they conducted a modest agitation within the party during the next few years on behalf of a more "progressive" attitude toward social reform. Like other reformers before them, they harked back to the example of Disraeli, and with no more than the usual exaggeration of political rhetoric claimed not only that the Beveridge Report was "the very essence of Toryism," but even that "perhaps the Party's greatest tenet is, as it has always been, the elevation of the condition of the people."[3] Forcefully reasserting a Disraelian maxim, Quintin Hogg warned his party during the Beveridge Report debate : "If you do not give the people social reform, they are going to give you social revolution."[4]

If the crux of the party's adaptation was its acceptance of the financial burdens of the postwar Welfare State, hardly less important from the viewpoint of public policy was the Conservative adoption of the methods and responsibilities of the Managed Economy. By economic management I mean that system of directing the economy which emerged in the last years of Attlee's Government and which relied primarily, although not exclusively, upon the concepts of national income analysis to define its problems and upon the broad influences of fiscal policy (and, under the Conservatives, monetary policy) to solve them. Interwar Con-

---

[9] 386 H.C. Deb. 2015–20 (16–18 February 1943).

[1] Forward by the Right : A Statement by the Tory Reform Committee (London, 1943), p. 11.

[2] Moved by James Griffiths. 386 H.C. Deb. 1965–73.

[3] Viscount Hinchingbrooke, Full Speed Ahead : Essays in Tory Reform (London, 1944), p. 9.

[4] 386 H.C. Deb. 1818 (16 February 1943).

servatism had taken major steps toward control of the economy. Wartime practices had equipped government with an elaborate system of quantitative planning, supplemented by primitive Keynesian methods at the Treasury, while Labour's ancient orthodoxy saw in public ownership and public administration still a fourth broad method of economic direction.

Which of these methods, or how much of any of them peacetime Conservatism would accept and use was by no means decided as the war came to an end. The period of transition was not the question : it was generally agreed that most of the wartime system would have to be maintained during demobilization and reconversion. But looking farther ahead, Churchill told the party that "at the head of our mainmast, we, like the United States, fly the flag of 'free enterprise.' "[5] And during the campaign of 1945, as the authors of the Nuffield study observe, the Conservative stress on free enterprise in comparison with Labour's vision of a planned economy produced "a real difference of economic theory."[6] To be sure, the freedom that Conservatism foresaw for the economy was qualified by the prospect of large measures of state intervention. If coal, gas, electricity, and transport were not to be nationalized, they were nonetheless to be subjected to central "help and guidance," while agriculture would continue to enjoy "stable markets and prices" and land use and the location of industry would be controlled.[7] Nevertheless, in 1945 Conservatism had not made a clear and definite commitment to either the Welfare State or the Managed Economy.

ACTORS AND MOTIVES

By the time the Conservatives took office in 1951 these ambiguities had been resolved and, as the actions of Churchill's Government showed over the next few years, Conservatism had adapted to Labour's "peaceful revolution." The process of adaptation has familiar contours. It was, in the first place, a reaction to the new electoral situation revealed by the crushing defeat of 1945, which the Conservative recovery of 1950 and 1951 reversed only to the extent of leaving the two parties almost evenly matched in the country and in the House. The force of electoral considerations

[5] London *Times*, March 16, 1945.
[6] McCallum and Readman, *op. cit.*, p. 53.
[7] *Mr. Churchill's Declaration of Policy to the Electors.*

in bringing the "New Conservatism" to the fore and keeping it there was readily acknowledged by party leaders—in what they said publicly as well as privately. With pain David Eccles told the House during the budget debate of 1950 that they could now see "the driving force of a working class budget in all its undisciplined humanity and in all its shapeless suicidal power."[8] Although this signalized the defeat of the old "middle class virtues," it was, he concluded, an implication of universal suffrage, reflected in the acceptance by Conservatives as well as Labourites of the public demand for expanding social services. With pride R. A. Butler in 1954 looked back on the years of opposition and compared what had been done then "to prepare the mind of the country and to educate our Party" with Disraeli's achievement. "As a result," he asserted, "we returned to power in 1951."[9] With calm Churchill showed that he shared a similar view of the electoral situation when he reminded the party conference that although "there are immense doctrinal differences" between the parties, nevertheless, "as each Party is supported by more than 12,000,000 voters they must have a great deal in common."[1]

In the process of adaptation, the party—meaning by this both the organized parliamentary party and the National Union—played a minor, supporting role. There were those who favored and those who opposed adaptation and a very great many who were ready to follow a strong lead in either direction. During the first two years or so after 1945 the party in both arenas was incoherent and confused. Although Churchill met regularly in the usual manner with his Shadow Cabinet, which consisted mainly of the principal ministers of his Caretaker Government of 1945, to agree on the line to be taken in Parliament, there was little consistency in Conservative views of what ought to be done in the various fields of economic policy. With regard to monetary policy, the former Chancellor of the Exchequer in the Caretaker Government, Sir John Anderson, in 1945 and 1946 fully approved of Dalton's policy of "cheap money."[2] By August 1947, on the other hand, leading Conservatives, including the Shadow Chancellor of the Exchequer, Oliver Stanley, were making "cheap money"

[8] 474 H.C. Deb. 239 (18 April 1950).
[9] Tradition and Change (London, 1954), p. 9.
[1] 1954 CPCR, p. 114.
[2] 414 H.C. Deb. 2019 (23 October 1945); 421 H.C. Deb. 1950 (9 April 1946).

a principal scapegoat of the economic crisis.[3] With regard to the proper balance between consumption and investment, there was vacillation and conflict. In April 1947, Brendan Bracken attacked Dalton for breaking his promise to use the American loan mainly for capital equipment.[4] A few months later, however, Conservative spokesmen were calling for fewer hardships in a sharp attack on the size of the investment program.[5] With regard to planning, they could at times claim that both parties accepted the necessity for it and at other times denounced it.[6] With regard to social expenditure and the consequent burden and incidence of taxation, the Conservative line was rather clearer. The Government, they said, was going ahead too rapidly with social expenditure and, in consequence, the burden of taxation bore too heavily upon industry and upon taxpayers of the professional and middle classes (Sir John Anderson giving particular emphasis to the grave dangers of equality). Yet at times Conservative spokesmen—for instance, Sir Anthony Eden when leading off for the party on the 1947 budget[7]—could claim that Labour's scheme of social services originated with the plans of the Coalition Government and that only differences of "degree" not "principle" divided the parties.

Nor did the party organization outside Parliament show any greater sense of direction. In November 1945, the Central Council, taking up the question of the party's future policy, followed the lead of Churchill, who delivered a vehement attack on the Labour Government and adopted a largely negative anti-Socialist line. Not long after, as "the first fruits" of this decision,[8] a strongly worded motion of censure was moved by the parliamentary party. Far from this tactic reflecting the interests of the business community, the chairman of the Federation of British Industries cut the ground from under the Conservative assault by announcing at about the same time that the leaders of industry were ready to cooperate with the Labour Government in carrying out its

---

[3] Oliver Stanley, 440 *H.C. Deb.* 1437ff (6 August 1947).
[4] 436 *H.C. Deb.* 348 (15 April 1947).
[5] See Comments of Oliver Stanley, 439 *H.C. Deb.* 1437ff (6 August 1947); David Maxwell Fyfe, 443 *H.C. Deb.* 449–53 (20 October 1947); Oliver Stanley, 444 *H.C. Deb.* 557ff (13 November 1947).
[6] Compare Lyttleton, 434 *H.C. Deb.* 1001 and Eccles, 434 *H.C. Deb.* 1214–17 (10 March 1947) with Lyttleton, 449 *H.C. Deb.* 631–9 (12 April 1948).
[7] 436 *H.C. Deb.* 101 (15 April 1947).
[8] *Annual Register, 1945,* p. 99.

economic policy and to help fit private enterprise into the Government's framework of action.[9]

At the conference of 1946, dissatisfaction with the party's negativism was marked especially among the Young Conservatives, and a resolution asking for a positive statement of party policy was passed with a large majority. On the other hand, the greatest ovation (next to Churchill's) was given a lady delegate's denunciation of controls and Churchill himself clung to the negative line, making a slashing attack on Socialism and strongly warning the conference that "the principles of our party are not up for auction."[1]

The initiative in resolving this confusion came from the small circle of top leaders. Within this circle there was a sharp clash, for the leaders, like their followers, were divided, not to say confused. But although the conflict was real, it was kept behind the scenes and the basic decisions were quickly made. By the time the *Industrial Charter* was published in May 1947, the main commitments, which were to govern the reconstruction of Conservative domestic policy, had been made. Concerned with "the future structure of British industry," the Charter was notable for its large acceptance of the nationalization measures of the Labour Government. Moreover, it accepted in a quite detailed exposition a far greater degree of planning and control than Conservatives had ever been willing to tolerate for peacetime. And while its main theme was industrial policy, it also committed the party to the new financial burdens of the Welfare State imposed by Labour's reforms. Indeed, the case for "strong central guidance" was grounded on its necessity for both control of the economy and expansion of the social services.

The leading figure in bringing about this adaptation was R. A. Butler. As a young man he had been influenced by his uncle, Sir Geoffrey Butler, a don, an author, and a Conservative M.P. who, it is said, opened young Butler's mind to "the importance of Bolingbroke in shaping the Tory tradition and in justifying the use of the State for political purposes."[2] But in R. A. Butler's early history within the party there was little to mark him out as an innovator. He had risen rapidly with the assistance of the personal

---

[9] *Ibid.*, p. 100.
[1] London *Times* (October 7, 1946), p. 2.
[2] Francis Boyd, *Richard Austen Butler* (London, 1956), p. 35.

patronage of Sir Samuel Hoare, a family friend. Far from a rebel, he had "acted in harmony with the central block of Conservative opinion," making "the preservation of the maximum of party unity" a constant purpose.[3] Unlike Harold Macmillan, he was not among the mutinous progressives of the 1930's who had urged on the Government the need for stronger planning and for economic expansion. On the contrary, he had been mainly occupied with foreign affairs and, in this sphere, as a junior minister, he loyally supported the appeasement policies of his chiefs. He had, to be sure, exceptional intellectual qualities, and Neville Chamberlain had indicated that Butler was to succeed him as the ministerial head of the Conservative Research Department.

Butler's concern with domestic affairs and social reform was, so to speak, an incidental result of Munich. For although Churchill kept him in the Coalition Government, he gave him no important wartime task, relegating him to the Board of Education. There Butler directed the framing and passage of a major statute in British educational history, the Education Act of 1944, which was warmly received not only by his party, but also by opinion generally. For much of the war he was also chairman of the new party committee on Post-War Problems. Again no rebel—he did not associate himself with the Tory Reformers—he nevertheless helped guide the party toward an acceptance of extension of the social services. In these ways he became identified with the tasks of peacetime domestic reform and, in November 1945, Churchill appointed him head of the revived Research Department and chairman of the party's Committee on Policy and Political Education.

It was a position with great opportunities. Churchill's successor would clearly be Eden, but the third place in the party leadership was open. Oliver Stanley, Macmillan, Lyttleton, and David Maxwell Fyfe, as well as Butler, were among the candidates. With the benefit of hindsight it can be seen that to make oneself the author of a reconstructed Conservative policy was a very promising way to move forward in this competition. And indeed by 1951 Butler had become the party's principal spokesman on domestic affairs and seemed to have established his claim to second place in the line of succession.[4] This is not to suggest that his action was dictated solely by the opportunities for advancement. Given his Tory background, it was natural that he should have a belief in the authority of the state and in social reform which his wartime tasks and achievements could only have enhanced. The point is that the structure of the situation of competition for the party leadership worked in harmony, rather than at cross-purposes, with such internal motivations.

Butler, as we observed earlier, once compared the adaptation of Conservative policy in the 1940's with Disraeli's achievement. He went on to note that while Disraeli had had to depend on his own personal efforts, the more recent work of "preparation and education" had been institutionalized. As compared with the party of Disraeli's day, the Conservatives of the postwar period had indeed developed an elaborate and far-flung structure of formal organization. To the ancient structure of Whips and Front Bench in the House of Commons had been added regular arrangements enabling backbenchers to meet, discuss issues, and keep in touch with and sometimes exert influence on their leaders.[5] Another means by which Conservative policy might conceivably have been influenced was the National Union's Advisory Committee on Policy and Political Education. Descending from the Post-War Problems Committee set up in 1941, it had in 1947 Butler as its chairman and a total membership of nineteen, including M.P.'s, peers, paid party officials, and prominent members of the National Union.[6] Finally, there was the Research Department, recently reconstituted by Butler and his talented "chief of staff," David Clarke, who was its director. Its high level of competence is suggested by the names of some of the members at this time: Reginald Maudling, Iain MacLeod, Enoch Powell.

ADOPTION OF THE INDUSTRIAL CHARTER

In the summer of 1946 Butler had already been discussing future party policy with Clarke as well as with other party leaders, such as Harold Macmillan and Oliver Stanley, whose views were similar to his own.[7] Current controversies suggested the subjects: plan-

---

[5] See R. T. McKenzie, *British Political Parties* (New York, 1955), pp. 55–62, and Peter Richards, *Honorable Members: A Study of the British Backbencher* (London, 1959), Chap. V, "Control of Policy and Administration."

[6] McKenzie, *ibid.*, pp. 211–213.

[7] Author's private information. In this account of the *Industrial Charter* I have depended very much on interviews with persons who were close to events at the time.

ning, nationalization, and in general the relation of government to industry. At about this time the extra-parliamentary party played its supporting role. The resolution passed by the conference in October asking for a statement of policy was, as one who was close to events recalled, a "red light" to the leadership, signaling the necessity for clarifying the party's position.[8] In response, Churchill appointed a committee to define "the Conservative attitude toward industry." This Industrial Policy Committee consisted of five members of the Shadow Cabinet (Butler, Macmillan, Lyttleton, Stanley, and Maxwell Fyfe), and four backbenchers (David Eccles, Derek Heathcoat Amory, Sir Peter Bennett, and J. R. H. Hutchison), with Butler as chairman and David Clarke as secretary.

With the assistance of the Research Department, this committee drafted the *Industrial Charter*. Outside sources were also consulted. Discussions, for instance, were held with groups of industrialists brought together by Area Agents of the party and a draft was circulated to representative business firms. There were remarks about "pink socialism," "nauseating socialism," and "totalitarianism"; but by and large the opposition from business circles was not vehement. Within the Shadow Cabinet fears were expressed, for instance, that the *Charter* might make it harder to raise money to finance the party and that some of its proposals might excessively strengthen the position of workers. But approval was won, including that of the Leader, a name was thought up by Butler, and the document was published. In the whole process the National Union's Committee on Policy and Political Education had played no significant part, its members merely being kept informed. Similarly, although the Shadow Cabinet of course included chairmen of the functional committees, the parliamentary party also played a subordinate role, with the *Industrial Charter* being put to a meeting of the parliamentary party for approval only after publication.[9]

The Leader's approval made the *Charter* "the official policy of the Party," to use Churchill's words before the conference later in the year. Yet the task of winning endorsement from conference

----

[8] At the 1947 conference friends of the *Industrial Charter*, in seeking to win over delegates, gave great emphasis to the fact that it was a response to the resolution of 1946. See, for instance, the comments of Thorneycroft and Maulding, 1947 *CPCR*, pp. 37 and 48. See also Lord Kilmuir, *Political Adventure : The Memoirs of the Earl of Kilmuir* (London, 1964), pp. 162-3.

[9] The *Industrial Charter* was published May 12th; the party meeting took place May 23rd.

required some management.[1] The opposition was expressed in two moves. One was an indirect assault and consisted of a motion offered by Sir Herbert Williams, attacking the economic policy of the Labour Government and demanding "a complete change of method and approach," which the mover interpreted to mean "the most drastic cuts in public expenditure" and the removal of "a vast number of controls." This clear implication of disapproval of the *Charter* was removed by an addendum that the delegates, given a strong lead by Anthony Eden, unanimously accepted. The more direct attack was a motion "welcoming" the *Charter,* but only as "a basis of discussion." This was dealt with by an appropriate amendment to which Butler lent his authoritative support. In consequence, the *Charter* was "welcomed" as "a clear restatement of Conservative economic policy" with only 3 dissentients out of some 5,000 delegates.

In managing the opinion of conference, the advocates of the Charter played on two themes : the appeal to authority and the appeal to the Tory tradition. In countering the indirect attack, Peter Thorneycroft reminded delegates that they must not fail to acknowledge the steps taken by the Leader to meet the wishes of the previous conference for a policy statement. His meaning was clear when he went on to observe that the *Industrial Charter* had been "launched by Mr. Churchill" and "defended on countless platforms by Mr. Eden." Mr. Eden then told delegates that the *Charter,* in his judgment, "reflects the greatest credit on its authors."

Similarly, in meeting the second attack, the friends of the *Charter* emphasized that it had already received the approval of the Leader and other party authorities. Calling up the ghosts of Bolingbroke and Lord Randolph Churchill, Butler appealed to the conference to accept "the main line of the Charter, which is strong Central Government policy" and to join him in a crusade "to capture the imagination of the working-people of this country." Eden's peroration displayed an even more striking use of the appeal to Toryism. After observing that Conservatives stood for individual liberty, the family, and the Christian virtues, he added :

We are not a Party of unbridled, brutal capitalism, and never have been. Although we believe in personal responsibility and personal

[1] For proceedings relevant to this account, see 1947 *CPCR,* pp. 35–43 and 46–54.

initiative in business, we are not the political children of the laissez-faire school. We opposed them decade after decade.

Where did the Tories stand when the greed and squalor of the industrial revolution were darkening the land? I am content with Keir Hardie's testimony : "As a matter of hard dry fact, from which there can be no getting away, there is more labour legislation standing to the credit account of the Conservative Party on the Statute Book than there is to that of their opponents."[2]

The adoption of the *Industrial Charter* was a decisive step in Conservative adaptation. This is not to say that the Charter could not have been abandoned if the forces which led the party to make these new commitments had radically changed in succeeding years. Its adoption itself indeed added a new and supporting force. All means of mass communication were used to publicize the new policy. For instance, within the first three months of publication, according to party officials, 2,500,000 copies were sold at 6d. a copy. Whether many of the recipients read much of the *Charter's* lucid, but earnest prose is not vitally important. Its symbolism was clear to party members and to the public. As one of its authors later recalled, it showed that in spite of the opposition of "brass-bottomed Tories," the party had advanced not only from its prewar position, but also beyond that of the election of 1945. Such expectations in the party and among the public were themselves a new force. Moreover, the growing Research Department—by 1950 it had a staff of fifty, of whom twenty-four were research officers—continued to feed memoranda to program-making committees of the Shadow Cabinet. Strengthened by the support of his "back-room boys," Butler continued his rise as party spokesman on domestic affairs.[3] The tradition of the "Tory democracy of Lord Beaconsfield and after him of Lord Randolph Churchill"[4] continued to be used to legitimize what might have seemed to many

[2] 1947 *CPCR*, pp. 42–3.

[3] Yet even while Churchill was making his Cabinet in 1951, it was "touch and go" whether the Treasury would go to Butler or Lyttleton. See Churchill's remarks quoted in Oliver Lyttleton (Viscount Chandos), *Memoirs* (London, 1962), pp. 341–4. For most of the time the Conservatives were in opposition, the Shadow Chancellor of the Exchequer and chairman of the Finance Committee of the parliamentary party was Oliver Stanley. Stanley, who died in 1950, was succeeded as chairman of the Finance Committee by Oliver Lyttleton, who many expected would be given the Treasury in 1951.

[4] From the Foreword by Churchill to *The Right Road for Britain : The Conservative Party's Statement of Policy* (July, 1949).

a new departure in British Conservatism. And the Leader, in spite
of his aversion to "detailed programmes," was prevailed upon to
authorize the long and detailed statements produced by the pro-
gram-makers as "a description of Conservative faith and policy,"
a "manifesto of our beliefs and policy," a "statement of Conservative and Unionist policy."[5]

Most important, the electoral situation remained promising,
but perilous. The sensitivity of the party leadership to these considerations was pronounced. One high-ranking Conservative, who
strongly opposed the new commitments, later recalled that in
the election of 1951, scenting victory, the party drew back
significantly—an analysis that is borne out by a comparison of
the proposals of 1950 with those of 1951. The victory of the
latter year, however, was flawed not only by the narrow Conservative majority in the House (321 out of 625) but also by the
fact that in the country the party had polled slightly less than
Labour (48 per cent as compared with Labour's 48.7 per cent
of the popular vote). As Churchill did not hesitate to admit, this
narrow electoral balance clearly affected his Government's policy.
That policy, which some observers summarized in the epithet
"Butskellism" in order to express the similarity of views between
the Conservative Butler and the Socialist Gaitskell, had in no
small degree originated with *The Industrial Charter*.

[5] Churchill's words, quoted, respectively, from *The Right Road for
Britain*, *This Is the Road*, and *Britain Strong and Free : A Statement of
Conservative and Unionist Policy* (October, 1951).

CHAPTER XII

The New Group Politics

By the early 1950's Labourites and Conservatives seemed well on the way toward executing a classic movement of a two-party system. From positions widely separating them on issues of substantial, even fundamental, importance, they had moved markedly toward one another. Within the Labour Party, as we have seen, powerful forces resisted this movement; and one could never say that British Socialism had quite deserted its ancient ideological orthodoxies. Yet on the scale of Left and Right, as defined in British politics, each party was shifting toward the center, as the party of the Left extended its appeal to groups on its Right and the party of the Right extended its appeal to groups on its Left. Class and ideological contours faded, while interest groups appeared as more prominent features of the political scene. It was against the background of these developments that R. T. McKenzie concluded in 1958 that "pressure groups, taken together, are a far more important channel of communication than parties for the transmission of political ideas from the mass of the citizenry to their rulers."[1]

We will examine the role of interest groups in the formation of Conservative social and economic policy in the 1950's and how it compared with the role of party. But before we turn directly to this question, it will be helpful to sketch the general outlines of group politics in the postwar period. From our previous account the two main features have emerged: the "realities of governing" that led Governments and parties to bargain with organized producers and the "realities of winning power" that led

[1] Quoted above, p. 303.

them to bid for the support of groups of consumers among the voters.

These two features were not separate parts of the political system. They were rather two different sets of relationships among the same entities. In one set of relationships, for instance, the groups were "producers," in the other, "consumers," but obviously most producers were also consumers and vice versa. It was primarily because government attempted to control or manage the economy that producer groups acquired power to influence policy. On the other hand, it was mainly because programs of the Welfare State appealed to groups as consumers that Governments and parties were incited to appeal for their support by means of these programs.

Yet the Managed Economy and the Welfare State were not two separate and distinct activities of the pattern of policy. Action to maintain full employment comes under both headings. A change in direct taxation is both a measure of economic policy (affecting prices, imports, saving, and incentives) and a measure of social policy (affecting the distribution of disposable income among various social strata). Depending, however, on how the political situation is viewed—from the perspective of the Managed Economy or that of the Welfare State—the flow of influence is seen to come, respectively, from producers or from consumers.

Moreover, the modes and channels of influence varied between the two sets of political relationships. Producers influenced policy largely through direct contact with the executive in what may be called a system of functional representation. The power of consumers was especially expressed through the system of parliamentary representation, in which party government was the dominating feature.

In sum, then, the two perspectives on the flow of power direct attention to the following relationships: 1) controlled economy : producer groups : functional representation : bargaining for cooperation and 2) welfare state : consumer groups : party government : bidding for votes.

PRODUCER GROUPS AND THE MANAGED ECONOMY

Viewed from Whitehall, the most powerful forces confronting (not to say arrayed against) a Government in this time were the organized bodies of producers representing the main sectors of the economy : trade unions, trade associations, and professional organizations. Pressure groups were nothing new in British politics, but in the twentieth century they had assumed a distinctively new form. In social base, structure, purpose, political tactics, relations with government, and the foundations of their political power they greatly differed from the transient, voluntary associations of like-minded reformers that sought to win Victorian Parliaments over to their schemes of legislation. We have already gained some idea of what these "Collectivist" pressure groups were and how they operated when we examined the bargain of 1948 struck between government, labor, and business. I will not try to call the roll nor to describe in detail their modes of organization and operation, all of which has been ably done by other writers.[2] I will, however, consider in general terms three questions : What were the bases of their political power? How was this power mobilized? Through what channels was it brought to bear on policy-making?

Bases of Power

We begin from the fact that these groups were based on a productive function. Typically, their members consisted of wage-earning or salaried employees with the same or related occupations; of business enterprises concerned with a common product, process, or activity; of professional people with similar training and *expertise*. To say that performance of a productive function endows persons or groups with political power is to call up the shades of syndicalism—and rightly so. For in spite of its exaggerations and utopianism, the syndicalist analysis has great relevance to the structure of power in the modern state. According to that analysis, the political power of the producer group rests on its ability to refuse to perform its function in the economy. In

[2] See Allen Potter, *Organized Groups in British National Politics* (London, 1961); J. D. Stewart, *British Pressure Groups : Their Role in Relation to the House of Commons* (London, 1958); Samuel E. Finer, *Anonymous Empire : A Study of the Lobby in Great Britain* (London, 1958); Harry Eckstein, *Pressure Group Politics : The Case of the British Medical Association* (London, 1960); Peter Self and Herbert J. Storing, *The State and The Farmer* (London, 1962); Graham Wootton, *The Politics of Influence : British Ex-Servicemen, Cabinet Decisions and Cultural Change, 1917–1957* (London, 1963).

Britain the extreme use of this power in the "general strike" had been attempted only once, and then only halfheartedly, and after 1926 the syndicalist prescriptions rapidly lost their appeal.

These prescriptions, to be sure, presumed that government, if not entirely laissez faire, would not be deeply engaged in regulating, planning, or managing the economy. The syndicalist, therefore, was obliged to suppose that producer groups could influence government only indirectly by coercing the whole community. But the syndicalist analysis is also relevant, and certainly more realistic, in the era of the mixed economy. For insofar as government has committed itself to intervention in the economy, it must have access to or control over instrumentalities that are in the command of producers. In a totalitarian system this dependence on the cooperation of producers can be minimized, though not entirely eliminated. But in a free country, as government extends its powers over the economy, it must at the same time so act as to win a substantial degree of consent and cooperation from the groups being regulated. "The greater the degree of detailed and technical control the government seeks to exert over industrial and commercial interests," E. P. Herring wrote more than a generation ago, "the greater must be their degree of consent and active participation."[3]

Legal theory may tell us that the state is sovereign, particularly in Britain where the authority of Parliament is unlimited by constitutional restraints. Hence, when Parliament commands, all persons and groups must obey and, if control over a certain sector of the economy is authorized by law, the producers in that sector, whether organized or unorganized, must in theory comply. In this light, the extension of government intervention appears as a one-sided growth in state power. But there is also a flow of power in the other direction.

ADVICE

The most obvious instrumentality which producers command and which government needs is advice. Advice includes sheer information : for instance, the statistical data without which neither the regulation of a particular trade nor management of the economy as a whole would be possible. But the advice that government seeks from producers consists also of their technical knowledge

[3] *Public Administration and the Public Interest* (New York, 1936), p. 192.

and judgment. Obviously no ministry engaged in economic control can have staff large and specialized enough to enable it to make policy and administer it without the advice of the producers in the sector concerned. "The form and functioning of British Government," Professor S. E. Finer has written, "are predicated upon the assumption that it will be advised, helped and criticised by the specialist knowledge of interested parties."[4]

When, for instance, the Poisons Board considered modifications of the Poisons List and Rules, it sought the advice of the trade and had, therefore, since 1930 maintained close relations with the Association of British Chemical Manufacturers. For similar reasons, when the Ministry of Food was drafting the hygiene regulations of a new Food and Drugs bill it consulted with the relevant trade association, the Cake and Biscuit Alliance, as a result of whose representations various amendments were made to the original proposals.[5] Again, when the Minister of Transport, acting under wide delegated powers, revised the regulations on construction and use of motor vehicles, he regularly sought and received the advice of the Society of Motor Manufacturers and Traders.[6] Even in the case of the most important of the "peak" organizations of British industry, the Federation of British Industry, most of its relations with departments were concerned with questions on which it could bring to bear the technical knowledge at the command of its staff and members. As Professor Finer reported after a study—"based on file after file of dusty minutes" —of the Federation's relations with government, "overwhelmingly its persuasion is concerned with technical and administrative minutiae," rather than questions of general public policy.[7]

The need of departments for such technical advice and criticism is of long standing and has typically resulted from the piecemeal intervention characteristic of Radical politics. But the technical "know-how" of producers has also been indispensable to that kind of economic planning which depends on physical programing and direct control. This was a major reason for the fact that

[4] S. E. Finer, "The Political Power of Private Capital," Pt. II, *Sociological Review*, new ser., Vol. IV, No. 1 (July, 1956), p. 14.
[5] *Industrial Trade Associations: Activities and Organization* (London, 1957), pp. 77 and 82.
[6] See the Society's annual reports, *passim*; for example, *Fifty-First Annual Report and Accounts* (1952), p. 13.
[7] "The Federation of British Industries," *Political Studies*, Vol. IV, No. 1 (February, 1956), p. 67.

during the war the general type of control in the Ministry of Supply was a converted trade association. Knowledge of the technical aspects of a trade or occupation, however, shades off into knowledge of economic conditions and relationships. Producer groups are sources of what Allen Potter has called "market intelligence," "facts and opinions about what is happening and is likely to happen" in their sector of production and its relations with other sectors.[8] Hence, even as the government relaxed its methods of control over the economy as a whole and turned toward the methods of economic management, it continued to need access to this broader "economic knowledge" possessed by producers.

The strategy of economic management is "situational" in the sense that its essential technique is to obtain a desired result not by direct command or request, but indirectly by manipulating the economic situation confronting producers and consumers. A remark that one of Britain's planners made to me in the early 1950's illustrates the difference. "We are rather disillusioned with physical programming," he said. "We prefer to get results not by commanding what must be done, but by putting out a piece of cheese and trusting that some particular mouse will go after it." National income analysis provides the basic framework for such "situational" control. A certain change in direct taxation, which changes the disposable income of consumers, will presumably have some roughly calculable effect upon imports, private saving, and incentives. Similarly, a change in interest rates will have an effect upon the flow of capital to and from Britain, a movement in wage rates upon prices, an expansion or contraction of government current expenditure upon the level of employment, certain tax remissions upon investment by firms and so ultimately upon productivity. On such matters, government can learn a great deal from its professional economists. But often ministers and officials have also found it necessary to seek the judgment of representatives of the productive sectors involved.

Immediately after the war, for instance, a principal element in the Labour Government's economic policy was the export drive. One possible source of greater exports was the motor car industry; and the question of what action the government might take to encourage the export of motor cars was an urgent subject

[8] *Op. cit.*, p. 193.

of discussion in the advisory committee established by the Ministry of Supply to provide a means of regular consultation between the government and the industry.[9] According to the industry representatives, British purchasers of cars were discouraged from buying larger models because the annual tax on use was based on engine size. As a result, the British industry was geared to the production of a smaller car that did not compete well in foreign markets with the larger American car. Therefore, they advised that if the annual tax were put on a flat-rate basis, demand would shift toward a larger car and the industry would accordingly direct its production toward a product with better sales possibilities abroad. Indeed, the main producers on the committee, while they made no promises, indicated that if the Government made such a change in taxation they would "include in their forward plans provision for the development and quantity production of a larger model."[1] The committee was persuaded and ultimately so also was the Chancellor of the Exchequer, who in 1947 changed the annual tax to a flat-rate basis, apparently with beneficial results for British exports.

Planning based on direct physical control faces the problem of winning the acquiescence of the controlled to the scheme of behavior imposed on them. "Situational" planning avoids this problem by allowing the controlled to follow their normal market behavior. Since, however, such planning also seeks to guide that behavior, it confronts the new problem of foreseeing how controlled sectors will respond to manipulated changes in the situation. To ask the advice of producers about such questions may seem to invite replies that are less than impartial. Both sides, Government and producers, are acutely aware of the dangers of the temptation to "bluff." A Director-General of the F.B.I., for instance, characterizing the advisory work of the organization as an exercise in "the art of persuasion," declared that the first essential was to create and maintain "confidence on the part of the Government in one's *bona fides*."[2] Such consultation is, to

[9] For composition and terms of reference of this committee, see below, pp. 338–9.
[1] *National Advisory Committee for the Motor Manufacturing Industry: Report on Proceedings*, Ministry of Supply (London, H.M.S.O., 1947), p. 14. For this example generally, see the *Report, passim;* also the *Annual Report* for 1947 of the Society of Motor Manufacturers and Traders, p. 7, and P.E.P.'s *Industrial Trade Associations*, p. 50.
[2] Sir Norman Kipping, *The Federation of British Industries* (London, 1954), pp. 4–5.

be sure, rather like asking the mice just how much cheese it would take to get them to run in a different direction. But after all, who would know better?

ACQUIESCENCE

In seeking to control the economy government needs not only the advice of producers, but also in many instances their active cooperation in carrying out a program or policy. The producers may be brought directly into administration, as trade associations were during the war. Or they may be employed individually in carrying out a program, as in the case with doctors under the National Health Service. Or again, even when producers in a sector are not directly engaged as agents of government, a program may require their wholehearted acceptance if it is to be effective, as the system of price control during and after the war needed to have from businessmen something more than mere grudging consent to "the law." And referring generally to the effectiveness of direct controls, the authors of the Radcliffe Report observed that

it is necessary in this context to remember that the post-war controls themselves depended much on voluntarism. If it can be shown that there are good and sufficient reasons in the public interest why controls should be imposed, they can be effective for a short time without an elaborate administrative structure.[8]

The relations of the Labour Government and the iron and steel industry will illustrate how the refusal of such cooperation, as well as of advice, may be used by a producer in resisting government policy. In 1947, Hugh Dalton recalls, the Government "began to negotiate" with the companies over its plans for nationalization of the industry. In response the steelmasters "threatened that if we nationalized the industry, they would retain Steel House, its staff and its records, and so make the work of a new Public Board almost impossible."[4] In their approaches to Attlee, according to Dalton, "they seemed to have some success," Attlee charging Morrison with looking into the possibility of measures less than nationalization.[5] When in 1948, after much chopping and

---

[8] Committee on the Working of the Monetary System, *Report* Cmd. 827 (London, 1959), para. 184 (Radcliffe Report).
[4] *High Tide and After : Memoirs 1945–1960* (London, 1962), pp. 248–9.
[5] *Ibid.*, p. 249, and *Herbert Morrison, An Autobiography* (London, 1960), p. 296.

changing, the Government finally announced its intention to nationalize, the representatives of the steel companies withdrew in protest from the Iron and Steel Board, which had been set up as a controlling body for the industry.

Whether or not these reprisals by the industry affected the form in which Labour nationalized the industry, they did not, at any rate, prevent its being taken into public ownership under the Act of 1949. At this juncture, the industry intensified its policy of noncooperation. The leaders of the steel industry boycotted the public corporation established to own and control the industry, refusing to serve on it and dissuading all important figures from serving. Moreover, the industry's trade association, the British Iron and Steel Federation, refused to permit representatives of the public corporation to sit on its Council, on its committees, or even on the two trading companies of the Federation that respectively controlled imports and exports and disposed of surplus steel.[6]

What would have been the ultimate outcome of this "strike action" by the industry against nationalization we cannot know, since shortly thereafter the Conservatives returned to power and the industry was denationalized. For our present analysis, however, the important fact is that these sanctions of noncooperation by the industry had come close to paralyzing the public corporation's "control over the policy and operations of the publicly-owned companies" and its ability to "discharge [its] duties under the Act." In its first report the public corporation said :

It was clear to the Corporation that to secure adequate control over the policy and operations of the publicly-owned companies and to enable the Corporation to discharge their duties under the Act they would require either to create an organisation independent of, but in part similar and parallel to, that of the Federation, or alternatively to come to some arrangement with the Federation which would afford the Corporation the benefit of the services and advice of the Federation and control of its policies in the public sector.[7]

This example illustrates the great difficulties in which noncooperation by an organized group can sometimes put government. Usually, neither government nor organized producers will push matters to a showdown. Anticipation of what might well

[6] For an account of these events, see Finer, "The Political Power of Private Capital," pp. 16–19.

[7] Iron and Steel Corporation of Great Britain, *Report and Statement of Accounts for the Period Ending 30th September, 1951*, para. 45.

happen, however, will affect their negotiations. Indeed, it is the anticipation by government of the need for such cooperation that makes it often accurate to refer to its relations with producers groups as "negotiation" and not merely "consultation."[8] In 1948, for instance, the Government could have contrived some means of imposing on business by law its proposals for reduction of profits, perhaps on the lines of the statutory limitation of dividends developed by Gaitskell in 1951. It preferred, however, a voluntary arrangement, even though this achieved only "restraint" on dividends and not reduction of profits. Similarly, in its relations with the unions at the same time, the Government was quite aware that, even if it had been able to hold its parliamentary majority behind a legally imposed policy, it would have had to have a substantial degree of voluntary cooperation from unions and workers if any policy regarding wages were to be effective.

In these instances the difficulties of an imposed solution were no doubt vividly before the minds of officials and ministers. But government may develop relations of cooperation with a key producers group in which there is such a gentlemanly give and take that no mention and little thought of sanctions are occasioned. The Conservative Government's relations with the City were of this character. In the years 1955–57, for instance, the Government from time to time called on the banks for help in carrying out its anti-inflationary policy by tightening credit.[9] In bringing about a restriction of bank loans, the Government could have invoked its legal powers under the Bank of England Act and given the banks unequivocal instructions. But it preferred the method of "jollying along," or what D. H. Robertson has called "ear-stroking"—that is, the use of "encouragements which are not quite promises, frowns which are not quite prohibitions, understandings which are not quite agreements."[1] The method is brought out in a minute from Prime Minister Eden to the Chancellor of the Exchequer, Harold Macmillan, in December 1955 :

As to this question of imports, I should be most reluctant to contemplate any return to licensing and Government control as I am sure you would be. Is it not, however, possible to get something of

---

[8] On the distinction between "negotiation" and "consultation" in British practice see Harry Eckstein, *op. cit.*, pp. 22–5.

[9] See Peter B. Kenen, *British Monetary Policy and the Balance of Payments, 1951–1957* (Cambridge, Mass., 1960), Chap. III, "The New Monetary Policy." See also *Radcliffe Report*, pp. 118–9, 142–50, 161–3, and 188.

[1] Quoted in Kenen, *op. cit.*, p. 200.

the same results by other methods? Cannot the banks, for instance, be given some indication from time to time that such and such materials are those for the import of which we should be most reluctant to see money advanced? If something of this kind were practicable I should much prefer it to import control.[2]

The banks were highly responsive—indeed, according to the Governor of the Bank of England, through whom the Government and banks formally communicated with one another, the British banking system was "the most responsive of any large banking system [in the world] to indications of official policy."[3] In turn the Government showed itself ready on some points to accommodate its wishes to the advantage and convenience of the banks. According to one authority on the history of monetary policy in this period, the methods of "ear-stroking" were successful, partly because bankers knew that the Government had powers of coercion in reserve, but also because "the bankers have received a considerable reward for cooperation in the form of higher interest rates."[4]

Similarly, the Chancellor could be responsive when his requests might cause the banks administrative difficulties. In the fall of 1957, for instance, while tightening the squeeze on credit, the Chancellor asked the banks to promise an all-round cut of 5 per cent in their loans. The execution of this scheme would rest with the banks, as each would have to decide which requests from its customers were to be refused or reduced. Anticipating much friction from such a task the bankers demurred. In the end the

[2] Anthony Eden, The Memoirs of Anthony Eden : Full Circle (Boston, 1960), p. 358.

[3] The Banker, November, 1956, p. 715. Report of speech at Mansion House on October 9th, 1956.

[4] Kenen, op. cit., p. 200. See also Harry G. Johnson, "The Revival of Monetary Policy in Britain," Three Banks Review (June, 1956). He writes : "The intimate small-group relationship between the members of the banking system, and the dominant position of the Bank of England, raise the question as to how far the revival of monetary policy can be accurately described as a return to control of the financial system by anonymous and impersonal market forces" (p. 10). And later : "A cynic might well argue that the return to flexibility is merely a façade, designed to improve the appearance and the public relations potential of an oligopolistic agreement, and to hide the fact that what has really been achieved has been to bribe the banks, by means of higher interest earnings, into enforcing directives which, in the less profitable days of cheap money, they were inclined to disregard as much as they decently could" (p. 11).

Chancellor settled for an agreement that bank advances simply would be frozen at their 1957 level.[5]

APPROVAL

How much bargaining power a producers group will have and how far it will try to use this power in its relations with Government will, of course, be affected by other factors than those we have been considering. Our concern has been to isolate those particular factors based on the productive function performed by a group that give it a bargaining potential. Broadly, they are the government's need for advice and for acquiescence. But there is also a third factor which is also specifically related to the performance of a productive function and which further helps account for that extreme hesitation of departments and Governments—commented on by many students of British pressure politics—to confront an open and public break with producers groups. It is the attitude (one detects it not only among officials and ministers, but also among M.P.'s and members of the general public) that such organized groups have a "right" to take part in making policy related to their sector of activity; indeed, that their approval of a relevant policy or program is a substantial reason for public confidence in it and conversely that their disapproval is cause for public uneasiness. It is in short an attitude reflecting the widespread acceptance of functional representation in British political culture. It coexists, of course, with a general adherence to standard constitutional doctrines asserting the sovereignty of Parliament and the exclusive right of ministers to make final decisions, subject to Parliament. If forced into a sharp and systematic formulation, that attitude would be in conflict with these doctrines—as indeed the actual practice of negotiation modifies in fact the sovereignty of Parliament. Yet as a current of opinion it is nevertheless a real force, restraining the hand of Government and strengthening the hand of organized producers.

Such an attitude, for instance, helps account for a peculiar

[5] Andrew Shonfield, *British Economic Policy Since the War*, rev. ed. (London, 1959), pp. 254–5. "On the industrial side, the banks on the whole managed to avoid positive reductions of existing advances, though they had to be discouraging to applications for new advances." Hence, "the blow fell not on projects already in train but on capital projects in their earliest planning stages. . . . It was not, that is to say, the current level of demand that was affected; rather, action was upon the possible prolongation and development of the boom." *Radcliffe Report*, pp. 162–3, para. 460.

"convention" that emerged in the relations of the Government and the National Farmers Union after the war. From the beginning of the annual price review, Professor Self has observed, "the Government emphasized that the final decision over agricultural guarantees was exclusively its own, as constitutionally it was bound to be." At the same time, "a convention soon emerged whereby the Union gave a formal endorsement of some kind to the final settlement," a confirmation which the Government, whether Labour or Conservative, was able to win each year throughout the postwar years until 1956.[6] The interesting point is that ministers, far from finding this endorsement a political liability (suggesting, as it might to an old-time Radical, that a "sinister interest" had triumphed over the common good) welcomed and used it when publicly defending their agricultural policy, a practice which, as Professor Self notes, itself further strengthened the understanding that Government ought to secure such endorsement.

A similar and perhaps even stronger attitude, according to Professor Harry Eckstein, has affected the relations of the Ministry of Health and the British Medical Association. In analyzing why these relations have so often consisted not in mere consultation, but in negotiation, he has found two attitudes of particular importance. One is "the widespread belief . . . that technical experts (practitioners) have some singular competence even in regard to social policies and administrative forms that touch upon their fields of practice." The other is the "persistent corporatism" of British political culture, which results today in the fact that "functional representation . . . is not only tolerated, but even insisted upon." From these two broad attitudes springs that "frequent normative insistence on negotiations between government and 'voluntary' associations on matters of policy" which has been particularly pronounced in the relations of government and organized medicine.[7]

In postwar Britain the cooperation that government needed from producer groups took various forms. I have identified them broadly as advice, acquiescence, and approval. To identify them and illustrate their use do not tell us what in general their role has been in British government. But our analysis does, I think,

[6] Self and Storing, *op. cit.*, p. 63 and *passim*.
[7] *Op. cit.*, p. 24.

show quite clearly that producer groups have a power to affect policy-making that is quite separate from their position in the system of parliamentary representation and party government. We may prefer to call some relationships influence rather than power. When, for instance, a producers organization by rational argument persuades a department to take a new line, we may wish to call this influence, since the group has not won its way by use of a sanction. But what I have been particularly concerned to show is that producer groups do have sanctions—the denial (in various degrees) of advice, acquiescence, and approval—which can cause, to put it mildly, "administrative difficulties" and which, by anticipation, endow the group with bargaining power in its relations with government.

The source of this power is not the fact that the group or its members has a role—for instance, as voters or contributors to party funds—in the system of parliamentary representation, but derives from the group's performance of a productive function. Should such power, therefore, be called "economic power"? That would have been the appropriate term to characterize the sanctions which inhered in producers according to the old syndicalist analysis. In essence those consisted in the power to coerce government indirectly by depriving the economy of an important service. The sanctions of producer groups in the Managed Economy do not take that form. They arise from the fact that Government has taken over functions once performed by the economic system, in particular, by its market mechanisms. We can say that governmental action has become part of the economic process; or that elements of the economic process have been taken over by Government. From their position in the "mixed economy" resulting from this interpenetration of polity and economy, producer groups derive their new powers.

Mobilization of Power

If producers are to use these new powers to influence Government and, indeed, if Government is to obtain the cooperation necessary for the Managed Economy, producer groups must be organized. Very large firms, it is true, have usually maintained regular contacts with departments independently of the representational efforts of the trade associations to which they belonged. As our examples have shown, however, the relations of Government with producers were normally with a nation-wide organization. By means of such organization the group achieved a capacity for unified decision-making and action. How far it has such capacity for unified behavior, how far it has mobilized its power as a producer group—we may call its degree of concentration.

Concentration cannot be measured on a single coordinate. One dimension is "density,"[8] that is, the per cent of eligibles, such as individuals or firms, that have been organized. Thus it is possible to calculate for a certain category of producers at a certain time an index of density (for example, in 1953 42 per cent of the total working population of Britain belonged to trade unions) and make comparisons with an earlier period or another country. A high degree of density, however, is compatible with a situation in which there is a low degree of unity because the organized are divided into many separate bodies. A second dimension of concentration, therefore, is amalgamation, taking this to mean how far the organized have been brought together in one body, whether by outright merger, federation, or other similar arrangements. Although amalgamation can be high when density is low and vice versa, in fact, over time the trend among producer groups in Britain has been toward an increase of concentration on both coordinates. It is possible, of course, for an organization scoring perfectly in indices of density and amalgamation to be a clumsy and distracted giant. Still, the measurable aspects of concentration serve to mark out the long-run trends.

TRADE ASSOCIATIONS

Trade associations, as we have observed, already existed in mid-Victorian times. Then, as later, their purposes were only in part political, including such functions as the collection and dissemination of information among members, the coordination of steps to mitigate competition, and the representation of employers in relations with trade unions, as well as the advocacy of the interests of a branch of industry or commerce before government. They did not appear in any number until the latter years of the nineteenth century, but from that time the trend toward concentration had been continuous, paralleling the rise of big government, big business, and big unions.

Unlike British labor, British business did not produce a single

[8] I am indebted to Professor S. E. Finer for the notion of density as a dimension of concentration.

"peak" organization. On the whole, commerce was organized separately from industry. By the 1950's, the Association of British Chambers of Commerce, founded in 1860, had grown to include some 100 constituent chambers including 60,000 members, some of which, incidentally, were manufacturers. Retail merchants not embraced by the A.B.C.C. had local bodies federated nationally in the National Chamber of Trade. In industry there were three "peak" organizations, the Federation of British Industries, the National Union of Manufacturers, and, for dealing with labor matters, the British Employers Confederation, whose 270 affiliates negotiated with 70 per cent of the employed population.

In the industrial sector, at which we will look more closely, concentration had gone very far. By the 1950's trade associations were virtually all-embracing in their membership : 90 per cent of the larger firms and 76 per cent of the smaller belonged to one or more of the 1,300 industrial trade associations.[9] Along with this increase in density had gone a strong trend toward amalgamation. Inter-industry organization achieved its first solid success during World War I with the formation of the Federation of British Industries and the National Union of Manufacturers. Tending to represent the larger firms, the F.B.I., by the end of its first year, included 62 trade associations and 350 individual firms; by 1925, 195 associations and 2,100 firms; and by 1957, 283 associations and 7,533 firms. By the latter date most manufacturing firms were directly or indirectly affiliated with the organization, which now represented some six sevenths of all industrial concerns employing more than ten workers.[1]

Particularly important in the world of industrial trade associations were some thirty or forty larger associations, each of which covered a complete industry. Leading examples, some of which we have encountered in previous pages, were : the Society of British Aircraft Contractors; the British Man-Made Fibres Federation; the Association of British Chemical Manufacturers; the Federation of Master Cotton Spinners Associations; the British Engineers Association; the British Iron and Steel Confederation; the Society of Motor Manufacturers and Traders; the British Non-Ferrous Metals Federation; the Cake and Biscuit Alliance; and the British Plastics Federation. A principal purpose of these organizations was to achieve cohesion in the relations of their respective industries

---

[9] Computed from data in *Industrial Trade Associations*.
[1] Finer, *Anonymous Empire*, p. 9, and "The Federation of British Industries," p. 62.

with Government and in their memoranda or constitutions most mentioned the need to "speak with one voice" when consulting or negotiating with departments. Their success in reconciling intra-industry differences of opinion, however, was variable. Where the industry consisted of many small firms there was likely to be difficulty. On the other hand, a high degree of economic concentration, as in the motor car industry, iron and steel, and chemicals, enhanced the group's capacity for unified action.

In general, cohesion was promoted by the tendency of larger firms to have a preponderant voice in the affairs of their respective associations. This resulted not so much from provisions of formal organization, which might or might not give greater voting power to larger firms, but rather, as Professor Finer has observed, from "the businessman's general attitude that the bigger the firm, the bigger its stake and therefore its entitlement to 'the big say.' "[2] In the F.B.I., for instance, as he has shown, while the organization could not be said to be dominated by "a small clique of large firms," the big concerns clearly carried a great deal of weight. Their activity was particularly marked in the standing committees, "the true centres of policy-making."[3] In 1955, for instance, of the eighteen standing committees of the F.B.I., the chairmen almost without exception came from giant concerns, such as General Electric, the Steel Company of Wales, Courtaulds, Associated Electrical Industries, Imperial Chemicals, and Richard, Thomas and Baldwins, with Unilever alone accounting for four.[4] Thanks at least in part to such leadership, the F.B.I. was able to say that its "statements or representations carry the backing or acceptance of all important sections of industry." Sometimes a substantial divergence of opinion did emerge, in which case the F.B.I. would not attempt to "speak with one voice." The issues on which unanimity was not reached, however, arose "surprisingly rarely."[5]

TRADE UNIONS

Trade unions had shown a similar trend toward concentration. From late Victorian days, when they had embraced only a modest part of the working population, their membership had grown immensely. While this increase was by no means steady, over the whole period from 1892 to 1953 membership in all trade unions rose from 1,576,000 to 9,524,000, these figures representing an

2 "The Federation of British Industries," p. 71.   4 *Ibid.*, pp. 83–4.
3 *Ibid.*, p. 70.   5 Kipping, *op. cit.*, p. 4.

increase from 11 per cent to 42 per cent of the total occupied population. At the same time, amalgamation, which set in strongly after World War I, reduced the number of separate unions and produced the huge organizations of recent decades. By the 1950's, for instance, seventeen unions included 6,500,000 members, some two thirds of all union membership. This aspect of concentration was even more marked among the unions affiliated with the T.U.C., of which the six largest in 1952 included fully 50 per cent of the total affiliated membership.[6]

"The whole trend of union development," Professor B. C. Roberts has written, "seems to be towards the consolidation of union membership in a relatively small number of unions, each of which is gradually obtaining exclusive jurisdiction over a particular area of employment." Moreover, within the individual unions authority has tended away from the local and toward the national level, the general secretaries in particular benefiting from this centralization. Only by the creation of such "a dominating driving force" have some of the big unions, which include widely diverse elements, been cemented into cohesive groupings.[7]

Labour's peak organization, the T.U.C., had not had a serious rival since its foundation in 1868 and had weathered the various surges in union growth without disruptive splits such as that between the A.F. of L. and the C.I.O. in the United States. From 1894, when its affiliated membership, standing at 1,000,000, represented 65 per cent of all unionists, the T.U.C., with some ups and downs, increased that proportion until in 1953, with membership at 8,094,000, it reached 85 per cent.

Like the larger firms in the world of organized industry, the larger unions exercised great influence within the trade union movement. Within each of the nineteen groups from which members were chosen for the General Council, it was usually, although not invariably, the largest that were regarded as "most representative" and won seats on the Council. Moreover, in contrast with other unions represented on the Council, the very largest had more than one member. In 1952–53, for instance, the Transport Workers and the General and Municipal Workers each had three and the

[6] Transport and General Workers Union; Amalgamated Engineering Union; National Union of Mine Workers; General and Municipal Workers; National Union of Railwaymen; Shop, Distributive and Allied Workers. See T.U.C. *Report* 1953, pp. 14–61.

[7] B. C. Roberts, *Trade Union Government and Administration in Great Britain* (Cambridge, Mass., 1956), pp. 53, 114, 463.

Mineworkers and the Amalgamated Engineers each had two.[8] These were still the days, it will be recalled, of the Deakin-Williamson-Lawther triumvirate. In general, as Roberts has observed, the long-run trend has been toward growing authority on the part of the T.U.C. over its affiliated organizations.[9]

The long-run trend is undeniable. But this is not to say that the capacity for unified decision-making among both workers and employers is adequate to the tasks of Britain's present-day economy. The powers of the T.U.C. over its affiliates are not extensive. It has no power to intervene in the wage policies of individual unions; and its ability to bring about changes in union structure or to intervene in disputes between its affiliates is severely limited. As we have seen in an instance involving a major question of public policy, the wage restraint bargain of 1948–50, the unions as a whole were able to concert their action sufficiently to make an agreement and to keep it with good faith. The General Council, however, could not by its own influence and authority make this agreement and was obliged to call on a meeting of the union executives. Many of those who believe that a wages policy, and not mere wage restraint, must be a regular part of economic management have concluded that far greater centralization of power is necessary, in particular, a strengthening of the General Council.[1]

Channels of Influence

In the British political system one may distinguish four main structural elements, corresponding to four main phases of policy-making, on which a group might seek to exert influence : the electorate, the legislature, the party, and the executive. It is a commonplace of any study of British pressure groups that on the whole they focus most attention on the executive, meaning by this both civil servants and ministers. The exceptions are important. The most obvious is the way the trade unions have used the Labour Party and their own sponsored M.P.'s to promote both the "interests of labour" and the ideals of Socialism. Yet the unions individually and through the T.U.C. have, especially since win-

---

[8] T.U.C. *Report* 1953, p. 3.
[9] *Op. cit.*, p. 436.
[1] See, for instance, the analysis and proposals of Michael Shanks, *The Stagnant Society* (London, 1961), esp. Ch. IV, "Trade Unions in Trouble," and Ch. V, "A Radical Labour Movement"; and Andrew Shonfield, *op. cit.*, Ch. XI, "A Way Forward."

ning full governmental "recognition" during World War II, maintained close and continuous contacts with the executive. Along with other producers organizations, they are represented in a vast, untidy system of functional representation that has grown up alongside the older system of parliamentary representation. It is mainly through this system that the powers of advice, acquiescence, and approval are brought to bear on public policy.

The principal conditions that created and have maintained this system are two : on the one hand, those powers related specifically to the productive function performed by the members of the organizations and, on the other hand, the extension of government control over the economy. I find it impossible to give causal primacy to one or the other condition. Such organizations have used their producers power to bring about extensions of government control. Yet the extension of government control has itself elicited the bargaining potential of producers, endowing them with the ability to influence the manner and purposes of that control.

Consider, for instance, the growth of trade associations. Again and again in their history it has been a development in government policy that has stimulated their concentration. In the 1920's government encouraged them as a means of promoting "rationalisation." Later the tariff system created by the adoption of "the great policy" led to further growth and still closer contacts. Only associations, not individual firms, could negotiate with the Import Duties Advisory Committee, and the Committee, as we have seen, might require a *quid pro quo*—such as reorganization of the industry under the supervision of a strengthened association—as a condition for recommending protection. In both world wars, trade associations, sometimes formed at the instigation of government, performed important functions, being called on to provide expert advice and to serve as instruments of control. After 1945, particularly where government was carrying out programs involving direct regulation and control, it used trade associations for similar purposes, encouraging industrial producers in their efforts to "speak with one voice."

The principal formal channel through which producers organizations gained representation was the advisory committee—of which there were some 850 in 1958, according to a reply to a Parliamentary Question.[2] Not all these committees had such representatives nor, even when a producers group was in effect represented on a committee, were the representatives formally

[2] *Advisory Committees in British Government* (London, 1960), p. 11.

nominated by the relevant producer organization. The number of committees on which producer groups were in actuality represented, however, was formidable. In the 1950's these committees ranged from such high-level bodies as the Economic Planning Board, the National Joint Advisory Council of the Ministry of Labour, and the National Production Advisory Council on Industry (on which the relevant peak organizations—the T.U.C., B.E.C., and F.B.I.—were represented) to the multitude of committees attached to the main economic departments. The latter were connected with the system of "sponsoring" departments which grew up during World War II, and which meant that every industry and every branch of it, no matter how small, had a sponsoring department or section of one somewhere in the government machine.

To illustrate the composition and duties of one of these departmental advisory committees, we may take a brief look at the National Advisory Council for the Motor Manufacturing Industry, a body whose operations we have already had occasion to observe. Established in 1946, this committee was in 1955 moved to the Board of Trade, whose permanent secretary was its chairman. In addition to him, there were three government representatives from the Board of Trade, Ministry of Transport, and Ministry of Supply, respectively. The seven employers representatives, appointed on the recommendation of the Society of Motor Manufacturers and Traders, consisted of two from the "Big Six" among motor car manufacturers, one from the specialist producers, two from the makers of heavy commercial vehicles, one from the manufacturers of accessories and components, and one from the body builders, all these being either chairmen or managing directors of their firms. On the industry side there were also two officials of the Society of Motor Manufacturers and Traders, ex officio. The four trade union representatives were nominated by and came from the Amalgamated Engineering Union (one), the National Union of Vehicle Builders (one), and the Confederation of Shipbuilding and Engineering Unions (two). There was also one "independent" member.

The committee's terms of reference, which it will be noted excluded labor questions, were :

To provide a means of regular consultation between the Government and the motor manufacturers on such matters as the location of industry, exports, imports, research, design and progress of the industry.[8]

The subjects discussed in the committee would in part depend upon the shape of government policy. As we have seen, the export drive led to the discussion of a different basis for the annual use tax on motor cars. When scarce materials were being allocated, the industry might find itself obliged to defend its use of a scarce material such as copper or nickel. A topic that industry representatives felt strongly about was the heavy purchase tax on cars and, although this was a Treasury matter, they might bring it up in the committee in the hope of enlisting the support of the Board of Trade in their efforts to persuade the Chancellor of the need for reduction. Then there were questions of regulation, such as the rules governing the construction and use of cars, which the minister drew up and revised, acting under wide delegated powers and relying heavily upon the technical knowledge of the industry. Again, when the Government was about to engage in negotiating trade agreements with other countries, the industry might find the committee a convenient place to urge that an attempt be made to open larger markets for British motor cars.

While these committees, which brought together the sponsoring department and the producer organization, had practical value to both sides (and, moreover, by the symbolism of formal status enhanced the position of the consulted groups), they did not constitute the sole means of contact. Apart from such committees, although often around them, a great mass of daily, informal consultation had grown up. Private and public bureaucrats continually called one another on the telephone and discussed a problem on a first-name basis. As for luncheon, in the dining room of the Athenaeum, according to an official of one of Britain's largest corporations, "you can hardly hear yourself for the grinding of axes."

CONSUMER GROUPS AND THE WELFARE STATE

We get a rather different view of group politics in postwar Britain if we look at the political arena not from the perspective of

[8] *National Advisory Council for the Motor Manufacturing Industry : Report on Proceedings* (1947), p. 5.

producer groups and the Managed Economy, but from that of consumer groups and the Welfare State. The main elements and relationships revealed by this view are easy to grasp. We can readily imagine them if we take the view of the embattled political leader as he considers the realities of winning or keeping power, and his responsibility for leading his party to victory. Tensely aware of the narrow electoral balance between the parties, sincerely concerned to protect the public interest against the dangers represented by the other party, he ponders the differential response among voters to the benefits and burdens of the Welfare State and considers how a change, or promise of change, would affect the electoral allegiance of this group or that.

But we need not merely imagine these thoughts. Sir Anthony Eden has left us a candid record of them. "I wanted to feel that I had the country's support for the work I wished to do," he wrote when recalling his approach to the general election of 1955. "Nothing but the verdict of the nation at the polls could really give me that." Yet he was aware that "the margin was pretty narrow : a small percentage either way would decide." Favoring the Conservatives' "political case" were "three years of achievement by the Government" and "the prosperous condition of the country"—"in 1955 employment was at a very high level." Moreover, he states, "I knew that if we were to improve our position I must in particular get my message to the better skilled industrial worker, who could be expected to benefit from the kind of society we wanted to create." Against this background, Sir Anthony devoted "four-fifths of the space" of his election address to home politics, summing up what had been done "at home" as follows :

> "Earnings are higher;
> Savings are much higher;
> Taxes are lower;
> Pensions and social benefits have been increased;
> A million new homes have been built;
> Rationing is a thing of the past;
> There is variety and abundance in the shops.
> There is more hope, more choice, more freedom for all."[4]

Bidding for the Pensioners' Vote

It will be helpful to take one item from Eden's summing up and look more closely at its relation to the electoral problem.

[4] *Op. cit.*, pp. 299, 309–10.

A favorite object of the *Economist*'s scorn in the 1950's was what it called "the present habit of bidding for pensioners' votes before every general election." Recalling that in 1951 Labour had raised pensions only three weeks before polling day, in 1954 it found that again as an election approached, both parties were engaged in this competition. Labour, it held, had started the "Dutch auction," but the Conservatives had not failed "to raise the bidding in turn."[5]

That the *Economist* should explain these party decisions as "bidding for votes" does not prove the point. When, like the *Economist* in this instance, one is urgently, indeed furiously, pressing one's own views on a government, it is tempting to accuse ministers of yielding to pressure when they fail to follow one's advice. Yet given the narrow electoral balance between the parties (as late as April 1955, the Gallup Poll showed the Conservatives ahead by only one percentage point[6]) it would have been a wonder if there were not something of a "scramble for votes." Moreover, the elderly were a large and growing proportion of the population, some 4.6 million men and women being in receipt of retirement benefits under National Insurance. It would be callous to claim that the pensions were generous; in addition, their purchasing power was being continually eroded by inflation. Among these millions, in short, there was a large group to whom an increase would be a significant benefit.

The sequence and timing of party moves with regard to old age pensions as the election approached make it hard to believe that electoral considerations were not a major factor in the decisions of party leaders. The Conservative conference of 1953, to be sure, far from favoring greater benefits, viewed with concern the growing burden of old age pensions on the national finances and urged that steps be taken to make continued employment more attractive to the elderly.[7] Labour, however, made a strong move in the course of drawing up its new policy statement, *Challenge to Britain*, which was drafted by the N.E.C. and approved by conference in 1953. Debated and adopted under an unusual procedure, which enabled conference to amend particular sections and not merely to accept or reject the document as a whole, the draft submitted by the N.E.C. was altered on a number of significant points. One

[5] *Economist*, July 24, 1954, pp. 261-2; November 20, 1954, p. 627; December 11, 1954, pp. 883-7.

[6] *Ibid.*, May 7, 1955, p. 452.   [7] 1953 CPCR, pp. 91-4.

of these items, which concerned old age pensioners, underwent a gentle process of escalation that is worth tracing.

The original draft of *Challenge* had pledged that a Labour Government would make an annual review of the cost of living and on that basis restore the real value of old age pensions and other benefits under National Insurance.[8] On the agenda for the conference of 1953 were thirty-four resolutions and amendments dealing with this question, most of them giving special emphasis to the problem of old age pensioners and all but one asking for an increase in benefits.[9] The composite resolution based on them asked for an "immediate" increase and the establishment of a minimum "related to the cost of living."[1] In the debate, the supporters of the amendment based their case mainly on the claims of social justice and Socialist principle, e.g., "to each according to his need, from each according to his ability."[2] One speaker, however, an organizer for the National Federation of Old Age Pensions Associations, also delicately noted that "millions" of old age pensioners would be "listening in" on the radio report of the decision of conference on this matter. Starting from an acknowledgement of that fact, the N.E.C. spokesman, Edith Summerskill, observed that "what I am going to say now is of importance to every low-paid worker and to every beneficiary under the National Insurance scheme."[3] Dr. Summerskill then accepted the demand for an increase, which would be immediate and not dependent on an annual review, although, as she pointed out, this committed "our future Chancellor of the Exchequer to a very big expenditure of money, maybe in the region of £140 million."

The final version of *Challenge*, as revised by the N.E.C. in the light of the amendments made by conference, and published in December 1953, included the pledge of an immediate increase, but also, echoing the demand of at least one of the resolutions submitted to conference, went on to promise that benefits would be restored to the purchasing power they commanded "when the National Insurance scheme was introduced."[4] This statement left open the question whether the base year was to be 1946, when the

[8] *Challenge to Britain* (June, 1953), p. 23.
[9] *Agenda*, 1953 Labour Party Conference, pp. 52–4 and 112–3.
[1] *Composite Resolutions and Amendments*, 1953 Labour Party Conference, No. 39.
[2] 1953 *LPCR*, p. 189.
[3] *Ibid.*, p. 192.
[4] *Challenge to Britain* (December, 1953), p. 25.

Act was passed, or 1948, when payments under it began. Labour's pledge took final form when, questioned on this matter, the party declared that the base year was to be 1946.[5]

The Conservative response to this pledge was for a time delayed. The Government had excellent grounds : it claimed to be waiting on the reports from two inquiries, including that of a committee (under Sir Thomas Phillips) set up to review the problems arising from Britain's position as an aging nation. Presumably, therefore, its scheme could not be formulated until these reports were in. Yet as early as a pensions debate in July, and long before either report was available, the Conservatives had virtually met Labour's bid by indicating that they intended to make good to "old pensioners, the war disabled, the sick, and the unemployed the whole of the injury and loss they suffered in six years of Socialist administration."[6]

At the Labour conference in the fall, Dr. Summerskill, again mentioning the "millions of old age pensioners sitting around their radios" to hear the report on the conference, took the opportunity to "refresh" their memories with a restatement of what Labour had promised and then gladly accepted a resolution repeating that pledge.[7] Similarly, the Conservative conference, now that the lead had been given by the party chiefs in Parliament, asked for an immediate increase in old age pensions. Welcoming the motion, the Minister of Pensions and National Insurance again declared that the Government's plan, when announced, would enable Conservatives to claim that "we have made good to the war disabled, the sick, the unemployed and the old age pensioners the whole of the loss and damage which they suffered under the Socialists in the years from 1946 to 1951."[8]

In December the Phillips committee report was published, and in the same week the Government's scheme was introduced in Parliament.[9] This may hardly seem to have given time for serious consideration of the committee's findings. The Government, said the *Economist*, "harried by the Opposition," had "hustled" the committee into finishing its report, "so that it could be published in

[5] 1954 *LPCR*, p. 118.
[6] Osbert Peake, Minister of Pensions, in the debate of July 21, 1954. 530 *H.C. Deb.* 1393.
[7] 1954 *LPCR*, pp. 113–9.
[8] 1954 *CPCR*, p. 51.
[9] See 535 *H.C. Deb.* 146–148 (1 December 1954) and Cmd. 9338 for the increases and the timetable of their coming into effect.

the same week as the Minister announced the increases in pensions. But this was an empty form. The Phillips report has not been considered by the Government and probably will not be."[1] In any case, the Conservative scheme carried out the commitment to give a flat rate-increase in old age pensions and other benefits, which fully restored their purchasing power to their original postwar level. Opportunely, the new scales came into effect shortly before the general election of 1955. In the campaign, 71 per cent of Conservative election addresses referred proudly to the Conservative record on pensions, while 63 per cent of the Labour addresses looked forward to what pensions would be under a Labour Government.[2]

Consumer Groups and Government Policy

In speaking of "consumer groups," I am not using the term "consumer" in a technical economic sense, although I am thinking of persons interested in consumption. By a consumer group I mean a number of voters whose material well-being is affected in the same way by some measure of government action, actual or prospective. The main immediate source of a person's material well-being is his income from work or ownership. But in the Welfare State income is supplemented by benefits and reduced by burdens. The supplements—the "social dividend," if you like— may take the form of direct payments to the individual or of subsidies to community services, such as housing or education. Nor in identifying such groups should one confine one's attention to benefits conventionally regarded as constituting the Welfare State, although in the postwar years these have been by far the most important politically. An improvement in the road system, for instance, is a benefit to auto users, and the agitation of automobile associations for such benefits will be a political factor to be considered by party managers. In short, the groups benefiting or expecting to benefit from the "social dividend" constitute a complex of pressures supporting the vast pattern of expenditure of the Welfare State. The Government would like to reduce taxation, Enoch Powell, the Financial Secretary to the Treasury, told the 1957 Conservative conference. But to do that they must be able

[1] *Economist*, December 11, 1954, p. 883.
[2] David E. Butler, *The British General Election of 1955* (London, 1955), pp. 32–3.

first to reduce expenditure and the "minority whom a limitation of expenditure affects, is always more vocal than the majority who will ultimately benefit."[3]

Then, in addition to benefits, government action also involves burdens on the material well-being of voters and their families. The Welfare State consists not only of programs of services but also programs of taxation accomplishing some redistribution of income among persons and between objects of expenditure. Thus, for instance, those who pay income tax at the standard rate constitute a group to whose electoral behavior party leaders may be responsive. From the point of view of the economist, income tax is a powerful weapon of fiscal policy, and in a time of overexpansion an increase in income tax would seem to be one of the most effective ways of reducing the general level of demand. During the 1950's, however, Governments did not use income tax in this way, one reason being their anticipation of the negative political reaction of groups affected. "The most serious handicap of fiscal measures, as a method of operating on the level of demand," commented the Radcliffe Report, "is that individual tax changes, as distinct from the budget total, have to overcome opposition on varied grounds having nothing to do with the general economic situation" (para. 517, pp. 184-5). Or as Michael Shanks put it : "Political pressures on Governments to reduce income tax, or at least not to raise it, are apt to be very strong indeed—especially before an election."[4]

But the Government action that is relevant to the existence and activity of such groups does not consist only in separate measures. For instance, both full employment and the inflation that occurs when employment is overfull have an uneven incidence on the material well-being of voters and, depending upon this incidence, different groups of voters will hold Governments and parties responsible for the corresponding benefit or burden. Indeed, within the same household husband and wife may evaluate the same government action differently, the one as wage earner applauding the rise in wages resulting from an expansionary policy, the other as housewife deploring the rise in prices. The general point, however, is that when a government has taken intervention to the point reached in Britain, voters hold it responsible not only for additions to and subtractions from other income, but also for the trend of that "other income" as well. The programs of the

[3] 1957 CPCR, p. 44.   [4] Op. cit., p. 189.

Managed Economy will be the ground for electoral reaction not only among the producer groups they directly affect, but also among the consumer groups incidentally affected by economic policy.

In this view of consumer groups as actors in the political system, there are several points that are important. First, the behavior of these groups is a function of the interaction of polity and economy. By this I mean that one cannot understand their activity by trying to attribute it solely to conditions arising outside of and independently of the political system. On the contrary, this activity was shaped by programs that already existed and by the competition of parties in proposing developments of those programs.

Perhaps when discussing the early days of Radical social reform, one might need to change this emphasis and account for the demands of groups mainly on the basis of their experience in a newly industrialized economy. Even then, however, when explaining why certain demands were brought forward in the political arena and accounting for the form they were given, one would be obliged also to consider the political culture of the time.[5] At any rate, once the Welfare State had begun its rise, and certainly once its basic code of policy had been established, its programs did much to define the further demands made upon government and the boundaries of the groups making them. As benefits, these programs created a clientele which might well demand "more." As burdens, they created a clientele which might well demand "less." In one way or the other they provided foci around which the interests of the consumer groups affected could crystallize. Just as producer groups were often stimulated to organize and were given a role and a footing in the new system of functional representation by the extension of the Managed Economy, so also consumer groups were brought to political awareness and activity by the Welfare State.

Moreover, these programs were the subjects of a continuous and ardent party battle. The immediate experience of consumers told them where their wishes were not being met by existing policies : the newly married couple seeking in vain to find housing they could afford; the old age pensioner noticing his retirement

[5] See Samuel H. Beer et al., Patterns of Government : The Major Political Systems of Europe, rev. ed. (New York, 1962), pp. 56–7.

benefit buying less and less each year; the surtax payer reflecting that rates were hardly less progressive under the Conservatives than under Labour. But immediate experience had to be interpreted before it could become the basis of a political response. Some could do this for themselves. Those who belonged to a producer organization, whose members, as consumers, were similarly affected by Government actions, might find it providing such interpretation, pointing out which program or policy was to blame, proposing a specific remedy, and justifying the demand in terms of some view of the common good. But foremost in offering these interpretations were the political parties. Problems of housing, pensions, educational opportunity for youth, the cost of living, full employment, and heavy taxation provided major themes of their discussions of domestic affairs in Parliament and at elections. By pointing out where the material welfare of certain groups had been affected, showing what the causes had been, and proposing remedies, the parties' interpretations of these problems clarified and sharpened the demands of consumers groups among the electorate. These demands, in short, did not arise autonomously from the immediate experience of consumers, but very largely from the interaction of that experience with interpretations offered by organizations, especially the political parties.

The role of party in shaping public opinion has often been noted. It has been said, for instance, that a principal function of a major party is to aggregate the demands of a large number of groups in the electorate. Where party government is as highly developed as in Britain—I wish to emphasize—the role of party is much greater. Party does not merely aggregate the opinions of groups, it goes a long way toward creating these opinions by fixing the framework of public thinking about policy and the voters' sense of the alternatives and the possibilities. In turn, of course, the party may find itself under pressure from such opinion. And when in its competition for votes it responds to this pressure, the flow of influence seems to be in only one direction, from voters to party. But by taking a wider view we will see that the parties themselves, backed by research staffs, equipped with nation-wide organizations, and enjoying the continuous attention of the mass media, have themselves in great part framed and elicited the very demands to which they then respond.

Since the 1940's, for instance, British parties have been subject to a demand among certain sections of public opinion, particularly among wage earners, that they commit themselves to keeping down unemployment to a level of 1 or 2 per cent. This demand of "vulgar Keynesianism" arose from various sources. But obviously a principal one has been the propaganda (and, when in power, the action) of the parties themselves. Similarly, the demand that the cost of living be stabilized—particularly strong among groups with fixed incomes—has been sharpened and strengthened by the claims of both parties that the Government, as inflation continued from the late forties into the fifties, had the duty and the means to halt the price rise. Hence, when ministers and officials find their efforts to manage the economy hemmed in by pressure from these two blocs of public opinion, they are confronting what is in no small part a consequence of the intense party competition of the past decade or two.

The parallel with the effect of mass advertising upon the demands of consumers in the economy is irresistible. One is tempted to say that as great retailing organizations manipulate the opinion of their markets, creating the demands of which in economic theory they are supposed to be the servants,[6] so also the massive party organizations of Collectivist politics create the opinion which in democratic theory they are supposed merely to reflect. Thus the popular sovereignty of democratic theory is undermined by the same means as is the "consumers sovereignty" of liberal economics.[7] But this gloomy view of Collectivist politics neglects various factors, not least the role of producers organizations in eliciting, and in protecting against party manipulation, the political demands of their members. In any case, some degree of manipulation of opinion by parties may be the price paid for a representa-

[6] "As a society becomes increasingly affluent," writes J. K. Galbraith, "wants are increasingly created by the process by which they are satisfied. . . . Increases in consumption, the counterpart of increases in production, act by suggestion or emulation to create wants. Or producers may proceed actively to create wants through advertising and salesmanship." *The Affluent Society* (Boston, 1958), p. 158. Galbraith calls this the "dependence effect."

[7] Nigel Nicolson, a Conservative M.P. who was denied renomination by his constituency party because of his opposition to the Suez action, expresses great alarm over this tendency. Party managers and candidates, he declares, "use all modern means of mass-communication to create a mass mind which does not require to think and therefore ceases to discriminate," while the mass media and general education, rather than "discovering, instructing and expressing the public's point-of-view . . . have merely served to stamp it out from two huge rounded moulds." *People and Parliament* (London, 1958), p. 50.

tion of consumer interests. The power of organized producers in a modern democracy is readily seen and widely recognized. Indeed, many fear that, overshadowed by these giants of the Collectivist economy, the consumer group, only poorly organized, or perhaps not organized at all, will be unable to bring its interests forcefully to the attention of Government. But this view neglects the function of the tightly knit, competitive political party. Keenly on the scent of votes and pressed sharply by its rival in the chase, it probes every neglected thicket in the political landscape for its quarry.

However one may assess the merits, the fact is that not only political parties, but indeed the whole vast apparatus of modern government and politics has a role in forming the opinion by which it is supposed to be governed. In this respect the mixed economy is paralleled by the mixed polity. In the era of Collectivist policy, we cannot separate the sphere of government from that of the production of material goods and services. Neither can we in the era of Collectivist politics separate the sphere of government from that of the formation of public opinion—the sphere of "ideal production." As government policy has deeply penetrated the economic market place, so also have the massive concentrations of contemporary politics invaded the market place of ideas.

PARTY GOVERNMENT AND GROUP POLITICS

It is common enough in democratic political systems for competing parties to try to broaden their electoral support by appeals to consumer groups. But the process of "bidding" that one finds in Britain's postwar politics depended on a rather special combination of conditions. Among these conditions were the decline of class antagonism; the wide acceptance of the basic framework of the Welfare State and Managed Economy; and the narrow electoral balance between the parties that became noticeable as the Conservatives regained popular support in the late forties and was manifest in the results of elections and public opinion surveys during the fifties and into the sixties. These conditions set the stage for a competition between the two major parties focusing on group appeals. Insofar as a principal aim of a party is to win power, such a tactic in such a situation was highly rational. But before a party can act rationally in this sense, it must have, in a high degree, the capacity for unified decision-making. It must

have some system for considering the situation, deciding and stating authoritatively what its promises will be, and effectively carrying them out if it wins power in the state. Like the producer group
that possesses a strong potential for bargaining, the party must
mobilize and unify its resources for bidding. And in the Collectivist
period of British politics, just as one can trace the rise of concentration among producers groups, so also one can find a similar tendency to concentration in British parties.

One result has been the "mass party," embracing in its membership millions of persons; Labour in 1952 meticulously reported
a total of 5,849,002 as compared with the Conservative rounded
estimate of 2,750,000. While the number of dues-paying members
of the two major parties amounted to over one third of the total
vote cast in the general election of 1955, the huge majority of
these numbers were inactive, except to pay the modest dues
solicited from them and presumably to vote for their party at
elections. But even if there were on each side thousands rather
than millions of party activists,[8] they and the extra-parliamentary
parties to which they belonged constituted vast and elaborate organizations extending into virtually every constituency.

Yet these mass parties had managed in a remarkable degree
to "speak with one voice." To an Attlee harassed by Bevanite
rebels on the backbenches, in the constituencies, and among the
unions, or to a Macmillan assaulted by Suez rebels under the
leadership of a Cecil, this assertion may seem painfully laughable.
It is when we look at the situation in the light of what once prevailed—or what prevails in other parties such as those of the
United States—that we properly appreciate the degree of cohesion achieved. The rise of party unity in parliamentary divisions
is the most striking exhibit. From the mid-nineteenth century,
when it had fallen to American levels, party cohesion in Britain
had steadily risen until in recent decades it was so close to 100 per
cent that there was no longer any point in measuring it.[9] In the
House of Commons were two bodies of freedom-loving Britons,
chosen in more than six hundred constituencies and subject to

[8] R. T. McKenzie has suggested that the total "active" membership of
the Labour Party is less than 130,000. "Policy Decision in Opposition : A
Rejoinder," *Political Studies*, Vol. V, No. 2 (June, 1957), p. 182n. Elsewhere
he has estimated the "politically active" as "a hundred thousand or so in
each party." "Parties, Pressure Groups and the British Political Process,"
Political Quarterly, Vol. XXIX, No. 1 (January-March, 1958), p. 10.

[9] See above, Ch. VI, pp. 184-5, Ch. IX, pp. 257, 262.

influences that ran back to an electorate that was numbered in the millions and divided by the complex interests and aspirations of an advanced modern society. Yet day after day with a Prussian discipline they trooped into the division lobbies at the signals of their Whips and in the service of the authoritative decisions of their parliamentary parties. We are so familiar with this fact that we are in danger of losing our sense of wonder over them.

Writing of American parties, Stephen Bailey asks : "On matters of national policy, what individual or group speaks with authority for each of the national parties?"[1] In Britain, on the other hand, although the processes differed as greatly between the two parties as do the conceptions of Tory and Socialist Democracy, each party had means for deciding what it stood for and acting accordingly. Nor was this cohesion in utterance and act confined to Parliament. At general elections the party manifesto was accepted and supported by all candidates. Labour imposed this obligation by strict rule; the Conservatives were less explicit, but no less demanding. And in general the election addresses of candidates faithfully reflected the agreed party views, just as the votes of M.P.'s reflected the decisions of their parties and the actions of Governments bore out their election pledges.

These were in short "strong" parties. What were the consequences for the role of groups in politics? Sometimes it is argued that "strong" parties mean "weak" pressure groups and that party government in the British style is the enemy of group politics. And, to be sure, one can easily see how the ability of a party to make a decision binding on its M.P.'s could enable it to hold its majority against some group demand. But if a "strong" party can in this way more effectively resist group demands, so also can it more effectively yield to them. The more cohesive the party is in utterance and action, the more effectively it can bid for group support. It can control what promises will be made in its name and, once having made them, it can deliver the legislative votes needed to honor them. The mere structural fact of "strong" parties does not tell us what the role of groups will be. Indeed, given other suitable conditions, party government in the British style can be highly favorable to the rise of a politics in which "bidding" for the support of consumer groups by highly competitive parties is a major feature.

[1] *The Condition of Our National Political Parties.* Fund for the Republic Occasional Paper (New York, 1959), p. 8.

CHAPTER XIII

Party Purpose
and Government Policy

The role of producer and consumer groups in British politics since World War II can be abundantly illustrated. There is no problem finding examples to show that "bidding" and "bargaining" have influenced the policy decisions of parties and Governments. It is correct and necessary therefore to speak of the "new group politics" whether one is making comparison with the structure of power of the British political system in the nineteenth century or in the interwar period. But simply to examine the role of groups may give the impression that other forces were insignificant and that pluralism finally reigned. We need also to consider the role of party.

Party, to be sure, has a role in pluralist theory. As we have just observed, a party system including strongly unified parties on the British model is quite compatible with a situation in which their competition for group support is the major influence on party and public policy. In such a situation, and in keeping with pluralist theory, the essential purpose of the party is to win and hold authority in the state. Guided by this purpose, the "competing teams of potential rulers"[1] adapt their promises and policies to the wishes, overt or latent, of various groups in the society. From such interaction of groups with the competing party teams, according to the pluralist view, public policy results.

The theory of party government, however, breaks with pluralism by asserting that party policy is influenced not only by calculations flowing from the pursuit of power, but also by distinctive party conceptions of the common good. The Labour and Con-

[1] R. T. McKenzie, "Parties, Pressure Groups and the British Political Process," *Political Quarterly*, Vol. XXIX, No. 1 (January-March, 1958), p. 8.

servative parties differed in this respect during the interwar period and, indeed, during the whole Socialist Generation. But what was the case after the late 1940's? Did the new group politics lead to such a "convergence" of party positions as to eliminate any significant difference of purpose? With this question in mind we shall look at Conservative social and economic policy in the 1950's, making comparison with the Labour position where appropriate.

CONVERGENCE OF POLICIES?

One kind of evidence to help answer this question would be evidence of a major discontinuity in social policy after the Conservatives took power in 1951. And if we follow the guidance of Labour spokesmen, it is in this area that we would expect to find important contrasts in the purposes of the two parties. Before the Conservatives took office in 1951, Labour spokesmen freely prophesied that a Tory victory would lead to a wide attack on the Welfare State and a return to the mass unemployment of the 1930's. It is hard to know how seriously to take these campaign utterances. But certainly a central thrust of Labour attacks on Conservative social policy in the 1950's was that it was undermining the Welfare State and altering the distribution of income in favor of the rich as against the poor. In fact, however, throughout the 1950's Conservative Governments maintained very much the same priorities in social policy that had been established by Labour. The pattern of expenditure on the Welfare State and the distribution of its burdens through taxation changed hardly at all. Moreover, although all incomes were rising, it was not the rich who enjoyed exceptional gains in prosperity.

Between 1950—Labour's last full year in office—and 1959 expenditure on social services rose steadily. Taking this expenditure to consist of current welfare grants to persons and current welfare expenditure on goods and services by all public authorities, we find the total increasing from 1,537 million pounds in 1950 to 2,184 million pounds in 1955 and 3,171 million pounds in 1959.[2] This doubling of expenditure under the Conservatives hardly suggests an attack on the Welfare State. Since, however, the 1950's were

[2] Tabs. 35 and 43, *National Income and Expenditure* (London, 1960). The totals of welfare expenditure stated in the text omit housing subsidies, which rose from 72 million pounds in 1950 to 100 million pounds in 1955 and 116 million pounds in 1959 (see Tab. 43).

a time of rising national income, partly inflationary and partly
real, this increase in expenditure could conceivably be compatible
with a declining role for the social services in the economy as a
whole. A comparison with personal income, however, shows that
welfare expenditure remained proportionately steady, if anything,
increasing slightly. Personal income (before taxes) rose from
11,041 million pounds in 1950 to 15,729 million pounds in 1955
and 19,676 million pounds in 1959.[3] As a percentage of personal
income, welfare expenditures were 13.9 per cent in both 1950 and
1955 and had risen to 16.1 per cent by 1959.[4]

The expenditure totals cited above comprised many different
items. To list them will suggest the complexity and variety of
consumer groups benefiting from the Welfare State. They included National Insurance benefits, consisting of retirement
pensions, widows' and guardians' allowances, death grants and
unemployment, sickness, maternity, injury and disablement benefits. They also included postwar credits, war pensions and service
grants, non-contributory pensions, public assistance grants, family allowances, industrial services for the disabled, and expenditure on education, child care, and the health services.[5] Under the
Conservatives there were some changes in the relative amounts
spent on these items, family allowances, for instance, being pushed
up more rapidly than other expenditure. But on the whole the
pattern of expenditure and the flow of benefits to consumers
groups remained very close to what it had been under Labour.

All Government expenditure [Enoch Powell then the Financial Secretary to the Treasury, told the Conservative conference of 1958] is a
payment to somebody. In every branch of Government expenditure
there is a vested interest. Every form of Government expenditure has
its devotees and its defenders. . . . The minority whom a limitation of
expenditure affects, are always more vocal than the majority who
will ultimately benefit. Hence, it comes about that economy is popular
in the abstract, but has few defenders in the concrete.[6]

If we look at the distribution of the tax burden under the
Conservatives, a similar continuity of priorities appears. To begin
with, although Conservatives had lamented the heavy burden of

[3] *Ibid.*, Tab. 2.
[4] I. M. D. Little, "Fiscal Policy," in G. D. N. Worsick and P. H. Ady, eds.,
The British Economy in the Nineteen-Fifties (Oxford, 1962), p. 300, Tab. 9.
[5] *National Income and Expenditure*, Tabs. 35, 38, and 43.
[6] 1957 CPCR, p. 44.

taxation maintained by Labour, total net taxes as a percentage of gross national product fell only slightly between 1950 and 1959. In 1950 the figure was 34.5 per cent; in 1955, 31.6 per cent; and in 1959, 30.6 per cent.[7] After eight years of Conservative rule, in short, taxes were still taking almost one third of the national product. How was this burden shared among the various social strata? Was there, for instance, a regressive shift from direct to indirect taxes? With regard to the latter question, again we find little change. As percentages of national product, taxes on income were 15.5 per cent in 1950, 13.6 per cent in 1955, and 12.6 per cent in 1959. Taxes on expenditure also fell a little, the percentages being 13.6 per cent in 1950, 13.4 per cent in 1955, and 12.9 per cent in 1959.[8]

What about the effect on income distribution of Conservative changes in income tax and surtax? This is an involved question that tends to excite polemical answers. It cannot be adequately answered simply by ascertaining whether a person with the same income paid more or less tax under the Conservatives than under Labour. For one thing, when national income is rising (as in the 1950's), if there is a progressive income tax, it is likely that revenue will rise faster than government expenditure. Hence, a failure to change tax rates will be deflationary, and to keep the economy on the path of steady growth will require successive reductions in tax rates. Moreover, when incomes generally are rising, a person who continues to enjoy only the same money income is relatively lower in the income scale; hence, unless Government is increasing the proportion of personal income taken or is changing the scale of progressivity, such a person ought to pay a lower tax—and in fact, each person who was merely as well off in 1959 as in 1949 did pay less tax.

For our purposes, the correct question is whether a person who has enjoyed an average degree of prosperity pays a higher or lower tax. (Or, more precisely, whether a person who was in a certain income group at one date and whose income has risen by the same extent as the average rise of income per head is paying a higher or lower tax at a later date.) On this basis I. M. D. Little has calculated the effect of income tax and surtax in 1959 compared with 1949. At every level of "equivalent" income he finds only slight differences in the tax burden at the

---

[7] Little, *op. cit.*, p. 295, Tab. 5.   [8] *Ibid.*

end as compared with the beginning of the decade. The Conservatives did reduce a little the average proportion of direct tax collected, and these minor concessions mainly benefited persons with 1959 incomes ranging from £1,000 to £3,000, while income groups above or below this range paid the same or a little more. In general, however, the curves of effective tax rates on "equivalent" earned incomes in the two years were very much the same.[9]

The structure of taxation and the pattern of social service expenditure, to be sure, are not the only elements of Government policy that may affect the distribution of income. It is conceivable that the Conservatives might have maintained the priorities of Labour in these fields of social policy, while bringing about by their changes in economic policy (for instance, their greater reliance on market forces) a significant shift in pre-tax incomes in favor of the well-to-do. This, however, was emphatically not the case. Between 1949 and 1959 those who started off higher in the income scale gained much less than those who started off lower down. The average increase in personal income before tax was 80 per cent. Income receivers in the 1st and 5th percentiles, however, enjoyed an increase in pre-tax income of only 47 per cent and 63 per cent respectively, while pre-tax incomes of those in the 20th and 50th percentiles rose by 90 per cent and 100 per cent respectively.[1] Lack of statistics makes it much harder to estimate what happened to those below the median—i.e., the 50th percentile—but it appears that, although they probably increased their incomes by slightly more than the average amount, they did less well than those fairly close to the median.[2]

For the student of the politics of the Welfare State there is a related point worth noting. The 1959 pre-tax incomes of the 20th and 50th percentiles, where the most rapid increase took place, were £815 and £522 respectively. In this range were also found many of those "better skilled industrial workers" whom the Conservatives, according to Anthony Eden, were particularly

[9] *Ibid.*, pp. 279–81.

[1] *Ibid.*, pp. 285–7 and Tab. 8.

[2] *Ibid.*, p. 285, n. 2. For confirmation see also comment by Utting on a paper by Professor H. F. Lydall, "The Long-Term Trend in the Distribution of Size Incomes," *Journal of the Royal Statistical Society*, Ser. A, Pt. I, Vol. CXXII (1959), pp. 42–3.

anxious to attract to their cause.[3] This is not to say that the Conservatives deliberately initiated and brought about this greater relative increase among the lower income groups. As Professor Lydall has shown, that development was part of a long-term trend that had set in during World War II and continued under both Labour and the Conservatives.[4] We can only say that the Conservative leadership did not effectively offset this trend and that, judged from the viewpoint of their electoral calculations, it need not have appeared objectionable to them.

Between the social priorities of Labour and Conservative Governments, there were differences, to be sure. The Conservatives, for instance, virtually abolished food subsidies, but then they devoted relatively more funds to family allowances. When we make an overall assessment, however, it is the massive continuity that stands out. Moreover, so far as one can judge by the evidence already cited, it is plausible to hold that the shaping influences responsible for this continuity were those of group politics. The explanation might be put in the following terms : because of the growing national income and, during their early years, a favorable turn in the terms of trade, Conservative Governments were able to mitigate rapidly the austerity that had been associated with Labour's rule. At the same time, they maintained the Welfare State whose popularity with voters had been shown in the 1940's and to which the party had adapted while in Opposition, and as more resources became available, increased the flow of grants, goods, and services to the many beneficiary groups. In short, a comparison of the effects of Labour and Conservative social policy suggests that the will to power of the Conservative "team" plus the wishes and demands of these consumer groups provide the elements of a sufficient explanation of the course of Government action in the 1950's.

To try to locate the "differential" between the two parties by comparing what the Conservatives did with what Labour had previously done keeps our inquiry on the firm ground of actual performance. It does not, however, answer the question of what

[3] At the time of the general election of 1959 the *average* male manual worker was earning £13 3s. per week. On the basis of a 50-week work-year, that is a little over £650 per year. David Butler and Richard Rose, *The British General Election of 1959* (London, 1960), p. 12. See also *Economist*, September 10, 1955, p. 838.

[4] Lydall, *op. cit.;* see above p. 356, n. 2.

Labour would have done if it had held office at the later date. This is a hard question—although it is one that confronts every voter when he chooses between the parties at election time. Even in the British context, where the conditions of responsible party government greatly reduce the gap between the promises of a party in opposition and its performance in office, we cannot answer it with certainty. We can, however, make a reasonable effort by examining in more detail the course of Conservative policy in the critical period 1955–58, estimating the probabilities of Labour action on the basis of both its proposals at the time and its previous performance when in office. The focus of our attention will be on economic policy, but since economic policy and social policy are not two separate compartments of Government action, we shall also have the opportunity to observe possible differences in social priorities.

In the history of Conservative-Labour rivalry throughout the Socialist Generation, economic policy had stood at the center of their declared differences : briefly and on the plane of clichés, "private property and free enterprise" versus "common ownership and planning." In the 1950's Conservative denationalization of iron and steel and of road haulage were important changes of policy in this sphere; Labour's commitment to reverse these reversals was just about as convincing as the promises of an Opposition can be. The Conservatives also speeded up the process of dismantling physical controls begun under Labour and dispensed with some, such as controls on building and imports, which Labour almost certainly would have retained. Their break with "cheap money" and use of monetary policy was another departure.

Yet the continuity in the methods of economic management was one of the most remarked features of "Butskellism." Just as under Cripps and Gaitskell, the budget remained the main instrument for managing the economy. Thus, the Treasury could assure the Radcliffe Committee in 1959 that the "main reliance for the regulation of the pattern and total of effective demand has at least since 1948 been on fiscal measures, monetary measures being regarded as having only a supporting role."[5] And while Conservative Chancellors did not use income tax in their periodic attacks on excessive demand—a failure for which economists have

[5] Committee on the Working of the Monetary System, *Report*. Cmd. 827 (London, H.M.S.O., 1959), p. 184.

criticized them[6]—it should be remembered that neither Dalton nor Cripps had raised income tax or surtax in their disinflationary efforts of 1947 and 1948. The political unpopularity of such increases, one may suggest, is so great that given the order of magnitude and scale of progressivity of the tax structure in recent decades, they are not likely to be made except in time of war. Moreover, although the Conservatives did not resort to building and import controls in the middle 1950's, their use of controls over hire-purchase and over bank advances was so specific as to arouse severe criticism among the doctrinaire neo-liberals of the time.

THE CRISIS AND THE ALTERNATIVES

Rather than trying to locate a distinctively Conservative approach in the cautious "neo-liberalism" of the early 1950's, we can identify a much more informative contrast in party policy if we will examine how the Conservatives attempted to deal with the crisis that broke over the British economy in 1955. The immediate symptom was a turn for the worse in the balance of payments. Holding that excessive demand was at least in part responsible, the Government, beginning with Butler's autumn budget of October, and continuing into the early months of 1956, took steps to reduce public and private spending. As in 1947 the main attack was on investment, public and private, but other steps also reminiscent of the earlier effort were taken when purchase tax and profits tax were raised.

From the point of view of the present analysis, the central episode was the attempt made by the Government in 1956 to negotiate a bargain for wage-price restraint with organized labor and organized business. When this attempt failed, the Government slowly but unmistakably turned to a new policy for dealing with the wage-price spiral. In both actions, the attempted bargain of 1956 and the new policy of 1957–58, Conservatism revealed a set of priorities, social as well as economic, that distinctly contrast with those of Labour, whether we compare them with what Labour had done in the 1940's or with what it was proposing in the 1950's.

While the Government believed that excessive demand was one

[6] For instance, I. M. D. Little, *op. cit.*, pp. 273–8.

cause of rising prices, it also believed that rising wages were also very much responsible. For dealing with this aspect of the problem, it saw essentially two alternatives. One was a policy of deflation carried to the point at which unemployment would limit effective wage claims by "removing pressure on the labour market."[7] Such action would mean a break with the "full employment" commitment that Conservatives had honored in word and deed. In the eyes of Prime Minister Eden, this alternative was "politically not tolerable."[8]

The other alternative was some kind of agreement with organized labor and organized business—above all, with organized labor. For this Tory Government, that was not an absurd hope. From the time they assumed office, the Conservatives had taken the utmost care to cultivate good relations with the unions. Close contacts were maintained—indeed, trade unionists were appointed to consultative committees more freely than under Labour.[9] Churchill, moreover, was "determined" that "there should be no industrial strikes during his period as Prime Minister." "Inspired by Mr. Churchill and executed by Sir Walter Monckton," the resulting policy of "compromise on wage claims," Lord Woolton goes on to recall in a melancholy tone, was the principal force along with heavy public and private spending that let loose the forces of inflation.[1] Wage claims, wage rates, and wage earnings rose buoyantly during the early 1950's. And while from time to time the Government asked in vain for restraint, not only did it not interfere with this upward movement on the wages front, but on critical occasions it took action to help the workers win their demands. Of the Government's intervention on behalf of the railway workers in 1953 and 1955, for instance, B. C. Roberts writes:

Twice the Transport Commission was thus compelled by the Government to settle claims at levels that would have led any private enterprise to go out of business. In each case the settlement established a pattern which was followed by other industries.[2]

[7] Prime Minister Eden in a minute to Harold Macmillan, Chancellor of the Exchequer in April 1956. Quoted in *The Memoirs of Anthony Eden: Full Circle* (Boston, 1960), pp. 362-3.

[8] *Ibid.*

[9] V. L. Allen, *Trade Unions and The Government* (London, 1960), p. 304.

[1] *The Memoirs of the Rt. Hon. The Earl of Woolton*, 2nd ed. (London, 1959), pp. 379-80.

[2] *National Wages Policy in War and Peace* (London, 1958), p. 155.

The General Council, to be sure, had not won acceptance of its budget proposals, as year after year it urged the Government to increase subsidies, lower purchase tax on essential items, and raise taxation on distributed profits.[3] Neither, however, had organized business had great success in influencing Government policy. The F.B.I.'s basic contention that the total of Government expenditure should be reduced had failed to halt the steady upward trend and in consequence the load of taxation still remained in its view "appallingly heavy."[4] The history of a more specific plea, the Federation's request for more generous depreciation allowances, is also illustrative. Tax law permitted businesses to calculate depreciation only on the basis of historical cost, but the continuous inflation of recent years meant that the actual replacement cost of depreciated assets was much greater. Combined with the very high rates of tax on profits, the Federation argued, the effect of inflation had been to make depreciation allowances inadequate to cover replacement and had "resulted in the running down of capital."[5]

While the Federation was pleased to report in 1949 that it had persuaded Cripps to increase the "initial allowances" from 20 per cent to 40 per cent,[6] it did not regard this device as meeting the problem since these allowances, which were in effect interest-free loans, concerned only new capital expenditure and did not increase the sum total of depreciation allowances.[7] It continued to urge its case for relief on successive Chancellors, being joined by the Association of Certified and Corporate Accountants and the Institute of Chartered Accountants and enjoying the strenuous advocacy of the *Economist*.

Writing of the factors that adversely affected the British economy in 1955–56, Norman Macrae characterizes "wage inflation" as "the one major internal economic evil which Butler quite signally failed to tackle during his otherwise admirable Chancellorship." *Sunshades in October : An Analysis of the Main Mistakes in British Economic Policy Since the Mid Nineteen-fifties* (London, 1963), p. 45.

[3] *Ibid.*, p. 151.

[4] *The Budget, 1954. Representations to the Chancellor of the Exchequer.* Federation of British Industries (February, 1954), p. 2.

[5] *Computation of Trading Profits for Taxation Purposes. Comment on the Report of the Millard Tucker Committee.* Federation of British Industries (February, 1952), p. 8.

[6] S. E. Finer, "The Federation of British Industries," *Political Studies*, Vol. IV, No. 1 (February, 1956), p. 79.

[7] *Computation of Trading Profits for Taxation Purposes*, p. 7.

The Conservative Government, however, did not respond favorably, and in 1955 a Royal Commission concluded that capital had not been eroded by inflation and that allowances between 1948 and 1954 had been greater than depreciation and replacement costs.[8] By then, however, the Government had introduced a radically new measure, the "investment allowance," which was in effect a subsidy to new investment. This measure was perhaps the most important example in the 1950's of the deliberate use of fiscal policy to further a specific end of economic policy.[9] Like the initial allowance, the investment allowance was designed not to deal with the alleged problem of capital erosion, but rather to promote expansion and modernization. The idea for it had certainly not originated with the F.B.I., which indeed received it coolly, as did the Royal Commission.[1] The source, it has been said, was "some Treasury economist."[2] We should note, however, the similarity with a proposal urged for some years by the T.U.C. that the Government encourage investment in essential industry by discriminatory depreciation allowances.[3]

THE ATTEMPTED BARGAIN AND THE NEW PRIORITIES

Against this background of its relations with organized labor and organized business, the Government, now headed by Eden, approached both sides of industry in the latter part of 1955. Its main drive for a "pact," however, was launched early in 1956 and continued into the summer.

Publicly, the Government hoped for a reduction in prices. Realistically, it did not expect to get more than agreements that would lead to "restraint in making wage claims and in fixing margins of profits."[4] In order to get such concessions from labor and capital, what would the Government offer? Eden himself wished to use the budget to make some reduction in the cost of living. He disliked the purchase tax increases and urged changes, such as a reduction in the beer duty. But neither the October nor the April budgets reflected these suggestions. The principal direct contribution that the Government was ready to

[8] See *Economist*, July 11, 1955, p. 915, and July 2, 1955, p. 53.
[9] See Worswick and Ady, *op. cit.*, p. 248.
[1] *Economist*, June 11, 1955, p. 915.
[2] Worswick and Ady, *op. cit.*, p. 248n.
[8] Roberts, *op. cit.*, p. 151.
[4] Eden, *op. cit.*, pp. 360–2.

make consisted of its action to restrain spending, both public and private. Ultimately it also intervened to hold prices in the nationalized industries. Otherwise, the role it attempted was that of winning wage restraint from the unions in exchange for price and profits restraint by business. In the latter effort it achieved no small success, but only on conditions that ruled out a bargain with the unions.

In their response to the Government's appeal for restraint, the initial response of both sides of industry was curiously similar. One might well have expected these two old antagonists of the industrial scene to put the blame on one another, the unions finding the source of inflation in "administered prices" serving excessive profits, while management held organized labor responsible for wage-push inflation. In fact, both blamed the Government, but for opposite reasons. "Too often," the General Council said in a memorandum to the Chancellor of the Exchequer in February 1956, "the responsibility for avoiding an income-prices spiral is put on to trade unions and employers."[5] Stating that "it is necessary to inquire more deeply into the causes of wage claims," the General Council then put the blame on the Government's dismantling of the machinery of control and planning and on its measures for redistribution of income. Under the latter heading, it referred to acts of "deliberate Budget policy" resulting in a rise in the cost of food and other necessities, mentioning specifically the purchase tax increases and the February cuts in food subsidies. Taking a positive line, the General Council then suggested that the April Budget "should make its contribution towards lowering the prices of necessities wherever possible"—a clear hint for the restoration of food subsidies—and could further help "people in the lower ranges of income" by raising the income tax exemption limit and increasing child allowances.

Reporting on their conversations with the Government at about the same time, the Federation of British Industries likewise observed that its spokesmen "emphasized once again to the Prime Minister and his colleagues that the cure of inflation lay primarily in H. M. Government's hands." In the view of the F.B.I., however, the "heart of the economy's problem" was "the high level of public expenditure, entailing a corresponding high level of taxation and resultant distortion of the economy."[6] In consequence, "a sub-

<hr>

[5] T.U.C. *Report* 1956, p. 262.   [6] F.B.I. *Report* 1956, p. 3.

stantial reduction of Government expenditures in all forms would
be the biggest single contribution they could make" toward
curbing inflation. This was, according to the F.B.I., the first of the
"two overriding factors" that governed "the ability of industry to
respond" to the Government's appeal. A second was "the need for
the policies and actions of the nationalized industries to coincide
with those sought from private industry."

The two peak organizations of producers had presented their
diametrically opposed conditions for a bargain, and in its April
budget the Government made its choice. Food subsidies were not
extended; on the contrary, the remaining subsidy on bread was
eliminated. Minor increases were made in family allowances, but
the tobacco tax was also raised. The only important income tax
relief went not to industrial workers, but to self-employed persons
purchasing retirement annuities. As for profits, the taxes on un-
distributed and distributed profits were raised slightly. Economically, it was a "neutral" budget, involving no change in total
revenue, but slight changes within the total, mainly as incentives
to save. An important step was taken, however, when the Chancellor pledged a further reduction of 100 million pounds in
Government expenditure.

The General Council's reaction was sharply negative : the
budget "should have been used to make a contribution towards
lowering the prices of necessities."[7] This did not mean, however,
that organized business was yet ready for an agreement. Late in
June the Chancellor announced cuts totaling 76 million pounds
toward fulfilling his promise of a 100 million-pound reduction in
Government expenditure. These were to be achieved by changes
that included running down defense stocks and increasing charges
for school meals.[8] About the same time the second of the "two
overriding factors" governing "industry's ability to respond" was
dealt with when the boards of the nationalized industries announced that, subject to various provisos, prices of their goods and
services would be held steady for a substantial period. "At that
stage it appeared to the F.B.I.," continues its report, "that the time
had come when private industry could and should play a like part,
and jointly with the British Employers Confederation, the Association of British Chambers of Commerce and the National Union
of Manufacturers, the Federation urged upon industry the wisdom
and desirability of exercising restraint in price policy"—even

[7] T.U.C. *Report* 1956, p. 264.   [8] *Economist*, June 30, 1956, p. 1259.

though this meant that "an exceptional risk" to profits must be accepted.[9] The statement was issued to the press on July 12th, at which time the B.E.C. also called for wage restraint as part of the common effort to hold down costs and prices.

The Government hoped for a cooperative response from the trade unions.[1] But although it continued its discussions with them during the following weeks, the hoped-for response was not forthcoming and at the Trade Union Congress in early September a resolution rejecting wage restraint was passed "with a great roar of approval."[2] The Government's attempt to negotiate an agreement with the unions had proved to be a total failure. In the following months, weekly wage rates continued their rapid rise. From 100 in January, the index rose to 106 in December 1956, and to 112 in December 1957.[3]

Perhaps no Government, Labour or Conservative, could have made an offer that would have induced the unions to accept wage restraint. Our question, however, is to compare Conservative action with what the evidence suggests that Labour would have been ready to do. The Conservatives, we may note, did achieve a "price plateau." Between July 17th and September 18th the retail price index rose only one tenth of a point. Indeed, between April and September there was a slight decline. It is impossible to say exactly how far this was due to the "cooperation" of organized business and how far to other factors, including the Government's restrictive policy. It is worth noting, however, that the plateau occurred between two periods of fairly steadily rising prices. Retail prices had risen sharply between February and April and then in mid-October resumed their climb.[4] Similarly, in the case of wholesale prices, while the index was a bit less steady, there was a plateau, the indices for such classic "administered price" industries as iron and steel and chemicals, for instance, showing virtually no change during the summer months.[5]

The behavior of prices during the critical period, in short, is

[9] F.B.I. *Report* 1956, p. 4, and statement issued to the press, July 12th. See also F.B.I. *Review* (August, 1956), p. 18.

[1] *Economist*, July 14, 1956, p. 109.

[2] *Annual Register, 1956*, p. 47.

[3] Tab. 148, *Annual Abstract of Statistics, 1958*. Central Statistical Office (London, H.M.S.O., 1958).

[4] Tab. 152 and 153, *Monthly Digest of Statistics*. No. 132 (December, 1956). Tab. 349, *Annual Abstract of Statistics, 1958*.

[5] Tab. 155, *Monthly Digest of Statistics, op. cit.*

consistent with the hypothesis that business firms on a wide front voluntarily followed the advice of their peak organizations. Although for a much shorter period, organized business in the summer of 1956 showed as great a capacity for unified decision-making and action as organized labor had shown under the wage-restraint bargain negotiated by Cripps. Nor, it may be added, was 1956 a year of soaring profits. On the contrary, net trading profits of companies showed a slight decline after several years of increase, while wages and salaries in all areas rose substantially, as did wages in manufacturing industry alone.[6]

What the Government would not do, however, was to respond wholeheartedly to the unions' suggestions for welfare and tax concessions.[7] Far from increasing subsidies, it proceeded to reduce those that remained on housing, bread and milk, and school meals. As a result, the price plateau, while impressive, was not backed up by the kind of assurance of Government action to hold down the price of necessities and protect the material well-being of organized workers that the unions might reasonably have expected to get from a Labour Government. From the autumn budget of 1955, criticism of this aspect of Conservative policy was one of the two main prongs of the Labour Party's attack on the Government. The first was on the Government's "doctrinaire" attachment to free enterprise and its refusal to use controls, especially building licensing and import controls.[8] The second was on the inequity of its social policy—"the sacrifice of social justice to self-interest"[9] —which raised the cost of necessities, especially food, and therefore stimulated wage demands.[1] It is relevant to recall that in 1949 Cripps, although deeply committed to the program of fiscal disinflation, had allowed food subsidies, already standing at 400

[6] Tab. 16 and 17, *National Income and Expenditure, 1963.*
[7] These suggestions were not made for the first time in 1955 and 1956. As Roberts notes, the T.U.C. had from 1951 "urged the Government to reduce the cost of living by increasing subsidies and reducing purchase tax on consumer essentials," *op. cit.,* p. 151.
[8] See, for instance, Harold Wilson, 545 *H.C. Deb.* 544 (28 October 1955); Herbert Morrison, 545 *H.C. Deb.* 698 (31 October 1955); Harold Wilson, 549 *H.C. Deb.* 74 (4 February 1956); Douglas Jay and Hugh Gaitskell, 549 *H.C. Deb.* 208 and 319 (21 February 1956).
[9] 1956 LPCR, p. 56.
[1] See, for instance, Hugh Gaitskell, 545 *H.C. Deb.* 404-5 (27 October 1955); Douglas Jay and Hugh Gaitskell, 549 *H.C. Deb.* 206 and 358 (21 February 1956); Harold Wilson, 551 *H.C. Deb.* 1029 (18 April 1956).

million pounds, to rise to 485 million pounds in order to hold down food prices and preserve the wage-restraint bargain of the previous year. I do not mean that the Conservatives ought to have promised to do precisely the same. I mention the comparison only to illustrate the kind of assurance the unions might have expected to get from a Labour Government but which the Conservatives would not and did not give them.

Organized labor, to be sure, was only one of the great producer groups with whom the Government was trying to arrive at an agreement. Commitments to welfare expenditure of a kind and magnitude sufficient to satisfy the unions would very probably have wrecked the Government's chances of negotiating a bargain with organized business. The F.B.I. had enjoyed only modest success in its lobbying efforts of the previous few years and now, put in a position where its cooperation as an organized producer group was necessary for the execution of the Government's plans, it firmly used its new-found leverage to obtain concessions. Increased food subsidies would hardly have hastened the announcement of July 12th. Admittedly, then, the Government's choice was not easy. The point is that it was a choice, and a distinctively different one, from what Labour would have made.

The Deflationary Alternative

Given this choice and the subsequent failure of a wage-restraint bargain, a second and more ostensible choice in policy followed. That choice consisted in a turn to the alternative that Eden had ruled out as "politically not tolerable," namely, a policy of deflation severe enough to create a level of unemployment that would limit wage claims. Throughout its negotiations of 1955 and 1956 the Government had maintained its commitment to "full employment" in that special sense which the expression had come to have under Labour and which meant that an unemployment rate much over 1 per cent was a signal for remedial action. Echoing Churchill's words in the manifesto of 1950, one could still regard "the maintenance of full employment as the first aim of a Conservative Government." Sometime in 1957—it would seem toward the middle of the year—the priorities shifted and price stability was given the highest place, even at the expense of a level of unemployment substantially greater than that tolerated by either Labour or the Conservatives during the previous decade.

The course of events needs to be only briefly sketched. From late 1956 the restrictive policy was slightly relaxed and Thorneycroft's budget of April 1957 gave only a "mild stimulus" to consumption[2] in the form of tax reliefs totaling 98 million pounds. Wages, however, continued upward. In the late spring, again sounding the inflationary alarm, the Chancellor renewed certain restrictive measures, and during the summer gave instructions that "a study should be made in the Treasury of the possibility of bringing about a measure of deflation in the economy."[3] A severe attack on sterling precipitated action in the form of a bank rate of 7 per cent, a "request" to the banks to hold advances to the average level of the preceding year, and further reductions in the public investment programs. The Government was determined to beat inflation, the Chancellor told the House. And, he added, "it is clear that we must sacrifice other ends of policy to secure that aim."[4] Unemployment, whose rise had been checked slightly in the spring, again began to climb in late summer and continued upward for the next year and a half.

In February the Cohen Council, which had been appointed to study prices, productivity, and the level of incomes reported this development with equanimity. Noting that unemployment had risen to 1.8 per cent in the previous month, it observed that "no one should be surprised or shocked if it proves necessary that it should go somewhat further."[5] About the same time, a new Chancellor, Heathcoat Amory, again affirmed that to strengthen the pound and to achieve price stability were "the dominating aims of the Government's economic policies and nothing whatever will take precedence over them."[6] In May unemployment in Britain reached 448,000, or 2.1 per cent of the work force.[7] In 1953, it will be recalled, a substantially smaller figure had called forth remedial action by the Chancellor. But Heathcoat Amory's budget of April 1958 made no significant concessions to expansion and in

[2] Worswick and Ady, op. cit., p. 48.

[3] Bank Rate Tribunal, Proceedings with Minutes of Evidence (London, 1958), Q. 10570 (Sir Roger Makins, Joint Permanent Secretary of the Treasury).

[4] 575 H.C. Deb. 47 (29 October 1957).

[5] Council on Prices, Productivity and Incomes. First Report (London, H.M.S.O., 1958), para. 135.

[6] Quoted in Economist, January 11, 1958, p. 89.

[7] Tab. 29, Monthly Digest of Statistics (June, 1959).

his speech he deliberately recognized that unemployment might well increase still further.[8]

It did. Rising to 621,000 in January 1959, the unemployment rate at that time reached 2.8 per cent of the total work force, the highest figure since the war.[9] The rise in unemployment was paralleled by a declining demand for labor, the number of unfilled vacancies falling from 380,000 in March 1956 to 181,000 in March 1959.[1] At the same time, the index of weekly wage rates, while it continued to mount, slacked off substantially in comparison with its previous steep climb. In 1956 it had risen seven points; in 1958 it rose only four.[2] At the end of the latter year, the *Economist* could approvingly comment that although December was traditionally the month when the unions pushed forward their most favored claims, in this December, with only a few exceptions, "all is quiet on the wages front."[3] Wholesale prices were also subdued. The index of manufactured products, which had risen sharply in 1956, leveled off in 1957 and from January 1958 to January 1959 rose by less than one point.[4]

The shift of priorities in Conservative economic policy, it hardly need be said, was no revolution. Toleration of a 2.8 per cent rate of unemployment was not a major attack on welfarism. Compared with American experience or with the expectations of Keynesians during the war, it could be considered an index of a most satisfactory condition of full employment. Moreover, the deflationary policy of 1957–58 was not permitted to trench on Conservative priorities for the social services. This was in essence the issue over which Thorneycroft resigned in January 1958. The amount involved was not vast—some 50 million pounds. But adherence to Thorneycroft's proposals—which he called a matter of "principle" —that estimates for the coming year be held to the level actually spent in the previous year could, as R. A. Butler said at the time, have overturned "in the course of a few days, policies in social welfare to which some of us have devoted our lives."[5]

But the character of the choices in economic and social policy

---

[8] *Economist*, April 19, 1958, p. 189.
[9] Tab. 29, *Monthly Digest of Statistics* (June, 1959).
[1] *Ibid.*, Tab. 33.
[2] *Ibid.*, Tab. 161.
[3] December 27, 1958, p. 1140.
[4] Tab. 166, *Monthly Digest of Statistics* (June, 1959).
[5] Speech to his constituents the day after Thorneycroft's resignation. Quoted in Worswick and Ady, *op. cit.*, p. 58.

made by Conservative Governments between 1956 and 1958 is quite clear. And while we may wish to say that the differences from what Labour would have done are only marginal, it cannot be denied that these differences are distinctive and reflect contrasting conceptions of the common good. With a touch of melodrama, Andrew Shonfield wrote that in 1957 the Conservative Party "had reverted (it is to be hoped temporarily) to the worship of its primitive idols." The objectives of the new policy, in his view, were not economic, but rather social: "stability was an end in itself, the condition for an orderly society with a hierarchy of relationships that were comfortable and fixed."[6]

CLASS AND CONSERVATISM

In examining these episodes of Conservative decision-making, we have considered the action of two elements : on the one hand, the action of organized producers, specifically labor and business, and on the other, the action of the Government or, in political terms, the Conservative leadership. While we have detected a distinctive party purpose in Conservative decisions, we have not, however, looked at the role of the party apart from its leadership. What was that role? To what extent was the leadership affected by the action of their backbenchers in Parliament and of the party in the country? This question not only rises out of our concern with the distribution of power in the party. It is also suggested by the Socialist interpretation of Conservatism. For if the Conservative Party is in some sense the party of the middle and upper classes, one might well expect its party organization to function as a main channel by which these classes brought influence to bear on the policy decisions of the leadership.

That Conservative backbenchers in Parliament and active members in the country are overwhelmingly from the middle and upper classes is too obvious to be greatly strengthened by quantitative study. One needs only to visit a party conference and spend some time in the Visitors' Gallery in the House, observing manners, dress, and accent. A rudimentary knowledge of English social differences will suffice to make plain the "class character" of Conservatism. The contrast with Labour delegates and M.P.'s, although they are by no means exclusively working class, only heightens the impression.

[6] *British Economic Policy Since the War*, rev. ed. (London, 1959), p. 248.

The Party Conference

"There they were," wrote the *Economist* of the Conservative conference of 1957, "—the clergyman's wife, the small employer, the retired service officer, the county lady—the softly respectable representatives of suburban and rural but not industrial England. The middle classes, they said and cheered themselves as they said it, are the backbone of the nation. . . ."[7] In the postwar period a good three quarters of what the public opinion analysts call the middle classes voted Conservative.[8] And while constituency parties might occasionally have a baronet (more likely his lady) among their active workers, it was from this middle stratum that they typically drew their officers and the "representatives" they sent to the annual conferences. Among the latter, industrial Britain was not entirely without a voice. A sprinkling of working-class accents was present, thanks in part to the strenuous efforts of the Trade Union section of the party organization. Noticeably absent, however, were "top people" from the ranks of employers and managers. At the Labour Party conference, the leaders of the major organized producers interest aligned with the party, the trade unions, were a conspicuous and often dominating element. But although the leaders of finance, industry, and commerce are no less partisan in their political preferences,[9] they played virtually no part in the public gatherings of the Conservative organization. Wealthy men still were a major source of party funds[1] and noblemen still adorned the conference platforms, but the main body of the four thousand or so delegates on the floor was no more than solid middle class.

Because of this peculiarity of its composition, the Conservative conference, even if it were permitted by the party statutes, could

[7] October 19, 1957, p. 1957.

[8] For a summary of the postwar voting pattern, see table compiled by Dr. Mark Abrams and quoted in Butler and Rose, *op. cit.*, p. 10.

[9] John Bonham found that in 1951 the "top business section," consisting of 140,000 sole proprietors and 180,000 directors, general managers, and other top administrators, voted 10 to 1 for the Conservatives as compared with Labour. *The Middle Class Vote* (London, 1954), p. 138.

[1] Frank C. Newman, "Money and Elections Law in Britain—Guide for America?," *Western Political Quarterly*, Vol. X, No. 3 (September, 1957), pp. 590–1, 596–8; S. E. Finer, "The Political Power of Private Capital," *Sociological Review*, new ser., Vol. IV, No. 1 (July, 1956), p. 6; William B. Gwyn, *Democracy and the Cost of Politics in Britain* (London, 1962), pp. 240–5.

not seriously advance a claim to a role in party policy-making comparable to that asserted by the Labour Party conference. As representatives of the party workers in the constituencies, however, delegates did have a claim on the party leaders. Moreover, they could also warn of the grievances felt by the millions of middle-class voters whom the delegates resembled in occupation, social status, and outlook. In short, the potential for a "middle class revolt" was present, and between 1955 and 1958 there was reason to think it might materialize.

In the latter months of 1955, after the "credit squeeze" had been inaugurated, the Conservatives' popularity, as measured by the Gallup Poll, fell below that of Labour, where it stayed until it began an unsteady recovery in the latter part of 1958.[2] By-elections conformed to this trend, showing a sharp swing away from the Conservatives.[3] Various patterns of voting behavior accounted for these reverses, but beginning with the Tonbridge by-election of June 1956, when the Conservative majority fell by some nine thousand votes in a strongly Conservative suburban constituency, the major reason was clearly large-scale abstentions. Many observers took these abstentions to be the expression of mounting discontent among the middle classes—"the Government's naturally most loyal supporters," in the words of the *Economist*.[4] And such was the warning lesson drawn from them by many delegates as they assailed the Government with increasing sharpness at the conferences of 1955, 1956, and 1957.

The rhetoric of these utterances matched, for class consciousness and class antagonism, any of the more extravagant outbursts by champions of the working class at Labour conferences. The Roman Empire had fallen, one lady delegate reminded the conference, because the middle classes were "crushed out."[5] "And," she continued, "remember what Viscount Hailsham said last Saturday night, that Christian culture was brought into this country by St. Augustine and St. Columba and should be the foundation of our national life. And how are we going to carry on that Christian culture if you are to strangle the middle classes—the creative artists?"

[2] Butler and Rose, *op. cit.*, p. 40.
[3] *Ibid.*, Appendix 6.
[4] June 16, 1956, p. 1077.
[5] This and the following quotations are taken from Official Reports of the Conservative conferences of 1955, 1956, and 1957.

The theme was developed by many speakers. The middle classes —the "harassed middle classes"—were the "backbone" of the country, "the guardians of this country's culture." Their virtues were to be "thrifty," "hard-working," "responsible," and yet "their standards of living have plummeted down over the past 15 years." In contrast, "a lot of our working people" have shown a "lack of responsibility" and through the power of their trade unions have been able to "repeatedly blackmail and coerce their employers into granting wage increases." Hence, "the root cause of inflation and the rising cost of living is rising wages with no rise in productivity." "I wonder," mused a delegate, "can it be that we are slowly reverting to the law of the jungle where might is right and where the one who snarls the loudest collars the choicest pickings? For that, to me, seems to be the precise object of some of our trade union leaders."

But while trade unions and working people were the principal objects of attack, from time to time resentment was also directed against "those privileged people on the management side who draw the minimum taxable salary, but receive the maximum non-taxable allowances." It was not the grievances of managers and executives or of big business that were voiced at these conferences, but rather those of "the bank employees, the smaller barristers, teachers, shop managers and . . . clerical workers" and especially of "the fixed income group," such as "old age pensioners, retired civil servants, retired bank officials, retired local government officials and business house pensioners." Understanding the term in this sense, delegates warned that "unless something is done for the middle classes they will abstain at the next general election and that will be a very bad day's work for us."

This wave of middle-class discontent, which can be traced not only in the speeches at conference, but also in resolutions submitted by constituency associations, rose sharply in 1955, persisted during the next two years, and by 1958 had subsided. Did it have any detectable influence on Government policy? Specifically, can we attribute to this pressure the Government's reluctance to accept the trade unions' terms for a wage-restraint bargain? There is no reason to think so. In the first place, although the Government was sharply criticized, the "rebels" were unable at any time to pass a resolution against the wishes of the platform, although some observers expected this to happen in both 1956 and 1957. Even a resolution urging the Government to do no more than pursue "a realistic economic policy which will stabilise the cost of living and also of wages" failed to win a majority.[6]

Although conference, as ever, called in general terms for a reduction of Government expenditure and of taxation, virtually no word was uttered against the Welfare State and its growing expenditures. Indeed, in the critical year of 1956, when the Government was reducing food subsidies, it presided over an increase in welfare expenditure of some 200 million pounds.[7] To be sure, these increases, as ministers took care to remind conference, for the most part followed automatically from existing legislation in such fields as retirement pensions, the health service, and education. But it was not beyond the Government's power, as in 1932, to take the legislative steps necessary to restrain them. The Conservative leaders, however, did not choose to do so, nor did the middle-class rebels of conference ask them to.

But what is perhaps most significant is the fact that the spokesmen for the middle classes did not by any means call for a hard-nosed, out-and-out policy of deflation. On the contrary, the "credit squeeze" was vigorously assailed and tax relief was demanded, the emphasis falling almost exclusively on incomes below surtax level. The surtax changes of 1957 did not meet this demand and the income tax reliefs of 1956 were minor. In general, the course of Government policy was hardly at all affected by the pressures of conference.

Backbenchers

The "class character" of Conservative backbenchers was even more pronounced than that of the conference. In the House elected in 1955, the Conservative side could claim an M.P. who at the time of his election was a working electrician, Mr. Ray Mawby of Totnes, "perhaps the first Conservative to have entered the House of Commons directly from a manual occupation."[8] Otherwise, the two parties in Parliament continued to display much the same contrasts in the social status and economic interests

[6] 1956 CPCR, pp. 65 and 76.
[7] Tabs. 35 and 43, National Income and Expenditure, 1960; and I. D. M. Little, Fiscal Policy in Worswick and Ady, op. cit., Tab. 9, pp. 299–300.
[8] David E. Butler, The British General Election of 1955 (London, 1955), p. 44.

of their members that had been remarked for a generation. As usual, the most striking contrasts were in the fields of business where Conservatives led by 101 to 34 and of manual work where Labour led by 97 to 1.[9]

These figures pertain to all M.P.'s. Our concern, however, is with the relation of Conservative backbenchers to their leadership; and thanks to a study by Professor Finer and his colleagues we have an analysis of the social composition of the former body during the later 1950's.[1] Classified on the basis of occupation, these 270 Conservative backbenchers comprised the following groups: Business, 60 per cent; Farmers, 8 per cent; Professions, 22 per cent; and Miscellaneous, 9 per cent. In the business group, which comprised some 163 of the 270 M.P.'s studied, 88 were directors of public companies, while 58 were directors of private companies, a distinction that corresponds very roughly to the division between big business and medium or small business.[2] Classified on the basis

[9] *Ibid.*, p. 43. The contrast in social and economic status between the two parliamentary parties elected in 1955 can be seen in this summary of the tables compiled by Butler, *op. cit.*, pp. 42–43. For a detailed account, person by person, of the business connections of M.P.'s in the Parliament elected in 1959, see Andrew Roth, *The Business Background of Members of Parliament* (London, 1963). For an excellent general discussion, see W. L. Guttsman, *The British Political Elite* (London, 1963), Chap. X, "Leadership in the Conservative Party."

Occupation	Conservative	Labour
Professions	159	100
Business	101	34
Workers	1	97
Misc.	83	46
Totals	344	277
Oxford/Cambridge	182	46
Public School	260	62
Eton	78	4

[1] S. E. Finer, H. B. Berrington, and D. J. Bartholomew, *Backbench Opinion in the House of Commons 1955–59* (Oxford, 1961), Chap. 3, "The Conservative Party."

[2] *Ibid.*, pp. 22 and 80. Finer's comparison between Labour and Conservative backbenchers on the basis of occupation is as follows:

Occupation	Conservative (in %)	Labour (in %)
Business	60	10
Farmers	8	—
Workers	—	33
Professions	22	31
Misc.	9	26

of education, the best single index to social status, Conservative backbenchers included 199, or 74 per cent of the total, who had attended public schools, nearly half of these having gone to the exclusive Clarendon schools. University graduates comprised 62 per cent, Oxford and Cambridge alone claiming 50 per cent.

These summary data confirm what many studies of the social and economic composition of the parliamentary party as a whole have shown again and again over the years. With regard to the economic interests represented by Conservative M.P.'s, however, one further point may be mentioned. For among them one finds not only the "interested M.P." who, as in the nineteenth century, was connected with the world of business by ties of ownership or management, but also members who were linked with business organizations, usually trade associations. For the sake of illustrating the wide variety of associations involved, some examples from the House elected in 1955 may be mentioned. Taking only those who were past or present officers, or members of governing bodies, one finds the following associations represented by one or more M.P.'s : the Association of British Chambers of Commerce, the International Chambers of Commerce, the British Empire Chambers of Commerce, the National Union of Manufacturers, the National Farmers Union, the British Iron and Steel Federation, the British Empire Producers' Organization, the Society of Motor Manufacturers and Traders, the National Tyre Distributors Association, the British Medical Association, the Institute of Bankers, the Road Passenger and Transport Association, the Parliamentary Committee of the Empire Industries Association, the National Sheep Breeders Association, the National Dairymen's Association, the Scottish Landowners Federation, the National Association of Municipal Grocers, the Federation of Master Cotton Spinners' Associations, the Caterers Association, the Press Association, the Newspaper Society, the Residential Hotels Association, the Council of British Hotels and Restaurants Association, the Westminster Chamber of Commerce, the Leeds Chamber of Commerce, and so on.[3]

The point need not be labored : if the middle and upper classes or the owners and managers of business were looking for M.P.'s drawn from their own ranks, they could hardly have asked for more adequate representation on the Conservative backbenches.

[3] Data from *The Times House of Commons, 1955* (London, 1955).

Moreover, if backbenchers wished to serve these economic and class interests, they had at hand new structures of organization that could be used for the purpose. Party unity, always comparatively high among Conservatives, had risen in the present century to the point at which cross-voting was almost unknown. But as the party in this respect had grown outwardly more monolithic and the outward appearance of its leaders' power correspondingly greater, an inner transformation had taken place. Beginning after World War I, a framework of organs had been elaborated through which backbenchers had acquired the opportunity to consult regularly with the leadership on questions of policy. The 1922 Committee, formed after the election of that year, was intended, in the words of one of its founders, to be "a rein upon the leaders," who, it was felt, had led the party astray in the period of Coalition under Lloyd George.[4] At first, exclusively a backbenchers' organ, communicating with the leadership through the traditional Whips, the Committee in time drew the leaders into a quite close relationship, in the 1950's the Leader himself often appearing before it, even though he was Prime Minister.

In the interwar period, as before, backbenchers had from time to time formed *ad hoc* committees of M.P.'s interested in some branch of policy, such as foreign affairs, social policy, or agriculture.[5] In 1946 a comprehensive system of functional committees, which covered the major fields of public policy and which reported to the 1922 Committee, had been established.[6] While these committees were headed by members of the Shadow Cabinet if the party was in Opposition, when it took power, they, like the 1922 Committee, elected their own officers. Before them also, although again only at the invitation of the committee, ministers frequently appeared to explain and, if necessary, to defend their policies. While formal votes were not taken, Whips attended and the chairman interpreted the sense of the meeting to the leadership. The committees had staff assistance from the Conservative Re-

[4] Author's interview with Mr. Walter Elliot, M.P. (Cons.) 1918–45 and 1946–58.

[5] W. Ivor Jennings reports that while the Conservatives were in Opposition in 1924 and 1929–31, some of the committees that backbenchers had created on their own initiative were converted into "semi-official Opposition committees," while other committees were formed, with the result that "each Department of government had facing it a committee of Opposition members." *Parliament* (Cambridge, Eng., 1948), pp. 168–9.

[6] Finer *et al.*, *Backbench Opinion*, p. 3.

search Department and frequently met with representatives of organized interest groups to discuss current questions of policy. Considering the opportunities this framework gave backbenchers to concert action and to assert their views, one might conclude that the ordinary M.P., deprived increasingly of his independence in voting, had sought to right the balance somewhat by demanding a greater voice in the decisions to which he would be bound by the stringent requirements of party unity.

These committees were the scene of much activity. Groups of backbenchers that were formed to urge a particular view on the leadership—such as the One Nation group or the Suez group—at times used these committees to forward their views. Moreover, M.P.'s who had a special concern with a certain field because of their occupation or membership in an outside organization often devoted particular attention to the functional committee covering that field. Active businessmen, for instance, were particularly prominent in the Trade and Industry Committee, while teachers took much interest in the Education Committee, and farmers and rural landowners in the Agriculture Committee. In any case, whether through this committee system or by other means, backbenchers did from time to time force the Government to make changes of policy. "Over and over," wrote one Conservative M.P. and ex-minister with reference to the 1950's, "I have seen cases where the Government were forced to swallow their pride and to back down on some issue under the pressure of backbench action. . . ."[7]

There is no doubt that backbenchers had the opportunity to exert pressure on the Government, that they frequently attempted to do so and from time to time succeeded. The question is : How much significance should we attach to this activity? To what extent was backbench opinion responsible for important features of Government policy? The privacy shrouding the meetings of backbench committees and the relations of backbenchers and ministers makes this a hard question to answer with precision. But informed observers have reported a number of cases of successful pressure on Government economic policy. Even if we run the risk of exaggerating the degree of backbench influence by accepting these reports as correct, the instances to which they refer qualify as no more than minor concessions.

[7] Enoch Powell, "1951–59 : Labour in Opposition," *Political Quarterly*, Vol. XXX, No. 4 (October-December, 1959), p. 336.

Three examples taken from the years with which we are particularly concerned will illustrate the point. In 1955 the Minister of Agriculture, Fisheries, and Food backed down on a proposed reduction of the White Fish subsidy. The reason, it appears, was that he found not only the Labour Party opposing the reduction because it harmed "the small man," but also a number of his own backbenchers. A meeting of Conservative M.P.'s from the fishery constituencies with the minister was highly critical, some even threatening to defy the Whips and vote against the statutory order making the reduction. As a result, the minister withdrew the order and issued a new one, which changed the proposal to the extent of restoring half the cut originally proposed for the smaller vessels.[8]

In 1957 the Government withdrew the clauses of the Electricity Bill of that year, which would have given the Central Electricity Authority power to manufacture electrical plant. The Monopoly Commission had reported that private manufacturers made a practice of fixing prices of such equipment, and the clauses in the bill were intended to enable the public corporation to act if prices were fixed against it. Pressure centering in the Conservative Fuel and Power Committee, according to the *Economist*, caused the minister to accept arguments he had previously rejected and to "surrender" to backbench demands.[9]

Another instance that was widely commented on arose in the same year during the course of the passage of the Government's controversial Rents bill. Under Clause 9, some 800,000 tenants renting properties at over £30 a year (£40 in London and Scotland)—in short, "middle class" rents—were to have their rents decontrolled six months after the passing of the bill. The Labour Party opposed this clause along with the whole of the bill. But in addition, a number of Conservative backbenchers were uneasy, and a group of about a dozen put down an amendment postponing decontrol for five years. After some hesitation, the minister responded by extending the period from six to fifteen months.[1]

This incident took place in February 1957, while middle-class discontent was in full flood, massive abstentions at the North Lewisham by-election only a few days earlier having cost the

[8] S. E. Finer, *Anonymous Empire* (London, 1958), p. 64.

[9] *Economist*, April 6, 1957, p. 64.

[1] *Economist*, January 19, 1957, p. 185; January 26, 1957, p. 272; February 23, 1957, p. 624; and Finer, *Anonymous Empire*, p. 70.

Conservatives a seat, the first such loss not only by this Government but by any Government since 1939. As the reverses continued, discontent grew on the back-benches, with complaints in the field of economic policy focusing on mounting demands for a "middle class budget."[2] Writing under the heading "A Budget to Turn the Tide?," one of Britain's most experienced political journalists reported that in response to "the demand for immediate concessions to the middle classes" among backbenchers,

the signs are multiplying that Ministers are going to make concessions—not next year or some time or never, but in the April budget. It may be that they no longer have a choice. From now on Mr. Ted Heath, the Chief Whip, is going to be told that a tough Budget will split the Party.[3]

Anticipating the budget, the T.U.C. asked for purchase tax reliefs and the F.B.I. saw the need for early action to stimulate the economy. When the budget came, however, far from being designed to stimulate the economy, it was regarded as restraining demand by some 100 to 150 million pounds more than in the previous fiscal year;[4] and far from making concessions to middle class incomes below £2000 as asked by backbenchers, it gave its main relief to surtax payers, roughly the business executive class. After this rebuff, what then happened on the back-benches? A few weeks after the budget, the journalist who had previously seen signs of concessions or a party split found that, although the swing against the Government continued in the constituencies, the morale of the parliamentary party was "higher than at any time since Mr. Macmillan became Premier." Conservative backbenchers, he reported, had "absolute trust in their beloved leader. . . . At the moment there is nothing the Prime Minister cannot do with his followers."[5] Middle-class protests, although actively taken up by M.P.'s, had hardly any more success through this channel of influence than through conference.

When the relations of the Conservative parliamentary party with the National Union are being discussed, it is often said that

---

[2] *Economist*, March 16, 1957, pp. 885 and 895.
[3] Hugh Massingham, "Political Diary," *The Observer*, March 10, 1957.
[4] So it was interpreted by the *Economist*, April 13, 1957, p. 107.
[5] Massingham, *The Observer*, April 28 and May 12.

the parliamentary party is "dominant." This is fair enough. But to be able to say that Conservative M.P.'s have more influence by far than conference delegates does not entitle us to overlook the crucial differences in the role of the backbenchers and the role of the leadership within the parliamentary party.

Backbenchers have frequently played a very important part in the selection and removal of the Leader and at times their revolts have badly shaken his tenure.[6] At first glance it would seem that to have power of this kind and in this degree would open the way for backbenchers to a major role in policy-making. So large a part in granting and revoking the Leader's authority must constitute, it would seem, a sanction for effectively influencing what he does with that authority. Yet in Tory theory this conclusion does not follow : so long as one is a leader it is one's right and duty to lead. This rule is expressed most sharply in the norm that policy decisions are the prerogative of the Leader. But it also applies to the party leadership as a whole. This body under its Leader may take counsel as widely as it chooses within the party and outside the party. But it is expected to act on its "independent judgment."

We know that in fact the leadership will not only hold consultations, but also make concessions. As a rule, however, these concessions are not of major importance. Over the years, whether the party was in power or in opposition, the Conservative backbenchers have not exercised significant control over major aspects of Conservative policy. In the aftermath of Suez a Conservative backbencher gave a judicious summary of the relationship. He granted that there was "action and interaction." "Members are affected in varying degrees by the criticisms of their constituents. This in turn affects the nature of internal discussions within the party which in their turn affect the views and outlook of the Executive." Sometimes there is danger of the extremists becoming "pace-makers." Against this danger the "real safeguard" is "the resolution of the Prime Minister, backed by his Cabinet, in major matters to heed only the national interest and to disregard party and personal pressures." And in fact this backbencher found that the problem of the relation of the party and the leadership was "normally dealt with by a combination of consultation and minor concession on the one hand, and on the other by firm resolution

[6] R. T. McKenzie, *British Political Parties* (London, 1955), *passim.*

to stand by Cabinet decisions objectively reached on issues of major importance."[7]

On the one hand, he perceived leaders who consult closely with their followers and concede to them on minor points; on the other hand, he perceived followers who give their loyal support and confidence to their leaders, except in the rare and extreme case when they feel that these leaders no longer merit that confidence and must be replaced. It would be hard to ask for a better statement of ancient Tory doctrine as applied to modern political practice.

The Leadership

The strong continuance of Toryism in the Conservative Party is confirmed not only by the distribution of power between leaders and followers, but also by the social composition of the leadership. Our previous account has indicated the considerable "social distance" between the members of the party conference and the parliamentary party. Moreover, within the parliamentary party there was in the 1950's, as in earlier generations, a marked gap in social status between the backbenchers and the leaders. Of the Eden Cabinet of 1955, for instance, two thirds had been to a "Clarendon" school as compared with only slightly more than one third among backbenchers between 1955 and 1959.[8] The touchstone of Eton suggests an even wider distinction. Among 1955–59 backbenchers, slightly more than 18 per cent had been at Eton, but in the Cabinet formed in 1955, the figure was over 55 per cent—fully ten of the eighteen members. Furthermore, we may note that not only were four of the Cabinet in the House of Lords, but also of the remaining fourteen in the House of Commons, ten were directly related to noble families.[9]

Backbenchers themselves sometimes professed to be puzzled by this gap. One former Conservative M.P., having noted that the

[7] Letter from W. S. Shepherd, M.P., to *The Observer*, January 6, 1957.
[8] Data on Cabinet based on *The Times House of Commons, 1955*. For backbenchers, see Finer *et al.*, *Backbench Opinion*, pp. 77–8. The "Clarendon" schools are the nine great public schools singled out for inquiry by the Clarendon Commission of 1861–64: Eton, Winchester, Westminster, Charterhouse, St. Paul's, Merchant Taylor's, Harrow, Rugby and Shrewsbury. They are the most prestigious of the public schools.
[9] P. A. Bromhead, *The House of Lords and Contemporary Politics* (London, 1958), p. 42.

cult of "inequalitarianism" among English voters makes the social composition of the Conservative membership of the House "radically different" from that of Conservative voters, then found himself puzzled by the further question : "Why are Conservative Ministers so unrepresentative of the Conservative Members?"[1] He could only give as an answer the personal taste of the then Prime Minister, Mr. Macmillan. If so, it was a personal taste that had been shared by many Conservative Leaders before him, as the social gap between front- and back-bench was anything but recent in origin. If, for instance, the Cabinet of 1955 seems exceptional in its preference for Etonians, we should consider the fact that of all Conservative Cabinet ministers between 1918 and 1955, precisely 56.7 per cent had been at Eton.[2] Figures for backbenchers alone are not readily available, but the disparity between front- and back-bench is clear from the fact that, from 1918 through 1951, only about one fourth of all Conservative M.P.'s were Etonians.[3] The figures for 1955 were almost exactly the same : Etonians in the Cabinet, 55.5 per cent; Etonians among all Conservative M.P.'s, 23 per cent.[4] By the 1950's, to be sure, the hold of the aristocracy over office in the Conservative Party had slacked off a bit from what it had been in the nineteenth century, and while about half of Balfour's Cabinet of 1902 had been aristocratic, by the 1950's the proportion was down to about one fourth.[5] Over the years, however, a substantial social gap between the leadership and backbenchers had been as prominent a feature of the Conservative Party as the fact, more frequently commented on, of wide social distance between M.P.'s and Conservative voters.

Distinguished from its followers by superior social status, yet engaging in continuous "parley" with them, the Conservative

[1] Christopher Hollis, "The Conservative Party in History," *Political Quarterly*, Vol. XXXII, No. 3 (July-September, 1961), p. 223.

[2] Philip W. Buck, *Amateurs and Professionals in British Politics 1918–1959* (Chicago, 1963), p. 121.

[3] J. F. S. Ross, *Parliamentary Representation*, 2nd ed. (London, 1948), p. 255, and *Elections and Electors* (London, 1955), p. 417.

[4] Data on Cabinet based on *The Times House of Commons, 1955*. For all M.P.'s, see Butler, *General Election of 1955*, p. 42.

[5] See above, Ch. IX, and Harry Eckstein, "The British Political System," in Beer and Ulam, eds., *Patterns of Government : The Major Political Systems of Europe*, 2nd ed. (New York, 1962), pp. 121–2, 195; and W. L. Guttsman, *The British Political Elite* (London, 1963), pp. 95–96.

leadership in the postwar world, as in earlier generations, decided what the party would stand for and authoritatively spoke in its name and committed its energies. This body, itself hierarchically ordered around the Leader and intricately differentiated among various voices with unequal weights, was overwhelmingly the main locus of decision-making in the party—and that was the case whether the party was in power or in Opposition.

The Tory tradition thus gave the party chiefs wide authority to lead and to govern. It did not, however, leave them entirely without guidance as to how they should use that authority. For although there is no Conservative ideology, there is a Tory conception of purpose. With regard to crucial elements of the general social order, Toryism offers an old and powerful design. As we noted when examining Disraeli's thought, the two main themes in this design are inequality and security. In their concern for security, Conservatives and Socialists have a good deal in common. It is with regard to the question of equality–inequality, as Socialists continually assert, that the main contrast between the parties appears.

Right as they are in this perception, Socialists, however, make a mistake if they interpret this conflict to be concerned primarily with economic condition and the distribution of material goods. For Toryism's essential concern is with something much more important—the distribution of power. This concern is explicitly political in one form : the theory of Tory Democracy. But the basic Tory premise that any field of social activity necessitates inequality—that "order requires hierarchy"—gives Toryism a concern with the distribution of power in society generally. Private property is one form of power and, confronted with the Socialist attack, Conservatives have defended it. But the defense of hierarchy is not limited to private property or dependent upon its existence.

If, for instance, private property were abolished and the means of production, distribution, and exchange were taken over by the state, the question of how power was to be distributed in the society would still remain. It would need to be answered not only with regard to the conduct of government proper, but also with regard to all economic and social activities. Hence, there would still be an opportunity for the advocates of hierarchy to assert their claim. Indeed, if we accept Tory sociology, the necessities of social order would continue to require hierarchy and in that sense the ancient message of Toryism would be as relevant to a socialized society as it has been to a welfarist, capitalist, mercantilist, or indeed feudal society. In the Socialist Commonwealth, in short, Conservatism might well disappear, but Toryism would have the chance to make another of its Phoenix-like adaptations.

CONCLUSION

Political Ideas
and Political Behavior

In postwar Britain, the new group politics—the group politics of the period of Collectivism—came to maturity. Through an intricate system of bidding and bargaining, consumer and producer groups exercised major influence on public policy. At the same time, the ideological gap between the parties narrowed as Labour's retreat and the Conservatives' advance left the two parties occupying the common ground of the Welfare State and the Managed Economy. Along with this decline in ideology, class antagonism, as compared with the interwar period, also greatly subsided. Already in 1951 an American reporter could speak of the election campaign as "the lull before the lull." A little later R. T. McKenzie concluded that

the "agreement on fundamentals" is very nearly as great as it has ever been in the modern history of British parties. . . . Two monolithic structures now face each other and conduct furious arguments about the comparatively minor issues that separate them.[1]

Yet great moral ideas did continue to inform political conflict. The problem of describing British politics in this period is to do justice to both features: on the one hand, the powerful thrust of the new politics of group interest and, on the other, the continuing dynamic of ideas.

This clash of ideas persisted in two spheres. First, as I have argued, the social priorities of the Conservative Party, however much qualified by the compulsions of group politics, continued

[1] *British Political Parties* (London, 1955), pp. 581 and 586.

to be informed by an essential Toryism. In the Tory acceptance of the social goal of security and the political means of strong government, Conservatives had much in common with Socialists. But the Tory belief in economic and social inequality put a fundamental principle at issue between them and Labour. For however ambiguous Labour's commitment to the utopian goal of fellowship had become, British Socialism was at least "about equality." This conflict, moreover, was not simply a difference in moral preferences, nor a conflict merely of values. On each side the vision of what ought to be was integrated with views of what could be. For the Tory the principle of hierarchy involved not only a belief in social and economic inequality, but also a wide-ranging sociology of how human affairs must be managed if any hard and worthy task were to be accomplished. The sociology of the Socialist was radically opposed. For baffled as he may have often been by the practical tasks of democratizing economic planning, industry, education, and social relations generally, his fervent ideal remained the classless society.

Also, the conflict between the parties extended from these contrasting visions of the purposes of government to a deep-seated opposition over how the process of government in the broadest sense should be conducted. Not that the disagreement was total : on the contrary, both parties accepted the basic legal structures, the basic parliamentary conventions, and the main contemporary practices of party government and functional representation. Yet for all this agreement there was between Tory and Socialist a conflict over the meaning of the party system, the constitution, and democracy itself that one might well call fundamental. Conceivably this conflict, which I have examined as the contrast between Socialist Democracy and Tory Democracy, could have been purely theoretical, a set of ideological remnants or useful rationalizations, not in fact corresponding to the realities of the distribution of power in the respective parties. The verdict, however, of those chapters in which we examined for different times and contexts the respective processes of party policy-making was that behavior by and large corresponded closely with idea.

One of our themes was how Old Tory authoritarianism had adapted to successive waves of voluntarism and liberalism until finally there emerged that curious hybrid—contradictory in name, but operational in practice—Tory Democracy. Giving a large initiative to leaders and the largely passive function of control to followers, while joining to the modern idea of mass participation the older doctrines of independent authority, class rule, non-programmatic decisions, and strong government, this conception characterized with reasonable fidelity the mode of governance of a typical Conservative Government as well as the Conservative Party. On the other hand, insisting that not merely control, but also the initiative itself must in some real sense be exercised by the rank and file, the Socialist ideal of democracy sharply departed from the Tory.

One may well think that in the nature of men and society the Socialist is the harder ideal to achieve within a party, as within a political system (which is what Tories have always believed). The major test case in the period with which we are concerned is presented by the legislative program of the Labour Government of 1945–51. When one seriously asks where this program came from and how it achieved its authoritative place as a party commitment, one cannot avoid examining a long historical development that goes back to the party's very inception. Whatever may have been the actual role of that ultimate integer, the member of the rank and file, the vigorous group action of the party's components in this development demonstrates a degree of pluralistic democracy that is worlds apart from the elitism of the Conservatives. For good or ill, moreover, throughout its disordered 1950's, Labour continued to display its lack of a true elite and its obsessive commitment to intraparty democracy. I conclude that in practice as in theory, in the actual distribution of power as in their reigning conceptions of authority, the two parties were deeply opposed.

The influence of the new group politics on public policy was substantially conditioned by these conflicts of principle between the two major parties. But the role of ideas was not confined to defining the basic issues of party conflict. There was also a system of political values and beliefs that were peculiar to this Collectivist period and generally shared throughout the community. These ideas, as we have seen, legitimated party government by two purposive, strongly united, and elaborately organized parties— along with functional representation by similarly concentrated producers organizations. The reigning ideas of Collectivist politics also extended to a new and distinctive conception of public policy, which, differing not only from Liberal laissez faire but also from

Radical social reform, expressed the responsibility of the state for the welfare of the economy as a whole. The predominance of these ideas in the culture of the time meant that, within the political community, while there was division—and I mean sharp and significant division—there was also consensus.

In the behavior of not only parties, but also pressure groups, these Collectivist values and beliefs were institutionalized. Producers, whether workers or employers, for instance, generally agreed that organizational concentration was the proper and most effective means of carrying out their common business. Both producer organizations and government departments commonly expected that they ought to be joined in close and constant consultation. Moreover, the very interests themselves—"the self-oriented goals"—that these groups pursued in their political action were shaped by an acceptance of Collectivist perspectives. In short, what kinds of organization groups would adopt, what modes of political action they would follow, and what ends they would pursue were dependent upon the legitimating ideas of Collectivist politics. To recall these observations is merely to confirm again the assertion of the opening pages : Political culture is one of the main variables of a political system and a major factor explaining the political behavior of individuals, groups, and parties.[2] In Collectivist politics as in Old Tory, Old Whig, Liberal, and Radical politics, a distinctive system of political ideas informed the decisions of individuals and guided the behavior of their political formations.

To give such weight to ideas is not to overlook the role of the "blind forces" in history. One of our main concerns has been to detect the unanticipated consequences of reigning ideas of the Collectivist period. In particular, I have been concerned with how both the organizational concentration of parties and producer groups and the extension of the pattern of policy have often converted what was an intended process of mere advice and counsel into one of negotiating and bargaining. In conception, the practices of functional representation do not infringe on the sovereignty of Parliament; in fact, bargaining with major producer groups may at times lead to a kind of extra-parliamentary legislation. The possibilities of conflict in this relationship are real and continuing. They may, for instance, be heightened by that re-

[2] See above, p. x.

cently created agency of functional representation, the National Economic Development Council, where representatives of the two sides of industry meet directly with ministers to discuss such questions as economic growth. "If Neddy settled policy effectively," Lord Bridges has observed, "it would be taking a lot of power from Parliament . . . if Parliament insisted on settling economic policy Neddy would be rendered ineffective."[3]

Finally, it must be said that to emphasize the role of ideas is not to play down the fact of conflict in politics. I would indeed assert that a peaceful and orderly political process does require as an essential condition the presence of substantial consensus on values and beliefs in the political culture. In such a situation ideas have a powerful stabilizing effect on the system. Yet it is also ideas that can most violently disrupt a political community when they divide it over fundamental moral concerns and fail to provide a bridge of consensus. In quieter times it was possible to scoff at the notion that political man could be moved by "abstract ideals."[4] After experiencing the ravages of ideological passion in the recent past, however, we are hardly inclined to deny that, for good or ill, for peace or war, men's visions of legitimate authority and the common good have a dynamic and sometimes terrible power over their behavior. Happy the country in which consensus and conflict are ordered in a dialectic that makes of the political arena at once a market of interests and a forum for debate of fundamental moral concerns.

[3] *Crossbow*, Vol. VII, No. 25 (October-December, 1963), p. 27.
[4] See Charles Beard, *The Economic Origins of Jeffersonian Democracy* (New York, 1915), p. 3.

The Modernizing of British Politics

THE PROCESS OF MODERNIZATION

The term modernization is a question rather than an answer. The question is whether one can find in Western societies of recent centuries and in the process by which they arose a type or model that is useful for general comparative study and analysis. Following a well-trod path, I shall say that the key concept is rationalization.[1] By rationalization I mean the growth of scientific knowledge in a broad sense and the impact of this knowledge upon culture and social structure. By rationalism I mean the cultural foundations of this process—the beliefs and values defining and supporting the pursuit of scientific knowledge and its use to control the natural and social environment.

Knowledge has extended human control and enhanced the sense of human competence since men first made tools and established laws. In this sense, rationalism begins with man himself, Homo sapiens. It has, however, gone through many phases. Ancient and medieval men were not unaware of consequences and in their teleological inquiries sought knowledge of the laws of nature and society. Modernity, however, was produced by a special kind of knowledge, viz., knowledge that was not only systematically ordered, but also empirically founded. With appropriate qualifi-

[1] I am following, above all, Max Weber. I also found very helpful Talcott Parsons' statement, "Institutionalized Rationalization and 'Cultural Lag'," in *The Social System* (Glencoe, 1951), pp. 505–20.

cations we may call it scientific. We recognize that within this broad definition science has had various meanings and has been organized by different paradigms. We need to include in it much that was theoretically crude, such as the expanding folk technology of the early Industrial Revolution, or methodologically ambiguous, such as the political science of a Locke or Hobbes.

For the purposes of this present study, we also need to distinguish the highly developed science, both natural and social, of recent decades which is producing the "scientific revolution." This new stage of scientific and technological achievement has heightened the impact of rationalization, tending to produce a "post-industrial" society and possibly also a "post-collectivist" politics.[2] Especially in the trend to professionalization of economic and political activities, we find forces that promise to transform British politics.

Rationalism and Voluntarism

As the cultural basis of rationalization, modern rationalism has been a principal force producing directly and indirectly some of the main features of present-day society, such as industrialization and bureaucratization. Yet one must not try to make it explain too much. Major traits of the modern polity derive from other sources. With regard to attitudes and values, one of the most important sources has been voluntarism. By voluntarism I mean the view that human wishes are the basis of legitimacy in constitutional structure and in public policy. For contrast we may compare it with the classical and medieval notion that authority derives its moral force from some source outside the human will, such as divine command or a teleological order.

Rationalism, the notion that men have the ability scientifically to control nature and society, does not logically entail voluntarism, the notion that men ought to design their environment, natural and social, to suit their own purposes and wishes. Yet in the rise of political modernity, the two are closely associated. For in-

[2] I take the expression and idea of a "post-industrial society" from Daniel Bell. See his suggestive notes on this topic in *The Public Interest*, Nos. 6 and 7 (Winter and Spring, 1967).

stance, the conception of law-making which is central to modern political culture includes both the rationalist and the voluntarist themes. It includes the notion that men can use their empirically acquired knowledge to control events—as, for instance, when they accept the findings of an Adam Smith as to how to increase the wealth of the nation. It also expresses the attitude that public policy should be based on human wants, such as the consumers' satisfaction of Smithian economics. As theories of means and ends respectively, rationalism and voluntarism are closely associated in the modern spirit.

One result of this association has been to give a wide scope to the process and products of rationalization. For the application of science and technology to economic, social, and political problems may greatly alter the conditions of life in those spheres, requiring far-reaching adaptations of norms and values. Voluntarism eases the process of making virtues of such necessities. We see its work in those frequent occasions when in the history of modernization —for instance, the rise of industry—conditions which were totally unplanned and initially repulsive soon came to be regarded as pleasurable and right. Thanks to voluntarism, alienation from such unintended consequences of some new pattern of human activity has often proved to be only a passing phase.

Some people may regard this as demeaning. But consider the alternative. If pre-modern attitudes prevailed in the context of a developing technology, the resulting conflicts between the old rigid discipline and the pressures of development would be severe. Indeed, insofar as pre-modern attitudes have survived, modernization in the West has frequently been marked by a special kind of conflict to which Parsons has given the name "fundamentalist reaction." [3] In Britain these conflicts have usually been milder than in most countries of the West. Yet they have occurred and even today in some spheres of political development, one can discern this typical strain of modernization. One can often see it in the tenacious assertion of old class identities by members of both upper and lower strata in opposition to a more pragmatic attitude toward parties and policies.

[3] See Parsons, op. cit., and also "Certain Primary Sources and Patterns of Aggression in the Social Structure of the Western World," in Essays in Sociological Theory, Pure and Applied (Glencoe, 1949).

Democracy and Rationalization

Along with technological advance in economic, social, and political spheres, a leading characteristic of modern Western history has been the rise of popular government, and discussions of the modern polity usually include a tendency toward democratization as an important variable of the model. I accept this analysis, subject to two qualifications. In the first place, I should insist that modern democracy has various sources, some quite independent of the process of rationalization. Certainly, we may not neglect the sheer creative power of the political imagination and the influence of its products—a *Social Contract* or a *Communist Manifesto*—in stirring previously passive masses to make new demands for citizenship. Secondly, however, we need also see that often rationalization is intrinsically related to the degree of participation. This relationship may prove to be negative, as, for example, when the further rationalization of public policy in the form of economic planning makes popular control more difficult and so reduces participation. Yet in harmony with the actual historical trend in the past, it is more instructive to stress the situations in which rationalization and democratization are mutually supportive.

Purely on the plane of cultural development, there seems to be such a tendency in the basic orientations of modernity. Rationalism, as understood here, is compatible with elitist conclusions, such as the Liberal position that some men are rendered by situation, if not endowment, incapable of the intelligent objectivity necessary to justify a share in power.[4] Similarly, voluntarism on the face of it seems to leave open the question, Whose wishes are to govern? An elitist answer could be conceived which put so high a value on the wishes of a few that the many would be wholly excluded from power. Fascism would fit this pattern.

Yet to accomplish this discrimination among human wishes, some criterion other than voluntarism has to be brought in. In other words, voluntarism itself sets up no barrier to the extension of political power. On the contrary, in contrast with classical and medieval notions, there is in voluntarism an openness that readily

[4] See above, pp. 34-5.

becomes a tendency toward democracy. Perhaps the reason is simply that while it is hard to deny that knowledge of the good, on which pre-modern conceptions based authority, is unequally distributed throughout society, it is self-evident that every man has wants to satisfy. If we are faithful to human appetite as our standard of valuation, we are pretty sure to come out with an equalitarian view of the ultimate foundations of power.

A more interesting tendency arises from situational rather than ideal forces. This tendency illustrates the broad proposition that the structure of public policy itself sometimes requires that certain groups be given power. When we study the rise of popular government, for instance, we commonly concentrate on the struggle of the excluded group for access to influence and authority. We examine, for instance, how it acquired the instrumentalities—money, organization, or knowledge—which enabled it to force its way into the active political community. Yet we should also recognize that such a group's chances of success may have been greatly increased because the polity needed its participation. It has been cogently argued, for instance, that the Reform Act of 1867 was necessary in order to make possible the consent and co-operation of the skilled working class for the new phase of government intervention that was being inaugurated.[5] Nor is this general possibility confined to modern times: the rise of Parliament itself has been interpreted as "self-government at the king's command." [6]

The case that interests us here occurs when the change in public policy has resulted from rationalization, i.e., a further use of instrumental knowledge by government to control events. A major illustration is provided by the rise of the system of functional representation that characterizes British politics in the Collectivist period. The Welfare State and especially the Managed Economy of recent decades simply could not operate without the advice and co-operation of the great organized producer groups of business, labor, and agriculture. And the history of these groups displays the powerful influence of government in calling them into existence, shaping their goals and endowing them with effec-

[5] By Professor H. L. Beales of the University of London in a private conversation.

[6] A. B. White's book with that title.

tive power. The point is relevant to Britain's current problems. For at the present time the burdens and complexities of economic planning require an even greater mobilization of consent.[7]

In general, the flexible and constantly changing control typically exercised by government today cannot be effective in a population governed by rigid norms or unthinking custom, but must on the contrary meet with the active response and understanding of affected groups. Moreover, the more rapid the development of technology, and so of consequent social change and government adaptation, the more continuous and intimate participation must be. In this sense, modernization involves not only a wider extension but also greater intensity of participation.

Yet the tendencies are not all in one direction. Looking to the future, we can expect that in Britain as in other Western countries the ever greater reliance upon scientific and professional knowledge in politics and government will enhance the influence of those who have such expertise. Also, needless to say, it can hardly fail to diminish the influence of those without it. Thus arise the dangers of technocracy in government, party, and pressure group.

Stages of Modernity

Rationalism and voluntarism characterize the modern spirit in politics and generally pervade attitude and behavior so far as a polity is modern. They did not, however, win their victory all at once, but gradually expanded their influence in broad but fairly well-marked stages. The typology of five kinds of politics presented in Chapters I–III can be used to mark this development.

First, some general comment about this scheme of classification. The most important fact to be brought out is that it is based upon political culture, or more specifically upon the orientations of the persons and groups whose behavior is being identified and classified. In this sense, the models of this typology can be called "ideal types," meaning by this that they show the derivation of these patterns of political behavior from the ideas and ideals of the persons concerned.

[7] I have discussed this in "The British Legislature and the Problem of Mobilizing Consent," in Elke Frank, ed., *Lawmakers in a Changing World* (Englewood Cliffs, N.J., 1966). Reprinted in Bernard Crick, ed., *Essays on Reform, 1967* (London, 1967).

Needless to say, in the study of society you do not always find a high degree of correspondence between intention and behavior and in such cases may find it more helpful to base your analytic models upon a pattern of unintended consequences. Although, as I shall emphasize at a later point, the models of this typology do have important unintended consequences, there is sufficient conformity of orientation and behavior to make the former a major basis for describing and explaining the latter. As I said in the Introduction, I found in political culture the most useful clues to developing a scheme of classification of parties and pressure groups in different periods of British history.[8]

In particular, the characterizing idea for each type of political behavior is a theory of representation. These theories of representation belong to more inclusive conceptions of authority laying down how power ought to be distributed and defining who may legitimately take part in governing and how they may do so. It is also evident that the orientation of each type of politics associates these notions about power with ideas about the purposes for which power may be used. In other words, a conception of purpose is linked with each conception of authority by means of certain pervasive values and beliefs.[9] Thus, for instance, the individualism and rationalism of the nineteenth-century Liberal shaped his approach to political action as well as to economic policy.

This effort to classify parties and pressure groups shows that political formations vary with elements of political culture in many important respects, such as structure, tactics, social base, and so on. Moreover, it suggests the general hypothesis that insofar as orientation determines behavior, all the main elements of a political system develop in harmony with these characterizing ideas of political culture through the various stages of modernization. My concern here has been to point out the interdependence of conceptions of authority and conceptions of purpose. While the focus of the scheme of classification is on the former, the names chosen to designate each type indicate the wider area of values and beliefs that is involved. These larger implications of

[8] See above, p. xi.

[9] I have discussed conceptions of authority and conceptions of purpose in relation to political culture in my introduction to *Patterns of Government: The Major Political Systems of Europe*, rev. ed. (New York, 1962), especially pp. 32-8.

the scheme are evident when we use it to outline the stages of political modernization in Britain. A table identifying these stages and showing the parallel development of ideas about power and about policy will be helpful.

Type of Politics	Conceptions of Authority		Conceptions of Purpose
	Modes of Representation		
	Common Interest	Particular Interests	
1. Old Tory	Monarchy	Functionalism	Mercantilism
2. Old Whig	Parliamentarism	Functionalism	Mercantilism (external)
3. Liberal	Parliamentarism	Associationism	Laissez faire
4. Radical	Popular Sovereignty	Associationism	Laissez faire (interventionist)
5. Collectivist	Party Government	Functionalism	Welfare State-Managed Economy

The premises of Old Tory political behavior were still essentially medieval, reflecting the ancient faith of the "Great Chain of Being." Although law-making was practiced, under the influence of a powerful monarch and newly centralized government, on a far wider scale than before, it was still restricted, in theory by the notion of a fixed and unchanging order of man and nature, and in fact by conscious imitation of a hierarchic and corporatist past.

Our focus on modernization makes the Old Whig model a fascinating example of transitional politics. Its basic orientation is modern. For although much of the Old Tory ideal of hierarchy and corporatism is retained, the premises have shifted radically, permitting far greater scope for human contrivance and changing circumstance. Statecraft is neither deductive nor metaphysical, but highly empirical, and though confined to the possession of a few, the modernity of its purposes was made clear by Burke when he declared that "government is a contrivance of human wisdom to provide for the satisfaction of human *wants*."[1] This fitting of new intellectual foundations to old superstructures eased the transition to the heightened modernity of the nineteenth century, as we can see by a comparative look at France, where a sudden passage from *ancien régime* to Liberal and Radical politics produced shocks from which the country has not yet fully recovered.

[1] "Reflections on the Revolution in France," *Writings and Speeches*, Vol. III, p. 310.

On the plane of ideas, nineteenth-century Liberalism and Radicalism constitute a kind of culmination of political modernity. Among the champions of these doctrines, the faith in science and the faith in democracy achieved an emphasis that has not been exceeded. Laissez faire, to be sure, was a doctrine of governmental withdrawal from control. It reflected, however, a growing commitment to, and understanding of, the scientific approach to the study of the economy, as well as a correspondingly greater systematic knowledge of how the economy operated. In the very different circumstances of the twentieth century, this same rationalist orientation led to the massive reassertion of economic management and control of Collectivist politics. Similarly in nineteenth-century political thought, modernity is expressed in an unambiguous acceptance of human will as the source of legitimacy—for the Liberals, the will of rational, independent men, for the Radicals, the will of the people. The Socialists would say that in the British context Radical democracy could never fulfill its populistic ambition until it had been transformed by a recognition of class politics. Still, as an ideal Socialist democracy is only an adaptation of the Radical commitment.

On the plane of ideas then, Liberal and especially Radical politics is just as modern as Collectivist and the corresponding political parties of the nineteenth century are no more traditionalist than those of the twentieth.

If in terms of political culture, modernity matured in the nineteenth century, nevertheless in the twentieth, modernization as a process continued on a more extensive scale and at an ever more rapid pace. Rationalist and democratic ideas advanced throughout the society, a principal example being the transformation of Toryism as from time to time it seized the leadership in widening the franchise and in pioneering economic control. But although this dominance of the modernist spirit made its consequences of ever increasing importance, these were rarely simple and straightforward.

Rationalization and Conflict

To speak of progressive modernization does not mean that one finds in British political development a smooth and steady movement in one direction, unflawed by conflict or dissension. There were, I grant, those curious mid-century lulls—the years around 1750, 1850, and 1950. Yet no significant stretch of time was free of deep-running conflict and one of the main uses of our five-fold typology is to help identify the ideological bases and issues of such conflict and show its importance. Even in the quiet times of the "Victorian compromise," for instance, Radicalism confronted Liberalism, and both faced Toryism, then on the verge of another of its invigorating renewals. As for the twentieth century, one of the major efforts of this book has been to show how the Collectivist period has been marked by a conflict over both power and purpose between Toryism and Socialism which I do not hesitate to call fundamental.

Sometimes these conflicts of ideals can be fitted fairly neatly into the formula of modernity versus tradition. This would be the case with Liberalism and Radicalism in their struggle against Toryism in the earlier part of the past century. But the tensions introduced by modernization sometimes cut across the alignment of parties. Such has been the case in the Collectivist period, when at a deep level in both the Conservative and Labour parties, modernizing forces meet with resistance. It will help to bring out some of the causes of development in British politics today and also to make the concept of modernization more concrete and usable if we will take a closer look at this conflict.

One way of stating the central concern of this book is to say that it is an attempt to put contemporary British politics in the context of the "organizational revolution." [2] Indeed, at one time I was tempted to use the term "organization politics" to describe my central topic, only to realize that this term would be even more open to misunderstanding than "collectivist." By "organizational revolution" I mean the rise of the large-scale, formal organization to a place of dominance in most spheres of Western society during recent generations. The leading example is the great business corporation. But as Weber pointed out in his discussion of "universal bureaucratization," [3] we see similar forms in government, the armed services, education, and politics.

This organizational revolution is a recent phase and striking

[2] Kenneth Boulding, *The Organizational Revolution* (New York, 1953).
[3] The phrase is Reinhold Bendix's in his discussion of Weber's views of the future of bureaucracy in *Max Weber: An Intellectual Portrait*, Anchor Books (New York, 1962), Ch. XIV.

instance of the process of rationalization. For illustration of the relationship we may consider briefly the rise of big business. Underlying the development of the large modern corporation there have been various causes, not least the search for market power in times of deflation. A principal continuing force, however, has been advancing technology. Although there are exceptions, "technological advance," as Parsons remarks, "almost always leads to increasingly elaborate division of labor and the concomitant requirement of increasingly elaborate organization." [4] New knowledge in some branch of production, for instance, leads to greater technical specialization as new tasks are created to embody new knowledge. As specialization develops, the problem of co-ordinating the various stages of production in time and space favors the creation of large units which can provide conscious planning and control over the constituent elements. Thus, the many small firms co-ordinated by the market are supplanted by the large, integrated firm essentially because it can better exploit the productive power of advancing technology.

In this way large organizations arise as a means of more effective use of growing knowledge. Another way in which technology may promote greater size should also be distinguished. This occurs as new techniques and instruments are developed for creating and managing large organizations themselves. A growing science of administration, supported by new means of communication and transportation, makes feasible the control of ever larger units. Modern bureaucracy, as Weber pointed out, is a highly efficient structure for the application of specialized, technical knowledge. At the same time, an improved knowledge of bureaucratic structures itself facilitates the creation of units which can more effectively perform this service. In other words, the technology *applied to* organizations as well as the technology *used by* organizations promotes an increase in size.

This distinction is useful in examining the central feature of Collectivist politics, the rise of political concentration, in the form of the mass party and the mass pressure group. Political formations of this type belong to the organizational revolution. Like other creations of this phase of modernization, they could have come into existence only when the technology applied to organizations provided the means for creating and managing such large

[4] *The Social System,* p. 507.

bodies of men and activities. Already in the nineteenth century, we see the skills and instruments that were making possible the growth of government bureaucracy and the business firm also being applied to the new political formations of the time. In the present century, the technology used by organizations no doubt has also had some influence in promoting political concentration by giving advantages in political competition to the large organization co-ordinating specialized organs.

But the analysis of contemporary Collectivist formations—I am thinking now mainly of the mass party, although what I have to say also applies in some degree to the great producer groups— vividly reveals that there may also be other foundations of organizational concentration. Specifically, when we examined the premises of action of both Toryism and Socialism we found powerful strands of pre-modern thought and feeling, centering above all on conceptions of class. These conceptions endow class with quite different functions, the Socialist regarding it as creating a horizontal division in society, the Tory looking on its as a means of vertical integration. Yet in each case a conception of class, whether it appeals to the solidarity of the working class or to the *noblesse oblige* and deference of Toryism, is integral to an orientation that supports the large, cohesive political party.

As the example of the business corporation shows, organizational concentration may be produced mainly by the technology of a new phase of rationalization. As the example of the mass party shows, however, concentration may also be based upon quite different forces of social integration, viz., class. To make the point more specific: the political formations of Collectivist Britain reveal a dual character. On the one hand, they use the basic organizational technology of the day, and show its typical features of a formal, centralized structure, co-ordinating specialized subunits. On the other hand, however, their moral foundations embody the very different values of class consciousness, descending in certain vital respects from an older, pre-modern Britain. This, of course, raises the question whether further modernization will erode these traditionalist elements.

Latent Function versus Operative Ideals

We will take up this question when we look at the possibilities of the future. I wish now to examine and illustrate in some detail another major type of conflict which is also a source of change and development in Collectivist politics. In the process we have just been describing, rationalization is hemmed in and conditioned by a traditionalist heritage. In the type of conflict we will now look at, the effort of control is caught up in its own unintended consequences.

In briefest terms, the conflict is between the purposes of political behavior and the unanticipated consequences of that behavior. These consequences need not be unpleasant even when they are surprising: there is sometimes a kind of objective serendipity in the historical process. But very commonly even those efforts which most successfully produce what we want also spawn a whole series of results that are unexpected and undesirable and require a new effort of control.

This irony of objective circumstance has dogged man's efforts to control his environment, no doubt, from the earliest time, providing him continually with new problems and so forcing new stages of development. Modernity, however, with its qualitative leap in the character of the control effort has heightened the dynamism of the process. On the one hand, the scientific approach has undoubtedly extended our knowledge of how to control events in both the social and natural environments. On the other hand, the very size of our growing apparatus of control sets in train massive reverberations that were not anticipated.

It is a commonplace of contemporary comment when we look at our cities, or our economies, or our international relations to say that we are continually threatened with being strangled, so to speak, by the unintended effects of our very attempts to breathe. Every wave of effort to control our environment itself creates a new environment which must be subjected to control. Indeed, it would seem that the larger the effort of control, the more substantial the new problems. Both aspects, the expansion of control and the "feedback" of unintended consequence, are intrinsic to the process of rationalization.

The model of Collectivist politics developed in this book illustrates this kind of conflict and how it impels development. In constructing that model I found myself going through two phases of analysis. My first task was to identify the basic orientations of political actors. In doing this I exploited the resources of the history of political thought, vulgarized so as to throw light on operative ideals. British Socialist thought helped me get a grasp of the premises of action of the Labour Party, especially during the "Socialist Generation." Tory thought, although as one would expect, more diffuse and less formalized in utterance, brought out the orientations of the central current of sentiment and behavior among Conservatives.

These premises of action of the two parties, although as opposed as the Tory and Socialist conceptions of class and community, legitimize theories of representation and theories of public policy with many elements in common. Both Tory and Socialist orientations support the practices of party government and functional representation and both legitimize substantial government intervention for economic management and social welfare. From these two sets of attitudes relating respectively to power and purpose comes a massive moral support for political concentration.[5]

In this kind of analysis, rather like the cultural anthropologist, one looks for the orientations or premises of action that support, perhaps through intervening levels of thought and feeling, a set of particular attitudes displayed in behavior. Although one is dealing with the intentional and purposive life of a community, the findings have explanatory value, insofar as they bring out the motivation on which behavior depends.

Another kind of analysis, however, was also involved in constructing the Collectivist model. The conceptions of party government and functional representation greatly help in identifying and describing the broad outlines of British politics in the twentieth century and in setting off certain of its distinctive features from those of the liberal and individualist nineteenth century. But as one looks into the political behavior of this more recent time, one also finds patterns not included in this description. One

[5] See above, Ch. III.

finds uniformities deriving from the structures and patterns legitimized by the operative ideals of Collectivist politics, but not intended by them. In other words, the model has not only manifest functions, but also latent functions.[6]

In identifying these latent functions and in tracing their origin and interconnection, organization theory proved useful. Economists in their study of economic concentration have shown how the size of the large corporation affects both its internal structure and its external relations.[7] These consequences of economic concentration can be summarized under four headings, two relating to internal effects and two relating to external effects: managerialism, bureaucracy, bargaining, and what Galbraith has called "dependence effect." While not exactly analogous, this pattern of relations in the economic field helped me find similar consequences resulting from concentration in parties and pressure groups and so to see the meaning and interconnection of patterns of behavior that had previously seemed unrelated.

The distinctive intellectual contribution of sociology, Robert Merton has said, is to be found in the study of unintended consequences.[8] In this sense this analysis of the "laws" of political concentration, i.e., of the latent functions of certain purposive structures, can be thought of as a kind of political sociology. Its subject is a particular aspect of the rationalization process, namely, the feedback of unintended consequences in large organizations.

Laws of Political Concentration

With the hunches and hypotheses suggested by these elements of organization theory, I was able to identify and order the unanticipated consequences set in train by the behavior patterns of party government and functional representation.[9] Very briefly, but more formally than in the text, I will summarize the findings.

---

[6] I take these terms from Robert K. Merton's well-known essay, "Manifest and Latent Functions," in *Social Theory and Social Structure* (Glencoe, 1949).

[7] I was particularly helped by the summary article by E. S. Mason, "The Apologetics of 'Managerialism'," *The Journal of Business of the University of Chicago*, Vol. XXXI, No. 1 (January, 1958), pp. 1–11.

[8] *Loc. cit.*, p. 66.

[9] See especially above, Ch. XII.

As has often been observed, the mass party, even if its inspiration is highly democratic, tends to separate leadership from the rank and file and to accumulate influence in the hands of an elite. The conventions of British cabinet government also work in this direction. But it is well to see that such tendencies toward *managerialism* also inhere in other large formations such as workers' and employers' organizations as well as political parties.

A major source of managerialism is the specialized and indeed professional skills which leaders must develop and exercise if they are to hold their organizations together and carry out their purposes. Organizational necessities of this kind help us explain the decline of the Labour Party conference and of the party's extra-parliamentary organization from the role given it in the party's image of itself and actually carried out in the earlier phases of its history. Such elitist tendencies cause little strain among Tories, whose ancient sociology accepts hierarchy as a law of orderly life. Insofar, however, as political managers win their status by achievement and by demonstrated capacities of expertise or professional knowledge, there may be a clash with certain Tory values.

Size and complexity in political formations as in other organizations also tend to promote *bureaucracy*, or, to use the more general term, formalization.[1] Sidney Webb's neat constitution of 1918, as elaborated and amended over the years, illustrates the point. On the Conservative side, the party and its leaders have shown themselves remarkably forward in the use of formal organization from the days of Disraeli through the era of Woolton. No doubt, however, there is greater reluctance than among Socialists to formalize the framework of vital decisions and authoritative positions, as shown by the long delay to establish an explicit set of rules for choice of a party leader.

Managerial bureaucracy refers to the effects of concentration on internal structures. Its effects on external relations are twofold. The operative ideals of functional representation legitimize and even require consultation between government and producer groups. The degree of concentration achieved by many of these groups in their respective fields means, however, that

[1] William H. Starbuck, "Organizational Growth and Development," in James March, ed., *Handbook of Organizations* (Chicago, 1965), pp. 477–80.

consultation almost inevitably becomes negotiation and, indeed, a kind of collective *bargaining*. The annual price review between the Government and the National Farmers' Union is a good example. Of even more importance are the repeated efforts of Governments to achieve agreement with trade unions and trade associations on an incomes policy from which, indeed, when the efforts are successful, a kind of "extra-parliamentary legislation" results.

When we look at the relations of the parties and the electorate, however, the appropriate term is "bidding" rather than "bargaining." These two fairly evenly matched parties make an intense effort to identify and attract every vote that might float. This leads to a great stress on group appeals. "The voter," as Lord Woolton once said, "is also the consumer." And one can conveniently think of these voters as consumer groups, the beneficiaries or prospective beneficiaries of the Welfare State. One result of this process of bidding is to enhance the role of the usually poorly organized consumer groups in the electoral and governmental process. At the same time there is a certain "dependence effect" as political parties shape the often inchoate wishes of these electors.

Bidding and bargaining characterize the relations of parties and governments with pressure groups. Political concentration in the context of wide government intervention also tends to shape the relations of the two parties to one another. This tendency bears on a major political development of recent years. In Britain as in most other Western countries during the postwar period, the intensity of political conflict significantly and rather unexpectedly diminished, leading to much talk of "the decline of ideology" and "consensus politics." Various conditions, especially economic, help account for this development. It is important, however, also to point out how this tendency is promoted by the objective political conditions under which the two mass parties must operate. Each party when seeking power must bid for the votes of many of the same consumer groups and when in power must bargain with most of the same producer groups. These are the hard realities of getting elected and of governing. Together they have worked to promote a certain *convergence* of party programs, lessening the ideological distance between Socialist and Conservative. With ideological contours fading, a new group politics appeared as a more and more prominent feature of the political scene.

One final tendency of political concentration—certainly unintended, though no longer unrecognized—which is of the most vital importance in present-day Britain must be mentioned. The new group politics that has arisen in recent years has very positive advantages as a counterbalance to the extension and centralization of government control that has occurred at the same time. It takes no very acute observer, however, to see that the danger may now be not oppressive efficiency, but *pluralistic stagnation*. I am thinking particularly of the reasons for Britain's economic problems. There are various helpful approaches to an explanation. The specifically economic is, of course, crucial, bringing out the exposed international position of the British economy, especially in view of the attempt to remain a world banker. A more popular explanation relates to cultural reasons and tends to put the blame on the "Old Freddies" of management and their fellow traditionalists among workers who are resisting modernization.

But the responsibility of the new group politics for the failure of the economy is far from negligible.[2] One major reason for the relative lag in economic growth has been the relatively low proportion of national product used each year for net new investment in manufacturing. This condition is not helped by policies favoring expenditure on consumption, private and public. Yet the more austere choice is by no means easy for a party in power constantly threatened by a competitor's bidding for the votes of the same consumer groups in which the Government itself has found support.

A related problem is inflation and its consequences. A major cause of Britain's recurring balance of payments crises has been price rises resulting from the pushing up of wage costs by trade-union pressure and by competition among employers for scarce labor. Bargaining with relevant producer groups, however, has not yet succeeded in winning the co-operation necessary for an incomes policy that could successfully restrain these inflationary forces. Yet without a considerable degree of such voluntary co-operation the appropriate economic policy cannot be effective.

In greater or lesser degree these political causes of economic problems afflict many of the other highly modernized societies

[2] I am summarizing from the article mentioned in footnote 7 p. 396, above.

of the West. If one is looking for irony, the situation abundantly illustrates how a higher and higher effort of rationalization can produce more and more irrationalities. The organizational revolution in politics and the extension of government planning are guided by the hope of strengthening man's control over man's fate. Let us not dispute that in comparison with selected times in the past there has been a net gain. Neither can we deny that the system generates massive dysfunctions.

These seven tendencies—managerialism, bureaucracy, bidding, bargaining, dependence effect, convergence, and immobilism, to give them brief titles—are latent functions of the model of Collectivist politics. The two major situational factors from which they flow are a high level of political concentration and a wide scope of government policy. In some instances, it is also relevant that there are two major parties and that they are fairly evenly matched in electoral strength. If one does not project too much on the term, one can think of the key propositions of this analysis as constituting "laws" of political concentration. They are continuous with much well-established organization theory and go on to develop certain hypotheses in a form that makes them testable in the context of other political systems.

This analysis helps us see and understand significant patterns of behavior in the Collectivist period. Moreover, it also brings out forces making for change and development. We will turn our attention more closely to this question by first considering what has been happening in the sixties and then going on to examine the possibilities of the future.

DEVELOPMENTS OF THE SIXTIES

In looking at recent developments of the sixties and the possible future, I will continue to make rationalization the focus of discussion. More particularly, I want to stress that new phase of recent years resulting from the explosion of scientific knowledge and its ramifying impact throughout society.

One of the most obvious effects is on the economy, where, as we are continually told, the scientific revolution has become the principal dynamic force, bringing about what one might call a growing professionalization of the mode of production, distribution, and exchange. Among other things, it continually reduces the number of manual workers and increases the white-collar class equipped with technical and professional training, a change in occupational structure that cannot help but have important effects upon parties and politics.

The scientific revolution, moreover, affects the polity not only indirectly through economic development, but also directly through government policy as our knowledge of society responds to the scientific impulse. Thus, for instance, not only in Government departments but also in the leading echelons of parties and pressure groups there is occurring a professionalization of policy-making as the social sciences are applied more and more to problems of public policy. Surely, the most weighty instance of the way knowledge can thus affect politics is the impact of Keynesian economics on the conflict of parties. Throughout the West and well before the era of affluence, this revolution in ideas dissolved the rigid doctrines of "capitalism" and "socialism," bringing old combatants into a wide area of agreement, as the emergence of Butskellism revealed to slightly astonished Britons in the early 1950's. Thus reason has had as much to do with reducing the class struggle as any material force.

Finally, perhaps the most interesting development of all arises from the growing knowledge of how to influence voters and win elections. By this means, the technology used by political parties promises to heighten the professionalization of vote-getting and thereby considerably to affect their structure and behavior.

It will be convenient to consider the changes of the sixties under the two headings of party government and functional representation.

Party Government

If one asks whether during the sixties there has been a further lessening of the ideological distance between the two parties, the answer is clearly yes. By the first months of—ironically—Harold Wilson's leadership and well before the party took power again, revisionism had carried the day in the Labour Party. As the quiescent conference of 1963 showed, the old Left that had fought the battles over nationalization and nuclear disarmament was spent.

The harsh defeats suffered by Gaitskell in 1959–60 when he

tried to alter Clause IV, the ancient pledge of universal public ownership, had demonstrated the power the old myth still held over the verbal behavior of the party. On through the years of the Wilson Government the old rhetoric continued to crop up, usually it seemed when someone needed an honorific term to moralize resistance to some hard specific of reform.[3] But in contrast with the heroic battles of the forties and fifties, it could no longer mobilize effective force in the party, except for the drive to renationalize steel. At the same time, revisionism, which had produced not much more than an eclectic set of group appeals in the program of 1958, *The Future Labour Offers YOU*, acquired a conceptual framework. This was set forth in the program adopted in 1961, *Signposts for the Sixties*, and in the manifesto of 1964, both of which based their proposals on "the scientific revolution," drawing out its implications of modernization, planning, and economic expansion.

On the Conservative side there had been at least an equivalent movement toward their opponents. After they had returned to power in 1951 the Conservatives showed that they accepted not only the Welfare State, but also a high degree of economic management. They still, however, rejected planning. Then under Macmillan, who had been a planner of old, they gave up their brief flirtation with "neo-liberalism" and launched the country on what they hoped would be a British version of French plannification. The central agencies were the National Economic Development Council and a National Incomes Commission, which meant an explicit commitment not only to planning, but also to that difficult but indispensable ingredient, an incomes policy.

After Labour took office in 1964, the two parties came to look even more alike. Innovation depended upon and in large part was measured by economic policy and, as of old, at the heart of the Government's economic problem were relations with organized labor. These relations and the policies they ineluctably led to belong with our discussion of functional representation. They should be mentioned here as representing a failure of party government. It had been hoped that the new organs of, and commit-

---

[3] For instance, Frank Cousins when moving a resolution against the pay freeze at the T.U.C. (T.U.C. *Report* 1966, p. 464) or Clive Jenkins in a motion attacking the Government's economic policies at the party conference (1967 *LPCR*, p. 69).

ment to, planning had put an end to the "corporative stagnation" of the fifties.[4] This did not prove to be the case. Although pursued with unbelievable patience and the utmost sensitivity to the feelings of the unions, incomes policy under Labour was significantly, but not sufficiently, more successful than it had been under the Conservatives.

Like the Conservatives before them, Labour chose to protect the pound. Like the Conservatives also, Labour, failing to obtain adequate wage restraint, was obliged to resort to the deliberate creation of unemployment in what proved to be a futile effort to defend sterling. After devaluation, the old pressures for consumption continued, as under the Conservatives, to show their power, making the necessary cuts late, if not too little.

The cause of nuclear disarmament had generated the New Left of the early sixties, of which the C.N.D. was the principal champion. But the test-ban treaty and the election of that Leftist Harold Wilson as Leader caused this agitation to subside and in 1963 the "New Left" clubs, of which there had been scores in and outside London, simply fell apart. In succeeding years, the character of Government policy—unredeemed, moreover, by success—might have been expected to prompt a resurgence of the Left, stiffened by trade-union allies. Opposition did grow in conference. By 1967 the floor could beat the platform on such questions as the American war in Vietnam and the Greek dictatorship, hardly crucial or unprecedented sorts of defeats. More significant was the way conference approved the Government's economic policy by only a miniscule majority and went on to pass a motion sharply hostile to its wage-price effort.[5]

In Parliament the economy package of January, 1968, consequent upon devaluation, probed old sensitivities—prescription charges, school-leaving age, free school milk—leading to the most serious uprising since the party's return to power. On the crucial vote twenty-one left-wing M.P.'s—about 6 per cent of all Labour M.P.'s—publicly abstained.[6] As one of the dissidents observed, these numbers demonstrated that the Left was weaker than ever

[4] See the intelligent discussion in Peter Pulzer, *Political Representation and Elections: Parties and Voting in Great Britain* (New York, 1967), pp. 143–4.

[5] For the texts of the two resolutions, see 1967 *LPCR*, pp. 163 and 171; for the votes, p. 201.

[6] House of Commons Debates, 18 January 1968.

before.[7] Certainly, neither in numbers, weight, nor ideas did it compare with the roaring opposition of Bevanite days, or even with the rebels of the Attlee régime, who in November, 1946, for instance, put down a highly critical amendment to the Address which attracted 57 Labour signers—14 per cent of the total—and about the same number of public abstainers.[8]

Class Politics

If class ideologies had declined, class politics on the other hand continued to flourish. By class politics I mean primarily class voting, although I also include other partisan behavior such as party membership. If we take manual and non-manual occupations as identifying, respectively, the working class and the middle class and ask each of the two groups has divided its support between the two main parties since the war, we find that in spite of policy convergence, affluence, professionalization, and the rest, the various indices of class voting have remained remarkably high and stable. Alford's index of party voting, for instance, which had stood at 37 in 1945, still read 35 in 1962, dropping slightly to 31 in 1964.[9] In the elections of both 1964 and 1966 there were slight shifts in middle-class strata to Labour, with the result that "the class polarisation of the British electorate was perhaps fractionally reduced."[1]

If by class voting we mean correlation between voting and class, the most striking thing about the British figures is the inability of Labour, the avowedly working-class party, to carry a great deal more than a majority of that class. Strongly supported

[7] Mr. Hudson Davies, quoted in *The Guardian*, 1 February 1968, p. 1.

[8] Ivor Bulmer-Thomas, *The Growth of the British Party System*, Vol. II, 1924-1964 (New York, 1966), p. 164.

[9] For the years 1945 and 1962, see Robert R. Alford, *Party and Society: The Anglo-American Democracies* (Chicago, 1963), p. 348; for 1964, see Seymour R. Lipset and Stein Rokkan, *Party Systems and Voter Alignments: Cross-National Perspectives* (New York, 1967), p. 87 and n. 51. Gallup data for the years 1945-1964 show the same stability of class voting. See Henry Durant, "Voting Behaviour in Britain, 1945-64," in Richard Rose, ed., *Studies in British Politics: A Reader in Political Sociology* (London and New York, 1966), p. 123.

[1] D. E. Butler and Anthony King, *The British General Election of 1966* (London and New York, 1966), p. 265.

by the middle and upper classes, the Conservative Party survives and thrives in the age of democracy only because of its massive following in the working class. But this too signifies a kind of class voting, insofar as a major ingredient in working-class Conservatism is the deference voter. The political behavior of this large section of the working class shows the continuing vitality of the classic Tory theory that class serves to integrate society vertically rather than dividing it horizontally. Depending on the stringency of the definition, anywhere from a quarter to a half of working-class Tories can be classified as "deferentials." [2] When we realize that roughly half the Conservative vote has come from the working class, the importance of this kind of class voting is evident.

One of the most interesting questions to the student of political modernization in Britain is the future of political deference. It would surely seem to be doomed by the joint action of pragmatic rationalism and democratic egalitarianism. Yet its future is not quite so obvious. Recent painstaking surveys have shown how very complex the attitudes of deference voters are. There is in them an element of pure ascription: the notion that the right to rule belongs to certain persons simply because of who they are— "the old king's son," or, as contemporary working-class Tories sometimes still say, "they're my guv'nors."

But normally the deference voter does not disregard consequences. He identifies the people to whom he defers by certain well-known signs of class status—accent, dress, family, certain kinds of education, not to mention handwriting, table manners, time of dining, and whole style of life. This is Bagehot's "charmed spectacle which imposes on the many and guides their fancies as it will." [3] But contrary to Bagehot, the deference voter's response is not simply one of subconscious, non-rational inference. On the contrary, he is thinking instrumentally and in terms of means and ends. He takes these signs of class status to indicate superior political ability and to promise better performance, basing his rea-

---

[2] Robert McKenzie and Allan Silver, *Angels in Marble: Working Class Conservatives in Urban England* (Chicago, 1968), p. 164n.; and Eric Nordlinger, *The Working-Class Tories: Authority, Deference and Stable Democracy* (London, 1967), pp. 65–6.

[3] Walter Bagehot, *The English Constitution*, World's Classics Edition, (London, 1928), p. 237.

soning on such things as genetic inheritance, family training, and education at elite public school or ancient university.

To think this way may well be old-fashioned, but it is not transparently stupid. While it is clearly arguable, it is certainly not irrational to prefer as your ruler a man with this background to a man without it who has worked his way up in the world.

The deference voter, in short, is by no means a simple-minded traditionalist destined to be forced out by modernity. On the contrary, it takes no great imagination to see how his attitudes could become highly functional to a technocratic society in the future. In justifying his preferences, for instance, he gives great stress to education and to its product—"brains," "a good headpiece." A technocratic elite likewise bases its claim to authority on education, although, to be sure, education in scientific and professional specialties. If, however, the British upper classes could sufficiently adapt their educational system to the scientific age, deference might continue to be offered to their offspring, real and adoptive, and perhaps even on a wider scale in that more modern society. As the longevity and past adaptability of the "class system" should warn us, we may not think of its future solely in terms of cultural lag.[4]

Although class voting in both senses persists, the continuing rationalization of the economy is causing changes in occupational structure that could have important political effects. The shift from manual to non-manual jobs continues markedly. In manufacturing alone, for instance, between 1954 and 1964, the per cent of administrative, technical, and clerical workers rose from 18.4 per cent to 23.1 per cent.[5] From 1951 to 1961 the index of scientists and engineers more than doubled.[6] These changes in the economy have, of course, affected the trade-union movement. Although white-collar workers are being widely and rapidly unionized, losses in the declining occupations, such as mining, shipbuilding, and textiles, have been severe, and between 1953 and

[4] See above, p. 393.
[5] Royal Commission on Trade Unions and Employers' Associations, *Written Evidence of the Ministry of Labour* (London, 1965), par. 27 and Appendix V, p. 51.
[6] *British Journal of Industrial Relations*, Vol. IV, No. 3 (November, 1966), p. 307.

1963, although the total of employees went up 9 per cent, trade-union membership rose only 4 per cent.[7]

Such changes in occupational structure must surely affect political behavior. The most plausible expectation would be a shift toward the Conservatives as more people move into conventionally middle-class jobs. The relationship, however, is not simple. The movement from manual to non-manual employment has been going on for a long time. From 1931 to 1951, for instance, manual workers declined as a per cent of the work force from 70.3 per cent to 64.2 per cent, while white-collar workers rose from 23.0 per cent to 30.9 per cent.[8] Yet in this period Labour more than doubled its membership and won its greatest electoral victory.

Parliamentary representation may reflect the rise of technical and professional sectors in the occupational structure. Among Labour M.P.'s, candidates elected in 1965–66 showed a striking increase in professional occupations and university background,[9] and in general since the war the per cent of Labour M.P.'s with working-class backgrounds, far lower than during the interwar period, has markedly declined.[1] In social representation as in program, the two parties are tending to converge.

The same broad forces of rationalization in political and economic spheres work to make the parties also more alike in structure. Assembling, as it does, representatives of the main elites and resources of the party, Labour's conference cannot help but have far greater influence than the Conservative meeting of representatives of the local activists alone.[2] Moreover, the commitment to intraparty democracy remains strong, helping to block reform of the awkward arrangement which prevents the Labour Leader from having direct control of the party bureaucracy and forces him to work through the National Executive, a body chosen by conference and often including dissidents from his leadership.

In contrast, the Conservatives have brought a greater degree of co-ordination into what Lord Woolton once called their "ramshackle" organization, pulling together under the party chairman

[7] Royal Commission, *op. cit.*, par. 28.

[8] *British Journal of Industrial Relations, loc. cit.*, p. 306.

[9] Butler and King, *The British General Election of 1966*, p. 210.

[1] Richard Rose, *Class and Party Divisions: Britain as a Test Case,* Survey Research Centre, Occasional Paper No. 1 (University of Strathclyde, 1968), p. 28 and Table 1.

[2] See above, pp. 233–4.

and his deputy not only, as in the past, organization and publicity, but also research, intraparty propaganda, and the vital new functions of survey research and public relations. Yet the major change in the method of choosing the Leader, now a genuine election, clearly broadens the circle of control and influence at the top. Moreover, the Tory Leader now meets regularly and frequently with his Shadow Cabinet, which tends not only to systematize but also in a degree to democratize the exercise of his authority. At conference itself, he no longer merely appears majestically for an address at the end, but sits through all sessions.

Professionalism and the Mass Party

Two more developments relating to structure need to be considered. The first relates to party membership and to a decline which may portend a major change in the character of the parties.[3] The Conservatives do not keep an exact count, but between the early fifties and the early sixties their membership is said to have fallen from about 2.8 million to 2.3 million—although during the present phase of opposition it is thought to be rising again. On the Labour side, data is firmer and developments more serious. Individual membership reached a peak in 1953 of about one million after some years of steady growth. From 1953 to 1966, however, the figure dropped by almost 25 per cent. Trade-union membership in the party reached its peak in 1956, likewise after a long and steady climb. In the following ten years, although the trade-union total only fell off 2 per cent, it failed to keep pace with the work force, which grew by some 7 per cent. The Labour Party, in short, far from promising to embrace ever larger circles of the working class, suffered not merely a stop, but an absolute decline.

As affluence and further bureaucratization of the economy soften the old class lines, one could expect a decline of the mass party. A similar effect might well follow from the convergence of party policies. This relationship is familiar: a party reaches out to attract new voters, but in the process waters down the doctrine that had previously attracted and held its core of militants. To assess properly these explanations and the meaning of the declining

---

[3] I have benefited greatly from Leon Epstein's discussion in *Political Parties in Western Democracies* (New York, 1967), especially Ch. VI, "The Socialist Working-Class Party."

figures, however, we need wider and deeper research into the history of the local parties. We recognize, of course, that only a small fraction of the millions reported by each party are in fact active party workers. What we do not know is whether and how far there has been a decline in this core of active partisans.

Among M.P.'s and observers it is frequently said that enthusiasm has greatly declined on both sides in the localities, substantially reducing the ability of local parties to meet traditional obligations, such as the maintenance of the marked register. On the other hand, Labour Party officials will point out that as their local parties have found new sources of income, such as bingo and football pools, the membership drive is not as important as it was in the past. Certainly, central-local finance in the Labour Party gives no clear sign of declining intensity of support, the per capita financial contribution from the local parties to the national party having just about doubled during the period of declining membership.

One of the more portentous developments of the sixties may have a bearing on these changes. This is the further professionalization of major party functions, especially the making of party policy and the influencing of voters. For in political parties as in government itself, such developments raise the possibility of substantial technocratic shifts in the structure of power.

As for policy-making, although experts are abundantly and indeed increasingly used by both parties, they seem in the British fashion to have been kept in a subordinate role to the politicians. On the Labour side, although the subcommittees that drew up the programs and manifestoes of the sixties were studded with stars from the natural and social sciences, the basic decision to emphasize "the scientific revolution" was the product not of expertise, but of the common sense of party bureaucrats and leaders, principally Peter Shore and Hugh Gaitskell. Moreover, in spite of Harold Wilson's promise of a "white-hot technical revolution," it seems that his administration brought to Whitehall very little in the way of specific programs for the development of technology and its application to industry.[4]

In sharp contrast with their predecessors of the interwar years, Conservative leaders gave great and prolonged attention to pro-

[4] Merton J. Peck in Richard Caves and Associates, *Britain's Economic Prospects* (Washington, 1968), p. 448.

gram-making—at one time before the 1966 election there were thirty-six groups reviewing policy—but like Labour they heavily weighted their subcommittees with party representatives quite innocent of any expertise. The manifesto of 1966, however, had a specificity and detail in its identification of grievances to be remedied and groups to be relieved that could only have originated in expert knowledge.

One treads on delicate ground when one turns to the effects on party policy of the new professionalism of influencing voters and winning elections—specifically the use of survey research, advertising, and television—for even the most disinterested observer will not find it easy to fix clearly the line between opportunism and responsiveness. One may well agree heartily with Anthony Crosland and Mark Abrams in the early sixties when they are urging Labour to give up its old dogmas for issues in which voters are genuinely interested and yet also echo the sentiments of the Conservative publicity director, George Hutchinson, who said some time after his resignation following the election of 1964, "The duty of a political leader is to advocate what he believes to be right, not what market researchers prescribe for immediate popularity."[5] Both parties have exerted themselves to keep policy-making groups separate from publicity groups, yet the large and rapid growth in the use of the new techniques is hardly compatible with total isolation.

In both parties there was strong initial resistance. Tory statesmanship—George Hutchinson's remark catches the spirit—means that the task of the governing class is to govern and then to ask the approval of the people, on whose favorable judgment it can ultimately count. On the Labour side, the idea of conference as the voice of the working class is even less favorable to the use of survey research to identify the wishes of voters. The effectiveness of the new techniques in winning elections, however, finally broke through these obstacles.[6] In 1957 a slump in party morale and fear of slipping popularity led the Conservatives to make the first big step. In preparing and fighting the election of 1964 Labour followed suit, being greatly influenced by the scientific find-

---

[5] Quoted in Richard Rose, *Influencing Voters: A Study of Campaign Rationality* (London and New York, 1967), p. 156.

[6] Butler and King tell the story in their two Nuffield studies of the general elections of 1964 and 1966.

ings of Mark Abrams and the political judgment of Hugh Gaitskell. Indeed this change in means and tactics was part and parcel
of the revisionist triumph over the ideologues. In 1966 the Conservatives further expanded their effort, in their attempt to locate
"target voters," making a far more ambitious use of survey research than had ever been done before by either party. After its
burst of interest in the early sixties, Labour, on the other hand,
relaxed its use of survey research.

It is hardly likely that opportunism is any greater in either
party today than it was in the past. The important difference is
that party leaders now have much more effective ways of identifying the grievances and wishes of voters and rather more effective
ways of influencing their opinions by means of the mass media.
Even granting that policy-making is not altered, this knowledge
can greatly affect "presentation." In selecting the policies to emphasize in the 1966 campaign, for instance, the Conservatives did
not include education "partly because surveys indicated that the
target voters . . . were largely in favour of comprehensive
schools." [7] Joined with greater use of experts in identifying problems and proposing remedies, the new techniques in public relations refine and strengthen the process of group politics and so
add further strength to the forces making for convergence of
policy.

This major step in political rationalization may also affect the
future character of the mass party. Broadly, the effect of the new
technology is to enable central units to by-pass intermediary levels
and directly to assess and influence voters' opinions. This could
mean a shift of important functions, and therefore power, from
local parties to the central offices. Already there is evidence, especially on the Conservative side, that survey research has provided the central office with a counterweight to information from
agents overly influenced by partisan preconceptions. If the new
technology continues to shift functions to central agencies, the
local parties, and especially the local activists, will decline in importance. Conceivably in time, a new kind of technocratic cadre
party could take the place of the familiar mass party of Collectivist politics. At present we are a long way from that eventuality.
There are still important functions for local parties and still
enough class feeling to provide activists to perform them.

[7] Butler and King, *The British General Election of 1966*, p. 93.

Functional Representation

In revising his standard work on pressure groups in 1965, Professor Finer wrote: ". . . the most striking impression I have received is the stability and durability of the system it describes . . . broadly speaking, the same great organizations still hold the centre of the stage, continue to make the same sort of demands, and press them by the same sort of tactics." [8] With regard to functional representation, two developments, both continuous with past trends, deserve to be mentioned. The system of quasi-corporatism bringing Government and producer groups into intimate and continuous relationships has been still further elaborated and institutionalized, primarily through the extension of Government efforts to plan and control the economy. At the same time, the expert, the scientifically and professionally trained person, has continued to win a position of greater influence. In neither case, however, has the course of events been smooth, but rather, like British planning itself, punctuated by "stop" and "go."

Building on the foundations laid by Conservative Governments, Labour ambitiously extended the national commitment to economic planning. While in contrast with Conservatives they characteristically showed a greater willingness to intervene in the economy and to promote institutional reform, the planning system remained only "indicative." The purpose of the National Plan published by the new Department of Economic Affairs in 1965 was "to develop a co-ordinated, internally consistent set of projections of how the economy might develop to 1970 and thereby create expectations that would induce private economic decisions to conform to the projections." [9] Alongside N.E.D.C. and a score or so of little Neddies for particular industries, Labour, in what was perhaps its most important innovation, set up the National Board for Prices and Incomes, a body well staffed by experts, but also having representation from business and labor as well as Government.

Through these channels consultation between Government and producer groups was widened and regularized. A major change

[8] *Anonymous Empire: A Study of the Lobby in Great Britain*, rev. ed. (London, 1966).
[9] David C. Smith in Caves, *op. cit.*, p. 118.

facilitating this new level of contact was the crucial shift in the attitudes of organized business toward the acceptance of economic planning.[1] Even after the war, industry continued to be torn between its old principle of independence of Government and the new possibilities of exercising influence on it at the cost of closer association. Finally, in the early sixties a decision was made in favor of the latter alternative, reflected in the vigorous advocacy by the Federation of British Industries of economic planning for growth on the French model. Indeed, it was industry's acceptance of its new responsibilities in the N.E.D.C. that led to the amalgamation of the three main peak organizations—the Federation of British Industries, the National Union of Manufacturers (recently renamed the National Association of British Manufacturers), and the British Employers' Confederation—into one comprehensive organization, the Confederation of British Industry. Nor was this new commitment merely organizational: individual firms co-operated heartily in providing the massive information needed for Labour's National Plan.

In the sixties, however, as in the forties and fifties, the success of planning depended upon the restraint of inflation, a particularly acute problem for an economy in the exposed international position of the British. Again as in the past the new group politics caused difficulties. Looking backward to election promises and forward to a new political challenge, Governments showed reluctance to restrain consumption, private and public. Against the resulting background of excessive demand, it was even harder to achieve success in the effort to hold down forces making for inflation on the side of costs, especially wages.

Incomes Policy

With regard to this wage element in the inflationary pressure, the core of the problem was the attempt to devise an effective incomes policy. The prolonged and intricate bargaining over this question by the Labour Government with producer groups, especially trade unions, makes a fascinating chapter in the history of functional representation. For two years Parliament played a

[1] Professor Stephen Blank has traced this development in *Industry and the State: The Changing Relationship of Government and Industry in Britain* (unpublished Ph.D. thesis, Harvard University, 1968).

residual role, while the Government attempted to achieve its ends by agreement. Failure of this effort and the onset of acute crisis from mid-1966 forced the Government to intervene with even weightier legal powers. Yet even in this later period it was clear that these legal powers were unlikely to mean much if there were widespread dissatisfaction with the policy.[2]

At first glance this story illustrates the vast power of the great functional organizations of the modern economy. Yet it would only be part of the truth to think of them as organizational giants grappling with representatives of the public interest. For these giants themselves are often not masters in their own houses. The more fundamental lesson is to show once again the need for a deep mobilization of consent if planning is to succeed.

One reason for the failures of incomes policy consists in certain structural weaknesses, on the side of both trade unions and employers' associations, which throw light on the stage of political concentration reached by the British polity. Modern economic management entails the making of bargains that will be kept and this in turn means that there must be coherent and authoritative leadership on the part of the great producer organizations. Yet as compared with similar groups in such countries as Sweden, British producer groups have long been criticized for their lack of cohesion.

Among unions concentration has gone forward and today some 70 per cent of trade-union membership is accounted for by eighteen huge organizations.[3] The dynamics of union development seem to be inexorably eliminating the many small organizations, while the separatism of different crafts is in part being overcome by the further growth of general unions. At the same time, however, full employment has led to a shift of much significant collective bargaining in industry from the national to the plant level. Even if and when national organizations did accommodate their agreements with regard to wage rates to the criteria of incomes policy, "earnings drift" at the plant level continued to swell the forces of cost inflation.[4] The practices responsible for this tend-

[2] David C. Smith, "Incomes Policy," in Caves, *op. cit.,* p. 129.

[3] Royal Commission on Trade Unions and Employers' Associations, Research Papers, John Hughes, *Trade Union Structures and Government* (London, 1967), par. 85.

[4] Royal Commission on Trade Unions and Employers' Associations, *Report* (London, 1968), pars. 57 and 76.

ency are rooted in attitudes that go deep into British culture. First among them, as one American observer has put it, is "a proletarian spirit that seems conservative even by the standards of a traditionalist society." [5] Also in his opinion, sharing responsibility for the resulting underutilization of labor is "a tradition of paternalism" which leads management to feel that, in the words of one employer, its "first responsibility is to provide work for these chaps—to keep the shop occupied . . ." [6] Thus, in economic as in political behavior the ancient heritage of class consciousness shows its power.

As compared with the time when nationally agreed wage rates were virtually identical with earnings, these trends to decentralize collective bargaining have meant a real loss of authority to the national unions. Yet movements of earnings are still substantially influenced by the terms of wage settlements, so it remained vitally important for the Government in turn to try to influence those settlements. It did this with rather greater success after the introduction of legal powers and only then did earnings also respond, showing a rate of increase lower than could have been expected if there had been no incomes policy.[7]

Perhaps the most interesting development of all from the viewpoint of the student of modernization is the success of the Government's efforts exerted through the National Board for Prices and Incomes to promote "productivity bargaining," a kind of agreement which involves, for instance, a pay increase but in return for the surrender of restrictive practices. The Board, making a wide use of expert staff and consultants, brings its criticism and suggestions to bear on questions of this sort when it is considering wage demands. A context of situational pressures of which legal coercion is only one element seems to be giving considerable thrust to these step-by-step, grass-roots measures of modernization.[8]

The failure of planning to realize Labour's ambitious hopes also meant a setback for that professionalization of policy-making which is a growing characteristic of British as of other Western

---

[5] Lloyd Ulman in Caves, *op. cit.*, p. 332.
[6] *Ibid.*, p. 335.
[7] David C. Smith in Caves, *op. cit.*, pp. 131–4.
[8] Allan Flanders, the authority on "productivity bargaining," in a private conversation.

governments. If we look generally at the role of the scientist and scientifically trained person in British Government, we see that it has grown steadily during the past three decades, although by no means as greatly as in the United States. As has often happened to other groups and classes in the past, these strata have been elevated in power and influence because of the needs of public policy. During the war Britain gave scientists new and important functions. Since then the country as a whole has invested heavily in research and development—indeed, recently it has been spending more relative to G.N.P. than even the United States.[9] Although the many advisory committees that cluster around Government departments would seem to be primarily representational, they include a high proportion of scientifically trained people. The creation of the Ministry of Science and Technology has further improved their position within the administration, giving science policy a new coherence and making more effective the application of science and technology to industry.

When Harold Wilson took office in 1964, as we have seen, he came with large promises of bringing the scientific revolution to fruition in Britain. One immediate instance was the flocking of dons, particularly economists, to Whitehall, reminiscent of, and indeed consciously initiated from, American practice. If the original hopes for economic planning had been fulfilled, we can expect that the role of the professional would have been greater than it is today. It is possible that, following the French model, the great representational emphasis in British Government-industry relations would have been diminished, and the etatist emphasis enhanced, as many observers had urged.[1]

The shift in the position of the Treasury illustrates how the forces of innovation were blunted. Initially under Wilson the Chancellor of the Exchequer was deprived of membership on N.E.D.C., while the new Department of Economic Affairs was charged with drawing up the National Plan. The pressure of economic crisis, however, with its usual features of inflation and an international deficit, forced authority away from the new organs and back toward the Treasury, which although by no

[9] Merton J. Peck in Caves, *op. cit.*, p. 449.
[1] For example, Andrew Shonfield, in his *Modern Capitalism: The Changing Balance of Public and Private Power* (New York, 1956), especially Ch. VIII.

means as innocent of expertise as it once was, remains especially the home of the generalist and the non-professional amateur. By 1968 there was talk of abolishing Economic Affairs.

A Post-Collectivist Politics?

The sixties in Britain have brought no great departures from the model of Collective politics. Britain's politics, like Britain's problems, bear a remarkable resemblance to what they were ten or even twenty years ago. The incremental changes within the Collectivist model that I have tried to identify could in time bring about a qualitative change amounting to a new era. But change of another kind—reactive, discontinuous, and radical—is also possible. Two features of British politics that have become prominent in very recent years make this possibility worth considering: student rebellion and Celtic nationalism.

At first glance these two movements may seem quite unlike and unconnected. Yet each can be considered as a reaction to the increasing scale and intensity of rationalization in both government and society. Each shares an antagonism, not always reasoning, against bureaucratic and technocratic forces; against the impersonal, distant and faceless organizations of modern times. In each case also some of the supporters of protest and self-assertion put forward demands that would mean a radical break with the present manner and substance of British politics. Yet, extreme as these movements sometimes seem, it may well be that they will be contained by the basic structures and procedures of Collectivist politics. If so, we will probably look back on them as analogous to other movements that arose when the two main branches of modernity, rationalization and democracy, got out of kilter with one another, and will consider how they caused a readjustment rather than any far-reaching reform of the structure of power.

The gains that Celtic nationalism have made in terms of success in local elections and in party organization warn us not to underestimate its future prospects. The Scottish National Party now claims 100,000 members and has announced its intention to contest all seventy-one Scottish seats at the next General Election. Sober observers will speculate that not only Liberals but Labourites and Conservatives may be wiped out north of the Tweed.

Like the Scots, the Welsh nationalists at present have one M.P. Their party, Plaid Cymru, claims 30,000 members and is expected to enjoy growing success.

The grievances of Scottish and Welsh nationalists are not essentially economic. Current restrictive policies do bear harshly on areas of declining traditional industry. But while economic grievances sharpen, they have not created nationalist sentiment, which springs rather from fears that are genuinely cultural and which involve a sense of domination from a distance and loss of identity.

Nor is this upsurge of regional resistance confined to the Celtic fringe. In recent years localism has become a major principle of opposition, especially at by-elections. J. P. Mackintosh connects the anti-centralist tendencies:

For some, voting for Scottish Nationalist candidates is a method of protesting at the remoteness of modern government, its slowness, its frequent refusal to give explanations for decisions. This frustration has ample justification and some of those who feel it appreciate that their sentiments are the same as those of the residents of Essex who objected to the decision to site a major airport at Stansted. Everything said then, if the airport had been in Scotland, would have been excellent for Scottish Nationalist propaganda.[2]

If the Government, as seems very likely, takes major steps of decentralization in response to nationalist demands, it is quite possible that measures in the same direction will be taken on behalf of other regions. Even though a reaction to the rationalizing aspects of modernity, such a devolution of power would be another instance of that democratization of structure that modernity itself often calls forth.

Like the nationalists, student rebels also lack positive, long-term proposals. Moreover, as members of the large and rapidly growing university population they make complaint against bureaucratic and technocratic pressures. Between 1950 and 1965, the proportion of the age-group 20–24 who were enrolled in higher education more than doubled, jumping from 4 per cent to 8.5 per cent. In the four years from 1962 to 1966, membership in the National Union of Students, the official and long-

[2] "Scottish Nationalism," *Political Quarterly*, Vol. 38, No. 4 (October–December, 1967), p. 394.

established student organization, rose from 150,000 to 366,000. In this context of rapid growth, the advocates of "student power" produced the Radical Students' Alliance.

In the light of this vast increase in numbers, many students deny that they can be regarded as a privileged minority being educated at public expense, and claim instead that they should be treated as working adults, receiving grants as wages and sent to study in a university rather than work in a factory because this will be to the long-run benefit of society. Higher education, it is also claimed, is being subordinated to the manpower requirements and economic imperatives of a new kind of industrial society. Or as one activist put it, universities are becoming "battery farms for broiler technicians."

The phrase points to the new and vastly greater dependence of society upon trained manpower. Like other groups in the past who similarly found themselves controlling a key resource, British students have moved to expand their role in the structure of power. In October, 1968, in a proceeding entirely consonant with the spirit and norms of the Collectivist model, the N.U.S. negotiated an agreement with the heads of the thirty-seven universities of England, Wales, and Northern Ireland, providing for student participation in university management. The committees of "joint consultation" that have been set up have set to work on important questions of university government and administration. As of this writing, and in spite of some outbursts, the university scene in Britain has been peaceful as compared with the continent or the United States.

THE SHAPE OF POST-COLLECTIVIST POLITICS

If we turn back to the table on page 398 and look over the types of politics that have characterized modernization, we see a curious pattern. Each of the basic theories of representation has two main elements, one defining the mode of representation of the common interest, the other the mode of representation of particular interests. As we move from one type to another chronologically, however, we do not find a break with regard to both elements, but rather continuity in one mode of representation and innovation in the other. This means that between any two adjacent types there is an overlap in one mode of representation.

Moreover, innovation alternates, first with regard to one element and then with regard to the other.

Thus, when in the late eighteenth and early nineteenth century there was a shift from functionalist to associationist attitudes toward interest representation, the parliamentarism of Old Whig views, nevertheless, was carried over into the Liberal outlook. In the next phase, however, Radicals retained the individualist and associationist attitudes of the Liberals toward pressure groups, but made a sharp break from parliamentarism in their assertion of popular sovereignty. This latter view in turn had much in common with the Socialist idea of party government, while the new functionalism and pluralism marked a very different attitude toward the representation of interests.

If this pattern of alternation holds, the next major stage in the development of representation will bring innovation primarily in the way the common interest is formed and represented. Of course, the extrapolation of a pattern of the past does not bind the future. But it must be said that identifiable present tendencies likewise lead one to expect that the post-Collectivist phase, while retaining functionalism, will involve some kind of break from party government.

The further development of corporatism is surely to be expected. Planning is inevitable in an economy that seeks both stability and expansion. In the absence of a totalitarian bureaucracy —and to an extent even when one exists—such planning means that the enterprises and people that carry out the plans must be brought in on their formulation. To this extent, as planning develops, functional representation will likewise grow, becoming an even more important part of the representative system of the polity. The structure may become more centralized as has been the tendency in the past. Or it may functionally and territorially decentralize tasks that are now excessively burdening the center. The extension of control through some form of bureaucratic structure, however, seems hardly to be avoided. This tendency to corporatism has its roots in economic development, and in this respect the British political system is responding to forces that are bringing about very much the same sort of results in all Western industrialized states.

But corporatism cannot constitute a complete polity and must be supplemented by some other source of will and direction such as has come in the past from party government. In Britain, as in most other European countries, today's parties and party system assumed their present form and content at least two generations ago. Considering the profound changes that have taken place in these societies since that time we should hardly be surprised if radically new patterns were to emerge.

1. One of the more ominous possibilities was recently characterized by a friend of mine while speaking generally of the Western countries. He described it as "Caesarism based on technocracy because of the difficulties experienced by democracy in dealing with complexity." The demand for planning is inexorable —so runs this analysis—and produces an ever more technically sophisticated bureaucratic apparatus and mode of operation. The present régime of parties, however, is incapable of producing among the people the understanding and acceptance that will yield the decisions necessary for planning. A Caesarism, perhaps less authoritarian and more manipulative thanks to the new techniques of communications, will perform this essential function of forming the public will, no doubt in conjunction with a controlled and highly etatist system of corporatism.

2. This possible future is rooted in fundamental processes and problems of modernization, viz., the powerful thrust of economic rationalization and its conflict with similarly powerful demands for democratization—or a facsimile thereof. With it may be contrasted a tendency which has come into prominence more recently and which would disrupt the imposing dualism of the Caesaristic alternative with a radically new kind of dualism.

The pattern of policy of the Caesaristic alternative carries the impersonality and centralization of bureaucracy to a new height, legitimizing them with the authority of science and modern rationality. Yet, as the experience of Gaullist France has sharply reminded us, precisely this set of factors can produce a powerful reaction. There are precedents in the past. Reaching deep into the spirit of voluntarism, modernity has from time to time produced a romantic reaction that not only rejects the discipline of an objective ethics, but also the discipline of an industrial environment. In Britain, from the Luddites to D. H. Lawrence, different classes and times have shared this impulse of which student anarchism is only a recent flowering.

But if rebellious students are the most vivid exhibit, the possibilities of a regional or local politics are more serious and no less romantic. We can expect some such change if schemes of substantial decentralization are put into effect. The really radical possibility, however, that some foresee is a fundamental realignment of political forces along the lines of central-regional tension, producing perhaps a two-party system based not on the old division between classes, but rather upon a center-periphery cleavage. One observer of affairs believes that in Britain as on the continent, regionalism is very likely to have such an explosive future. For Anthony Sampson, "the battles against the capitals will grow all over Europe" as the centralized nation-state is by-passed on the way to a wider unity.[3]

3. Apart from the possibility of such radical discontinuities, incremental changes inherent in the Collectivist model could transform the system. If the parties continue to converge, conceivably they could produce a condition of "party duopoly without product differentiation." Further professionalization of leadership would reduce the power of militants and open the way to a highly flexible policy. Through two "catch-all" parties, competing teams of leaders would seek power on the basis of shifting coalitions of voters. Conceivably an "era of good feeling" could supervene in which the old dualism would be dissolved by the overwhelming dominance of one party. In view of Labour's gloomy prospects at the moment, it is not idle to speculate on this possibility of democratic one-party government. Broadly agreed on the basic outlines of the Welfare State and Managed Economy, a set of lively factions within this great catch-all party would contest for party and so governmental control. One is reminded of the C.D.U., or the Christian Democrats of Italy, or indeed not a little of the Tories during their recent long tenure of power.

4. The discussion of the catch-all party and of factions suggests a more radical alternative that should not be dismissed. This is the withering away of party altogether. Ostrogorski, it will be remembered, regarded party as the dead hand of traditionalism extended in a new form into the era of liberty. Instead of parties he would have preferred temporary "combinations of citizens"

---

[3] *The New Europeans* (London, 1969), p. 434.

shifting with issues and problems.[4] Without trying to follow his proposals exactly, we should at least consider the possibility that parties may become fairly dysfunctional and as a result decline and disappear.

Ostrogorski rightly remarked the traditionalizing effect of parties. By freezing voters in their adherence to a symbol, they prevent a flexible response to new problems. The continuance of class lines and class interests gave some justification to this stereotyping of political response. If we can suppose the decline of class, more flexible means of mobilizing opinion and changing the configurations of loyalty and support would be appropriate.

Such a development would seem to be a natural result of further rationalization of the political process. It has been observed that one of the marks of a modern society is that it produces and uses more special purpose organizations than does a traditional society.[5] I should like to suggest that modernization also brings a more rapid turnover in special purpose organizations. Modernity means a greater division of labor, but it also means, and especially in a highly technological age, a changing division of labor. In politics this could well be embodied in the rise of a new type of political formation consisting of a coalition of voters united by a common attitude toward a major problem, but dissolving and re-forming as such problems changed.

That such a type of political formation might be functional is suggested by the fact that in Britain, as elsewhere, we continually see how attitudes toward problems of major importance—especially the newer sort of problem, such as Europe or industrial modernization—cut across existing party lines and therefore may have trouble being clearly articulated or forcefully pushed. Moreover, there is growing evidence of great volatility in party support among voters, suggesting that they may be losing their old class-based partisan attachments and preparing for a more flexible —and rational—participation in politics. Looked at in this way,

[4] For Ostrogorski's penetrating analysis of how the party system stereotypes opinion, see *Democracy and the Organization of Political Parties* (New York, 1902), Vol. I, Ch. 8, Sections II and V; and for his "solution" of "temporary parties for a single issue," Vol. II, "Conclusion," Sections X–XIV.

[5] Arthur Stinchcombe, "Social Structure and Organizations," in James March, ed., *Handbook of Organizations,* p. 145.

the political party, far from being a permanent feature of the democratic polity, is a transitional form between traditionalism and a mature modernity.

5. In the end, as in any discussion of British politics, one comes back to the question of class. In Britain class trails with it ancient habits of thought and feeling. Even those who rebelled against the class system of industrial capitalism acquired their sense of class identity and solidarity not only from those objective conditions, but also from a much older heritage. In this sense class diminishes as modernization proceeds.

Yet it is a great error to think of class in Britain as merely an inert remnant of the *ancien régime*. It is not alone ancient habit that has kept it alive all these centuries, but also active function, social and psychological. In this sense there has been and still is a great deal of modernity in much of British traditionalism.[6] For many people, for instance, there is psychological security and comfort in class: in automatically having membership in a certain kind of human community by birth and breeding, in knowing exactly where one stands socially in relation to others, in not being continually driven by the social ethos to be "upwardly mobile."

Strong as may be these cultural and psychological conditions favoring class, however, it also requires some current and objective focus for its survival. One such focus consists of differences in material well being and style of life. Quite conceivably affluence could spread to the point where this basis of class and class politics had vanished. Another focus consists of the relationship of individuals to the ownership of the means of production. "Universal bureaucratization" continually erodes this difference by making employees of more and more members of the economy.

But class also, and I am inclined to think this is the most important meaning of the term, rests on differences of power[7]—and these show little promise of disappearing. In this sense an objective focus will remain for the old class habits. Moreover, there

[6] This general point in relation to modernization studies and especially India has been powerfully and sensitively developed by Lloyd and Sue Rudolph in *The Modernity of Tradition: Political Development in India* (Chicago, 1968), especially the introduction.

[7] I accept the general argument of Ralf Dahrendorf in *Class and Class Conflicts in Industrial Society* (Stanford, 1959).

also will remain an old issue of fundamental moral importance: How should power be distributed in society?

Conceivably, the two parties could become irrelevant to British politics if they were contesting nothing but the distribution of material goods and services. Similarly, if that myth of universal nationalization produced by the political imagination of the early Socialists were the party's only reason for being, Labour might well see the time when it had no future.

But Tories and Socialists also confront one another as advocates of distinctive attitudes toward the distribution of power. Conflicting views of equality and inequality have divided political forces in Britain for many generations. The question goes to the roots of the meaning of modernity itself. Embodying such powerful historical and moral forces and focusing on major structural features of the technocratic society, the old party dualism would seem likely to have a long, vigorous and useful future.

Index